S0-CAF-731

Culinary Nostalgia

Culinary Nostalgia

Regional Food Culture
and the Urban Experience in Shanghai

Mark Swislocki

Stanford University Press
Stanford, California

Stanford University Press
Stanford, California

©2009 by the Board of Trustees of the Leland Stanford Junior University. All rights reserved.

No part of this book may be reproduced or transmitted in any form or by any means, electronic or mechanical, including photocopying and recording, or in any information storage or retrieval system without the prior written permission of Stanford University Press.

Printed in the United States of America on acid-free, archival-quality paper

Library of Congress Cataloging-in-Publication Data
Swislocki, Mark.
 Culinary nostalgia : regional food culture and the urban experience in Shanghai / Mark Swislocki.
    p. cm.
 Includes bibliographical references and index.
 ISBN 978-0-8047-6012-6 (cloth : alk. paper)
 1. Cookery--China--Shanghai--History. 2. Food habits--China--Shanghai--History. 3. Cookery, Chinese--Shanghai style. 4. Shanghai (China)--Social life and customs. I. Title.
 TX724.5.C5S98 2009
 394."20951--dc22

                            2008029119

Typeset by Bruce Lundquist in 10/14 Minion

For Maya

Contents

Illustrations

Weights, Measures, and Currencies

jin (catties):

Ming: 1 *jin* = 20.7 ounces

Qing: 1 *jin* = 20.9 ounces

li ("Chinese miles"):

1 *li* = 1/3 mile

liang (*taels*):

1894–1904: 1 *liang* = approximately 1/3 £

yuan, jiao, fen (Chinese currency units):

ca. 1930: 18 *yuan* = $5 US = £ 1

1 *yuan* = 10 *jiao* = 100 *fen*

SOURCE: Immanuel C. Y. Hsu, *The Rise of Modern China*, Sixth Edition (New York: Oxford University Press, 2000); Frederic Wakeman, Jr., *Policing Shanghai, 1927–1937* (Berkeley: University of California Press, 1995); Endymion Wilkinson, *Chinese History: A Manual* (Cambridge, MA: Harvard University Asia Center, 2000).

Acknowledgments

IT IS A PLEASURE to thank the many individuals who have shaped the research and writing of this book, as well as the institutions that have provided financial support.

I was blessed as a graduate student at Stanford University to study Chinese history with a remarkable team of professors who taught me the importance of both Sinology and social and cultural analysis: Timothy Brook, Albert E. Dien, Charles Hayford, Harold Kahn, Ellen Neskar, and Lyman Van Slyke. I remain most grateful for their guidance and instruction, their enthusiastic support of my interest in food history, and for the trust they put in me to explore this relatively uncharted historical terrain. I must also express special gratitude to Bryna Goodman, whose support and advice hold a deep significance for me.

My initial research on Shanghai food history was supported by a dissertation fellowship from the Committee on Scholarly Communications with China. Christian Henriot and Gail Hershatter provided helpful guidance while I was first formulating my research questions. Catherine Yeh generously shared valuable documents from her own research on Shanghai culture. In Shanghai, Xiong Yuezhi, Luo Suwen, Song Zuanyou, Cheng Zai, Xu Min, Yuan Jin, Ma Jun, and Lu Wenxue assisted me in innumerable ways during my stay at the Shanghai Academy of Social Sciences. I am also grateful to the leadership and staff of the Academy's Office of Foreign Affairs: Li Yihai, Zhao Nianguo, Tian Guopei, Ma Ying, and Jin Caihong. Shao Qin and the staff of the Shanghai Municipal Archives kindly filled my requests for research materials, as did the staff of the Shanghai Municipal Library. Zhu Gang, Xu Yuanqing, and Tang Jianing, of the Shanghai Cuisine Association, and Zhou Sanjin, of the Chinese Cuisine Association, kindly met with me to discuss the history of Shanghai restaurants and cookery. Zhang Wenyong, of the Shanghai History Museum, also shared his knowledge of Shanghai food history with me. Special thanks are due also to the general managers and head chefs of the Dafugui, Lübolang, Meilongzhen, Renmin, Xiao Shaoxing, Xinghualou, Xinya, and Yangzhou Restaurants, who took time out of their busy schedules to discuss the history of their restaurants, shared anecdotes about their training and professional lives, and provided valuable historical materials. Thanks, again, to Zhao Nianguo for making these meetings possible. I remain grateful, finally, to Daniel Buck, for helping me navigate a year of research in Shanghai.

Generous support from the Stanford Humanities Center Geballe Dissertation Prize Fellowship and the Giles Whiting Foundation provided support for the writing of the dissertation from which this book developed. My cohort in Chinese History at Stanford during these years—Fei Si-yen, Jiang Jin, Zwia Lipkin, Colette Plum, Reiko Shinno, and Wang Juan—contributed immeasurably to my thinking about Chinese history and culture. Emily Osborn and Angus Lockyer further helped me appreciate the possibilities of historical thinking and research. I also learned much about how to write about and study food from Amy Bentley, Barbara Kirshenblatt-Gimblett, Marion Nestle, and the other participants of the "Feast and Famine" colloquium at New York University's Department of Nutrition, Food Studies and Public Health.

Many people and institutions eased the difficult transition from dissertation to book. Columbia University's Society of Fellows provided a stimulating environment in which to reformulate my doctoral dissertation. Without the encouragement of Paul Cohen and Matthew Sommer, I might never have developed what I originally envisioned only to be a long article into its present book form. The support of Dorothy Ko and Robert Hymes and their interest in my work has also been essential in ways that are hard to express. I am grateful to Sue Fernsebner for sharing her insights into material culture and for inviting me to present my preliminary ideas on this project at her 2003 Fairbank Center workshop on urban spectacle; to Jiang Jin for the opportunity to share a portion of this book at the 2005 Eastern China Normal University conference on urban culture in China; and to Paize Keulemans for the same at the 2005 AAS panel on the sensory landscape of the nineteenth century city. Wen-hsin Yeh pushed me in valuable ways to clarify my thinking about cuisine. Michael Chang and Eugenia Lean offered characteristically sound guidance regarding many matters of scholarship and interpretation. Chen Luying, Huang Weijia, Lo Shih-chieh, and Wang Hongjie provided valuable assistance reading several documents. Deborah Cohen, Daniel Kim, and Michael Vorenberg offered essential professional advice during the writing and publication process. I am also grateful to Nicolás Wey-Gómez for reminding me, at a crucial time, about what really matters in this line of work.

A Brown University junior faculty sabbatical provided much needed time to write the book manuscript. A faculty fellowship from the Cogut Center for the Humanities provided time and space for making my final revisions. I am grateful to Brown University and to James McClain and Kenneth Sacks for the leave time from my regular teaching responsibilities during these semesters, and to Michael Steinberg, Leslie Uhnak, and Kit Salisbury for making my time at the Cogut so stimulating and comfortable.

The final manuscript has been enhanced by the insights of many readers. For their comments on all or parts of the manuscript, I thank my colleagues in the Department of History at Brown University: Deborah Cohen, Mary Gluck, Evelyn Hu-DeHart, Tara Nummedal, Ethan Pollock, Seth Rockman, Robert Self, Naoko Shibusawa, Kerry Smith, and Vazira Zamindar. A timely conversation with Eugenia Lean helped me reformulate Chapter Five, and Alexander Cook's reading of a draft of the same chapter helped me refine my argument. An opportunity to test-run the book's introduction at the Department of History at Johns-Hopkins University saved me from numerous intellectual blunders and helped me produce a much more satisfying product; I am grateful to Tobie Meyer-Fong for making that opportunity possible, and for her intellectual and professional support. Dorothy Ko and Joanna Waley-Cohen provided extremely helpful comments on the full manuscript. I am sorry if I have not been able to incorporate all of their suggestions into the final version.

I am grateful also to Muriel Bell of Stanford University Press for her support of this project, to my editor, Stacy Wagner, and to the many other members of the Press who have helped guide this project through the final stages. Thanks to Lynn Carlson for designing the map on page 33. And to Clea Liquard for her last-minute and invaluable help with proofreading.

Family and friends provided so much over the years that is impossible to detail here. This book would not have been possible without your guidance, curiosity, and support.

I must express special gratitude to my colleague in Comparative Literature at Brown, Dore Levy. Her insights into Chinese culture and literature enriched

my understanding of the material and enhanced the final product tremendously. Her enthusiasm and her intellectual and professional guidance during
the last year of writing have made an immeasurable difference. Would that all
junior faculty find such a mentor in a senior colleague.

I am so grateful, finally, to my wife, Maya Allison. Her remarkable sense
of story structure helped me work through countless story problems and has
made the final product much more satisfying to read. Her love, support, and
confidence has been inspiring.

Introduction:
Thinking about Food
in Chinese History

AS CHINA EMBARKED on the period of "opening and reform" after the death of Mao Zedong in 1976, the country's diverse regional food cultures, decimated by decades of food shortages, communal canteens, and restaurant mismanagement, quickly sprang back to life. In Shanghai, new restaurants serving regional specialties were among the most numerous and successful early private enterprises, and monotonous state-run restaurants resumed the regional character for which they had been celebrated before the "proletarianization" of restaurants and food culture during the political frenzy of China's Cultural Revolution decade (1966–76). The city's venerable Yangzhou Restaurant took the extra step of creating a special "Dream of the Red Chamber" banquet menu, featuring well-known Yangzhou dishes that appear in the famous eighteenth-century novel of the same name. Within a few short years, restaurants became important meeting grounds for communities of fellow-provincials to gather and reminisce about old times over a meal of hometown cooking, as well as places in which city residents could connect with China's many regional food cultures and the country's culinary heritage.

This resurgence of regional food culture in China was more than just a recuperation of earlier food traditions or a response to the tedium and deprivation of material life under socialism. What I call "culinary nostalgia"—the recollection or purposive evocation of another time and place through food—is a time-honored Chinese tradition. Even in Shanghai, China's most "modern" city, culinary nostalgia took many forms and was an integral component of urban culture at each stage of the city's development. In the late nineteenth century, city residents mourned the loss of Shanghai's most famous specialty foodstuff,

the Shanghai honey nectar peach, and thereby the fading of the city's historical garden culture to urbanization and Westernization. During the Republican
period (1912–49), when civil war tore apart the Chinese body politic, Shanghai
residents turned to food once again, this time to the city's many regional Chinese restaurants, to connect with their country's rich heritage, and to imagine
for themselves how such a culturally diverse country might be held together.
The tradition of culinary nostalgia continues today, in "Old Shanghai" theme
restaurants that link city residents to an image of Shanghai's former glory, while
the city itself is transformed into a global destination of the future.

This book argues that regional food culture was intrinsic to how Chinese
connected to the past, lived in the present, and imagined a future. It focuses on
Shanghai—a food lover's paradise—and identifies the importance of regional
food culture at pivotal moments in the city's history, and in Chinese history
more generally. Looking at how the Chinese in Shanghai thought about food
reveals how they viewed their relationships with other places, whether other
regions of China or the Western world, and how they experienced the many
changes the city underwent through several centuries. By identifying nostalgia as an enduring theme of late imperial and modern Shanghai food history,
this book builds on recent studies of the city that have challenged the idea of
Shanghai's essentially "modern" or "Westernized" character. Indeed, when seen
through the lens of its food history, the city emerges as a deeply nostalgic place
and one much more beholden to—indeed committed to—"traditional" ways
of life than previously imagined. Food was not the only object of nostalgia in
Shanghai's history, but food's importance for Chinese articulations of nostalgia
more generally make Shanghai's food culture an especially rich window onto
the nostalgic side of city life.

Thinking about the Shanghai experience as part of a wider history of food
in China further draws into relief one of the most remarkable, yet rarely remarked upon, features of Chinese history during the past two centuries: the
enduring appeal of "traditional" foodways and their regional manifestations
during periods of often rapid and drastic social and cultural change. The significance that Chinese have attached to foodways and diet has of course changed
many times, and in many important ways. But regional foodways remain a core
component of cultural identity in China. This book seeks to explain why, by
examining both the tenacity of regional taste preferences and the almost limit-
less flexibility that food provides as a vehicle for constructing a sense of home
and imagining an ideal society.

Culinary Nostalgia

Nostalgia, a term that characterizes a wide range of mnemonic and evocative practices, is a tricky word. At the very least, it connotes a problem, rather than a solution, a pathology, rather than a critical frame of analysis for looking at the world. Coined in 1688 by the Swiss medical student Johannes Hofer (1669–1752), *nostalgia* referred to a new medical condition that first made its presence among displaced peoples, especially soldiers, of seventeenth-century Europe. Nostalgia became epidemic in Europe in the wake of the French Revolution, which transformed the foundations of thought and society and, as Svetlana Boym notes, "appeared to unchain a yearned-for future," driving a wedge between experience, what people knew to be true about the world around them, and expectation, what they anticipated the world becoming.[1] Advocates of Enlightenment concepts of progress sought to guide this anticipation in ways that pushed people and society "forward," and only the Romantics provided a widely recognized way of valorizing the past as a source of hope. The Romantics elevated folk art and local customs to the level of the heroic and, in so doing, made nostalgia into a virtue. But they also gave birth to the trappings of modern nationalism.[2] Today, *nostalgia* most commonly suggests a form of self-deception, a false sense of an idealized place that never was.[3]

In China, where there are several rough equivalents for the English *nostalgia*, such as *huaigu* and *huaijiu*, the idea has generated far fewer detractors and a long record of well-respected practitioners.[4] These practitioners may be effectively divided into "restorative" and "reflective" types.[5] Among the former, who are distinguished by their efforts to effect a "transhistorical reconstruction" of a lost world, must be counted Confucians, who based their notions of the ideal state on a series of representations of the early sage kings, Yao, Shun, and Yu, and the early Western Zhou (1045–771 B.C.). Reflective nostalgics, by contrast, "thrive in . . . the longing itself, and [delay] the homecoming—wistfully, ironically, desperately." Among the most revered of China's reflective nostalgics is the poet Tao Qian (A.D. 365–427), whose "Record of the Peach Blossom Spring" (Taohua yuan ji) yielded the trope of a perfect lost world, Wulingyuan. Nobody ever seriously doubted that Wulingyuan existed—that was beside the point. Instead, debate centered on where it was, and how to get there.[6] Indeed, few Chinese considered nostalgia itself to be a problem, at least not until the late nineteenth century, when Chinese elites, grappling with shifts in the balance of world power, concurred with their European counterparts that the "Chinese attachment to the past" was a source of weakness, rather than strength. European somatology threatened to remake the Chinese world in its own image.

In Europe, or at least in the Protestant West, history's moralists have looked no more favorably upon epicures than they have upon nostalgics, on the grounds that an undue interest in the pleasures of eating and drinking reflects a moral failing. In this regard, the British diplomats and traders who led the charge to "open China" shared something with Confucians, for whom food mattered deeply, but as ritual and a source of social stability, not as pleasure. The Confucian classics and early texts of Chinese political philosophy are replete with discourse on food. These include depictions of Zhou food rituals in the *Book of Rites*, as well as observations about the interrelationship among food, human nature, and social order. Thus, as the *Guanzi* observes, "If the state has an abundance of wealth, people will come from afar; if the land has been opened for cultivation, they will settle down. When the granaries are full, they will know propriety and moderation; when their clothing and food is adequate, they will know [the distinction between] honor and shame."[7] Still, most Chinese, Confucianism notwithstanding, are epicures, for whom no food tastes better than that of their hometowns. In this regard, Chinese have firmly held their ground against the universalizing discourse of modernity. Of all the forms of nostalgia that Chinese reformers and modernizers have condemned during the past century and a half, only culinary nostalgia has emerged almost entirely unscathed.

The idea that food can evoke another time and place has been a modernist truism ever since Marcel Proust, in *Remembrance of Things Past*, transported his readers to the Combray of his narrator's childhood by the alchemical effect of mixing, on the tip of the narrator's tongue, a few crumbs of madeleine with a sip of warm lime-flower tea.[8] In China, Confucians and epicures alike engaged in such reverie, well before the development of a discourse on the modern. For them, food evoked images of an ideal society and, in its absence, a model either for establishing one, or for understanding the sources of its want. China's restorative nostalgics dreamt of a world in which, "the grain will be more than can be eaten," and "the fishes and turtles will be more than can be consumed," so that "people may nourish their living and mourn for their dead, without any feeling against any." Accomplishing this, according to Mencius, was "the first step of royal government."[9] More reflective types were drawn to Tao Qian's Wulingyuan, whose path was lined with peach blossoms, or to the mythical kingdom of Penglai, where immortals were said to travel to banquet, and where the Queen Mother of the West cultivated the fruits of immortality. Few Chinese dreamers ever expected that they would find their way to Penglai, but the many scholars, officials, exiles, sojourning merchants, and migrant workers who made late imperial China into one of the most mobile societies of early modern times were especially prone to culinary nostalgia. On their long journeys away from home, as Bryna Goodman has poignantly remarked, they left behind "the special way of speaking and the unique forms of dried tofu or sweet cakes of their village; passing through neighboring counties with still comprehensible dialects and recognizable dishes; and finally arriving in strange places where words were unfamiliar and palatable food hard to find."[10] They fed their nostalgia in somewhat more mundane ways than, say, the Tang (618–907) poet Wang Wei (701–61), who sought to "create within himself the contentment and equilibrium imputed to the folk of the land of the Peach Blossom Spring."[11] But the regional restaurants, specialty food shops, and networks of fellow-provincials that followed in their wake and catered to their needs provided sojourners with a sense of home in a foreign land. In the process, as this book illustrates, they shaped the course of history in late imperial and twentieth-century China.

In the twentieth century, the Chinese Communist Party (CCP) made food into a trope of the failings of the past or present, and of the promise, instead, of the future. "Speaking bitterness" (*suku*) campaigns, during which the party instructed disenfranchised peasants to speak out freely about the abuses they suffered at the hands of landlords, dug up many painful memories of hunger. During the Cultural Revolution, sent-down youth even participated in "eating bitterness meals," at which peasants recalled their bitter past over unappetizing meals to facilitate the youths' reeducation.[12] These memories served as a useful foil for the more just world that the party promised to provide for China's poor, a socialist utopia replete with bountiful harvests and plump healthy babies, suggesting that, as far as food was concerned, the Communists were only trying to deliver what Confucians, or so they argued, failed to provide.[13] Yet with food a powerful sense of time and place may be wrought from even the most wretched circumstances. Take, for instance, the recent popularity of Cultural Revolution theme restaurants, where former sent-down urban youth gather over plates of rustic fare and reminisce about hard times engaging in manual labor in the countryside.[14] In China, culinary nostalgia has been a valuable framework for articulating both ideology and utopia, and for learning how to live with the consequences of the one or the absence of the other.

The significance that Chinese have attributed to food, and in particular to cherished specialty foodstuffs and regional cuisine restaurants, is the focus of this book. To understand how these themes played out in Shanghai, and to identify the conjuncture and disjuncture between Shanghai's food history and that of China more generally, this introduction first assesses the state of scholarship on regional food culture in China.[15] I then chart a new framework for identifying the historical significance of food as a symbol of place, and as an object through which people understand and make sense of the world around them. As will be seen, the history of food as a symbol of place has a long history in China, where regional food culture has been an important component of personal and group identity, and of both dominant accounts of the past and counter-narratives written from the "margins." This introduction then closes with a preliminary overview of the ways in which Shanghai city residents and commentators on Shanghai society have engaged with food culture to identify and remake the image of Shanghai itself.

National and Regional Food Culture in China

Chinese attach great importance and meaning to their hometown food culture. Visitors to China throughout history have been struck not only by the preferences that Chinese from one part of the country express for the foods of their native region, but also by their reluctance, and even professions of inability, to eat the food of another region. As one Republican-era Chinese interpreter of food culture in China explained to Shanghai's English-reading public: "The cuisine of a locality is a reflection of the surrounding topography, and the mode of living of the inhabitants. . . . Chinese from the far mountains of Sichuan do not have their food prepared in the same way as natives of Shanghai. . . . There is variation from north to south . . . and again from east to west . . . . The main products of the place must of necessity form the basis of the people's food, and their cooking is built around the ingredients produced in their own district."[16] Of course, all food has some local characteristics. In the context of French cuisine, this is explained by the concept of *terroir*, a term that denotes the special properties that the soil of a particular place imbues in local products, especially wine.[17] Seeking to identify the "importance of food itself in Chinese culture," K. C. Chang once observed, "That Chinese cuisine is the greatest in the world is highly debatable and is essentially irrelevant. But few can take exception to the statement that few other cultures are as food oriented as the Chinese."[18] One could add to Chang's point that in few places have conversations about regional food culture been as historically significant as in China. It is not that such conversations do not take place in other parts of the world. But just as Philip Kafalas notes about the prevalence of tropes of nostalgia in the history of Chinese letters, so with the question of discourse on regional food: "There seems to be a difference of degree."[19]

The importance of regional foodways to the process of self- and place-formation in China is a recognized area of Chinese culture. Yet the historical significance of differences in regional food culture, and of the ideas that Chinese have formulated about these differences, has not yet been integrated into the study of Chinese history. This significance has been recognized but also partially obscured by some pioneering scholarship on the history and anthropology of food in China, including the landmark 1977 essay collection, *Food in Chinese Culture*. The essays in this collection are rich and nuanced and reward multiple re-readings, but as Charles Hayford pointed out in a review of the collection, there is a fundamental tension in the volume between those contributions that emphasize continuity in food culture in China and those that emphasize change over time.[20] The editor, Chang, tries to strike a balance, noting, "First, continuity vastly outweighs change . . . . Second, there are enough changes to warrant some preliminary efforts to give the periodization of Chinese history a new perspective." Chang initially cedes ground on the second point, "to let [the] authors speak for themselves in regard to the major events in each of the periods." But he then posits three thresholds of major change: the "beginning of farming"; the "beginning of a highly stratified society, possibly in the Hsia [Xia] dynastic period [ca. 21st–18th c. B.C.] and certainly by the Shang period of the eighteenth century B.C."; and a third, some three thousand years later, "happening right in our own time," in the "truly national distribution of . . . food resources," during the People's Republic.[21] Chang recognizes that, in between the second and third stages, "Most changes involved the geographic movement of peoples with their particular food habits," but adds that "truly important changes having to do with total alignment of society are very rare."[22]

The overall effect of Chang's assessment is contradictory. On the one hand, there is a set of enduring core elements of "Chinese" food culture, such as Chang's notion of the "*fan-cai* principle"—according to which Chinese diets are understood to consist of a base of grains and other starch foods complemented with vegetable or meat dishes. On the other hand, there are many remarkable developments, at both empire-wide and regional levels, of indeterminate significance. With regard to "Chinese food culture" in the aggregate, Edward Schafer's contribution to the collection identifies a Tang "revolution" in attitudes toward "foreign manners and customs," which "ultimately led to the richness and variety of modern Chinese cookery." Michael Freeman, moreover, suggests that Song (960–1279) capital cities witnessed the creation of a self-conscious "cuisine" as something understood to be distinct from mere cookery. But when Schafer's and Freeman's suggestions regarding change are followed by a chapter on Yuan (1279–1368) and Ming (1368–1644) food that identifies the overall pattern of food culture in China as one of "limited change within stable patterns," the overall effect of the earlier contributions is effectively neutralized.[23] Moreover, we are left with a recasting, through the history of food, of the once-conventional, but now largely discredited, image of China's abortive "medieval" modernity. It also remains unclear just what significance to attach to the "geographic movement of peoples with their particular food habits."

Some greater clarity may emerge by adapting the insights of recent scholarship on China that denaturalizes the category and space of the nation, and by further applying these insights to our study of the idea of the region.[24] First, a nonnationalist perspective will make it possible to identify geographical and chronological frameworks that help explain broad patterns of change during the three to four thousand years spanning Chang's second and third threshold. After all, Shang territories included neither Sichuan nor the Guangdong region, two territories that provide, for many, definitive components of Chinese cuisine. And as Chen Mengyin, a Hong Kong food writer who published under the pseudonym Tejijiaodui, pointed out more than four decades ago, what we know today as Sichuan cuisine did not begin to take shape until the late seventeenth century, and Cantonese cuisine did not acquire the high status it is accorded today until the early twentieth century.[25] Moreover, what came to pass for "Northern" and Huaiyang cuisine—which along with Sichuan and Cantonese cuisine constitute the so-called "four great culinary traditions" (*sida caixi*) of China—certainly did not exist in even the Zhou, Han, or Tang, let alone the Shang. Indeed, leaving aside questions of temporal origin and comparative assessments of quality and taste, the wider prestige of "Northern" cooking, commonly identified as being synonymous with Shandong (Lu) cooking, is attributable largely to the patronage of Shandong (and to a lesser extent Henan) chefs by the Manchu emperors, especially the Qianlong emperor (r. 1735–96), of the Qing (1644–1911).[26] How then might we characterize some of the changes in the intervening periods between the eras marking Chang's second and third thresholds?

Viewing Chinese food culture from the level of imperial capital cities, we might adapt the approach of Valerie Hansen's *Open Empire*, which identifies broad shifts in the geographical orientation of imperial formations in China. Seen in this light, the cosmopolitan food culture in Tang Chang'an may be best seen as the culmination of a "Western facing" food culture, whereas that of Song Kaifeng and especially Southern Song Hangzhou mark a transition to an "Eastward facing" food culture that is itself discontinuous in significant ways with the northern steppe, Southeast Asian, and American orientations and influences that become so important to food culture in the Yuan, early Ming, and late Ming, respectively.[27]

Second, it will also be helpful to rethink what is commonly meant by "regional food culture" in discussions of food in China. Regional diversity in Chinese food culture is most commonly characterized in axioms that postulate the existence of either "four great culinary traditions" (*sida caixi*)—generally taken to be Cantonese, Sichuan, Huaiyang (or Jiangsu), and Northern (or Shandong)—or "eight great culinary traditions" (*bada caixi*), adding Anhui, Fujian, Hunan, and Zhejiang cooking to the first four. Complementing these are notions of "minor" cuisines, such as that of the "eight minor culinary traditions" (*baxiao caixi*). Yet, as a number of scholars have pointed out, these categories obscure as much as they clarify because one such term might encompass cooking styles that are as different from one another as they are from a style represented by another term.[28] E. N. and Marja Anderson have noted that yet another classification system posits five great regional cuisines—although the five change depending on the classifier—and suggest that this reflects "little more" than "an interesting demonstration of the Chinese obsession with grouping everything by fives." For the purposes of their own analysis, they "added at least three more schools of cooking," on the ground that they "have appreciated [them] as worthy of equal rank."[29] Such gestures, however, only reinforce the relative arbitrariness of such classification systems. Moreover, Chinese have themselves historically been well aware of the inadequacies of these terms. Thus, when Republican-era restaurant critics wrote in general of Shanghai's "Cantonese cuisine" (*Yuecai*) restaurants, they acknowledged that doing so was to engage in a kind of shorthand for different cooking styles within Guangdong Province, where one would more rigorously distinguish Chaozhou and Guangzhou varieties of Cantonese cuisine.[30]

The effort to classify "great" and "minor" culinary traditions is further complicated by shifts in collective assessments of regional cooking. Anhui cooking is generally considered one of China's "eight great culinary traditions," but

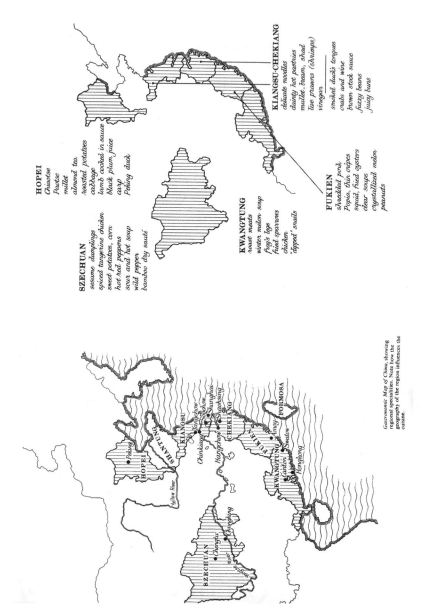

HOPEI
Chiaotse
millet
almond tea
roasted potatoes
cabbage
lamb cooked in sauce
black plum juice
carp
Peking duck

SZECHUAN
sesame dumplings
spiced tangerine chicken
sweet potatoes, corn
hot red peppers
sour and hot soup
wild pepper
bamboo dry sauté

KWANGTUNG
roast meats
winter melon soup
frog's legs
fried sparrows
chicken
"dipped" snails

KIANGSU-CHEKIANG
delicate noodles
dainty hot pastries
mullet, bream, shad
live prawns (shrimps)
vinegar
smoked duck's tongues
crabs and wine
brown stock sauce
fuzzy beans
juicy buns

FUKIEN
shredded pork
Popia, thin crêpes
squid, fried oysters
clear soups
crystallized melon
peanuts

Gastronomic Map of China, showing
regional specialities. Note how the
geography of the region influences the
cuisine.

Figure I.1 "Gastronomic Map of China," Representing Selective Regions: Hebei (Hopei), Jiangsu (Kiangsu), Zhejiang (Chekiang), Fujian (Fukien), Guangdong (Kwangtung), and Sichuan (Szechuan).

SOURCE: *Chinese Gastronomy,* by Hsiang Ju Lin and Tsuifeng Lin, by permission of the K S Giniger Company, New York.

in Republican Shanghai, Anhui cooking was best known for inexpensive and large portions, and its status has fallen even further in present-day Shanghai. Dafugui, an Anhui restaurant that first opened in Shanghai during the late nineteenth century, is one of the oldest extant restaurants in the city. Yet today its menu offers few traditional Anhui dishes and includes many dishes from the repertoire of Shanghai cuisine, a cooking style that some now consider to be, at the very least, one of China's "eight minor culinary traditions," and possibly even the new flagship cuisine of the broader Huaiyang region. This decline in the status of Anhui cuisine may account for its omission, for example, from the very learned and thoughtful 1969 *Chinese Gastronomy*, by Hsiang Ju Lin and Tsuifeng Lin. This text included a "Gastronomic Map of China" that illustrated regional specialties of Chinese cuisine (see Figure I.1). But the map is itself remarkable for the many blanks it contains and for the way it obscures not only Anhui cooking but all regional styles west of major coastal regions, except for that of Sichuan.

Such shifts in status, and the lack of fit between categories of cuisine and culinary practice, beg the question of how these categories came about in the first place and when, where, and why they are put to use. As Taiwan historian Lu Yaodong points out, regional cuisines often do not acquire a clear self-conscious definition as something distinct, different, or "authentic" (*zhengzong*) until the purveyors of different cuisines come into contact with one another and seek to differentiate the qualities and flavors of their variety of cooking from others.[31] Moreover, if local food culture is such an important component of a sense of self and place, how has it come about that Chinese have also concluded that these various regional cuisines constitute a broader "Chinese" culinary tradition? Indeed, as some of the best cookbooks point out, some culinary traditions that are today considered a part of the repertoire of Chinese cooking as a whole, such as that of Yunnan Province, have more in common with Southeast Asian cooking than with any other variety of regional cuisine in China.[32] As the present book shows, even Cantonese cuisine seemed foreign to mid-nineteenth-century men of Jiangnan who first encountered it in Shanghai. What conclusions, finally, have Chinese drawn from recognition of this diversity? To answer these questions, this study considers the terms used to designate regional cuisines as discursive constructs rather than as simply analytical categories, and I examine where, when, and why claims for gustatory difference or distinction are made.

Two Traditions of Regional Foodways

The copious documentary record on food in China provides many insights into cultural constructions of place in discourse on regional foodways. Broadly speaking, this discourse speaks of two different forms of food culture: one centered on local specialty foodstuffs, and a second on regional restaurants. The two traditions are sometimes related, because the cuisine served in a Cantonese restaurant, for example, is often prepared with ingredients that were originally particular to the Guangdong region. But there are also important differences in discourse on these two forms of food culture, as well as in the kinds of source material through which regional foodways may be studied. To highlight these differences, the two traditions are distinguished here. What links the two, for the purposes of the present discussion, is not so much their culinary relationship, but the way that people from a particular part of China identified both specialty foods and cuisine as a manifestation of local culture and of the importance of their home regions.

Among the most valuable sources of information about regional food culture and of regional food consciousness are gazetteers (*fangzhi*).[33] Gazetteers were a genre of history writing that grew out of central government record keeping and biographical literatures on local worthies. By the Yuan, they were perhaps the most important record of a region's historical significance. Gazetteers provided imperial authorities with detailed accounts of the territories under their jurisdiction and aided local officials in administration, but they were also, above all, representations of place. Their focus was usually a geographical administrative unit, such as a county or prefecture, and they organized copious amounts of information into categories such as changing borders, topographical features, famous places, official buildings, waterworks projects, records of omens, chronicles of natural and manmade disasters, academies and schools, temples, officeholders, fiscal information, granaries, markets, military institutions, biographies of local figures (officials, chaste women, military men, doctors, and monks), and local crops and products.[34] County-level gazetteers (*xianzhi*) provided the raw materials for gazetteers of higher-order units of administration, such as prefectures (*fuzhi*) and comprehensive gazetteers of the entire realm (*yitongzhi*). Local notables and county-level officials often compiled county gazetteers in response to a directive from prefectural or central authorities, but the gazetteers themselves reflected the hometown sentiments of the men who compiled and wrote them. As Timothy Brook explains, "The compiler of a local gazetteer placed before his reader a comprehensive edited archive of the history and geography of his local area," which "stood in a sense as proof that the area was culturally developed. By doing so, [the gazetteer] strengthened the claim of native sons who went out into the national bureaucratic or cultural world to be taken seriously."[35]

The section of the gazetteer most responsible for spreading word of local food products carried the title "*wuchan*," or "crops and products." The term was a standard chapter title for gazetteers by the Song and accounted for everything from raw materials, such as local varieties of fruits and vegetables, to processed specialty foods, known as *tuchan* or *techan*.[36] The following excerpt, from the Jiaqing-era (1796–1820) *Gazetteer of Zhujing* (Zhujing zhi), illustrates the ways in which the genre provided a framework for locals to boast about the high quality of local crops and products: "The crabs are smaller than in Pandang and Fenhe, but the taste is actually superior. Bamboo shoots are a product of Zhaofen; they are fragrant and crisp, plump and white, and not inferior to [those of] Yushan."[37]

The straightforward tone of the entry is typical of the genre and may have had its origins in one of the earliest extant uses of the term *wuchan*, in the Jin dynasty (265–420) poet Zuo Si's (c. 253–c. 307) "Three Capitals Rhapsody" (Sandu fu) a long poem in the "rhyme prose" (*fu*) genre. As David Knechtges notes, "Zuo Si was especially critical of the hyperbole, exaggeration, and lack of verisimilitude that characterized the works of the Han [206 B.C.–A.D 220] *fu* poets." Zuo Si's criticism of his predecessors is worth citing at length for what it reveals about the impulses animating record-keeping of local crops and products:

When Xiangru composed his "Imperial Park," he referred to "black kumquats that ripen in summer." When Yang Xiong composed his "Sweet Springs Palace," he described "jade trees green and virescent." Ban Gu in his "Western Capital Rhapsody" remarked about catching "paired-eye fish." Zhang Heng in his "Western Capital Rhapsody" told about the playing *Hai-ruo* [ocean monster]. . . . These writers contrived rarities and wonders in order to embellish their writings. If we examine the fruits and trees mentioned, we find they do not grow in that soil; and if we look at the supernatural creatures, we find they do not come from the specified place. In terms of rhetoric, it was easy to produce gaudy ornament, but as far as meaning is concerned, their works are vacuous and lacking veracity.

. . . When I first thought of writing the "Three Capitals" in imitation of the "Two Metropolises," for the mountains and streams, cities and towns, I consulted maps. Birds and animals, plants and trees, I have verified in gazetteers. . . . Why have I done this? . . . Without the truth and facts, what can the reader believe?

Furthermore, fixing tribute according to the nature of the land is specified in the "Documents of Yu" [from the *Classic of History*]. "To distinguish between things and set them in their proper place" is something the *Classic of Changes* carefully considered. For now, I have only lifted one corner and arranged the form and generalities, all in conformity with the words of the ancients.[38]

For Zuo Si, crops and products needed to be identified and assessed properly not only because it was what the ancients expected, but because doing so defined the relationship between the imperial center and the various components of the wider realm, as well as that between Heaven and earth.

Writing more than a millennium later, Shanghai's gazetteer writers were similarly concerned with defining this relationship and maintaining cosmic order. As the crops and products entry in the 1524 *Shanghai County Gazetteer* (Jiajing Shanghai xianzhi) noted, "Heaven bears things in accordance with the land. Examples are provided here to illustrate the pattern."[39] The 1683 edition, like Zuo Si, traced this need to classical precedent: "The *Book of Odes* recognized grasses and trees, birds and beasts; the "Document of Yu" listed fine and coarse bamboo, *jun* and *lu* bamboo, the pearl-oyster of the Huai, and the turtle of the Yangtze. All provided a livelihood for the people and were products of the land. Therefore, although trifling, they must be detailed."[40] Centuries of such "detailing" and "pattern-illustration" made regional food culture into a powerful vehicle for imagining community, and for projecting images of local culture upward toward the emperor and outward to other regions, linking the world of the image makers to a larger empire, or civilization, and its history.

Locally, people understood that Heaven could only bear things in accordance with the land's particular *fengtu* (literally, wind and soil), a *terroir*-like notion that conceptualized places as local "expression[s] of a pervasive correlative cosmology." *Fengtu* accounted for the way that "human beings replicate the natural world," as well as for particular emanations of art, literature, and aspects of everyday life, such as social customs and diet and food preparation.[41] The idea of *fengtu* even inspired medical thinkers to postulate regionally differentiated forms of human physiology that required distinct forms of medical treatment.[42] Despite the appearance of influential strains of philosophical and scientific skepticism toward the principles of correlative cosmology during the seventeenth century, the idea of *fengtu* remained pervasive, both as an aspect of human experience, and as an explanatory device.[43] As one early-twentieth-century observer remarked with regard to the food preferences of the people of Anhui,

Anhui people are especially fond of fatty [foods]. The taste of [local food] is so fatty that, when visitors first arrive from other places, [they find the food] so greasy that they cannot eat it; while Anhui people, on the contrary, consider it delicious. It is said that this is related to the natural environment and climate, and that were diets not like this, it would not be possible to maintain healthy digestion.[44]

In any given place, *fengtu* mattered for locals and nonlocals alike. Non-Anhui natives, not having been raised in Anhui *fengtu*, were incapable of eating Anhui cooking, and Anhui natives were only able to survive on Anhui foods, even when not in Anhui. Anhui people constituted some of the wealthiest and most mobile merchant groups in late imperial China, and historical records indicate that everywhere Anhui merchants went, so did Anhui entrepreneurs, opening Anhui restaurants to meet their fellow-provincials' native-place taste preferences and dietary needs.[45] These establishments helped sojourning Anhui merchants maintain a close relationship to their hometowns and compensated for the foreign *fengtu* they encountered along their commercial routes.

The need for such establishments, felt not only by Anhui merchants, but by all sojourners in imperial China, was a driving force of the development of restaurants, the second important tradition of regional food culture in China. The earliest houses of public dining in China for which there are reliable records date to Tang times. Weary travelers and pilgrims sought rest and refreshment at Taoist or Buddhist monasteries. Officials found food and lodging in hostels known as *guan*, a near homophone for the term "official" (*guan*), the term for "hostel" being rendered in print with the addition of the graphic radical for "food," "to eat," or "to drink" (*shi*). Such hostels, as Schafer notes, were not always exclusive establishments and were generally located in the heart of commercial districts, near "marketplaces, mansions, and boat moorages." They were distinct, however, from establishments known as *jiudian* (wine shops), also called *jiusi* (wine houses) or *jiulou* (wine halls), that provided male patrons with entertainment, light snacks, wine, and prospects of companionship.[46] Such public venues for eating out were features of city life and followed the spread of trade across the empire in the form of the *lüdian*, or traveler's shop. "During the most prosperous part of the eighth century," Schafer writes, "when commodities were abundant, food cheap, and travel safe, there were restaurants (*ssu* [*si*]) all along the public roads 'to wait upon wayfarers with food and drink.'"[47]

Although the institutions of Tang public dining resemble the networks of taverns and inns that grew up in medieval and early modern Europe, restaurants in Song cities exhibited more distinct characteristics. Kaifeng, the political and commercial center of the Northern Song (960–1126), drew travelers and migrants from all parts of the empire, and a restaurant industry evolved there to meet the population's diverse food needs. Although food in China varied regionally before the Song, in Kaifeng these differences were embodied, for the first time, in a restaurant industry divided along regionalist lines; restaurants there served either "northern" (*beishi*), "southern" (*nanshi*), or "Sichuan" food (*Chuanfan*). "In [Kaifeng]," wrote Wu Zimu (fl. 1276) in his *Record of the Splendors of the Capital City* (Mengliang lu), "southern style noodle shops and Sichuanese tea houses were made for gentlemen from Jiangnan, who said they didn't care for northern food."[48] A similar configuration of restaurants emerged in Hangzhou, after the Song capital moved south in 1127.

The mobility of the domestic Chinese population spread regional cooking from one end of the empire to the other and heightened regional food consciousness. "To cook northern food in Hangchow [Hangzhou]," Freeman notes, "implied a conscious choice among possible ingredients and possible styles of cooking; it became, in other words, a style of cooking set loose from its local moorings and the product of a consciously maintained tradition."[49] These tendencies only heightened with the increased geographic mobility of the Ming and Qing, which was so great that it brought into being a new kind of sojourner's institution, the *huiguan*, or native-place lodge. *Huiguan* provided their members with social services ranging from the mediation of business disputes to the repatriation of remains, and they functioned as oases of home food culture in foreign lands. As Frederick W. Mote explains, "The *hui-kuan* [*huiguan*] had a staff of employees from the home locality, including cooks. The Su-chou [Suzhou] merchant or statesman residing temporarily at the Su-chou *hui-kuan* in Peking, at any of the important centers along the Grand Canal or the Yangtze, or at other important locations could expect to hear his Su-chou speech and to eat his fine Su-chou shop noodles and pastries for breakfast."[50] Such institutions helped familiarize cities for sojourners, while marking sojourners as "other" to the cities through which they traveled.

Food as Local Knowledge

Just how "other" a person was depended largely on access to material and symbolic resources, which provided social groups with opportunities to shape the regimes of representation through which regional food culture endowed a particular part of the Chinese realm with historical significance. In imperial China, accounts of local food culture in local gazetteers spoke, first and foremost, to the imperial center, which drew from their materials to create comprehensive gazetteers of the entire realm, creating a stabilized image of the relationship between the center and its peripheries. This meant that, ideally, gazetteers were updated in a timely manner, to register regime changes and to make it possible to incorporate local developments into a dynastic narrative. Accounts of foreign food items offered in tribute to emperors of China, recorded methodically into the "veritable records" of each dynasty, complemented this image of the empire and, in addition, identified the terms of the political relationship between the space of the imperial realm and that of its neighbors and trading partners. The ultimate arbiter of this narrative was Heaven because food culture, or any culture for that matter, could thrive only in a place that was favored by Heaven for its social, political, and moral rectitude. A local claim for recognition of Heaven's favor could pose a direct or indirect challenge to the imperial center. As we will see with the case of the Shanghai honey nectar peach, such claims also constituted assertions of superiority over other regions and claims to a cosmopolitan status.

In the twentieth century, the terms of such claims and counterclaims were transformed, when linear history replaced the dynastic model of history writing as the dominant mode of narrating time and space.[51] The subject of history itself shifted from the establishment and maintenance of imperial political authority to the emergence of the nation-state, the story of which insisted on the unfolding of a national culture. Accounts of national foodways written in a linear mode did not grant any special privilege to local food culture. Instead, they plotted stages in a national history of food that spanned the entirety of "Chinese" history, from remote antiquity to the present, emphasizing general topics such as food rituals and the history of food processing, especially agricultural techniques and crops.[52] These linear narratives provided challenges for chroniclers of local food culture, who developed new frameworks for asserting its historical significance. Although linear national history dominated academic and political circles, it did not maintain a monopoly on representations of the past. Accounts of local food culture provided important ways of either writing local history into national history, or of producing alternatives to linear history and a way of "rescuing history from the nation."

Food culture was thus part of a broader discourse on what Prasenjit Duara calls the idea of "the local." For Duara, "the local"—the nominalization is key—is "a site of authentic values of a larger formation, such as the nation or civilization." It refers not so much to specific locations, but to the conceptual framework through which Chinese attributed historical significance to particular places: villages, cities, provinces, even forests. Such attributions of historical significance linked the idea of the local to a sense of time, making in each case for a distinct "chronotope," a space "characterized by its own temporal rhythm." Duara takes as his case study Liang Shanding's 1942 novel *Green Valley* (Lüse de gu), in which Duara identifies three such chronotopes: the primeval Manchurian forest represents a "natural, cyclical time outside linear history"; Langgou valley, fought over by competing elites and state-building factions, represents the "linear time of the nation" in the making; and the city Nanmanzhang represents "the accelerating pace of capitalist change" in the international geopolitical context of Japanese colonial capitalism.[53]

Zhou Zuoren's (1885–1967) essay about his favorite hometown sweets, "Selling Candy" (Mai tang), illuminates the ways in which food operated as a subject of chronotopic discourse.[54] Zhou, a Shaoxing native who spent several years studying in Japan before finally settling in Beijing, was one of the leading participants in the great debates of the early-twentieth-century May Fourth–New Culture Movement, which promised to solve China's problems by providing Chinese people with a new culture to replace the old. Zhou soon broke with the mainstream of the New Culture intellectuals, however, because he was reluctant to embrace their dim view of China's past and feared the consequences of their insistence that writing serve the politics of nation-building. Instead, Zhou developed a long-term interest in Chinese local society through the study of history, anthropology, and folklore. This passion served him well after Japan's occupation of Beijing in July 1937. Unlike many Chinese intellectuals who fled Beijing for the interior, Zhou remained in the fallen city, reluctantly accepting the position of head librarian at Beijing University, and later becoming a member of Wang Jingwei's (1883–1944) pro-Japanese government. Zhou was later tried and sentenced by the Nationalist Party for "collaboration," but "Selling Candy," which traverses some four hundred years of history in China and Japan, resists easy identification with such motives.[55]

The essay, written in 1938, is a thought piece on how a representation of food is able to conjure a sense of place. Zhou begins the essay by discussing a reference, in Cui Xu's (1767–1846) *Random Notes on Poetry by Niantang* (Niantang shihua), to a certain variety of "night candies" that were sold on the streets of his hometown by the beat of a gong. After registering his disappointment that an important work on Shaoxing folklore and customs, the *Yueyan*, fails to mention this practice, Zhou remarks, "How much duller would life be for the little ones, because night candies and toasted pastry are two great favorites with the children; they all have to have them, whether street urchins or children of the rich." He then describes in loving detail how the various sweets are manufactured, the configuration and sound of the gongs, and the comings and goings of vendors, before noting, suggestively,

> Since I came to Beijing I have not seen these pastries anymore, because in the South rice is the staple food and these pastries were made of rice flour; the situation is completely different [in the north]. The things we ate when we were small were not always so tasty but later they seem to become extremely delicious. This is exactly the reason why I keep remembering all these candies and sweetmeats.[56]

Clearly, absence made the heart grow fonder, but the essay is no mere apology for the creative powers of memory. "Selling Candy" ends with a reference to Zhu Shunshui (1600–82), a Ming loyalist who "assimilated" to Japanese society after the Ming state fell to the Manchus. Zhu was revered in Tokugawa Japan (1603–1868) as a Confucian authority, and, many years later, by revolutionary Chinese for his anti-Manchu writings. Significantly, as Zhou notes, Zhu hailed from a neighboring Shaoxing town that sold the same candy.[57]

Zhou was clearly grappling with the problem of what it might mean to live in a part of China that had become, of all things, a part of the Japanese colonial empire. His solution was to make Shaoxing food culture into a chronotope that transcended the problems of the day. When Zhou wrote, the Qing had disaggregated into several semi-independent territories, and China proper, the component of the former empire that most concerned Zhou, was itself falling to pieces. A century of wars with foreign powers had littered China with alien outposts and leased territories, prompting fears that the country was being "carved up like a melon." Violent clashes between rival warlord factions and an intermittent civil war between the Nationalist and Communist Parties only exacerbated the fragmentation. Under the leadership of Chiang Kai-shek, the Nationalist Party had established a provisional sense of unity during the Nanjing Decade (1928–37), but by now the Nationalist government had fled Japan's assault on the national capital and had not yet re-constituted itself in the wartime capital of Chongqing. And though internationally recognized, the

Nationalists themselves laid waste to much of the land and many of the communities through which they passed during their inland retreat. For its part, the Communist Party had barely begun to establish a viable presence beyond its base areas near remote Yan'an, and had in any event fervently embraced the New Culture Movement's disdain for traditional ways of life. Memories of food that traversed vast spans of time and space—and that identified, in this case, a precedent for the role that Zhou had to play under Japanese occupation— made for a surer sense of home than any of the major political alternatives. Zhou's writings on food thus reveal a form of mnemonic and historiographical practice that sought to carve out a cultural realm that transcended the secular politics of empire, imperialism, and nationalism.

Shanghai, Modern and Nostalgic

Foodways, as this book shows, also helped Chinese in Shanghai construct their own nostalgic visions of the ways in which their hometowns, or the city itself, fit or did not fit in with dominant discourses of place and politics during the late imperial period and the twentieth century. The choice of Shanghai for a study of such nostalgic sentiment and food culture in China requires some explanation. Shanghai is not widely recognized for having a distinctive, or even remarkable, regional food culture of its own, at least not until quite recently. Moreover, Shanghai, more so than any other Chinese city, projects an image of China as "modern" or "cosmopolitan," a place wrenched free of the morass of the rest of China and its supposedly constricting past. Indeed, in *Midnight*, Mao Dun's (1896–1981) paradigmatic fictional account of the city, written and published in the early 1930s, the idea of a Chinese cultural past appears only fleetingly, embodied by the crippled and decrepit Old Mr. Wu, who arrives in Shanghai in the opening scene of the novel clutching a book titled *The Supreme Book of Rewards and Punishments*. When Old Mr. Wu dies later that night, from a heart attack brought on by the scandalously revealing clothing worn by the young and "modern" women of the family, his poet nephew remarks, "In this modern city of Shanghai he has done. He's gone, and good riddance. One mummy of old China the less." In response, the old man's niece musters no more than "pretend vexation," suggesting that even those who disagreed were, in fact, only faking it.[58]

This view of Shanghai, the city that Marie-Claire Bergère provocatively dubbed the "other China," and Rhoads Murphey called the "key to modern China," registers many important aspects of the city's history.[59] It has also inspired a sizable body of scholarship, on reformers and revolutionaries, the new press and the public sphere, political reform and civil society, capitalists and labor activists, and culture, including film, music, and literary modernism.[60]

The character of Shanghai's "otherness" and "modernity," however, only represents one part of the city's history. Shanghai turns out to have been very closely linked not only to its immediate hinterland, but to numerous far regions of China. It was also home to a population with employment, residential, and organizational patterns shaped decisively by rural and extra-local forms of culture and communication. People resided in new kinds of buildings, but their lifestyles, and the material conditions in which many city residents lived, often resembled those that prevailed in the countryside.[61] For much of Shanghai's history, native-place identity was a more salient form of personal and group identification than was the nation, or even the city itself. Moreover, regional identity and national identity were by no means incompatible.[62] These trends point to an urban culture that, contra Bergère, might well be called the "other Shanghai." It would be foolish to suggest that Shanghai did not represent the prospects and problems of what it meant to be "modern," to its own residents and to outsiders. But modern did not always mean "Western," and it would be a mistake to overlook the ways in which the "modern" or "Western" character of Shanghai made the apparent waning of "traditional" China all the more acute.

Nostalgia appears as a salient theme at virtually every stage and turning point of the city's history. The influential reformer Wang Tao (1828–97), for example, formulated highly influential ideas about political reform and citizenship. But he also wrote accounts of city life that were deeply infused with nostalgia for the Jiangnan culture destroyed by the mid-century Taiping Rebellion (1851–64).[63] The industrialization of Shanghai that followed the 1895 Treaty of Shimonoseki, which granted foreign powers the right to open factories in China, inspired numerous visual and literary representations of "Old Shanghai." These include a 1910 serialized illustrated guide to the "Three Hundred and Sixty Trades," published when many everyday street vendors and artisans were disappearing from the urban landscape, and such texts as Chen Boxi's 1924 *Compendium of Shanghai Anecdotes* (Shanghai yishi daguan) and Chen Wuwo's 1928 *Record of Things Seen and Heard over Thirty Years in Old Shanghai* (Lao Shanghai sanshinian jianwenlu).[64] Japan's occupation of Shanghai during the Second Sino-Japanese War (1937–45) moved many intellectuals in the city to identify as *yimin*, or "anachronisms," to carve out for themselves a "space of atonement" for staying behind in the city after it fell. They published their wartime writings in the journal *Reminiscences* (Gujin).[65] One period of Shanghai's history that is not clearly marked by an articulate and outspoken longing for the city's past is the Maoist period (1949–76). At that time, politics was predicated, in theory at least, on a repudiation of that past. Over time, however, even CCP officials recognized that, to maintain authority, they had to make important allowances for the popular forms of urban market culture that they had designed their policies to eradicate.[66] The widespread and oft-noted "Old Shanghai" nostalgia of the late-twentieth and early-twenty-first centuries turns out to be only the most recent chapter in the history of urban sentiment in a city that has long been a deeply nostalgic place.[67]

Few topics are better suited for exploring these themes over the *longue durée* of Shanghai history than is food culture. Shanghai foodways reveal vital links between Shanghai and other parts of the country, and the documentary record of food in Shanghai is replete with nostalgic sentiment.

Officially designated a market town in 1074, and then a market city in 1159, before becoming the county seat of Shanghai County in 1292, Shanghai grew into a city of more than two hundred thousand during Ming rule.[68] Already by this time, as Chapter One shows, Shanghai struck many city residents as a place that had lost or was losing its way, and local elites struggled to carve out a distinctive identity for the city. Shanghai faced many of the same economic challenges as other parts of the wider Jiangnan region in which it was located, particularly inflation and fiscal instability arising from the monetization of the Ming economy and, later, large infusions of silver from the New World.[69] As Craig Clunas has shown, such instability occasioned great new "anxieties about things," especially luxury goods, antiques, books, and other items through which China's elites cultivated a sense of distinction, but also such everyday commodities as foodstuffs.[70] Late-Ming commodity culture challenged the value and meaning of material objects and drew attention to their ability to disrupt more idealized ways of life. In Shanghai, the situation was exacerbated by the city's heavy reliance on imports for basic foods, like rice, which grew plentifully in the wider region, but not so well in Shanghai County, where, by the early seventeenth century, more than 70 percent of Shanghai's soil was in cotton.

Another crop that grew well in Shanghai, however, was peaches, a valuable and symbol-laden foodstuff that brought the city much needed cultural capital and offset the city's reputation as a one-crop commercial town. Peach cultivation took off in Shanghai during the mid-Ming period. The best of all Shanghai peaches were of the "honey nectar" variety (*shuimitao*), which grew famously well in the Gu family's Dew Fragrance Garden, located just inside the northwest arc of the city walls. Word of the Gu family peaches spread far and wide, even after Dew Fragrance Garden fell into disrepair and itself became an object of nostalgia. By spreading word of local peaches over the mid-Ming and early-Qing periods, local elites created an image of Shanghai as a peach garden paradise. Their writings evoked both the rural idyll of Tao Qian's "Record of the Peach Blossom Spring" and the famed Shanglin Garden, which Emperor Wu of the Han (r. 140–86 B.C.) had built to embody the cosmic significance of his realm. By likening Shanghai to these two places of the past, local elites represented Shanghai as a central place in the Chinese realm, and one where, in image at least, the uncertainties of Ming and Qing commodity culture did not predominate.

Idealized images of other times and places remained salient tropes of food writing in Shanghai after the city opened to foreign settlement and trade in 1843, but as Chapter Two shows, the object of nostalgia shifted to other, more geographically specific, parts of China, and to aspects of the city's own past. One of the factors shaping this shift was demographic change. Like most late imperial Chinese cities, mid-Qing Shanghai had many sojourners, from Fujian, Shanxi, and Zhejiang provinces, as well as the cities of Chaozhou and Huizhou. During the second half of the nineteenth century, however, Shanghai became the most demographically diverse city in China and home to a population of nonlocals that soon outnumbered the locals. The new population came to the city in three great mid-century waves of domestic migration, from Guangdong, Jiangsu, and Zhejiang; from overseas (initially from England, France, and the United States, but later also from Russia and Japan); and then more gradually from other parts of China. The immigrants settled heavily in Shanghai's foreign concessions, territories originally designated only for foreign settlement but that for logistical reasons became home to a Chinese population that far outnumbered the foreigners.

Unaccustomed to Shanghai foods and cooking, these newcomers did their best to produce or procure food comparable to what they had eaten from childhood in their native places, and a vibrant regionally and nationally diverse restaurant industry emerged to meet their native place needs. The new regional restaurants opened up all over the city, but the geography of the restaurant industry corresponded closely with urban demographics. Restaurateurs set up shop in areas of the city with large numbers of potential native-place patrons; Cantonese restaurants were most common in neighborhoods with large numbers of Cantonese residents, whereas Anhui restaurants were never far from the city's many pawnshops, which were owned and staffed by Anhui natives.[71] Restaurateurs attracted their clientele by catering to native-place taste preferences and by promoting their establishments as oases of regional culture.

This new demography was only one part of the story, however. The rapid growth of Shanghai coincided with and fed off the decline of several of China's largest and wealthiest cities. Shanghai itself soon became the wealthiest in the realm, and a place that struck many observers as a veritable "Penglai," home to an enthralling variety of new things, foods and otherwise. These novelties generated much excitement, but also new anxieties about the uncertainties of city life, prompting city residents, natives and newcomers alike, to identify ever more strongly with the idea of Shanghai as a "Wulingyuan," only now as an image of the city that was on the verge of being lost. The loss was rendered all the more poignant by the decline of local peach cultivation during the second half of the nineteenth century. Shanghai residents complained loudly about how peach hoarding drove up the price of the few samples of the cherished honey nectar variety that still remained, and they made the idea of the Shanghai past into a foil for the problems and dangers of the new metropolis.

In an ironic twist, as Chapter Three demonstrates, city residents even made Western food culture into a vehicle for shoring up a neo-traditional sense of Chinese culture. Western food first made an impression among Chinese residents of Shanghai during the late-Qing period. Chinese initially found Western food unpalatable and the use of knives at the table barbaric, but by the last decade of the nineteenth century, eating Western food evolved into the city's most visible food fad. Chinese entrepreneurs opened *fancaiguan*, or "barbarian food restaurants," on Fuzhou Road, Shanghai's main entertainment artery, and these establishments soon became de rigueur eating venues for the urban elites who patronized the brothels, theaters, and bookshops in the same neighborhood. Customers were initially drawn to these establishments in a quest for the exotic, but before long patrons, travel writers, and social commentators touted them as symbols of Shanghai's modernity.

Again, however, the excitement about new things—ingredients, serving ware, dinner tables, and other features of restaurant interior design—generated new anxieties, both about the things themselves and about the people with whom city residents most closely associated them. In the case of Western food, these people were Shanghai's courtesans. Courtesans were, in terms of fashion, the city's genuine celebrities, and their patronage of Western restaurants lent an aura that made Western goods into everyday objects of elite consumption.

Western food culture thus did present some city residents with an alternative way of life. But others found ways of containing these foreign goods and food-ways within conventional cultural frameworks. One late-Qing commentator, for example, interpreted the craze for Western food as a mere playing out of longer-term trends in food history in China, such as an interest in foreign food-stuffs that dated back to Han times. A more forceful response, and ultimately a more influential one, came from urban reformers and cookbook writers, who circulated new images of women to compete with the image of the courtesan. Women, these reformers urged, should not be eating out in restaurants, but should be home, cooking meals with their own hands, and purchasing as few prepared foods in the marketplace as possible. Like good Confucians (and citing the *Great Learning* to boot), the reformers argued that social order relied on a well-ordered home, and that women had an important role to play, as mothers and wives, in raising healthy, well-fed children. Western food, and in particular identifiably nourishing items like milk, became a symbol of a neo-traditional Chinese notion of family.

Experimentations with Western food aside, native-place taste preferences also persisted well into the twentieth century, but as Chapter Four shows, Shanghai's diverse restaurant industry also provided city residents with an op-portunity to encounter the broad sweep of China's culinary riches and heri-tage, and engage in forms of national culinary nostalgia. As guidebook writer Xu Guozhen noted in his 1933 *Shanghai Living* (Shanghai shenghuo), "If you want to eat foreign cuisine, go to a Western restaurant, and if you want Chinese, then it's even easier, what with Cantonese cuisine, Yunnanese cuisine, Fujianese, Sichuanese, Anhui, Beiping, and so on and so forth (just take your pick)."[72] In-deed, the city's regionally and nationally diversified restaurant industry defined the city's culinary landscape and became a part of the very idea of Shanghai. Whereas Shanghai guidebooks uniformly boasted of the city's great culinary diversity, the 1934 *Guide to Guangzhou* (Guangzhou zhinan) divided that southern city's restaurants into only two categories, "restaurants" (*jiulou*) and "restaurants serving food from other provinces" (*waisheng jiucaiguan*).[73] Shang-hai's restaurant industry thus presented city residents with an organic version of a Chinese "nationscape."[74] Restaurateurs even commodified popular motifs of regional culture and history for commercial gain, and different branches of the restaurant industry appealed to their customers by evoking a sense of the Chinese past: Beijing cuisine restaurants made their name by serving the food of the former Qing capital and dressing their court-Mandarin-speaking waitresses in imperial era costume, whereas Wuxi cuisine restaurateurs developed a special menu reminiscent of the "riverboat cuisine" (*chuancai*) for which Wuxi had been famous in the late nineteenth century.

Each of these gestures constituted an effort by city residents to find a meaningful place for different regions of the country in a composite vision of the nation. Though warlordism and civil war threatened to tear apart the body politic, city residents made the city's regional cuisine restaurants into a template for understanding their history as "Chinese" and for putting together the pieces of a national culture. To be sure, the high cost of much restaurant food made it difficult for many city residents to participate in this form of national culinary nostalgia. Moreover, these same years witnessed a mounting crisis of confidence in the urban market system to provide a meaningful and fair price system for even basic foodstuffs, let alone restaurant fare. Urban insiders thus took it upon themselves to write consumer shopping and dining guides that provided tips on how to get "the real thing for the right price," authentic versions of regional cuisine, rather than the overpriced banquet food on which the city's rich and powerful squandered fortunes. These guidebooks provided consumer solutions to the growing instability of Shanghai's economy. More profound solutions to the city's emerging food problems, however, would have to await the socialist transformation of urban food culture after 1949.

As Chapter Five shows, even the Chinese Communist Party, which assumed control of Shanghai in 1949, recognized the value of the city's many different forms, restorative and reflective, of culinary nostalgia, although the party also added its own distinctive varieties to the mix. The Communists came to power in the wake of Japan's wartime occupation of Shanghai (1937–45) and the four years of civil war between the Nationalist and Communist Parties that followed. By the end of these struggles, the Shanghai food economy lay in near waste, having been ravaged by inflation and black market manipulation of such key items of urban diets as rice. Concerned about restoring order to this vital city, which the Communist Party planned to turn into a model of industrial socialism, party officials sought complete control over the city's food supply. They rationed basic food items and socialized ownership of the restaurant industry, instructing restaurant managers to sell "mass" foods in place of the high-end goods and regional specialty dishes for which they had long been famous.

Yet, recognizing that city residents remained quite fond of regional specialty foodstuffs and cuisine, party authorities soon came up with their own ways of investing regional food culture with historical significance. These efforts assumed an increasingly important symbolic significance during the late 1950s and early 1960s, when the party failed to deliver the economic resources necessary for a socialist utopia in which food was plentiful. Party organizations thus became important patrons of the "mass" food culture that had once thrived in the neighborhood of Shanghai's City God Temple; they designated the city's leading restaurants "Old Time Establishments" and converted them into model work units; and they celebrated high-end restaurant chefs as model workers and heirs to long and valuable traditions of Chinese culinary artistry. In the long run, these chefs and their party patrons proved to be no match for the "proletarian power" of the Cultural Revolution decade, during which time most of Shanghai's high-end restaurants were reduced to serving everyday Shanghai fare. Yet, the peculiarities of the Cultural Revolution years should not blind us to the party's efforts to become a patron of the Chinese culinary past. Communists were clearly not all of one mind regarding what to do about the culture of food in Shanghai.

As discussed in the Epilogue, a little more than a decade into the post-Mao period, new images of Old Shanghai emerged. These new images of the old were, for the first time in the city's history, not centered on the rural idyll of Wulingyuan, but on the vibrant consumer culture of the 1930s, which the CCP and its supporters had vociferously criticized during the party's rise to power. This was an image of the Shanghai past appropriate and appropriated for Reform-era policies of market socialism. In Shanghai's restaurant world, this image is now embodied in Old Shanghai theme restaurants, the most pervasive manifestation of the commodification of food and history in Shanghai during the post-Mao era. It is also an inspiration for the new application of the term *Haipai* (or Shanghai faction) to the food culture of the city. This term had historically been applied to distinctive forms of late-Qing and early-Republican Shanghai theater, literature, and art. Now chefs and officials invoked it to identify long-term trends in Shanghai food culture more generally. By *Haipai*, these figures refer to an ever-evolving repertoire of fusion dishes that artfully combine techniques and ingredients from various regional Chinese, as well as non-Chinese, cuisines into a new whole.

As the Epilogue also shows, however, the rhetoric surrounding both Old Shanghai theme restaurants and the *Haipai* debate obscures an even deeper historical trend in Shanghai food culture, the enduring appeal of "family-style" (*jiachang*) fare that is commonly sold in "family-style" restaurants (*jiachang fandian*) all over the city. Historically, city residents distinguished Shanghai cuisine from other regional cooking styles, and there were many restaurants in the city that specialized in this style of cooking. But Shanghai cuisine itself had heretofore contributed little to public discourse about the idea of the city. Today, by contrast, family-style Shanghai cuisine restaurants are pervasive, and they continue to serve many of the dishes, such as "sticky eel" (*shanhu*), "red-braised pork shoulder" (*hongshao tipang*) and "vegetable rice" (*caifan*), that native Shanghainese have been eating since at least the nineteenth century. A key counterpoint to the Old Shanghai theme restaurant and *Haipai* visions of Shanghai's historical food culture, these family-style restaurants provide a comforting localization of the rapidly re-globalizing space of the city.

1

"Only Available in Shanghai"

The Honey Nectar Peach and the Idea of Shanghai in Late Imperial China

The provenance of the honey nectar peach is not known; some say Beijing, others say Kaifeng. No matter—after all, when a mandarin orange crosses the Huai River, it turns into a bitter orange; and when a plum crosses the Yellow River, it turns into an apricot. How could the relocation [to Shanghai] be good were it not for the rich soil and lively water? Whatever its origin is, it does not really matter.

Chu Hua, *Treatise on the Honey Nectar Peach*, 1814

TOWARD THE END OF HIS FIRST CHINA TRAVELOGUE, published in 1847, the Victorian botanist Robert Fortune reflected on the accomplishments of his "three years' wanderings in the northern provinces of China," remarking, "Amongst the more important of the acquisitions which I made in the vicinity of Shanghae, I must not forget to mention a fine and large variety of peach, which comes into the markets there about the middle of August, and remains in perfection for about ten days. It is grown in the peach orchards, a few miles to the south of the city; and it is quite a usual thing to see peaches of this variety eleven inches in circumferences and twelve ounces in weight. This is, probably, what some writers call the Peking peach, about which such exaggerated stories have been told."[1] Fortune traveled to China shortly after the signing of the 1842 Treaty of Nanjing, which opened Shanghai, along with four other port cities, to foreign settlement and trade. Fortune's charge, which he carried from the Royal Horticultural Society, was to collect specimens of twenty-two alimentary and ornamental plants. Fortune soon fell out with the Horticultural Society, but the 17,000 tea-plant seeds he shipped from Shanghai to Calcutta helped the East India Company establish Britain's first commercial tea plantations in India and establish itself as a major producer of this vital crop.[2] Plants such as the "Peking peach," along with "new azaleas, camellias, chrysanthemums, peonies, and new species of roses," which he shipped back to Britain, further bolstered the evolving British imperial self-image as a paramount "governor of nature" more generally.[3]

For Fortune himself, the Shanghai peach was a useful subject to turn to at the close of a book designed to expose myths about Chinese agriculture and simultaneously promote the significance of his own botanical discoveries.[4] On the one hand, there was no shortage of mythology and lore associated with the peach in China, for "hardly any other tree or fruit in China is so heavily overlaid with symbolism as the peach."[5] By the time of Fortune's arrival, peaches had been closely associated with the quest for immortality for two millennia, ever since the Queen Mother of the West chided Emperor Wu of the Han (r. 140–86 B.C.) for presuming that he could grow the peaches of immortality that she cultivated in her gardens in the fabled Kunlun Mountains. Several centuries later, the poet Tao Qian (365–427) immortalized the image of peach blossoms as a portal to a utopian paradise in his "Record of the Peach Blossom Spring." Peaches were also an important component of Chinese aspirations to create a cosmopolitan empire and were a symbol of "all the exotic things longed for and the unknown things hoped for."[6] On the other hand, although the dimensions of the Shanghai peach were somewhat more diminutive than those described by the Horticultural Society—"cultivated in the Emperor's Garden and weighing 2 lbs."—they also provided Fortune with an opportunity to boast of the bountiful crops and products that he witnessed first hand in Shanghai.[7] He acknowledged a challenge in this regard because he was writing in the wake of predecessors who had written with such hyperbole about the agriculture of southern China that it was not clear what terms were left for him to describe "the rich plains of Shanghae." By laying claim to a fruit that grew neither in the capital in Beijing nor in the more familiar terrain of the south, Fortune placed himself at the vanguard of a new phase of the European exploration of China and helped draw attention to the still relatively unsung Shanghai region.

What Fortune did not realize, however, was that he was a latecomer to a discourse about Shanghai that locals had themselves been elaborating during the past several centuries to represent Shanghai as a paramount governor of nature. Fortune pointed to a paucity of available words for describing the agriculture of the Shanghai region, but by the early nineteenth century Chinese writers had a distinctive vocabulary for describing the area's various "crops and products" and, in particular, the virtues of Shanghai's peaches. The importance of peaches to the idea of Shanghai is the subject of this chapter, which illustrates the ways in which representations of local food crops put forth the idea of Shanghai as a central place in the Chinese realm, and as a cosmopolitan space of its own, well before the transformation of Shanghai into an international treaty port and the arrival of men like Fortune.

This pre-treaty-port-era idea of Shanghai circulated in several bodies of traditional Chinese food writing produced by officials and local elites in and about Shanghai. Among the most important of these was the "crops and products" entry in local gazetteers, which contained historical anecdotes and poetry inspired by the area's products. Gazetteer writers played a key role in identifying the region's unique crops and products and, eventually, linking Shanghai's foodstuffs to a broader history of Chinese food culture. Local notables built on this baseline record in belles lettres (*biji*), in which they recorded their more personal assessments of the significance of Shanghai foodstuffs, and in turn influenced the content of subsequent gazetteers. By the seventeenth century, Shanghai was becoming famous for one product in particular, the Shanghai honey nectar peach (*shuimitao*), which was known to grow especially well in the local gentry Gu family's Dew Fragrance Garden (Luxiangyuan). Eventually, the Shanghai honey nectar peach became the subject of a botanical monograph, Chu Hua's 1814 *Treatise on the Honey Nectar Peach* (Shuimitao pu), the first ever on the peach in the history of Chinese letters.[8] The *Treatise* represented Shanghai as a place that was worthy of visits by immortals, and even associated Shanghai with Emperor Wu's Shanglin Garden, once described as a "microcosm of the whole far-flung realm of Chinese dominion and, in the end, of the universe itself."[9] Fortune, by substituting the Shanghai peach for the "Peking peach" he was originally sent to obtain, merely confirmed what locals already knew.

A study of the lore and local knowledge surrounding Shanghai's signature crops and products provides a valuable cultural history perspective on Shanghai in late imperial times. Shanghai's importance to Ming and Qing economic history is now well understood: its cotton was a key component of the economic development of the broader Jiangnan region, and its port was a major entrepôt for domestic trade.[10] Recent studies of temple construction and the intellectual communities that took shape around such figures as Xu Guangqi (1562–1633) also give the lie to the once-common impression that late imperial Shanghai was but a minor city "in a corner by the sea" (*haizou*).[11] Much less clear, however, is how Shanghai natives reconciled their own understanding of the significance of their hometown with the city's secondary, even tertiary status in the country's administrative hierarchy.[12] Shanghai natives were well aware of their hometown's symbolic deficiencies: it had never served as a major capital city, and it lacked the cultural pedigree of even many smaller and commercially less significant locales. Recognizing Shanghai's residents' own recognition of their city's middling status thus raises the more general question of how the inhabitants of mid-level cities in China sought to establish a distinctive reputation for their hometowns.

One of the ways that local boosters established a reputation for their hometowns was by glorifying local cultural accomplishments. The glorification of local culture was an empire-wide trend in late imperial China that is evident in such major cities as Beijing, Guangzhou, Shaoxing, and Yangzhou, as well as in smaller towns.[13] One force animating this trend was the increasing mobility of regional demographic groups, which spread their hometown regional cultural forms across the Chinese realm as they engaged in travel for official business, commerce, and itinerant labor. These sojourners might also become patrons of the local culture and history of the regions in which they settled.[14] There was, however, a more specific factor shaping the impulse to glorify local culture felt by the inhabitants of mid-level cities in Jiangnan, the wider region in which Shanghai was located. During Ming and early Qing times, even the region's most distinguished cities, such as Suzhou, became so "embedded in their regional hinterlands" that "it might be better to conceive of Jiangnan not as two or three major cities in a surrounding rural hinterland, but rather as an 'urban region.'"[15] Patterns of urbanization and trends in urban culture threatened to deprive late imperial cities of some of their distinguishing characteristics and made it even harder for the residents of newer cities, such as Shanghai, to establish a sense of the distinctiveness of their hometown. John Meskill's study of Songjiang Prefecture, in which Shanghai was then located (see Figure 1.1), suggests that many towns and cities there met this challenge by "taking advantage of nearby natural resources or the development of particular skills," and thereby "became known for special products": Huzhou was famous for bamboo wares, Jiaxing for smelting metals, Wuxi for clay figurines, and Yixing for teapots.[16] Shanghai, by contrast, had no such defining product.[17]

Garden building and the cultivation of specialty products provided some solutions for Shanghai elites. On the one hand, building gardens provided Shanghai elites with an opportunity to assert themselves as cultural equals to the residents of more notable cities. Gardens had been an important component of imperial identity since the Han, and were an increasingly important component of urban elite status in late imperial times.[18] On the other hand, because gardens could be tailored to the specificity of the location in which

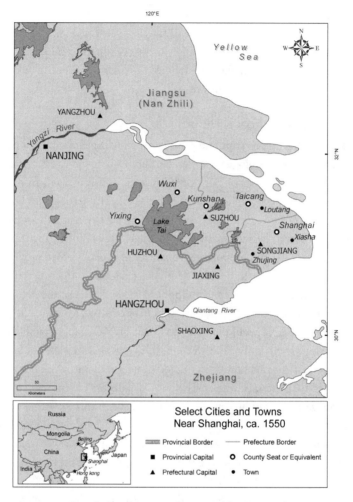

Figure 1.1 Shanghai and Surrounding Notable Cities and Towns during the Ming (1368–1644)
Map by Lynn Carlson

they were built, they also became vehicles for identifying a distinctive urban space and identity. Specialty products such as the Gu family's peaches helped further define that space as a place of cultural significance.[19] In their writings about Shanghai's peach gardens, Shanghai's local notables created an image for their city that placed Shanghai in a cultural genealogy of fruit gardening that dated back to the time of Emperor Wu of the Han. In so doing, they found a distinctive urban identity for the city and projected an image of Shanghai as a central place in the Chinese realm and the broader world. As extensions and elaborations of the longer and broader history of agricultural production in the Shanghai region, Shanghai's gardens and their finest product—the honey nectar peach—put Shanghai culture on the map.

Self-Sufficiency and Local Heroes

The history of Shanghai crops and products during the late imperial period is closely linked to the ecological, social, and administrative transformation of the place that became Shanghai, as the broader region evolved from coastal marshland to market town and then county seat. This process took roughly two millennia. Fortune described the plain of Shanghai as "one vast beautiful garden," its soil a "rich deep loam" that yielded "heavy crops of wheat, barley, rice, and cotton, besides an immense quantity of green vegetable crops, such as cabbages, turnips, yams, carrots, egg-plants, cucumbers and other articles of that kind."[20] At the start of China's imperial history, however, the region was a relatively undeveloped section of the ancient state of Wu. Much of the ground upon which Shanghai would emerge was then only unstable marshland, and beneath today's metropolis lies two thousand years of sediment and ocean detritus from the eastward flow of the Yangtze and Qiantang rivers and the westward flow of the East China Sea.[21] The city's origins are commonly traced to a fishing village called Hudu, founded during the Tang at the confluence of the Songjiang and Huangpu rivers, and which was sizable enough by the Song to warrant being designated a market town in 1074. The town was then located in Huating County, itself only recently established, and still subordinate to the town of Qinglong, the region's major port.

Before the designation of Shanghai County, in 1292, the region's crops and products entered the historical record as part of the history of Huating.[22] Word of Huating crops and products circulated as early as the third and fourth centuries, in historical anecdotes, poetry, and scattered references in comprehensive geographical treatises of the empire, but a coherent picture did not emerge until the publication of the area's first county-level gazetteer, the 1193 *Gazetteer of Yunjian* (Shaoxi Yunjian zhi), Yunjian being a secondary name for Huating. Three local holders of the *jinshi*, the highest degree in the civil service examination, Lin Zhi, Hu Linqing, and Zhu Ruchang, wrote the gazetteer. The gazetteer was then edited by Huating Prefect Yang Qian, who wrote the preface.[23] Yang's preface stressed just how important it was for Huating finally to have its own gazetteer, for although Huating had warranted mention in a number of important comprehensive gazetteers, these sources "only delineated the boundaries in broad strokes" and did not provide a meaningful record of the area's "former worthies, famous sites, population, tax contributions, streets and alleyways, [or] crops and products."[24]

The crops and products chapter of the *Gazetteer of Yunjian* represented Huating, first and foremost, as a self-sufficient and stable corner of the empire. At the time, the region's most famous products were cranes, perch, and water-shield (*Brasenia schreberi*, a small, purple-flowered aquatic plant of the fanwort family, prized as food in China), but gazetteer writing conventions required that the crops and products entry begin with the "five grains" (*wugu*). The importance of this convention would have been readily apparent to the three Huating *jinshi* who compiled the text, for their county would not have earned the honor of an official gazetteer in the first place were it not for the quality of its land, which several centuries earlier had made it promising terrain for establishing agricultural colonies for settlers from the north. Thus, the authors proudly cited the Tang poet Li Han (727–81), who, as prefectural secretary of Huainan, toured the Huating region in 770 and praised it as a successful example of southward agricultural expansion under the Daizong emperor (r. 763–80):

> Huating abuts the ocean near the Yangtze River. The terrain is flat and fertile, and it possesses products of the land and river. Li Han's "In Praise of the Meritorious Record of Military Land Development [in Jiaxing]" says: "In all of Wu, Jiahe has the most fertile soil." It also says: "As soon as Jiahe is harvested, the Yangtze and Huai [regions] are at peace."[25]

Jiahe (or Jiaxing) was one of the three jurisdictions that constituted Huating in Li's time, and four centuries later, Huating's gazetteer writers were happy to report that things there were much the same: "Today, as for profits from farming in Huating, fields are good for wheat; dry land is good for hemp. The towns in Jiahe are still the most fertile."[26] The land was rich enough to "provide for the everyday survival of the people: salt is boiled from water; reeds are planted for fuel; the earth is abundant in vegetables and mushrooms; the water has plenty of shrimp and crab. Of goods gathered by ship, seafood is abundant."

After describing the region's rich soil and abundant aquatic products, the authors strengthened the credibility of their claims by challenging doubtful remarks about the region's crops and products that circulated in other texts. They noted, on the one hand, that the late-tenth-century *Gazetteer of the World during the Taiping Period* (Taiping huanyuji), one of the earliest extant comprehensive gazetteers of the Chinese realm, had "acclaimed Huating's valleys for producing fine fish and water shield."[27] But, on the other hand, they also drew attention to references in this same text drawn from an earlier regional history, the Tang *Monograph on Wu Geography* (Wu diji), which struck them as so unlikely that they sought to set the record straight:

> In the entry for Kunshan County, the *Taiping huanyuji* also quotes the *Wu diji* as saying: "In winter rock cod (*shishouyu*) turn into wild duck (*fu*), while small fish grow to five inches and at the Autumn Sacrifices turn into sparrows." Of course, this comment is not based in fact but is a flight of fancy. Today Huating also has many wild ducks. When the Pride of India blooms, the rock cod arrive; before the frost has come, the sparrows are plump. Is this not because Huating was originally a part of Kunshan?[28]

By distinguishing fact from fantasy, the authors sought to strengthen the credibility of their assertions about Huating. For although they were delighted to claim products associated with Kunshan for Huating, they wanted to represent their hometown as a place that nonlocals could believe in too.

Although the idea of Huating as a self-sufficient region loomed large in the region's representation in the *Gazetteer of Yunjian*, the three Huating *jinshi* took their greatest pride not in the region's "five grains," or even in its rock cod and wild ducks, but in two other famous regional items, cranes and water shield, and in the integrity of the historical figure most famously associated with them—Lu Ji (261–303), a local statesman, general, poet, and author of the "Rhymeprose on Literature" (Wenfu). Lu had an impeccable local pedigree: his grandfather, the military commander Lu Xun, was named the marquis of Huating after securing Wu for the kingdom's founding emperor; his father, Lu Kang, served as grand marshal of Wu. When Wu fell to the Western Jin in 280, Lu Ji lingered for ten years in Huating, then a vast hunting estate of "clear springs and luxuriant forests," but later ventured north to the Jin capital at Luoyang, where he served several of the eight imperial princes competing for power during the War of the Eight Princes (291–306).[29] Eventually, Lu fell victim to false charges of treason and was sentenced to death. On the eve of his execution, he lamented that he would never again hear the cry of Huating's cranes.

Accounts and memories of Lu's lament, which began to take shape soon after his execution, were key components of local and extra-local perceptions of his persona and of his hometown. The lament was recorded in such official sources as the 648 *Jin History* (Jinshu), but also in Liu Yiqing's (403–44) *New Account of Tales of the World* (Shishuo xinyu),[30] a compendium of historical anecdotes and "character writing" covering the years 150 to 420. Character appraisal originated in the Later Han (25–220), "when leading local scholars evaluated and recommended candidates [for bureaucratic office] according to Confucian moral criteria," but by Lu Ji's time, it had "shed its political emphasis and evolved into a comprehensive study of human nature."[31] As the *New Account* rendition of Lu Ji's last words indicates, such appraisals came in a remarkably condensed, even cryptic, form: "When Lu Ji was defeated at Heqiao (Henan), he was slandered by Lu Zhi and sentenced to death (in 303). On the eve of his execution he sighed and said, 'Would that I might hear once more the cry of the cranes at Huating! Will I ever get to do so?'"[32]

The *New Account* tale drew two aspects of Lu's persona into relief. The first was his poetic sensibility, evident in the image of a man who invokes the image of the crane—a symbol of longevity in China—the night before he is to be put to death. The second was Lu's strong connection to his native place, which despite having been conquered by the Western Jin, possessed a reservoir of natural phenomena that outlived the vicissitudes of political change. Lu Ji had been taken captive, but his hometown culture, embodied in the Huating crane, was still free. Moreover, though Lu Ji lost his life, his lament for the Huating crane earned immortality for his native place.[33] Indeed, his lament made Huating's cranes into a byword for the region.

Word of Huating's second most famous product, water shield, also circulated around the figure of Lu Ji, in a second tale from *New Account of Tales of the World* cited in the crops and products chapter of the *Gazetteer of Yunjian*. Deemed a "remote" state with a "harsh terrain and humid climate" even by one of its own early kings, Lu Ji's Wu developed during the Three Kingdoms period (220–80) into one of the commercial, cultural, and political centers of China.[34] Lu's pride at this development, and of the relative sophistication of his hometown food culture, comes across clearly during a well-known encounter with Wang Rong (234–305), one of the so-called Seven Worthies of the Bamboo Grove and a general who served under the command of Jin and participated in the final campaign against Wu. The two met shortly after Lu first arrived in Luoyang, and as recounted in *New Account*, "Wang set before him several *hu*–measures of goat curd. Pointing them out to Lu, he asked: 'What do you have east of the Yangtze to match this?' Lu replied: 'We only have the water shield soup of Qianli Lake, but without adding fermented soybeans.'"[35] As the *Jin*

History account of this encounter added, "At the time people considered this a famous answer."[36]

Lu's answer has spawned a cottage industry of conflicting interpretations, with the conflicts centering on the meaning of the second half of the phrase, which others have rendered as "the salted beans (or legumes) of Moxia" (reading the phrase not as *weixia yanchi* 未下鹽豉, but as *Moxia yanchi* 末下鹽豉, and Moxia as the name of a town in Wu).[37] Both renditions yield a scenario in which Lu effectively rebuffs Wang, who dared to compare Wu food culture unfavorably with even the goat curd common to the diets of nomadic peoples of the northern steppe regions. When the closing phrase is read as "the salted beans of Moxia," Lu Ji's answer consists of two counter examples to Wang's unfavorable comparison and is relatively straightforward. However, when the same phrase is read as "without adding fermented soybeans," the text yields a much more powerful image of Lu Ji cleverly turning the table on Wang. As Shi Zhecun explains, Lu Ji likely realized that northerners like Wang were only recently familiar with water shield, a delicate vegetable that grew plentifully in the lakes of Lu's home region, and thus did not know how to prepare it properly in soup. In the Wu region, the soup is clear and delicate and does not call for the salty fermented soybeans that northerners added to impart extra flavor. According to this reading, what Lu Ji meant was: The only reason why water shield soup might compare unfavorably to goat curds is because northerners, lacking in sophistication, ruin it by adding fermented soybeans.[38] Lu Ji's home state of Wu may have suffered military defeat at the hands of the Western Jin, but by upstaging Wang Rong in an exchange about his hometown food culture, Lu Ji won the war of words, a victory that the *Gazetteer of Yunjian* was still celebrating eight centuries later.

Salt, Cotton, and Shanghai's Topographical Advantages

The *Gazetteer of Yunjian*'s image of the Huating region—that of a fertile, self-sufficient corner of the empire, with a number of well-known specialty items linked to key figures of Chinese history—was an important one for a recently established county, but it would not withstand the test of time, nor was it easily transferable to Shanghai. By the end of the Southern Song, the expansive land and growing population of Huating was difficult to administer, and in 1292 the new Yuan regime carved out five regions from northwest Huating into a new Shanghai County, promoting the former market town of Shanghai to the status of county seat. Upgrading Shanghai made good sense, because the shifting sands of the Yangtze delta had made Shanghai into the area's port of choice by the beginning of the Southern Song. However, the growing dominance of rice agriculture in the Yangtze river valley in the Song, Yuan, and Ming gradually weakened the cachet of soil fertility based on wheat and hemp production. Moreover, much of Shanghai's soil was too sandy and brackish to support broad-based rice agriculture, the seedlings of which are much more delicate than wheat, and centuries of hard work by officials and farmers did not succeed in fully transforming local soil conditions. Dike construction and the eastward thrust of the delta stabilized and raised the area's soil and prevented salt water from washing back over the coastal land plots.[39] But the result of this hard work was vastly different soil qualities in the eastern and western areas of Shanghai. To the west, the soil did became rich enough to grow rice intensively, but in the east, the soil remained sandy and suitable only for wheat, barley, beans, and hemp.

Rice was becoming the staple food of choice for all Huating residents, so villagers in the eastern regions had to develop products worthy of trade. They found one in the area's natural resources, salt, and a second in a southern import, cotton. These two products brought considerable wealth to the region, which in Yuan and Ming times prospered as never before, but they also created new challenges. As the region became increasingly dependent on trade networks for its food supply, its reputation as a place became vulnerable to criticism. In response, local gazetteer writers developed new representational strategies for celebrating the area's crops and products.

The development of the region's salt industry was a major turning point in Huating, and later Shanghai, history. It gave "early rise to local commercialization" of the Shanghai area, and it produced the region's first widely marketed specialty product.[40] The Huating salt industry developed as part of the state monopoly system. Huating's salines were part of the Liangzhe salt district, which along with the Huainan salt district constituted the "heart of the medieval salt administration."[41] Salt had long been an essential ingredient for food processing, but salt consumption also rose rapidly during the Southern Song, partly because of the rise in rice consumption (rice being the most saline-poor of all the major cereals), and partly because of the growing sophistication of cuisine, especially in the vicinity of the Southern Song capital of Hangzhou, which depended on the Liangzhe salines for its supply. The demand for salt continued to grow even after the national capital moved back north. As S. A. M. Adshead notes in *Salt and Civilization*, "The *Yuan-shih* [*Yuan History*] estimates that the nearly 20 million inhabitants of the metropolitan capitals of Liang-che and Chiang-tung, i.e., northern Chekiang and southern Kiangsu, consumed 10 lb of salt per head per year: the highest consumption figures suggested anywhere up to that time, and indeed until much later."[42]

Huating's and Shanghai's salines grew in several stages to meet this demand, and the region soon became famous for this commercial product.[43] During the Song, Huating's salt administrator oversaw production in three salines, in Pudong, Yuandu, and Qingdun; by the Southern Song, this number grew to five. By late Yuan times, the region's salt industry was so developed that it received monographic treatment in the *Illustrated Boiling of Sea Water* (Aobo tu), compiled by Chen Chun (1271–1368), the salt commissioner of the town of Xiasha, located approximately twenty kilometers south of the Shanghai County Seat.[44] Chen's text details the rendering of salt according the regional method known as *shahui fa*, which called for saturating ashes with sea water and then exposing them to sun and wind. Each of the work's forty-seven chapters describes and illustrates one stage of the production process, from the initial construction of hearths, through the sprinkling and exposing of ashes, to the boiling of the rendered brine, and the final transporting of the loose finished product. As Commissioner Chen noted in his preface, the region was especially well suited for this activity:

> In the west of Zhe, one hundred *li* east of Huating county, is [a place called] "Downward Sands" (Xiasha) which really looks like this. [Xiasha] is near the shore of the Great Sea-Wall (Datang), and cloaked and girdled by the Wusong and Yangzi rivers. When walking southeastwards, everywhere is salt land [unfit for cultivation]. [The practice of] boiling the sea [water here] for getting salt goes back a long time.[45]

The reorganization of the imperial salt administration during the early Ming placed the Songjiang Prefecture branch administration of the Liangzhe salt district in Shanghai County, where the salt fields of Xiasha continued to produce its especially fine salt, known to be "as white as snow." From that point on, the link between salt and the idea of Shanghai became so strong that, even as salt production gradually decreased during the mid-to-late Ming, "the history of all the rural towns dating back to the Song was told . . . as a history of the salt trade."[46]

Cotton, the next product for which the area became famous, intensified the commercialization of the Shanghai region. Tradition credits Shanghai native and peasant woman Huang Daopo with introducing cotton to Shanghai.[47] After more than two decades of sojourning in Hainan, Huang brought the cotton technology she learned from the Li people of that southern island back to her native place. Cotton, previously imported from Fujian and Guangdong, grew especially well in the brackish soil in eastern Shanghai. For a short while, rice agriculture remained dominant in the western villages, and the eastern villages substituted cotton for salt in their trade for rice, but before long cotton dominated the agricultural economy of the western villages too. Word of Shanghai's desirable "nankeen" cotton eventually spread internationally, but well before then, its reputation was made domestically, and Shanghai cotton was sought out by buyers north and south. North China merchants came to Shanghai carrying cash to buy their share of the market, and merchants from Guangdong and Fujian came bearing sugar, which they sold locally to pay for theirs. The Ming and Qing states were also major purchasers of Shanghai cotton.[48] By early Qing times, cotton crops occupied roughly 70 percent of the arable land in Shanghai county.

Cotton made Shanghai into one of the wealthiest counties in the country, but also a place increasingly dependent on long-distance trade for its basic foodstuffs, leaving the region's poor especially vulnerable. Land-holding patterns created marked social inequalities, and cash-cropping left the county "immediately affected by any drop in demand from distant provinces."[49] In times of plenty, a moral economy distributed food to the land poor by means of a manorial system, providing for tenants who "desire to do the farm work but do not have enough food." During leaner years, however, the system broke down. As one mid-sixteenth-century commentator noted, "What in times past was called 'mutual aid and sustenance' changed into mutual suspicion and enmity."[50] Enmity could quickly lead to "rent resistance and violent uprisings," by which point sheer desperation was not far around the corner.[51] As Shanghai native Ye Mengzhu lamented, describing conditions in 1641, as the Ming was on the verge of collapse, "With Shantung smitten by famine and rebellion, and Honan even more severely disrupted, the people in our region had to exchange their children to eat, or break up corpses and steam them."[52] There could have been no more powerful picture of a world turned upside down than Ye's image of villagers forced to eat their own ancestors.

Many local notables, however, viewed such episodes as exceptional events, and Shanghai gazetteer writers of the Ming period fought the growing impression that theirs was a one-crop town. Thus, even as cotton production increased during Ming rule, gazetteers emphasized the diversity of Shanghai agriculture. The list of crops and products in the 1504 *Shanghai Gazetteer* (Hongzhi Shanghai zhi), the earliest extant Shanghai specific gazetteer, contained the names of thirty-four grains and legumes, thirty-nine medicinal plants, twenty-seven fruits and nuts, forty-five flowers, thirty-three tree varieties, eighteen varieties of bamboo, forty kinds of vegetables, eleven breeds of domesticated animals, thirty-seven different birds, forty-eight varieties of fish, and seventeen different kinds of finished goods, including salt and honey.[53] In the 1588 *Shanghai County Gazetteer* (Wanli Shanghai xianzhi), the number of items listed in each category was even greater.[54] For the men who compiled such lists, there was no question but to represent Shanghai as a rich land, closely integrated with the cycle of the agricultural seasons. The 1524 *Shanghai County Gazetteer* (Jiajing Shanghai xianzhi) opened its discussion of Shanghai crops and products by listing the "five grains" grown there, indicating that, just as in the other regions of Songjiang Prefecture, in Shanghai too "there are three moments of ripening: early ripening, mid-autumn ripening, and late ripening."[55]

What motivated such representations of Shanghai crops and products? Were these men simply engaging with a textual tradition that required gazetteer entries on crops and products to begin with a discussion of the five grains? Were they concerned that their home region looked too much like the kind of commercial society that was generally frowned upon in the Confucian tradition? Or were they engaging in a form of ideological obfuscation to protect local landholders, who were in a position to gain from the cotton trade, at the expense of farmhands, who might have been better off growing their own food? The answer to each question seems to be yes.

The men who compiled Shanghai's gazetteers were closely linked to the creation in Shanghai of a gentry society. Following Timothy Brook, this gentry may be defined as a critical mass of degree-holding lineages that are "conscious of [their] collective privilege and status" and who seek to "redefine high status away from pure wealth in favor of the more constructed standard of gentility."[56] Tang Jin, editor of the 1504 edition, earned his *jinshi* in 1496 and became the "doyen of Shanghai society" after his official career ended in 1519; Zhang Zhixiang, who edited the 1588 edition, only held the degree of *shengyuan*, but his lineage "could claim more degree holders than any other lineage in the county."[57] Surely such men did not want their home region to be known as a one-commercial-crop town. In the long run, no crop would serve their interests better than Shanghai's peaches, but local elites did not recognize the value of peaches for serving these interests until some time after the publication of the 1588 Shanghai gazetteer. What, then, was a local gentryman to do?

One strategy that local gazetteer writers adopted was to enter into a dialogue with gazetteer writing conventions. Gao Qi, like gazetteer writers before him, began his entry on Shanghai crops and products with a discussion of the five grains. But Gao questioned the convention that prioritized the five grains in such gazetteer entries. He acknowledged that the convention had its merits, for "of all crops and products, none is more important than the five grains, and so they are listed first." One wonders, however, why Gao would have felt compelled to make such an observation at all if listing the five grains first in an account of the crops and products of Shanghai actually made good sense. Moreover, later in the entry Gao questioned the wisdom of a decree, attributed to Song Taizong (r. 976–98), that called for the exchange of products between north and south to prevent the rise of monocropping. Gao's line of questioning intimated that the five grains need not be seen as the key indicator of a region's character. Gao recognized the logic of the Song policy, but he added that it also ran contrary to an equally significant principle, which he explained as follows: "In our humble town, the climate and elevation differ in east and west, and different [crops] are planted [accordingly]." Gao then proposed that it might be more important "to make use of the climate and yield to topographical advantages (*yongtian lidi*)." This, he suggested, along with "minimizing expenditures" and "loving [the young] and supporting [the elderly]," was what "Mencius called the first step of royal government."[58]

Having identified a sanction for emphasizing the "topographical advantages" that prevailed in Shanghai, Gao devoted the bulk of his discussion of Shanghai crops and products to those items that thrived in the various microclimates of the region. He highlights the towns and villages that produced superior varieties of goods and drew attention to the rich diversity within the county: "The finest watermelons come from Yellow Earth Bridge"; "Mountain yams, bitter yam, and taro come from the west and north of the river"; "Peaches and plums are numerous in the river villages, while *gan*-oranges and *ju*-oranges are numerous in the lake villages."[59] When writing of products with a long history in the region, such as the cranes of Cranes Nest Village, he drew attention to the especially prized varieties, such as those bearing a "tortoise shell pattern," which he called a "product worthy of immortals" (*xianpin*). Climatic conditions also meant that some items were strictly seasonal, like the sparrows that locals considered a "delicacy," and which only "come off the ocean early in the winter." Finally, Gao paid considerable attention to Shanghai's many fish varieties, noting their sources and seasonal availability: perch from the Yangtze, plum fish at the time of the plum rains, shad before summer, pomfret and herring from the sea, shrimpfish and blowfish from the Yangtze and Huangpu rivers and the lake-shores, *zi* fish from the area's ponds, and finally, sturgeon, which swim up the Yangtze from the sea. Many of these weighed as much as one hundred catties (*jin*), and local fishermen liked to preserve the heads in salt.[60]

Gao found much variety to celebrate in Shanghai's crops and products, but he was trapped between the need to represent Shanghai in a positive light and an awareness that developments in Shanghai agriculture during the Ming had a mixed impact on the region's economy and society. In fact, Shanghai witnessed its worst famine to date between 1522 and 1523, scarcely two years before Gao issued his gazetteer. To strengthen his position, Gao thus also sought to anchor the rapidly changing and unstable society that Shanghai had become to a secure past, an impulse evident in his allusions to well-known anecdotes involving local heroes. In the *Gazetteer of Yunjian*, as discussed earlier, allusions to local heroes helped establish the pedigree of the newly emergent Huating county. In Gao's case, by contrast, they read more as an effort to identify a link to the past that transcends the recent transformation of the region from a self-sufficient land into a commercial economy dependent on multi-regional trade.

Consider, for example, Gao's reference to Zhang Han (fl. first quarter of fourth century), which appears in reference to Shanghai perch. Gao writes, "This is the fish that Jiying [Zhang Han] praised alongside water shield."[61] Zhang, like Lu Ji, hailed from Wu Commandery in the Kingdom of Wu and traveled to Luoyang to serve in the staff of northern princes. Unlike Lu, however, Zhang resisted the pull of an official career, and in a famous story related in *New Account of Tales of the World*, he justifies his decision by invoking his favorite hometown foods:

> Zhang Han was summoned to serve as an aide in the administration of the Prince of Qi, Sima Jiong (in 301). While he was in Luoyang, and saw the autumn winds rising, it was then that he longed for the wild rice, water shield soup, and the sliced perch of his home town in Wu. He said, "What a man values in life is just to find what suits his fancy, and nothing more. How can he tie himself down to an official post several thousand *li* from home, in pursuit of fame and rank?" Whereupon he ordered his carriage and proceeded to return home. Shortly thereafter the Prince of Qi was defeated and killed (302). His contemporaries all claimed Zhang was clairvoyant.[62]

The choice of allusion was a careful one. For Zhang, hometown crops and products were the objects that defined his true and eternal self. They pointed his way home, and they provided him with a sanctuary from the uncertainties of history. For Gao, these same objects provided a missing link between the Shanghai of his own day and of the region's increasingly remote past, anchoring a changing Shanghai to enduring products of the land, rather than solely to imports like cotton.

Garden Culture and the Shanghaiing of the Honey Nectar Peach

By the mid-Ming, Shanghai's gazetteer writers, members and makers of an emerging gentry society, had created an idea of Shanghai as a place that, because of its "topographical advantages," was notable for crops and products indigenous to the area. This image of Shanghai provided local gentry with a source of local pride and a sense of their connection to the longer history of the region, even as the growing dominance of one nonnative crop, cotton, brought great changes to Shanghai. By the end of the Ming, Shanghai would be famous for another import, peaches, which would become the local specialty food item about which Shanghai natives were most proud, and about which non-Shanghai natives knew the most. Peach cultivation in Shanghai had a two-fold significance: it strengthened local elite claims about unique conditions in Shanghai that produced specialty food products; and it provided gentry with a framework for asserting a slightly different kind of relationship to history. No longer content to rest on the laurels of the accomplishments of men of the remote past, local gentry in Shanghai began to represent their home region as one that had distinctively enhanced the accomplishments of the past.

The social and cultural context for this transformation in the idea of Shanghai was the emergence of a garden culture in Shanghai during the last century of Ming rule. Garden-building in Shanghai was shaped by local events and broader trends unfolding during these years in all of the major cities and suburbs of Jiangnan. The trends included the commercialization and growing wealth of the Jiangnan region, which facilitated a building boom in gentry villas and gardens. This building boom, as Craig Clunas has noted with regard to Suzhou, was shaped decisively by a new discourse on garden culture that characterized gardens as sites of aesthetic refinement and that elided the productive

potential of gardens as orchards, as well as the relationship of the gardens' owners to the relations of agricultural production.[63] Shanghai County exhibited
all of these trends, but garden culture in Shanghai was also shaped locally, by
the building of walls around the Shanghai county seat in 1553.[64] The impetus
to build the walls was largely defensive—pirates attacked the city in 1552 and
local elites convinced imperial authorities of the need to provide Shanghai with
this defining feature of administrative cities. But after the walls went up, the
county seat became an increasingly attractive location for gentry settlement.
Largely from within this newly walled space, Shanghai's gentry participated in
the Jiangnan garden building boom and sought to create a semblance of a rural
idyll inside the city limits.

The Ming garden boom in Shanghai yielded at least eleven gardens of note,
each distinguished by a particular aesthetic feature.[65] This feature was often
signaled in the garden's name, as in the case of the Plum Blossom Garden and
the Peach Garden. Yet, even gardens with names less suggestive of their features
were organized around such objects of connoisseurship. The Yu Garden, the
only late-Ming garden that has survived to the present day, possessed a sub-
stantial collection of extraordinarily shaped rocks. The Southern Garden contained a creek with a hidden connection to the Huangpu River and was unique
for incorporating into its design the sound of ebbing and flowing tidewaters.
The Banjing Garden was renowned for its forest of fragrant trees.[66] Thus, many
of Shanghai's mid-Ming gardens conform to the pattern that Clunas identifies in Suzhou. Dew Fragrance Garden, which produced the peaches for which
Shanghai would become famous, also conformed to this pattern during its
early history, but it ultimately departed from this trend.

Dew Fragrance Garden was one of the first gardens built during these years.
The garden was the undertaking of Gu Mingshi (*jinshi* 1558), whose highest official posting was as steward of seals, a position that placed him in the central
government agency that kept track of the emperor's seals, tallies, and stamps.
Mingshi was the younger brother of Gu Mingru (*juren* 1529), the head of the
Gu household, whose official career peaked when he served as commissioner
of Daozhou (today's Lingling, Hunan Province).[67] In 1559, to mark and enjoy
his retirement from office, the older brother built an estate in Shanghai, known
as the Ten-Thousand Bamboo Retreat (*Wanzhu shanju*). The younger brother
then built his garden on an undeveloped piece of adjacent land. Mingshi reportedly conceived of the name for his garden when he recovered a stone bearing the characters "dew fragrance creek" (*luxiangchi*) while digging a pond on

the garden grounds. The characters had apparently been etched in the rock by the esteemed Yuan calligrapher and rock collector Zhao Mengfu (1254–1322), who once lived in Shanghai County.[68] By choosing Dew Fragrance as the name for his garden, Mingshi established a clear relationship between his garden and the Shanghai past at the very moment of the city's sixteenth-century transformation.

The Gu family that built and maintained the garden became famous for several family products—peaches, embroidery (*Guxiu*), and a special preparation of pickled vegetable (*Gucai*)—but the garden's early reputation was as a site for repose and aesthetic appreciation. Local enthusiasm to secure such sites for Shanghai is evident in Shanghai poet and book collector Zhu Chaqing's (d. 1572) essay on Dew Fragrance Garden, of which there are two extant versions.[69] The longer of the two versions, which sheds light on local sentiment regarding the significance of Dew Fragrance Garden, opens by noting, "Shanghai was only recently established as a named place. It lacks the antiquity of a Zhengpu [in today's Henan Province, where the Daoist figure Liezi was said to have lived] or a Wang River [in Shanxi, where the Tang poet Wang Wei built a villa]."[70] Lu Ji, Zhu adds, once had a splendid villa in the Shanghai region, but he had left home, never to return, and so Zhu was pleased that his hometown was now accumulating gardens worthy of comparison with famous sites of the Chinese past.

Zhu's description of the garden, as illustrated by the following excerpt from the shorter version, emphasized the many opportunities it provided for relaxation and the aesthetic appreciation of natural and cultural refinements:

> The garden plot is large and shaped like a coiled earthworm. It is the most splendid in the county. Upon entering the garden, the lane plunges one hundred paces and is lined with willow and elm, which form a green shade so luxuriant that it is possible to take walks on a rainy day without an umbrella. If you turn to the east, there is the Hall of the Mountain of Abundant Spring, [which is] fitted intricately with brilliant partitions. If you make to leave the building and go further east, stones are piled up at the exit [at the far end of] the courtyard. The Hall of Blue Ripples is cool and refreshing, spacious and clean. At the foot of the Hall great stones are placed like chess pieces. Behind the Hall is a mound of earth [planted with] lofty pines, juniper, and fir . . . called Glimmering Green Mount.[71]

Zhu's account, of which this is only a short excerpt, contains all of the trademark features of the late-Ming discourse on gardens. Ample attention is paid to objects, natural and manufactured, that represented a high level of scholarly refinement. This is a beautiful space and an intellectual space, and it attested to the fact that even though Shanghai did not have a long tradition of learning (local elites in Shanghai had a short, if noteworthy, history of success in degree earning), Shanghai should not be thought of merely as a commercial society.[72] The longer variant of the essay expanded on this theme by noting the "tripods and caldrons, stringed instruments and wine goblets, and many volumes of old and new illuminated books" that were stored in the Hall of Blue Ripples, as well as the garden's many "sweet smelling fragrant flowering trees."[73] Zhu would no doubt have been pleased to know that the prominent Ming poet Wang Shizhen (1526–90) made Dew Fragrance Garden the subject of a poem, and that the poem was proudly entered into subsequent Shanghai gazetteers.[74]

The aesthetic refinements of Dew Fragrance Garden attracted the attention of Shanghai natives and garden lovers like Wang Shizhen, but in the long run, the Gu family's crops and products, and particularly the fruit of one of the flowering trees that the Gu family grew in its garden, became the most powerful icon of Shanghai's virtues. To be sure, peaches were also valued for their blossoms. Thus, local literatus Ye Mengzhu noted of Shanghai's Peach Garden, that it was "not inferior to the triumphs of Xuandu and Wuling," the former being a Daoist monastery in Chang'an famous in Tang times for its glorious peach blossoms, the latter a reference to the self-sufficient earthly paradise of Tao Qian's "Record of the Peach Blossom Spring."[75] But in the case of the Gu family garden, the peach fruit was most valued. The peach fruit was especially useful for highlighting Shanghai's "topographical advantages." Shanghai's brackish soil may not have been suitable for extensive rice cultivation, but it proved ideal for peach trees. Once they realized this, Shanghai's gentry found peaches, and the Gu family's honey nectar variety in particular, to be an especially fruitful crop for touting positive images of their home.

Locals first drew the connection between Shanghai's peaches and its topographical advantages in belles lettres. One such local was Zhang Suowang (1556–1635; *jinshi* 1601), a member of the Zhang lineage involved in the production of the 1588 *Shanghai County Gazetteer*. Zhang's *Notes on Reading and Plowing* (Yuegeng yulu) proudly claimed the honey nectar peach for his home area: "The honey nectar peach only exists in my hometown (*wuyi*), and those produced in Steward of Seals Gu's western garden are especially delicious. The taste ranks second to fresh litchis. There is also a kind [of the honey nectar variety] called Red-When-Thunder-Strikes (*leizhenhong*). These develop a red hue whenever there is a thunderstorm and are even more rare."[76]

A second local figure to highlight the garden's peaches was Ye Mengzhu, for whom Dew Fragrance Garden was best seen as a fruitful site nestled in the heart of an elite family with typical stories of success and failure. As Ye notes, Gu Mingshi "established the family on the basis of success in the civil service examinations," but Mingshi's son, Huihai, became too "accustomed to a life of luxury" and spent his time making "every effort to select only the best in clothing and food for his day to day living, and in this way outdo and distinguish himself from his contemporaries." Still, Ye provides a uniformly favorable impression of the Gu family's products, remarking, "The garden had peaches that were not inferior to Wang Rong's plums, and [the family produced] pickled vegetables that were superior to the salted beans of Moxia. The ladies of the house embroidered with an ingenuity that rivals the work of Heaven and when entertaining guests could play songs on the zither that could hold back the clouds. . . . As of today, more than one hundred years have passed, and the Dew Fragrance name has become famous throughout the world."[77]

Zhang's and Ye's remarks echoed and built upon the repertoire of images and references that the region's gazetteer writers had invoked over the centuries to broadcast positive images of their corner of the Chinese realm. Zhang, echoing Gao Qi's notion that local growers must "make use of the climate and yield to topographical advantages," represents the honey nectar peach as an embodiment of the particular climatic conditions of the region. Here was a product that was not native to the region but that nonetheless throve there and was even improved upon by means of a remarkable local atmospheric effect. By ranking Shanghai's peaches as second in taste only to fresh litchi, a famous and cherished fruit of the south, Zhang placed Shanghai very high in the pantheon of fruit-growing regions. Ye's reference to "Wang Rong's plums" and the "salted beans of Moxia," also echoed earlier gazetteer discussions of the region's crops and products, while departing from them in significant ways. The Wang Rong to whom Ye refers is the same northern prince whom Lu Ji humiliated by suggesting that northerners could not appreciate southern foods. For the authors of the *Gazetteer of Yunjian*, Lu Ji's encounter with Wang Rong provided evidence of the relative sophistication of Wu culture. For Ye, by contrast, the anecdote is a measure of just how far his home region had come. By Wang Rong's plums, Ye refers to a well-known story about Wang Rong's precocious intelligence, in which a seven-year-old Wang is "acclaimed for his divine intelligence even in his youth" for having a discerning eye for the quality of fruit.[78] To Ye's mind, the Gu family's preserved vegetable and peaches were superior to even the finest products of days gone by, and Shanghai no longer needed to draw evidence from the remote past to provide it with a worthy reputation as a place. It was now a place that had improved upon the past.

Through the efforts of men like Zhang and Ye, it was as a fruitful site that word of Dew Fragrance Garden would spread the farthest, and before long the honey nectar peach would be identified as a crop that was, as Zhang himself put it, "only available in Shanghai." Although originally a northern product, the honey nectar peach became associated with the Hangzhou area during the Southern Song.[79] It was also listed as a local product in at least five prefectural gazetteers before the Yongzheng era (1723–35), and the Kangxi-era (1661–1723) *Comprehensive Gazetteer of Jiangnan* (Jiangnan tongzhi) associated the variety with Wang Xijue's (1534–1610) Nanyuan Garden, in Taicang, Jiangsu Province.[80] But though the *Comprehensive Gazetteer* dates the variety's cultivation in Taicang to roughly the same time that it was first grown in Shanghai, the paper trail on the Nanyuan Garden peach ends with this same text. By contrast, the paper trail on the Shanghai variety continues well into the twentieth century, and the Shanghai variety was registered in texts with a national scope.

This paper trail began when Zhang Suowang's description of the peach was picked up by other writers, most importantly Wang Xiangjin (1561–1653), in his 1621 *Treatise on Many Fragrances* (Qunfang pu). Originally a record of Wang's own experience with gardening and the study of horticultural traditions, Wang's text was later expanded from thirty to one hundred chapters under the patronage of the Kangxi emperor.[81] Wang describes numerous peach varieties, some named for their color, others for the time of year in which they bloom or bear fruit, and yet others for their shape, such as the remarkable "mandarin duck peach," which bore a "double-lobed" fruit, mandarin ducks being a symbol of conjugal bliss. In Wang's opinion, however, few peach trees actually bore a fruit worth eating: "wild peaches" were good for medicinal purposes, but they were "small and very fuzzy" and had a "disgusting flavor," while the "October peach" was "sweet and sour and the flesh clings to the pit." The "plum peach," so named because it had the glossiness of a plum, fared better, but only because its "green flesh did not cling to the pit." Wang's entry on the honey nectar peach, however, repeated Zhang Suowang's praise from the *Notes on Reading and Plowing* almost verbatim, and Zhang's description of the honey nectar peach, thus transmitted by Wang, followed what was subsequently known as the "Shanghai honey nectar peach" for the next three centuries.[82] Searches of the major Qing (1644–1911) collectanea and encyclopedia collections yield numerous references linking the variety to Shanghai, as described by Zhang via Wang, but only one reference to the variety as grown elsewhere (that from the Nanyuan Garden noted earlier) after the development of the Shanghai variety.[83]

The reputation of Shanghai peaches and gardens also slowly moved up the gazetteer knowledge trail. The peaches are noted in the 1631 *Gazetteer of Songjiang Prefecture* (Chongzhen Songjiang fuzhi), and Dew Fragrance Garden earned an entry at the national level in the 1746 *Gazetteer of the Unified Realm of the Great Qing* (Daqing yitongzhi). The peaches themselves are noted in the 1820 revision of the same, where it says, "Peaches in Songjiang come from Shanghai. The honey nectar variety is the best."[84] With its reputation broadcast so widely, the Shanghai honey nectar peach also came, finally, to set the standard for how even other peach varieties should taste. Thus, the 1772 *Loutang Gazetteer* (Loutang zhi) boasted of Loutang's golden peaches by claiming that "the taste resembles that of the Shanghai honey nectar peach."[85]

Shanghai Crops and Products as Chinese Crops and Products

As heirs to the late-sixteenth and early-seventeenth century discourse on Shanghai crops and products, which earned Shanghai an empire-wide reputation, local elites in Qing times developed one final representational strategy for depicting the significance of Shanghai crops and products. Earlier in the region's history, local elites had written about the area's crops and products to put their region of China on the map, whether by depicting the region as a self-sufficient land linked to famous historical figures or by emphasizing the diversity of the region's native products and the power of the land to produce new goods. Qing elites, in contrast, wrote about Shanghai crops and products as if they were part of a broader and longer history of Chinese foodways and food writing. This new representational strategy proved useful in a number of contexts. It was the strategy of choice for the editors of the first Qing gazetteer of Shanghai, published in 1683. It was also a strategy to which local elites turned in the early nineteenth century. By this later date, Shanghai had become a key component not only of the Jiangnan economy, but of the broader imperial economy, and local elites struggled to retain Shanghai's distinction as a place. By writing about Shanghai crops and products in this new way, local elites could rest assured that their hometown crops and products had more than just a regional importance. They had become a definitive component of the history of the empire's crops and products more generally.

The first text on Shanghai crops and products to exhibit these tendencies was the 1683 *Shanghai County Gazetteer* (Kangxi Shanghai xianzhi). The emergence of a new representational strategy did not mean that former strategies were abandoned entirely. Thus, the entry on the five grains emphasizes the diversity in cropping cycles among villages in different parts of the county.[86] It also includes some mention of local notables. But the text registered the significance of local notables in a different way, by interspersing their names among references to the Chinese classics and other works of Chinese literature in which items of food were an important component or the central focus. Indeed, the entire entry is characterized by a new emphasis on such references, beginning with the very first line, which notes, "The *Book of Odes* recognized grasses and trees, birds and beasts; the "Document of Yu" listed fine and coarse bamboo, *jun* and *lu* bamboo, the pearl-oyster of the Huai, and the turtle of the Yangtze. All provided a livelihood for the people and were products of the land. Therefore, although trifling, they must be detailed."[87]

Earlier gazetteers, as discussed previously, cited sources that spoke directly to the Huating or Shanghai locality, such as the stories about Lu Ji, or Li Han's "In Praise of the Meritorious Record of Military Land Development." The editors of the Kangxi gazetteer, in contrast, drew its corpus of allusions from a much wider range of sources, many of which had no direct relevance to the Shanghai region. This new style of selecting allusions, by which the gazetteer characterized a crop or product by reference to its prior reference in another text, is evident, for example, in the opening section on the "five grains," which alone contains references to fourteen different texts or authors. Significantly, these references were interspersed with the names of local figures—such as literatus Lu Wenyu (Lu Shen), who built the first garden of note, the Houleyuan, in sixteenth-century Shanghai—with book titles and other prominent figures drawn from the full extent of Chinese history and geography. The references reached as far back as the Western Zhou (1045–771 b.c.) and to several different regions of the empire, including the Song poets Lu You (1125–1210) and Yang Wanli (1127–1206), natives of the Shaoxing region and Jiangxi, respectively, as well as the early Warring States (475–221 b.c.) *Rites of Zhou*, the Western Han (202 b.c.–a.d. 23) *Sayings of the States* (Guoyu), the early second-century character dictionary, *Shuowen jiezi*, and the Ming *Collection of Materia Medica* (Bencao gangmu).[88] This representation of Shanghai's crops and products provided a compelling image of a place that lay at the crossroads of Chinese history and geography. The image was so compelling that when the next edition of

Shanghai's gazetteer was issued in 1750, it reprinted the chapter on crops and products from the 1683 edition verbatim.

The enduring appeal of this new image of Shanghai was related to developments in Shanghai's social and economic history that integrated Shanghai more closely with other parts of the empire. These developments, which some locals welcomed but which others viewed as cause for concern, consisted of three main components: the revival of coastal trade, the proliferation in Shanghai of guilds representing nonnative merchants, and a restructuring of the local cotton trade. When the Qing rulers, in 1684, lifted the ban on maritime trade imposed during Ming rule, Shanghai, which "had the good fortune to be situated at the nexus of the three most important arteries of waterborne trade in the empire," became an increasingly important shipping port. It became "the major port of entry and exit for the produce and coastal traffic of the whole lower Yangzi region," and a stopping-off point for ships embarking from the southern ports of Fujian, Guangzhou, Ningbo, and Quanzhou and for northern destinations like Guandong, Shandong, and Tianjin.[89] This transformation of Shanghai into a domestic entrepôt was further facilitated by the proliferation of *gongsuo* and *huiguan*, native-place and trade associations for sojourning merchants to the city. The first of these, the Guan-Shandong *gongsuo*, representing soybean and fertilizer shipping merchants from Shandong and Guandong, was established circa 1660. By the time Chu Hua published his *Treatise on the Honey Nectar Peach*, in 1814, at least seventeen such associations had been established in the city.[90] A small number of these represented local merchants, but the locals were soon outnumbered by merchant groups from Anhui, Chaozhou, Fujian, Ningbo, Qianding, and Shaoxing, who set up shop in the city at various points during the eighteenth century. Finally, although cotton remained Shanghai's most lucrative crop, local cotton merchants gradually lost control over the cotton economy: "In Ming times, the fabric market of Shanghai . . . was under the control of local fabric brokers, upon whom outside merchants had to depend for lodging and meals on their visits, as well as conducting business. This manner of doing business did not change until [the late eighteenth century, when] the 'guest' merchants hired their own agents and established their own permanent headquarters in town."[91]

Chu Hua, a sixth-generation descendent of a prominent Shanghai cotton merchant family—he describes one distant relative as "the richest man in the county" from late Ming to early Qing times—witnessed these changes in Shanghai's economy first hand, and was determined that Shanghai retain an identity as a distinct place, even as it became an increasingly integrated component of the society and economy of China.[92] To this end, Chu wrote a lengthy reference work on Shanghai, as well as treatises on Shanghai's two most important crops, cotton and peaches.[93] Chu was clearly troubled by the loss of local control over the fabric trade, but he was proud that peach cultivation remained a distinguishing feature of his home region. A paucity of relevant source material for the eighteenth century makes it difficult to determine how many and how widely peaches were cultivated in Shanghai during these years. More clear is that, by mid-Qing times, the distinguishing sites of peach cultivation were different from those of late Ming times.

By the time of Chu's writing, in the early nineteenth century, the Gu family garden that had made Shanghai's peaches famous was long gone. The decline of Dew Fragrance Garden was a combined product of patterns of late Ming decay and the Qing conquest. Among the most prominent families in Shanghai in the sixteenth century, the Gu family seems not to have been able to reproduce the examination successes of the generation of Gu Mingshi and Gu Mingru in subsequent years.[94] It is not possible to date the deterioration of the family's garden with precision, but by the first few years of the Qing, as Ye Mengzhu notes, "the walls to the garden were all in disrepair and of the pavilions [that marked] the scenery, only one tenth remained." By 1656, "the famous garden had become overgrown with weeds." Then, at the beginning of the Kangxi era (1661–1723), the Qing state appropriated the site, using it to house a unit of the navy and as a residence for civil authorities, before finally converting it into a military barracks. As Ye Mengzhu lamented, "The hills were leveled and the dells filled in; the dry weeds crushed and the rotten wood smashed; the quarters went up freely and swiftly; and before too long it resembled but a barricade. Today, it is a garrison for soldiers who have returned home from overseas and the barracks built there are truly a worthless place, overgrown with thorns and brushwood."[95] Chu Hua himself lamented that the former site was now but a military training ground known as the Nine-*mu* Field. Traces of the garden's past could still be found in a few rocks and ponds strewn throughout the site, but, "alas, not one tree remained of the [once] beautiful and luxuriant [site]."[96]

Chu also reports, however, that in his time heirlooms of the Gu family peaches were thriving in four other Shanghai locations. Some of these orchards apparently stretched out over ten *mu* of land, but the best peaches now reportedly came from Li Yunjia's (1766–1826) Wu Garden, located in the southwest corner of the city. Li Yunjia, a close associate of Chu Hua, was a merchant, book collector, and calligrapher who played a key role in Shanghai's cultural life during the late-eighteenth and early-nineteenth centuries.[97] Li held only a *gongsheng* title, but he served a term in the Court of Imperial Entertainments (*Guanglusi*), and as a court archivist (*dianpu*), an assignment for which his hobby as book collector had well prepared him. Li's posts and his book collection, which reportedly numbered some 6,000 titles, brought him into close contact with men of higher rank and greater artistic and literary prominence. In 1803, with the help of another close associate, the multiple-term Shanghai Circuit Attendant, Li Tingjing, Li established the Wu Garden Society of Painting and Calligraphy (Wuyuan shuhuashe), an association of 133 painters and calligraphers, which lasted for some twenty years. The society's activities centered on the Wu Garden, which contained a peach orchard that Li purchased the previous year from a family surnamed Xing.[98] Li had more than purely financial motives for the purchase; his book collection originated, centuries earlier, with Zhu Chaqing, who wrote the description of Dew Fragrance Garden cited earlier, and Li must have known that Zhu's essay had filled out the garden's entry in local gazetteers ever since. By purchasing the garden and engaging in honey nectar peach cultivation in Shanghai, Li was able to forge a link of his own to Shanghai's gentry past.

Chu Hua's *Treatise on the Honey Nectar Peach*, which Li worked hard to get published, fulfilled two linked purposes. First, the body of the treatise, written by Chu Hua, documented the techniques by which Li and his fellow peach growers revitalized Shanghai peach cultivation and kept their orchards productive. It drew attention to the particular features of Shanghai that made it hospitable to peach cultivation, and it built on the repertoire of texts that Shanghai's local elites had produced over the previous centuries to put forth a positive image of the city's topographical advantages. Its unique contribution to this body of literature was the focus on the techniques of local peach cultivation, through its discussion of which Shanghai emerges as a place that is home to a special knowledge regarding the cultivation of fruits. Second, the preface to the treatise, written by the poet Chen Wenshu (1771–1843), whom Li solicited for the task, elaborated on the idea that Shanghai's crops and products were part of a broader imperial history of crops and products. By writing the history of the honey nectar peach into the history of China's marvelous fruits and natural wonders, Chen secured for Shanghai the idea of a place that could produce such wonders too.

The Treatise

As Chu's *Treatise* attests, peach farmers faced the challenge of growing a difficult and idiosyncratic crop that required both an ideal environment and techniques for developing and perpetuating the crop over lengthy periods of time. Chu considered Shanghai to be an ideal environment, a point he made at the very beginning of the treatise by invoking and rewriting a well-known passage, of which there were already many variants, that originated in the *Spring and Autumn Annals of Master Yan* (Yanzi chunqiu), a collection of tales about the sixth-century B.C. statesman Yan Ying (Yanzi). In the original passage, which comes from a section of the text titled "The Robber from Qi," Yanzi, himself a man of Qi, embarks on a mission to the state of Qin. When the king of Qin learns of Yanzi's imminent arrival, he sets out to humiliate him, by binding and parading before Yanzi's audience a man of Qi who has been arrested for robbery. When the king remarks, "So the men of Qi are robbers," Yanzi replies that they only became robbers after having come to Qin, where they were transformed by the environment. This is just as the king of Qi found, Yanzi explains, when he ordered that a mandarin orange tree, a southern crop, be transplanted to the north: "When it bears fruit, it is no longer a mandarin orange but a bitter orange. They look alike but taste different."[99] Yanzi's point was that a just social and political environment was essential to the cultivation of good people. Chu changed the emphasis of Yanzi's analogy to make a point about the environment of Shanghai. Noting that some had speculated about the northern provenance of the honey nectar variety, Chu remarks that the provenance did not matter, because the "rich soil and lively water" of Shanghai made for a successful relocation.[100]

After identifying Shanghai as an ideal environment for peach cultivation, Chu's *Treatise* documents the techniques employed in Shanghai to grow a successful crop. The first step was to sprout new plants, which called for planting a ripened peach, "flesh and all," under just a few inches of earth ("if planted too deep, it will not grow") and fertilizing it with night soil. The first sprouts were then to be transplanted, to prepare the plant for grafting, otherwise the crop will produce a small and bland fruit, known locally as "dead" (*zhijiao*) honey nectar peaches. The graft was to be carried out only after the plant had grown for two or three years, and usually either before the Spring Equinox or after the Autumn Equinox. The local technique, as Chu noted, required considerable dexterity and ingenuity:

> Sever [the plant] two to three feet from the root, making a smooth cut with a sharp knife, not allowing any moisture to leak in. Then make an incision that

runs a little more than one inch downward where the bark meets the trunk. Then take a branch from the south[east] or northeast side of a [mature] honey nectar peach [tree], carve it into a horse-ear shape and warm it in the mouth. Seal it well around the incision with paper and encase it in mud. Then cover [the seal] with a *ruo*-bamboo leaf to protect it. Wait for the plant to survive and then remove the bamboo leaf covering, letting the mud and paper gradually fall away of its own accord.[101]

Once the graft had taken, the plant required constant attention. Its roots were likely to sprout fresh buds that had to be removed, "otherwise the plant will grow weak and produce fruit indistinguishable from a wild peach."[102]

Peaches, Chu noted, were different from other fruit trees and presented growers with a unique set of challenges. Most fruit trees had to be irrigated upon bearing fruit, but if the standard procedure were applied to a honey nectar peach, "the fruit will fall off immediately." This matter was so crucial, Chu insisted, that the plants were not to be irrigated "even if there is a drought and rain doesn't fall for several months." Instead, if the branches and leaves showed signs of withering, the roots were to be covered in a thin coating of river mud. Peach tree bark was also especially troublesome and was prone to drying up even in a healthy tree, in which case it was necessary to carve openings in the bark to "generate circulation." Peach tree roots, finally, were shallow compared with those of other fruit trees, and they withered as the plant aged. The only solution required a long-term commitment, cutting away the tree as soon as the withering began, and then the following year, when the sprouts reappeared, cutting the tree back again: "Only after cutting the tree back three times will the root run deep in the earth and last a long time."[103]

The hard work was well worth the effort, however, for the peach blossoms and the fruit. The blossoms came first and, as Chu explained, distinguished the plant from others of its kind. Like other fruit-bearing trees, the honey nectar peach bloomed a single-petal flower, and thus one might expect a bloom inferior to multiple-petal flowers, but Chu insisted that although "the honey nectar peach blossom is but a single-petal [flower], its beauty surpasses [that of] a common peach." Indeed, the blossom defined and gave shape to the springtime vista, with peach blossoms "stretching as far as the eye can see." The blooms were so beautiful that people compared them to the plum blossoms of Dengwei, a waterway town on the outskirts of Suzhou where plum trees were reportedly planted as early as the Han, and the apricot blossoms of Mount Panshan, made famous by their description and rendition in the early-Qing Buddhist Monk Zhipu's *Gazetteer of Panshan* and *Illustrations of Red Apricots.*[104]

Last, but not least, there was the fruit, which locals eagerly anticipated, and for which there were elaborate criteria—regarding their size, color, and shape, and the time of year at which they were picked—to distinguish the best examples from the merely average. Peaches with "white fuzz and a round bottom" were considered excellent. Some peaches might be asymmetrical, but if the shape were caused not by worms but merely a split pit, then the peach could still be eaten, although it would be "slightly inferior." Some peaches had a yellow hue and bore a red tip; if they had the right fragrance, then these too were deemed "worthy of the name." These, however, were not to be confused with peaches that were a "pure yellowish white," for "it is commonly noted that these are not real honey nectar peaches." Only those peaches that ripened on the branch matured into a fruit with the perfect appearance, fragrance, and taste, although Chu allowed that a peach that had "fallen from the branch to the ground due to a sudden wind or rain was still sweet if eaten before ripening." The only viable alternative was to wrap such peaches in fabric and store them in a vessel to ripen, after which they were called "cave peaches." When a peach was ready for picking, Chu explained, "it can be peeled and then eaten . . . its fragrance wafting up the nose, while sweet juice splashes on one's hands." Many vendors who sold peaches on the marketplace considered the larger peaches the best, but peach growers, Chu explains, knew this to be false, and that "if the roots are mature and the fruit is on the small side, its taste will be twice as good [as a larger fruit from a younger plant]." As for the phenomenon of the honey nectar peach turning red in a thunderstorm, Chu guardedly noted, "Everybody values them tremendously, but actually, only one or two peaches per tree present such a pattern."[105]

The Preface

Chu Hua's *Treatise* identified the techniques by which local growers had made a northern crop a specialty of Shanghai, as well as the criteria according to which locals evaluated and appreciated Shanghai's most famous specialty foodstuff; it was the task of the writer of the preface, Chen Wenshu, to identify the broader historical significance of the crop. Chen wrote the preface at Li Yunjia's request, after Li gave Chen a copy of the text, along with a gift of peaches from his garden. Chen was an appropriate figure for the task. In addition to serving a term in the imperial Institute for the Glorification of

Literature, he had served in Shanghai in an official capacity around the time that Chu wrote his treatise. Though not an especially famous writer in his own right, Chen had established a reputation as an important patron of poetry, and of women's poetry in particular.[106] Through this work he became identified as an heir to a tradition most closely associated with the poet and critic Yuan Mei (1716–97), a distant relative. Given Yuan Mei's reputation as a consummate critic of all matters pertaining to gardens and food, Chen's authorship of the preface, therefore, immediately drew Chu Hua's peach treatise into a broader genealogy of food writing.[107] In Chen, Li Yunjia also found a poet capable of identifying the larger significance of Shanghai's honey nectar peaches. Chen's preface did this in two ways. First, it identified a need for a study of Shanghai's peaches, a need that, Chen noted, Chu's treatise ably met. Second, it built on the local tradition of locating Shanghai crops and products in the history of Chinese letters by locating the Shanghai honey nectar peach in a constellation of marvelous fruits and the literature that celebrated them.

It was remarkable and regrettable, Chen noted, that the peach had not already become the subject of a botanical monograph. Indeed, monographic treaties abounded for citrus fruits, litchi, plums, peonies, chrysanthemums, orchids, and roses, as well as other symbol-laden crops, such as bamboo, but not for peaches.[108] Chen noted that the honey nectar peach variety was not unique to Shanghai; it had been grown in Hebei and Shandong, and was so widely available in Jiangnan that it seemed to him that, "Wherever my cart goes, there I find the sweet fragrance of honey nectar peaches." But it also made sense that it would be Shanghai's peaches that occasioned such a text, because "Of all the good places in Jiangnan, Shanghai's are the best." Chen also found Chu Hua to be up to the task of producing the work and filling in this glaring gap in the literatures of botany and connoisseurship. Chen praises Chu's work for being "concise and methodical and of high quality," and he even compares Chu with model agriculturalists of the past. The most notable of these was the pseudonymous author of the *Book of Planting Trees* (Zhongshu shu), who took his name from Liu Zongyuan's (773–819) allegory, "Biography of the Gardener Guo Tuotuo" (Guo Tuotuo zhuan). Guo was known to have "Tao-inspired skill that brought him the patronage of all the rich and noble citizens of the capital."[109] Chen also likened Chu to a holder of the office of Supervisor of Forestry and Hunting (Yuheng), whose charge was to protect valuable products of the land.

The kind of land that Chen saw being protected in Shanghai is evident in the constellation of marvelous fruits that Chen cited to provide a context for recognizing the historical significance of Shanghai's peaches:

> Crab apples come from Huayang, pomegranates from Dunxun. The finest specimens of delicate dates come from Pangtang; the most famous streaked apricots come from Penglai. None are not [named] in Lu Ji's *Elucidation* or Ji Han's *Prospect*, listed in the forests of the "Seven Stimuli," or enumerated in the "Three Capitals." The most detailed "Record of Oranges" is Yanzhi's; premier among "Rhapsodies on the Litchi" is Jiuling's. Zijian wrote his poem on sugarcane, Xiaowei his letter on the apple. Those experts who have sought out different kinds [of fruit] have classified them and determined their essential characteristics as accurately as the jade balance.[110]

Chen's constellation of fruits, texts, and figures asserted Shanghai's status as a special kind of place. It was a place with native sons who contributed to a body of literature associated with the highest echelons of Chinese culture, and it was a place that had a certain cosmic significance. Chen's many references to distinct bodies of food writing placed Chu in a genealogy of literature that was a part of the process of magnifying and glorifying the realm. The implication of cosmic significance derived from the qualities associated with the four fruits Chen mentions at the opening of the preface. For the purpose of explicating how the allusions created this context and set of associations, it will be helpful to begin with the scholarly literature and poetry Chen cites and then conclude the discussion by focusing on the four fruits.

Word of marvelous and delicious fruits had spread throughout China over the years in a rich and diverse body of food writing, including scholarly exegesis, treatises, poetry, and personal correspondences, that Chu's text was now joining. Among the earliest extant texts in this tradition was Lu Ji's (266–301) *Elucidation of the Plants, Trees, Birds, Beasts, Insects, and Fishes in the Book of Odes* (Maoshi caomu niaoshou congyu shu). (The author of this text should not be confused with the Lu Ji discussed earlier, although it was probably not lost on readers that he was also a man of Wu.) The *Elucidation* formalized a long tradition of scholar-officials seeking to identify the plants and animals mentioned in the *Book of Odes*, a project that Confucius had encouraged in the *Analects*.[111] Each entry of the work "takes a four-character phrase from of the [odes] and adds a commentary seeking to identify the plant in question."[112] Lu's text was soon followed by Ji Han's 306 *Prospect of the Plants of the South* (Nanfang caomu zhuang), a regional botany of Guangdong, Guangxi, and Yunnan, and a pioneering work of a separate tradition of Chinese food writing that focused on the uses and values of unfamiliar foodstuffs and plants that Chinese botanists encountered in their travels to the south, following the southward movement of Chinese colonists and settlers.[113] Ji Han's *Prospect* contributed significantly to the process by which the foodstuffs of once foreign lands were written into and made a part of Chinese history. By citing these two foundational texts, Chen suggested that Chu's *Treatise* made him the heir to a core component of the Confucian tradition, and that Shanghai's peach growers should be admired for perfecting the cultivation of a fruit that was not native to their region.

Fruits were among the most written about subjects of poetry in the history of Chinese letters, and Chen sought to associate Chu's treatise and Shanghai's peaches with outstanding examples from this tradition. These poems included Mei Sheng's "Seven Stimuli" (Qifa) and Zuo Si's "Three Capitals Rhapsody," in both of which fruits function as part of a wider constellation of enticements and marvels.[114] Of all the poems Chen cites, however, the closest link to Chu's own project was with Zhang Jiuling's (678–740) "Prose Poem on Litchis" (Lizhi fu). Zhang, a native of Guangdong Province, wrote his prose poem about his favorite food at a time when northern Chinese still considered Guangdong a cultural backwater. By drawing attention to one of his hometown products, Zhang celebrated the "unappreciated (by northerners) glories of his native region" to "effect a reorientation of traditional geographic prejudice."[115]

Turning to the four fruits in Chen's preface, we can now piece together exactly what kind of image of Shanghai Chen was putting forth. The first two fruits to which Chen refers, crab apples and pomegranates, entered China through fringe territories or foreign lands and evoke histories of the incorporation of these fruits into the Chinese realm. Crab apple trees were native to present-day Sichuan Province, once part of the so-called Huayang region that also included Yunnan and Guizhou provinces, as well as parts of Gansu, Shaanxi, and Hubei. Crab apples were most commonly appreciated for their flowers. Daoist literature, however, also endowed the fruit and tree with certain cosmic properties. This is evident in the discussion of the crab apples of Huayang in the text to which Chen alludes, the *Biographies of Grotto Immortals* (Dongxian zhuan), a collection of biographies of seventy-seven Daoist immortals. This text, likely compiled late in the period of the Northern and Southern Dynasties (420–589), observes,

> Zhan Shanggong [an ancient Daoist worthy] studied the Dao in Fulongdi [today's village of Yuchen, Maoshan Town, Jiangsu Province]. [There] he planted

crab apples that enveloped his place of residence. Time and again he explained to other worthies: "Long ago I enjoyed the delicious taste of crab apples in Huayang, and while I was still savoring the memory, all of a sudden three thousand ages had elapsed." Later Guo Sichao [a Qin worthy] settled here [Fulongdi] and also planted the "five fruits." Shanggong said: "This place is perfect for planting crab apples. The variety called "Lucky Village Crab Apple" can prevent pestilence.[116]

The passage contains several noteworthy features. First, crab apples were, clearly, a means of achieving immortality. Second, they were also a resource for safeguarding communities, by virtue of their ability to appease the God of Pestilence (*Wenshen*) and bring luck to one's native place. Finally, there is a striking parallel between Zhan Shanggong's relocation of the crab apple from Huayang to his abode in Jiangsu, where the plant is said to have flourished, and Chu's positive appraisal of the relocation of the honey nectar peach to Shanghai. The allusion thus provided a model for representing Shanghai as a place to which immortals would travel and in which harmony between the worldly and otherworldly prevailed.

Like the crab apple, the pomegranate, a symbol of fertility and a valuable medicinal product, was also a fruit and flowering plant rich in associations in Chinese letters, and it also entered China from a distant land.[117] Dunxun was a Southeast Asian state located on territory that today constitutes a part of Myanmar. With a coastline that Chinese records describe as spanning "one thousand *li*," Dunxun became an important point of embarkation for the south seas and a marketing center for neighboring and distant states. As the seventh-century *Liang History* (Liangshu) notes, "Dunxun connects over land to the east with Jiaozhou [north Vietnam and China's Guangxi Province] and to the west with states outside the pass, such as Tianzhu [India] and Anxi [Persia]. . . . Every day more than ten thousand merchants [from these places] converge [at Dunxun markets]. There is no rare item or precious object that is not available."[118] The *Liang History* does not name pomegranates specifically as a product of Dunxun, but they were a well-known product of Persia and likely became associated with Dunxun marketplaces through Persian trade there. The *Liang History* does, however, mention an indigenous tree that "resembles the pomegranate of Persia," from which an alcoholic beverage was manufactured. For whichever reason Chen chose to link the pomegranate to Dunxun, his allusion provided a model for highlighting another of Shanghai's virtues: it was a place that trade had made a meeting place for valuable crops and products, and which thereby enriched the wider realm.

In contrast to Huayang and Dunxun, Pangtang and Penglai, the sources of the second two fruits noted in the preface, were mythical lands, both of which were associated with the Queen Mother of the West and figured prominently in tales of Emperor Wu of the Han. Word of the delicate dates of Pangtang appear in the first century *Record of Caves of Mystery* (Dongming ji), one of three monographic accounts of Emperor Wu's quest for immortality, where they are said to come from the mountains of Pangtang and "bear fruit once every ten thousand years."[119] The *Record of Caves* discusses the dates as a core component of a larger ceremony Emperor Wu conducts in the magnificent Pavilion for Summoning Worthies. First, a special Persian incense made from the fragrant *quanmi* herb (of which a small amount burns continuously for three months) is lit on the pavilion altar; then, the dates of Pangtang, a pit of which the Queen Mother has offered in tribute to Emperor Wu, are presented; finally, a lamp of the hemp-like *fangyi* grass is lit and emits a purple light. Once the stage is set, exotic animals enter the pavilion and play among themselves, while a goddess presents a jade hairpin that subsequently transforms into a white swallow. The date pit is of special significance because the queen presents it to the emperor with her own hands, in sharp contrast to another famous occasion when she chided him for trying to make off with the pits of her famous peaches. Significantly, the queen's gesture provided the date with a secondary name, *Wohezao*.[120] *Wohe* means literally, "to grasp the kernel" and refers first to the pit, but metaphorically to the crux of an issue. The queen's offering was thus certainly a compliment to Emperor Wu, as it suggested that he was capable of going straight to the heart of a matter. Chen's allusion to this encounter suggested that Shanghai, famous not for dates but for peaches, was worthy of the finest variety of a fruit denied even to the Han emperor during one of his quests for immortality.

Emperor Wu also figures in the account of the fourth and final fruit to which Chen alludes, Penglai apricots. Word of this specimen had spread via Liu Xin's (c. 50 B.C.–A.D. 23) *Miscellaneous Notes on the Western Capital* (Xijing zaji), a collection of tales of the capital of the Western Han. Discussing the "famous fruits and strange trees" of Emperor Wu's Shanglin Garden, Liu notes that the garden contains "streaked apricots and Penglai apricots." Chen seems to have conflated the two fruits, but of all the fruits he cites in the preface, these made the clearest connection between Shanghai peach cultivation and the emperor's commitment to cultivating fruit for cosmological purposes. The Shanglin Garden had several purposes: it was a hunting park, in which the emperor was able to demonstrate his martial prowess; it was a manifestation of his patronage of agricultural accomplishments, by which he demonstrated his ability, as a leader, to connect with the peasantry and the officials whose meritorious service created conditions for a good harvest; and it was an environment to which he could invite immortals to stop and rest, thereby securing his own position as a sage.[121] As Liu explains, "When the garden was first built, officials came from far-away places [outside the Nine Prefectures] and each presented [the emperor] with famous fruits and strange trees."[122] One source indicates that the garden covered three hundred *li*, and that items presented in tribute exceeded three thousand specimens in number. Liu Xin counted ten varieties of pears, seven of dates, ten of peaches, fifteen of *li*-plums, seven of *mei*-plums, two of apricots, three of tong tree, as well as ten trees of apple, pipa, orange, and pomegranate, and many more obscure items of which there were fewer varieties. Of the apricots Chen cites in the preface, it was said that the blooms of one tree contained five colors and the blossoms six petals (whereas most apricot blossoms have only five), and that the fruit was enjoyed by the immortals of Penglai.[123] By associating Shanghai's honey nectar peach with such fruits, Chen identified it as a fruit worthy of the Shanglin Garden, and thereby Shanghai as a place that was heir to the Shanglin tradition. It was a jurisdiction with inhabitants committed to securing an agricultural foundation for the realm, and a place worthy of visits by immortals. Chen's allusions thus put forth the idea that Shanghai had indeed become a "microcosm" of the Chinese realm, and of "the universe itself."

2 A Tale of Two Cities
Food Culture and the Urban Ideal in Late Qing Shanghai

The four directions are all provided for in Shanghai restaurants. Sweet and crisp, savory and rich—there is something there for everybody.
Wang Tao, *A Supplement to Record of Visits to Courtesan Houses in a Distant Corner By the Sea*, 1873

When visitors come they mistake it for a small Taoyuan;
branches and fragrance envelope the marshy plain.
The sight of flowers occupies spring for three hundred years;
to this day people still talk about Dew Fragrance Garden.
Zhang Chunhao, *Folksongs of Shanghai Seasons*, 1873

AT THE *GENG* HOUR on the eighth day of the third month of the *ren-yan* year of the reign of the Daoguang emperor (5:00 P.M. on March 19, 1843), a man fell out of the sky and landed in Huangdu Town, in Jiading County, Jiangsu Province. His face was disfigured beyond recognition, and frightened town residents cried out for an official investigation. Before long, it was ascertained that the man was a casualty of a massive explosion that had cast him through the air all the way from the Shanghai County Seat, a distance of some seventy *li*. The explosion took place in the Shanghai Munitions, which was located in the northwest corner of the city. The munitions were part of a new set of defensive measures the Qing government adopted after the signing of the 1842 Treaty of Nanjing, which ended the Opium War (1839–1842) and outlined new parameters for international relations with Britain. At the time of the explosion, the munitions held more than forty-five thousand catties (*jin*) of gunpowder. No wonder then, that when the gunpowder suddenly ignited, as local literatus and Shanghai native Mao Xianglin recalled in his 1874 *Record of Leftover Ink* (Moyu lu), "Thunder pealed and shook the ground, heaven and earth were cloaked in darkness, and even things close at hand could not be distinguished. Smoke as thick as ink was seen from afar and rose up to reach the cloud line, while the houses nearby were all turned to ash."[1]

Some suspected the work of traitors, but whatever the cause of the explosion, it exacted a heavy toll, and the disfigured man who fell from the sky was not the only casualty. Rui Yongsheng, the brigade vice-commander in charge of the munitions, had just come home from visiting a friend. He was reportedly loosening his belt when the explosion sounded, and "no sooner had he heard the noise and hurried to respond than he was wounded in the forehead by a flying tile." Rui managed to drag himself to safety, but it took him a full month to recover. Less fortunate was Zhang Kongan, a candidate for the post of commissioner of the munitions, who had arrived only a few days earlier: "When the fire was extinguished, Zhang's corpse was found lying beneath the eaves, his face burned by fire, and his body covered with wounds." Others were crushed and killed by falling debris, and one man was found lying "face down across the rear railing of the Autumn Water Pavilion," a recently restored site of the nearby Dew Fragrance Garden. As tragic as these losses were, at least these bodies could be buried intact, unlike the corpse of the runner He Bing, a local man whose labor services had recently been transferred to the munitions. The initial search yielded no trace of He; then, "Suddenly, somebody [found] a leg hanging from a tree." They identified He's leg by his shoes and socks, but "the rest of his flesh and blood was in bits and pieces and could not be distinguished." Other fatalities included ten members of a regiment of soldiers from Anhui that had been lodging in the Autumn Water Pavilion and a Buddhist nun from the Long Life Nunnery located just to the north. It was the darkest day in Shanghai history since British forces put the city into a state of siege in June of the previous year during the closing battles of the Opium War.

The explosion, like the Opium War and the treaty that ended it, marked the end of one era and the beginning of another. The Treaty of Nanjing has long been viewed as a turning point in Shanghai's history. It opened Shanghai to foreign residency, and local officials soon demarcated the boundaries of new foreign settlements to the north of the county seat, across the Yangjingbang Creek, paving the way for the internationalization of the city. Originally earmarked for foreign residence only, these settlements soon became home to thousands of Chinese refugees and opportunity seekers, who were pulled and pushed to Shanghai by the combined forces of commercial prospects and popular rebellion in neighboring provinces. Although Shanghai was not a small city at the time of the signing of the treaty—with a population of roughly 240,000, it ranked in the top twenty of the largest cities in China—by the end of the century, it was the wealthiest and most international city in the realm, and its foreign settlements were "routinely talked about . . . in terms of the paradise of Penglai, Island of the Immortals."[2] This was not the first time in Shanghai's history that it was likened to Penglai, but in this case, the term was inspired by the "electric lights densely covering" the foreign settlements, and the term Penglai henceforth attached to the foreign settlements alone.

Penglai, however, was not the only metaphor for the urban ideal circulating in late nineteenth-century Shanghai. The years that witnessed the rise of the foreign settlements were also marked by intersecting histories of loss. The first of these histories began with the explosion in the Shanghai Munitions. In addition to taking many lives, the explosion demolished the site of Shanghai's Dew Fragrance Garden, which lay adjacent to the munitions. The famous garden itself had fallen into a state of disrepair during the late Ming, and the site had been remade into a military facility in the early Qing. But memories of the garden had nonetheless continued to animate the idea of Shanghai as a garden city, and a number of local figures had even recently rebuilt the garden's Autumn Water Pavilion. The explosion thus dealt a considerable symbolic blow. This blow, moreover, was soon compounded by a more general sense that the county seat, which once constituted the heart of Shanghai, was losing its prestige relative to the foreign settlements. Many in the county seat remained powerful politically and economically, but culturally, for those who celebrated settlement life, the county seat looked like a backwater, "walled up and resistant to the new lifestyle, modern city management, and improvements such as roads and sewage systems springing up just over Yangjingbang Creek."[3]

Newcomers who settled in Shanghai beginning in the mid-nineteenth century brought to the city their own sense of loss. Many were, initially, only there as sojourners, seeking opportunities for employment or commercial gain. The sense of loss that they felt was a natural by-product of the sojourning way of life, which required long stays away from home. Their hopes for a return home, however, were dashed by the violent march of the Taiping Rebellion, which ravaged southern China from 1851 to 1864. The rebellion destroyed the homes and hometowns of many of Shanghai's sojourners, and left countless other refugees in its wake. These sojourners and refugees would soon become more permanent fixtures of Shanghai. They were key players in the spectacular growth of the new Shanghai of the foreign settlements, as well as its history's most influential chroniclers. However, as they learned about the history of their new home, they joined native Shanghainese in mourning the transformation of Shanghai from a serene garden city into a decadent and potentially dangerous metropolis. Natives, sojourners, and refugees alike made Dew Fragrance Garden into an important symbol of an Old Shanghai, for which the most suggestive metaphor was not Penglai, but Wulingyuan, the rural idyll and mythical lost world of Tao Qian's "Record of the Peach Blossom Spring."

Few topics better illustrate these two images of Shanghai—Penglai and Wulingyuan—than the views of natives and newcomers on the developments of Shanghai food culture. Before the rise of the foreign settlements, Shanghai food culture was distinctly local, if by no means provincial, and centered on its specialty foodstuffs—perch, water shield, and the delicious and evocative Shanghai honey nectar peach. After the rise of the foreign settlements, restaurants became defining elements of urban food culture. The settlements' streets teemed with itinerant food peddlers who carried their "kitchens" on shoulder poles and catered to commoners, and banquet rooms in high-end restaurants and courtesan halls became key social arenas for urban elites to assert their status. Reflecting the relatively conservative eating habits of newcomers to the city, as well as the need of newcomers to recreate the hometown culture they had left behind, restaurants at both the high and low ends of the industry initially catered to native-place tastes and functioned as nodes of immigrant community formation and urban segregation. Over time, however, city residents used restaurants as vehicles for exploring real and imagined cultural differences among the city's population and for developing new ideas of the city. When viewed from this perspective, Shanghai was indeed a Penglai, a place where, as the Shanghai sojourner Wang Tao noted, "There is something for everybody."[4]

Yet, newcomers such as Wang Tao—who produced the travelogues, urban guides, illustrated magazines, and popular fiction that celebrated the new culture of the settlements—could not shake their sense of loss, and they sought anchors of continuity for solace. They found some sense of continuity in the native-place food culture provided by the regional restaurants of the foreign settlements. But they also found comfort in the food culture of the Shanghai county seat, which connected them to the past of the city that they now called home. In so doing, they joined native Shanghainese, like the folklorist Zhang Chunhua (19th century), in insisting that the Shanghai county seat had a history that "people still talk about," even, perhaps especially, as the Shanghai of the foreign settlements became more international and "modern" than any other city in Chinese history.[5] Together, native and newcomer made icons of Shanghai's former food culture—the Shanghai honey nectar peach and Dew Fragrance Garden—into foils for the problems of the new metropolis, and an image of an ideal state and society. The contradictory images of Shanghai as Penglai and Wulingyuan mapped onto the two main sections of what had become a dual city—the "modern" foreign concessions and the former, more "traditional" county seat—the contours of which food culture was key to delineating. The fit, however, was not perfect in either case, and that only made culinary nostalgia more acute.

The Making and Meanings of a Dual City

Not all was well in Shanghai when Huang Mian, the sub-commissioner of Shanghai, enlisted local support to restore Dew Fragrance Garden's Autumn Water Pavilion in 1836. But as the act of restoration itself indicates, Shanghai natives and officials were committed to the status quo of their city—its domestic trade networks, its signature gardens, and its relationship with its past. The recent collapse of the international cotton market had led to a sharp drop in demand for the city's main commercial crop, which for the past five decades had been traded on the world market through merchants in Guangzhou. But when Hugh Hamilton Lindsay, a commercial representative of the British East India Company, visited Shanghai in 1832, "he counted 400 Chinese junks, averaging between 100 and 400 tons entering the port weekly during July 1832." The city was, according to one estimate, "one of the leading ports of the world."[6] European merchants and government officials who had grown frustrated with the Canton System, which restricted European trade with China to the southern city of Guangzhou (or Canton), sent the occasional mission north to renegotiate the terms of the China trade and find new markets for their merchandise. Those reaching Shanghai, however, did not make much progress. Lindsay's demands and bribes made little headway even with local authorities and failed to earn him the audience he sought with provincial and central government officials.[7] Sub-Commissioner Huang thus had little reason to imagine that Shanghai's northern suburbs, then only sparsely populated, would soon become the site of a glittering new metropolis that overshadowed the former county seat.

Confidence in Shanghai was not shaken until well into the Opium War, when on June 11, 1842, the British *Nemesis* pulled into the city's harbor during one of the war's closing battles. British troops took the city with relative ease and after five days of occupation evacuated and continued their march north (although not before sampling the delicious fruit that grew in the city's gardens, in which they camped during their short stay).[8] The occupation, though brief, sent shock waves throughout Shanghai society and raised awareness of a new threat to its inhabitants' sense of order. As indicated by the important local chronicle of these events, Cao Sheng's *Reminiscence of the Bitter Suffering During the Barbarian Disaster* (Yihuan beichang ji), "The inhabitants were thrown into a panic. . . . For several days rumors proliferated, describing imminent disaster and dwelling on terrible atrocities that could be expected." Few Shanghai residents actually died in the struggle, but "Locals remembered the firepower and lawlessness of the *yangren* [Westerners], which convinced authorities and population alike that these foreigners were dangerous."[9]

Such impressions loomed large in the eyes of local officials, among the most important of which was the Shanghai Circuit Attendant Gong Mujiu, who from 1843 to 1847 was responsible for managing Shanghai's foreign affairs. Gong felt that Chinese and non-Chinese should remain segregated, but the Treaty of Nanjing, which provided for foreign residence in Shanghai and the other treaty ports, made Chinese-foreign mixed residence a real possibility, because the treaty did not identify any separate territory in which the foreigners were to reside. A number of the earliest foreign arrivals found lodging within the walls of the county seat, but eventually Gong and George Balfour, the British consul, signed the Land Regulations of 1845, which mapped out the boundaries of a British settlement in the sparsely populated northern suburbs. American and French settlements soon followed, the former eventually being joined with the British to form the International Settlement.[10] The Land Regulations contained a segregation provision that prohibited Chinese from residing in settlement territories, and by moving foreigners out of the county seat, Gong successfully handled this chapter of Sino-foreign relations.

Gong's handling of this matter proved to be a short-lived success, however, as Chinese officials ultimately failed to stop Chinese from moving into the settlements. Chinese sought refuge in the foreign settlements in the wake of two major disturbances: the Small Swords Uprising (1853–55) and the Taiping Rebellion. The Small Swords was a local affair that began with the capture of the county seat by a coalition of Shanghai-based Guangdong and Fujian secret societies and ended with the looting and burning of much of the county seat by Qing troops. Many fled the county seat immediately after the outbreak of the disturbances, and "the settlements became at the same time the refuge of the Chinese authorities and of the wealthy native merchants."[11] Many Chinese returned to the county seat after the rebellion was put down, but others stayed behind. Chinese authorities remained opposed to the idea of mixed residence, but leading figures in the foreign community saw an opportunity for financial gain and revised the Land Regulations in 1854, removing the 1845 segregation provision. The revised regulations granted Chinese the right of residence and the opportunity to lease land in the foreign settlements, but they prohibited Chinese from buying and selling it. The revision paved the way for a larger and more diverse influx of Chinese refugees in the wake of the Taiping Rebellion. Refugees from Nanjing had begun trickling in after the Taiping armies captured their city in 1853; many more came later from Suzhou, Hangzhou, and Ningbo after these cities fell during 1860 and 1861.

The two uprisings transformed the population of the settlements and, ultimately, the status and idea of Shanghai as a city. Despite the potential the Chinese refugees provided for financial gain, the rapid increase in the Chinese population of the foreign settlements initially caused concern among the foreign residents, many of whom felt that the foreign jurisdictions were turning into Chinese slums.[12] Sanitation and public security were among the most pressing challenges caused by the flood of refugees. Settlement authorities met these challenges by establishing a jail and court system, drafting guidelines for Chinese business operations, and building a public health infrastructure of hospitals and waterworks.[13] From the foreigners' perspective, these measures helped transform the International Settlement into a "Model Settlement." For the many Chinese who relocated there, Shanghai's foreign settlements provided not only a refuge from civil unrest, but also commercial opportunities and prospects for employment.

Meanwhile, the Shanghai County Seat also acquired a new identity as one of China's most important urban administrative units. Much property had been damaged during the Small Swords Uprising, but the city walls, government offices, and key social and economic institutions were quickly rebuilt.[14] This recovery was later enhanced by the selection of Shanghai as the site for the new Foreign Inspectorate of Customs (later the Imperial Maritime Customs). Shanghai assumed even greater importance in the hierarchy of Qing administration after the quelling of the Taiping Rebellion, because it was the only urban center in the region that had not been badly damaged by the rebellion. It became the "main center of administration for the defense of Jiangsu Province" and the site of key new institutions of learning and manufacture: the Interpreters College (est. 1863), which taught Western languages and technology; the Jiangnan Arsenal (est. 1865), the director of which was the Shanghai Circuit Attendant; and the Longmen Academy (est. 1865), which taught a curriculum of Confucian philosophy and Western science.[15]

These developments significantly affected the way the city's leading image makers, foreign and Chinese alike, represented Shanghai's history and life in the county seat.[16] Foreign impressions of the county seat before and immediately after the Treaty of Nanjing had generally been quite favorable. Lindsay had boasted of Shanghai's potential as an international port to help make the case for the expansion of Britain's China trade. His optimistic assessment of the city was echoed by the botanist Robert Fortune, who stopped in Shanghai during the first of several journeys through China. In addition to the delight Fortune took in Shanghai's peaches, he describes many delightful days and evenings spent wandering around the county seat soon after the city was opened to foreign residence. On one of these nights, he attended an elaborate banquet in a private residence, for which the tables were "covered with a profusion of small dishes, which contained all the finest fruits and vegetables of the season, besides many of the most expensive kinds of soups, such as the celebrated bird's-nest and others."[17]

During the 1850s and 1860s, however, foreign impressions of the county seat changed markedly. Attempts by county seat officials to intervene in settlement life irritated settlement authorities, and now that the settlements provided foreign traders with the gateway to the China market that men like Lindsay had fought for, foreigners in Shanghai no longer needed to represent Shanghai as a vibrant native port. Instead, taking full credit for Shanghai's newfound importance, they described Shanghai as decidedly rural and economically undeveloped. Typical of these accounts was *The Times* correspondent George Wingrove Cooke's *China: Being 'The Times' Special Correspondence from China in the Years 1857–58*, which depicted Shanghai as a European settlement surrounded by a vast rural setting, where the cycle of the seasons rather than urban rhythms set the pace of life:

> Beyond the limits of the European settlement the rich alluvial plain on which Shanghai stands extends for twenty miles without a hillock. We must admire the fertility of the soil and the industry of the people, but there all our gratification must end. . . . The land is parceled out into little patches of cotton; and as the plant must be sown wide, the interstices are filled with beans, or by some vegetable that will find a market in Shanghai. . . . There are patches of maize and leguminous plants of many kinds. . . . The old women will sit under the eves of their cottages cleaning and winding, which, indeed, is their normal occupation all the year through; the able-bodied part of the family, having cleared their legumi-

nous crop, will plough up the ground, and either prepare it for wheat, or, if the situation is favorable, will bank up the land and let in water to prepare for rice. The wheat is off the ground in May or June, and the cotton is again sown.[18]

Before long, Shanghai's foreign residents would describe Shanghai as having been a mere fishing village before the signing of the Treaty of Nanjing.

There was a certain element of truth to the foreign rhetoric, because it usually referred specifically to the transformation of the northern suburbs into a new urban area. Moreover, as will become evident, such foreign rhetoric dovetailed in surprising ways with some Chinese accounts of the city. But for the foreigners, this new rhetoric meant that "Shanghai" should refer only to the territory of the former northern suburbs, and not to the former county and county seat. When speaking directly of the county seat, foreign residents of Shanghai did so in decidedly unflattering terms, disregarding the county seat's recently enhanced role as a center of Qing initiatives to manage the growing foreign presence. A common view, as expressed in the 1867 *Treaty Ports of China and Japan*, was that "except as an exemplification of the extreme of native filth and squalor, the city of Shanghai has nothing to repay a visitor for the discomfort of penetrating its narrow and unsavory precincts."[19]

Chinese impressions of the county seat, and of its status relative to the foreign settlements, were more mixed. Officials and residents with vested interests in the county seat viewed the growing influence of the settlements as an irritant, and as a potential threat to their moral and political authority.[20] They communicated their sense of their own relative importance in representations of the city's space, for example, maps that did not include the boundaries of the settlement territories.[21] They thus obscured the presence of the foreign settlements as much as foreign rhetoric obscured that of the county seat.

For many Chinese newcomers to the city, however, the settlements were not so much a threat as a source of fascination and wonder, and were, for all intents and purposes, "Shanghai." Thus, in the preface to his 1876 Shanghai travelogue, *Miscellaneous Notes on Travel in Shanghai* (Huyou zaji), Ge Yuanxu, a fifteen-year Shanghai sojourner from Hangzhou, explains that the book "only records material pertaining to the settlements," because this was the place to which "both merchants and officials love to come for a visit."[22] Although an important exception to this rule will be discussed later, Ge's overall marginalization of the county seat in his representation of Shanghai was part of a wider pattern that is evident even in more specialized accounts of the city, such as Wang Tao's writings on Shanghai courtesans. A native of Fuli in Jiangsu Province, Wang first came to Shanghai in 1848 and wrote three accounts of the Shanghai *demi-monde*, of which he was a regular patron. His first account, bearing a preface dated in 1860, addresses courtesans of the former county seat, whereas the second and third, dated 1873 and 1878, focus on the evolving rituals of courtship and the lives of famous courtesans in the foreign settlements.[23]

These two competing views of Shanghai—one centered on the settlements, the other on the county seat—were drawn starkly in representations of Shanghai foodways. Ge's *Miscellaneous Notes*, for example, represents Shanghai as a modern day Penglai, where such new technologies as the steamboat had made it possible to eat foodstuffs from all over the country, well ahead of the local growing season:

> Steamboats from Guangzhou take only five or six days to arrive in Shanghai. The climate in Guangzhou is warm. Melons and fruit ripen early, and transport by steamboat is convenient. The Shanghai markets have cucumber in the First Month, watermelon in the Fourth Month, and fresh fruit like litchi, longan, wampi, mango, banana, kiwifruit, pineapple, coconut, and *gan*-oranges all arrive before the local season. As for the apples, snow pears, and grapes from the north, and the white olive, *fuju*, and sugarcane from Min—in autumn and winter they are bound and shipped to the market, where they are piled high in abundance.[24]

This profusion of fruits arriving in Shanghai from points north and south stands in stark contrast to discussion of Shanghai fruits in the 1872 *Shanghai County Gazetteer* (Tongzhi Shanghai xianzhi), the first gazetteer written for Shanghai since the creation of the foreign settlements. Like Ge's list of fruits, that of the gazetteer was also extensive—it included peaches, persimmons, apricots, *mei*-plums, *li*-plums, *chen*-oranges, citron, *dai*-oranges, pomegranates, apples, grapes, loquat, gingko, dates, *ling* water chestnuts, *biqi* water chestnuts, and figs.[25] And when writing of Shanghai's peaches, the authors were especially proud, noting, "Peaches come in many varieties . . . but only the honey nectar peaches of Mr. Gu's Dew Fragrance Garden and Huangniqiang are the best. . . . The skin is thin, the fruit sweet, and they melt in the mouth. Those marked with tiny red dots are especially prized."[26] Yet nothing of significance distinguishes the list of fruits in the 1872 gazetteer from that found in the 1750 *Shanghai County Gazetteer* (Qianlong Shanghai xianzhi).[27] The language used to describe the honey nectar peaches in 1872 was also borrowed from the 1750 edition.

Ge's travelogue and the 1872 gazetteer, two of the earliest texts to put forth comprehensive views of Shanghai after the Treaty of Nanjing, represented Shanghai in strikingly different ways. The disparity between the two is rooted in an important generic difference: the former emphasizes articles of consumption available in Shanghai, whereas the latter catalogs those items that were actually crops and products of Shanghai. But the two representations of Shanghai clearly mapped onto different parts of the city and county and created images of two distinctly different places. The settlements Ge describes consisted of a rapidly growing and multinational consumer society that industry had helped break free of the routines of the agricultural calendar. The Shanghai that the 1872 gazetteer depicts, by contrast, was a productive place, still growing the same old fruits, and closely in sync with its past. Like Huang Mian in 1836, the gazetteer editors remained committed to the city's heritage, despite the new opportunities and institutions that prevailed both in the foreign settlements to the north and in the county seat itself. The meaning of that heritage was slowly changing, however. In the early nineteenth century, locals wrote of Shanghai's crops and products in ways that evoked Shanghai's cosmic significance and cosmopolitan status. By the 1870s, however, the foreign settlements' leading image makers, men such as Ge, Wang, and other authors of urban guidebooks, were redefining the terms of what it meant to be cosmopolitan.

Restaurants and the Idea of Cosmopolitan Shanghai

The regionally and nationally diverse restaurant culture that sprang up in Shanghai during the second half of the nineteenth century provided guidebook writers with a working template through which they could depict Shanghai as a new kind of cosmopolitan place. Ge Yuanxu's account of steamboats bearing fruits to Shanghai from all over the empire suggests that the process by which the foreign settlements became a meeting place of cultures was relatively seamless. This process, however, was strained, and it was not complete by the beginning of the twentieth century. The newcomers to Shanghai spoke different languages, they prayed to different gods, they ate different foods, and they organized themselves into institutions that were often oriented more toward their native place than to the city itself. Regional allegiances were not necessarily barriers to more inclusive models of social and political community, but differences were hard to bridge, and the process of bridging them was not unidirectional.[28]

Restaurant culture was a key part of this process, facilitating immigrant community formation and cross-cultural interaction, but also the construction and reification of ideas about regional cultural difference. These developments were most evident in the restaurant culture of the foreign settlements, which had an especially diverse population and a more dynamic restaurant industry than the Shanghai county seat had. Thus, guidebook writers focused their attention largely on settlement restaurants. However, a close examination of the discourse on Shanghai restaurants produced within the foreign settlements also indicates that settlement residents had an interest in overlooking the restaurant culture of the county seat, and that by doing so they were identifying core and marginal communities within the city. The guidebooks thus provide a window onto the historical context that shaped the new cosmopolitan ideal.[29]

The restaurant industry that sprang up in the foreign settlements during the second half of the nineteenth century was profoundly shaped by immigration patterns and the needs and taste preferences of Shanghai's immigrant communities. The more sizable of these communities were made up of sojourners from Suzhou, Ningbo, Nanjing, Tianjin, Anhui, and Guangdong.[30] Among the earliest of Shanghai's new restaurants was the Cantonese Tanhualou, which first opened in 1851 and later grew into the high-end restaurant known as the Xinghualou. The first proprietor was said to be a Cantonese commoner, who, from a one-bay shop front, sold inexpensive Cantonese fare to customers on their way to and from work in Cantonese trading houses—cured meat and roasted duck over rice by day, and five-spice congee and duck congee by night.[31] The restaurant later expanded, and its owner hired the famous Cantonese chef Li Linghai to provide fancier food to meet the needs of the city's growing Cantonese merchant community.[32] Other early regional establishments were the Suzhou snack food purveyor Wufangzhai and the Ningbo cuisine Hongyunlou.

Restaurants were key to the maintenance of native place culture and community among sojourners. As Bryna Goodman has noted in her study of Shanghai native place sentiment, a loss of access to native place food was understood to have serious implications. One native of Xiangshan, Guangdong Province, seeking to explain the regrettable existence of prostitutes from his hometown in Shanghai, argued, "because of their separation from their native place, the moral character of these individuals had deteriorated." As he remarked, "They were kidnapped young from Xiangshan to serve in Shanghai in these despicable professions. . . . When they came to this foreign place they drank the water and ate the food, and their language changed. Their hearts also changed."[33] Native-place taste preferences structured the surface of city life well into the twentieth century. Describing Shanghai's Ningbo restaurants in the

1930s, guidebook writer Wang Dingjiu observed, "The taste of Ningbo food does not suit the appetite of most people, and so other than Ningbo and Shaoxing people, customers from other native places do not enjoy [eating in them]." In Wang's time, many of the larger Ningbo restaurants went by the same name, Zhuangyuanlou, which made them easy for fellow provincials to identify, and just as easy for non-fellow provincials to avoid. Once inside, Ningbo sojourners in Shanghai were comforted by the taste and smell of the cooking and by the familiar furnishings, as Ningbo establishments were outfitted in chairs and tables made of *huhuang* wood, the trade of which Ningbo people dominated.[34]

Despite the divisions in city life that regional restaurants marked off in most parts of the city, a small number of commercial neighborhoods brought city residents from different parts of the country together. These were the neighborhoods centered on the busiest thoroughfares of Shanghai's foreign settlements, first Baoshan Street and later Fourth Avenue (also known as Fuzhou Road). To social commentators, these streets exemplified the prospects and problems of the new kind of consumer society that foreign settlement Shanghai was becoming. Wang Tao described Baoshan Street as a "lair for spending money," where "lanterns blazed brightly from dusk till dawn, and [night] was no different from day. Whatever you want to eat or drink, ask and it will be prepared without delay."[35] Ge Yuanxu and later Huang Shiquan's 1883 *Record of Dream Images of Shanghai* (Songnan mengying lu) described Fourth Avenue in similar terms, the latter noting that "Every evening, as the sun sets in the west, the proud horses approach from the east, and the women resemble clouds [filling up the sky] as they parade up and down the street."[36] By the time of Huang's writing, Fourth Avenue had become the heart of the Shanghai demimonde; it also had the highest concentration of restaurants in the city. Some operated as ancillary businesses from which brothels ordered food, others were independent establishments that served the customers of the publishing houses, book stores, teahouses, and theaters that lined both sides of the street. Fourth Avenue remained the heart of the high-end restaurant industry through the beginning of the twentieth century. Of the thirty-two high-end restaurants listed in the "English Settlement" section of the 1907 *Register of Chinese Merchants in Shanghai* (Shanghai huashang hangming buce), seventeen had Fourth Avenue addresses. The rest were located on nearby streets no more than three blocks away to the north, east, or west.[37]

The Baoshan Street and Fourth Avenue neighborhoods provided adventurous eaters with an opportunity to sample regional cooking styles from several different regions of China. As Wang Tao put it in 1873, "The four directions are all provided for in Shanghai restaurants. Sweet and crisp, savory and rich."[38] Wang refers specifically to Nanjing, Tianjin, and Ningbo restaurants, as well as one successful Shanghai establishment, the Taiheguan, that served "northern and southern food." Writing ten years later, Huang Shiquan notes the addition of high-end Suzhou restaurants.[39] Chi Zhicheng's 1893 *Dream Images of a Visit to Shanghai* (Huyou mengying) added Anhui and Cantonese establishments to the mix, and described the Shanghai restaurant scene as a veritable orgy of culinary diversity and excess:

> Among famous establishments, Taiheguan comes first. . . . Otherwise, for Tianjin restaurants there is the Zhonghe, and for Ningbo restaurants, the Hongyun and Yiqing, where the courtyards are crowded with carriages and the seats are full of beautiful women, but which when all is said and done do not measure up to the Suzhou Jufengyuan on Fourth Avenue or the Nanjing Fuxingyuan on Baoshan Street, which truly stand out from the rest. These two establishments contain tens of dining rooms, upstairs and down. In the middle [of each] is a main hall, flanked by parlors and pavilion rooms; the scale is immense and the decor exquisite. Books, paintings, and couplet scrolls make it the picture of elegance. On special occasions, guests are summoned by invitation. Banquet tables are spread [throughout the hall] and promptly set with delicacies from the seas and hills. Lanterns are strung up at the front gate, and music with drumbeats greets the guests as they arrive. For more common banquets of one or two tables, decorative screens with flower and bird motifs separate [the different parties], and the tables are covered with a profusion of meat and fish dishes, each prepared as exquisitely as the next. By the time the lanterns are lit . . . there is practically a river of wine and a forest of meat, and the steam [from cooking] fills the room like a dense fog.[40]

Ge Yuanxu assisted less experienced restaurant patrons and newcomers to the city by listing in his travelogue the names of the dishes for which each restaurant, and thereby region, was famous (see Figure 2.1).[41] Ge's list was later reprinted in the 1898 *Illustrated Guide to Shanghai Entertainment* (Haishang youxi tushuo), which suggests that Chinese elites made sampling the cuisine of different regional restaurants into an important form of urban amusement.[42]

Wang, Ge, Huang, and Chi represent Shanghai as a place characterized by a seemingly endless profusion of culinary diversity, but their guidebooks are also marked by a distinctive uniformity and pattern of exclusivity that register

Region	Restaurant Name	Dishes
Tianjin	Qingxinglou	Roast Duck, Red-braised Shark's Fin, Mixed Red Braise, Braised Sea Cucumber, Tofu with Dried Shrimp, Tofu-sautéed Eggs, Blanched Tripe in Consommé, Assorted Steamed Buns, Sautéed Sliced Fish, Pork with Rice Noodles
Jinling (Nanjing)	Xinxinlou	Shark's Fin in Clear Broth, Yunnan Ham, Braised Gluten, Spring Vegetables, Steamed Egg Custard, Shaoxing Wine, Roast Duck Soup, Roast Young Duck
Jinling	Fuxingyuan	Shark's Fin in Clear Broth, Steamed Fresh Fish, Sautéed Minced Squab, Huizhou Meat Balls, Assorted Cold Meats, Fruit Cocktail, Sliced Liver Soup
Shanghai	Taiheguan	Roast Duck, Blanched Tripe in Consommé, Rolled Cuttlefish, Dried Fish Maw in Consommé, Deep-fried Diced Chicken, Steamed Buns, Pork Ribs, Stir-fried Julienne of Cuttlefish
Ningbo	Hongyunlou	Yellow Croaker Soup, Blood Clam Soup, Stir-fried Eel, Stir-fried Turtle, Roast Duck, "Purple-canopy" Braised Pork
Ningbo	Yiqinglou	Yellow Croaker Soup, Clam Soup, Stir-fried Eel, Tofu Stew with Shrimp Brain, Ham, Red-braised Turtle

Figure 2.1 "Famous Dishes from Shanghai Restaurants"
SOURCE: Ge Yuanxu, *Huyou zaji. Shanghaitan yu Shanghairen* (Shanghai: Shanghai guji chubanshe, 1989).

patterns of elite interaction, the persistence of native-place residence patterns and taste preferences, and some of their own assumptions about what constituted core and marginal aspects of Chinese culture. All four writers characterize Shanghai's restaurant culture as diverse, but the range of cuisine on which they focus is relatively narrow compared with the actual food offerings on hand in the city. All four betray a bias toward restaurants serving the "Jiang-Zhe" cuisine common to their native place—Wang and Huang hailed from Jiangsu Province (Fuli and Nanhui, respectively), Ge and Chi from Zhejiang (Hangzhou and Ruian)—and Tianjin cuisine. The prominence they give to Tianjin cuisine is likely because of the close relationship between Shanghai's Tianjin commercial elite and merchants and bankers from Jiangsu (and Nanjing in particular), a relationship embodied in the northern-southern cuisine Taiheguan.[43] The Tianjin-Jiangsu connection may also lie behind the intimation that Ningbo restaurants did not measure up to Jiangsu and Tianjin establishments because Ningbo bankers constituted a competing commercial interest group. Of course, the distinctive flavors of Ningbo cooking, which derive from liberal use of fermentations and techniques for accenting the inherent saltiness of seafood, and which sets Ningbo cuisine apart from Hangzhou and Ruian varieties of Zhejiang cookery, may also have made Ningbo cuisine less appealing for non-fellow provincials (indeed, what made Ningbo restaurants notable was not the food but the carriages lined up outside and the beautiful women). Their location in the French Concession, away from Fourth Avenue but close to Shanghai's largest community of Ningbo natives, was also likely a factor.

The biases of the guidebook writers are most evident in their conspicuous omission of Anhui establishments and their exoticization of Cantonese establishments. The omission of Anhui restaurants from the guidebook literature on Shanghai was related to the location of the leading Anhui restaurants in the city. Anhui establishments were among the earliest restaurants to open in Shanghai after the signing of the Treaty of Nanjing. They were the initiative of a network of sojourners from Jixi, in southern Anhui Province, who over the previous century had built a string of restaurants in the region stretching from Huizhou, the largest city in southern Anhui, to Jianxing County in northern Zhejiang Province, a short distance to the south of Shanghai. Huizhou merchants were among the wealthiest and most mobile in the region, and Jixi entrepreneurs followed close behind, carving out for themselves a specialized business niche to meet the native-place taste preferences of Huizhou merchant communities. Jixi restaurateurs opened several establishments in the vicinity of the old county seat: at least two in 1851, three more in 1864, and then one more in 1869.[44] Anhui establishments did not spread to the foreign settlements until 1892, when the Dingfengyuan opened on Fourth Avenue, which explains why they are mentioned only in Chi's 1893 *Dream Images*, and then only in passing. Restaurants inside and near the former county seat were simply not visible to the writers of Shanghai guidebooks, and thus not a part of the idea of cosmopolitan Shanghai that the guidebook writers were creating.

Guidebook writers took more careful note of Cantonese establishments, but in ways that distinguished them from other kinds of regional Chinese restaurants in the city. Cantonese merchant associations were initially among the most powerful in the city.[45] Cantonese restaurants opened in Shanghai soon after the signing of the Treaty of Nanjing, and by the early 1850s, a sizable Cantonese community had formed in Hongkou, in the northwest corner of the original American Settlement. One might therefore have expected Cantonese restaurants to feature more prominently in guidebook depictions of Shanghai restaurants. Hongkou, however, was relatively remote from the Fourth Avenue neighborhood on which guidebook discussions of restaurant cuisine focused. Moreover, the status of the Cantonese community in Shanghai had been severely compromised by the role of Cantonese rebels and sympathizers during the Small Swords Uprising, and the community had not yet fully rehabilitated its public stature. It is also possible, finally, that Cantonese restaurants did not make a considerable impact on guidebook writers because Cantonese restaurant culture, if not Cantonese cuisine itself, was still relatively undeveloped compared with that of more northern regions and did not assume a distinctive shape until the late-Qing period.[46]

These three factors, however, only partially explain the guidebooks' representation of Cantonese cuisine. Another important factor was the relative foreignness of Cantonese foodways to the men who wrote Shanghai's leading guidebooks. For example, Ge Yuanxu, who did not include any Cantonese restaurant offerings in his listing of "famous dishes from Shanghai restaurants," did discuss "Cantonese teahouses" in his travelogue, but as a separate category that emphasized their remote location and their unusual, if delicious, food offerings:

> Cantonese teahouses have opened in Hongkou. In spring of *bing-zi* [1876] north of Jipan Street, the Tongfan teahouse opened for business. Though the establishment is not expansive, the place settings consist of glittering gold and green tea ware. [The teahouse] also sells tea snacks and sweets, congee with raw fish as morning approaches, steamed rice noodles, and every kind of delicious lunch snacks, as well as lotus seed porridge and almond junket at night. It can be seen that other places have their own distinctive flavor (*tachu bieju fengwei*).[47]

Evidently, a Zhejiang native like Ge considered, and wrote for an audience that considered, Cantonese foodways to come from a kind of "other place."

Just how "other" Shanghai's guidebook writers considered this place is suggested by the way that Chi Zhicheng, also of Zhejiang, combined his discussion of Cantonese restaurants with his remarks on Western restaurants. Chi characterized Shanghai's regional restaurant industry as a defining element of the city's nightlife. He also complained, however, that differences among certain branches of the industry had become muted over the years, because of the taste preferences of "heavy-jowled and pot-bellied [customers] who have to eat rich food to be satisfied." Shanghai's regional restaurant menus thus become dominated by the "heavy flavors" of such dishes as "red-braised sea cucumber, red-braised shark's fin, and roast chicken and duck." As a result, "for the most part, the cooking and seasoning in Suzhou, Anhui, Ningbo, Tianjin, and Nanjing restaurants is more or less the same." In contrast, he noted, "As for Western restaurants and [Cantonese] *xiaoyeguan*, those who 'dip a finger' in them and have a taste are surprised by something they have not encountered before."[48] On the one hand, Chi was praising Cantonese establishments for their relative novelty, but on the other, by pairing them with Western food, he reveals just how novel, foreign even, he found the food culture they represented.

Chi might have associated Cantonese with Western food because at the time of his writing, the late nineteenth century, many of the city's leading Western restaurants were owned and operated by Cantonese entrepreneurs. It is also possible that Cantonese establishments were simply part of a different kind of food culture than that which historically prevailed in Jiangnan cities. One variety of Cantonese establishment, the *xiaoyeguan*, or "night market," brought a major change to the city's food culture. Explaining the special word by which Cantonese restaurants were designated, one late-Qing writer sought to clarify the original meaning from a similar term with which it had become confused: "Cantonese night markets, not to be equated with what are commonly called midnight snacks (*xiaoye* 宵夜), take their meaning from [the phrase] 'to fritter the long night away' (*xiaomo changye* 消磨长夜)."[49] Although it is not entirely clear how common such establishments were in Guangzhou and other cities of Guangdong Province, establishments like *xiaoyeguan* simply had not existed in the old Shanghai county seat, which seems to have carefully enforced Qing curfew regulations against lighting fires at night.[50] *Xiaoyeguan* were thus a distinctly new component of Shanghai food culture. Even the word that designated this particular style of restaurant was unfamiliar and had to be explained.

Shanghai's *xiaoyeguan* initially opened in the Cantonese neighborhood in Hongkou; by the early 1880s, they had spread to Fourth Avenue, prompting guidebook writers to note them and to emphasize the differences between the food culture of Cantonese and other, presumably more normal, Chinese. Thus, Chi notes that in contrast to most places in China, where three meals are taken per day, "Cantonese only eat two meals a day, so mid-way through the night they add a meal, which is why it's called a *xiaoye*."[51] *Xiaoyeguan* were especially popular among late night theater-goers, and during wintertime, as one of their more novel features was the presence of a warm stove on the table top at which customers did their own cooking: "A blazing hot coal [is placed] in the stove and boiling broth in the pot. It is up to the customer to cook items like sliced fish or spinach and feed himself. When combined with getting drunk on wine, all customers like this. And when the meal is over, [the customer] feels full and warm."[52] By the end of the Qing, these establishments had become such a common feature of Shanghai that they were counted among other features of city life as "Shanghai Phenomena."[53] However, the eventual widespread popularity of *xiaoyeguan* should not obscure their early significance as a marker of Cantonese foreignness. Chi's final suggestion, that these establishments were "something that travelers [to Shanghai] can also 'dip a finger in,'" reveals that even Chi's idea of a traveler to Shanghai, and thereby the audience for his description of the city, was a non-Cantonese.

The Jiangsu and Zhejiang men whose writings were most influential in shaping ideas about the vibrant and diverse culture of the new Shanghai thus used food culture to delineate the space of Shanghai in two distinct ways. First, by depicting Cantonese food as all but foreign, they delineated core and fringe elements of settlement life and of the "Chinese" food culture that gathered in the settlements. Despite the common refrain that China has "four great culinary traditions"—northern, Sichuan, Huaiyang, and Cantonese—such a notion was clearly not operative among Shanghai's Jiangsu and Zhejiang guidebook writers, for whom Cantonese food still was a relative novelty. Second, by ignoring developments in the county seat, such as the proliferation of Anhui establishments, Shanghai's guidebook writers suggested that the only significant developments in Shanghai foodways, and thereby in the city's culture, transpired in the foreign settlements. Their image of Penglai was thus not one to which all Chinese would want to travel to banquet.

Conspicuous Consumption in the County Seat and Foreign Settlements

Ye Tingjuan, a native of Xiangshan, Guangdong Province, who assumed the post of Shanghai county magistrate in 1872, bore the brunt of both of these prejudices. His record of political patronage and hosting banquets, however, indicates that he had his own repertoire of techniques for using food culture in socially suggestive ways: to strengthen his position in the county seat, to accrue cultural capital for his office, and to bolster the image of the county seat relative to the foreign settlements. This record reveals that although settlement elites located the heart of Shanghai food culture in the Jiang-Zhe cuisine restaurants of the Baoshan Street and Fourth Avenue neighborhoods, county seat elites had their own ways of making food culture perform the work of status maintenance and representing the food culture of Shanghai. Significantly, Ye's techniques do not merely represent some type of conservative holdover, but reveal a close engagement with different constituencies in the city. Indeed, his gift-giving and displays of conspicuous consumption provided Ye with a vehicle for building relationships and for distinguishing himself from the new settlement elites. They thus provided valuable markers of the different kinds of elite lifestyles taking shape in the two parts of Shanghai.

As the top-ranking official in the Shanghai County Seat, Ye had to cultivate relationships with a wide range of constituents, something he accomplished through ceremonial exchanges of gifts that often took the form of food. Ye faced several challenges to his rule during his tenure as magistrate. During his second year in office, he brought a storm of criticism and ridicule upon Shanghai's Cantonese community when he sided with a Cantonese native place association in a suit it helped bring against a star of the Shanghai theater world, Yang Yuelou, who was accused of engaging in an illicit relationship with a young girl of Cantonese origin.[54] The following year, Ye drew fire for assisting French troops in the suppression of the Ningbo Cemetery Riots, which broke out when the French Municipal Council, the governing body of the French Concession, brought forth a proposal to build new roads that ran through the cemetery attached to the Siming Gongsuo, a powerful native-place association for Ningbo sojourners in Shanghai.[55] Finally, Ye was faced with a "massive protest" organized by gentry landlords and village heads opposed to his efforts to secure labor services for the Sanlintang Dredging Project.[56]

Ledgers from Ye's office provide a record of gift-giving to maintain relationships with constituents involved in each incident. To cement his ties with his Guangdong fellow provincials, which were strained by the Yang Yuelou case, he gave gifts of tea and wine, specialty hams, and fresh litchis (a Guangdong delicacy). To the French Consul, who intervened on behalf of the Siming Gongsuo and ultimately ordered the French Municipal Council to redraft its construction plans, Ye gave eighteen bottles of wine. To local gentry, he often gave gifts of fine books and ink, but also assorted specialty snack foods.

Perhaps because incidents like these challenged Ye's credibility as a county magistrate, he worked especially hard to portray himself as a paragon of Confucian virtue who, despite the demands of office, remained at least a filial son. This was an image of himself that he publicized once a year by throwing grand birthday celebrations for his mother. The parties Ye staged for his mother, in 1873, 1874, and 1875, were among the most elaborate banquets in the city's history.[57] The third, held on the occasion of her seventieth birthday, was especially grand and occupied the center of the county seat for several days. Ye's mother's birthday fell on the twenty-fifth day of the ninth month, but the celebrations began two days before, when lanterns and banners were hung up throughout the Yamen, and familiar guests came to pay their respects. On the twenty-fourth, there was a "pre-celebration," and then the formal celebration was held the following day. For these two days, Ye arranged for tea tables and performances of Sichuan *qing-yin* ballad singing. More than fifty notables came personally to pay their respects to Ye's mother, and the guest list, a veritable who's who of gentry and local officials, included Shanghai Circuit Attendant Shen Bingcheng; Feng Junguang, head of the Jiangnan Arsenal; Regional Commander Cai Jinzhang; and assorted gentry and office holders from nearby Nanhui County, where Ye had previously served two terms as county magistrate.

The icing on the cake was, of course, the banquet. Highest guests of honor sat at one of three tables serving the *shaokao* banquet, the centerpiece of which was a whole roast pig. Less-esteemed guests had to settle for a seat at one of the ten tables serving the swallow's nest banquet, the forty-one tables serving shark's fin (twenty of which were earmarked for fellow-provincials in Shanghai), the five tables serving medium-grade shark's fin, the thirteen tables serving second-best shark's fin, or the twelve tables serving sea cucumber. Also consumed at the banquet were eighteen barrels (*tan*) of wine and approximately one thousand bowls of noodles. Ye extended his largess to Yamen employees, who were invited to partake in the festivities, and even to prisoners and detainees in the county jail. County jail prisoners and detainees had been the beneficiary of Ye's mother's beneficence before, enjoying birthday noodles and several catties of pork on her previous birthdays, but this year they received their own tables. By casting such a wide net, Ye was portraying himself as a benevolent official concerned for the welfare of all city residents, but by throwing such an elaborate banquet, he was also sending a message to the denizens of the foreign settlements, who were creating a new style of banqueting in restaurants and courtesan halls and threatening to make the settlements into the dominant site of symbolic power in Shanghai.

Banqueting had long been a feature of Chinese elite sociability, for cementing friendships and professional relationships, and for special ritual occasions, such as weddings and birthdays. Before the creation of the settlements, banquets in Shanghai were generally held in private gardens, residences, or the halls of native-place associations, for even the more expensive restaurants in the county seat were large open spaces "crowded with hundreds of customers," hardly the kind of environment in which an elite family could stage an important event, or a group of elite men could strengthen close bonds.[58] The proliferation of restaurants in the Fourth Avenue neighborhood provided the

context for a new style of banqueting that took shape during the closing decades of the nineteenth century.

The new Fourth Avenue banquet culture evolved in and around the vibrant
courtesan culture of the Shanghai demimonde, where dinner parties were an
integral part of the courtship process between courtesans and their patrons.[59]
Courtesans in high-class houses generally greeted patrons with small plates of
watermelon seeds, nuts, and sweetmeats, a ritual skipped in lower-class houses,
where sex rather than courtship was the patron's principle objective. After a patron took an interest in a courtesan, he might place a call for her at a restaurant
to join a gathering of his friends. Although a courtesan might receive and fill
many such calls in one night, a patron could signal his interest and commitment to her by hosting a dinner party at her house. This was, "by far the most
important favor a client could do to secure his position with a courtesan. . . .
This costly gesture was taken as a sign of particular attachment. Such a dinner
party also gave the courtesan face in her community."[60] By accepting a patron's
offer, a courtesan indicated that she considered the relationship worth pur-
suing, and that it might eventually lead to something more permanent, such
as marriage. Taking a courtesan as a wife or concubine was not the objective
of every demimonde patron, but by hosting dinner parties in restaurants and
courtesan houses, a patron earned the companionship and public esteem of an
elite courtesan. Shanghai's leading courtesans were arbiters of urban taste and
culture, so earning that esteem marked a patron as a man of taste and culture.

The stages involved in working up to, planning, and finally hosting a dinner
party constituted a template of culture and power that underlay settlement life.
This is evident in late-Qing courtesan novels, such as Han Banqing's (1856–94)
The Sing-song Girls of Shanghai (Haishanghua liezhuan), that recount the inner
workings of Shanghai's demimonde in intricate detail. *Sing-song Girls* registers
some aspects of the cultural geography discussed earlier; thus, when some of
the main characters visit a Cantonese "restaurant-cum-brothel" in the north of
the International Settlement, they find that "the decoration was indeed novel
and distinctive, completely different from what they were used to."[61] With regard to food culture, however, the novel is most revealing when it demonstrates
the importance of banqueting etiquette to urban savoir faire, something sorely
lacking in the two figures on which the novel may be said to center, Simplicity (Zhao Puzhai) and his sister, Second Treasure (Zhao Erbao). Brother and
sister come to Shanghai from the countryside, and their experiences frame the
novel's main narrative, from Simplicity's first arrival in the city through Sec-

ond Treasure's nervous breakdown and tragic demise. As the novel indicates, the food culture of the demimonde provided residents of and newcomers to the foreign settlements with an opportunity to experience the Penglai side of Shanghai life, but this opportunity did not come without its risks. By highlighting the fantasies and fears of the two visitors from the countryside, courtesan fiction celebrated the conspicuous consumption of the foreign settlements and also drew into relief the dangers lurking in this new city.[62]

Food marks Simplicity's status as a man lacking in taste and culture from the outset of the novel. The inn where he resides is of a grade that provides no board for its lodgers, which is evident to everyone else in the novel and which identifies Simplicity as an ordinary traveler.[63] His first meeting with his Uncle Benevolence, his only family connection in town, is established over a "casual meal" that they eat in Benevolence's Flourishing Ginseng Store.[64] The description of the meal as "casual" signals the different horizons of expectation that Simplicity and Benevolence bring to the meal; the "four plates of cold cuts, two main courses, and a jug of wine" may be common fare for Benevolence, a successful urban entrepreneur, but not for Simplicity, who is repeatedly struck by the lavish meals eaten by the men in his uncle's social circles. Later that same day, uncle and nephew head off for dinner, where Simplicity gets his first glimpse of the world that he will soon long to be a part of. Bored with the conversation between Benevolence and his business partner, Simplicity wanders off, drawn by the "sound of lively music coming from the 'study' next door." Once there, he "peeped through the windowpane next door and saw six diners seated at a round table, surrounded by courtesans and their maids and servant girls. The women filled the room. . . . Simplicity Zhao watched, full of envy."[65]

The prospect of becoming one of those six diners taunts Simplicity for much of the novel. He is one of the few characters in the novel depicted eating alone, as on the morning after his first night's sleep in town, when he makes do with "a bowl of stewed pork noodles for 28 copper coins at the Fountainhead Restaurant on the corner of Pebble Road."[66] No sooner does he finish this lunch than he is shown to be out of sync with the rhythms of the demimonde. When he shows up at the Hall of Beauties at noon that day to call upon a courtesan named Jewel, the latter is surprised that he has already eaten, a fact that even Jewel's maid, Mama Yeung, notes derisively. Then, after realizing that the way to Jewel's heart is to throw a dinner party for her in her own establishment, he errs by suggesting that they be sure to invite Second Wang, a second-class prostitute he had met the day before through his fair-weather friend Rustic.[67] Simplicity's performance as host of the party, which is finally pulled together only through the interventions of his uncle, is so pathetic that Benevolence concludes Simplicity will not make it in the big city. Several weeks later, when Benevolence discovers that Simplicity is making ends meet by working as a rickshaw puller, scraping change together to feed himself, he decides to send him home to the country.

Simplicity's inability to navigate the food culture of the demimonde also calls his manhood into question. Second Treasure, Simplicity's sister, is enticed into the courtesan life by a demimonde regular, Fortune Shi, shortly after she comes to town to check on her brother. Although Simplicity's dim prospects are manifest in his inability to host a dinner party, Fortune's credentials are established by his command of urban food culture and etiquette. One night Fortune takes Simplicity and his family out to the opera and then sees the family home. Second Treasure sends Simplicity out to buy some snacks, but he returns with only "six bean curd dumplings, which he divided into three small bowls." Scolded by his sister for buying such meager fare, the brother is saved only when Fortune remarks, to Second Treasure's surprise and delight, that "bean curd dumplings are nice. I happen to like them." Then, "dispensing with any formality, he picked up a pair of bamboo chopsticks and manfully swallowed one down."[68] Having established his manhood by making a virtue of the very dumplings that marked Simplicity as a simpleton, Fortune takes Second Treasure out a few days later for her first Western meal, an occasion that helps mark her transformation from visitor from the country into a proper lady of the night.[69]

Second Treasure's transformation brought her and Simplicity a taste of the good life, but it also sets the family up for a fall. Thanks to Fortune's efforts, Second Treasure becomes the talk of the town, "with bookings for mah-jongg parties and dinner parties every night." Simplicity is delighted, for "The leftovers from the parties were sent over to Mrs. Zhao's room, where Simplicity was free to munch his way through all the delicacies. Stuffed to the gills with food and drink every night, he would fall on his bed and go out like a light, thinking he was in paradise."[70] Second Treasure's growing reputation eventually draws the attention of Nature Shi, a man who becomes her regular client and promises to marry her. To learn more about his prospective brother-in-law and help secure the proposal, Simplicity plies Nature's steward with "endless rounds of tea, opium, and snacks." Signs of trouble appear, however, when Simplicity buys Nature a gift of fresh peaches and litchis, which Nature refuses.[71] Desperate to secure a commitment from Nature, Second Treasure's mother makes her own offer of specialty foods, "choice teatime snacks from the Garden of Plenty," and "various imported candies, biscuits, and fruit" from the foreign goods store Hall and Holtz. This gift Nature accepts, and Second Treasure is greatly relieved. But by reading Nature's gesture as one of sincerity, she only highlights her and her family's inexperience. They are confident that, by accepting the gift offered by his "mother-in-law," Nature has indicated his intent to marry Second Treasure. Nature, however, soon leaves town and never returns. Second Treasure is not only heartbroken, but financially broken, having invested the family fortune on wedding preparations. Soon the Zhaos can barely afford to put food on the table. Despite all their efforts to earn a place for themselves in the urban world of Shanghai, the Zhao family remained, to the end, foolish and vulnerable rural folk.

Foreign settlement Shanghai thus presented the promise of Penglai, but as the century wore on a growing number of voices, among which must be counted that of Han Banqing, had began to wonder if the Penglai of the foreign settlements was anything more than a glittering façade. On the one hand, Shanghai provided a place in which refugees and opportunity seekers were "shielded from the conflagrations that were tearing China apart and consequently offered a haven where people could be safe and make money without the traditional social constraints or interference from Qing officialdom."[72] But there were also "antagonistic voices" that questioned the authenticity of this Penglai view of Shanghai, such as ballad-writer Chen Qiao, who in his 1887 *One Hundred Ballads of Shanghai* (Shenjiang baiyong) observed, "Upon entering Wusong port[,] one's horizon opens, one wonders whether one has not entered Penglai in this life; if Liu [Chen] and Ruan [Zhao] [from the Eastern Han dynasty] were brought back once again, they would have mistaken [what they see here] as the peach [the fruit that soothed all their earthly sufferings] and refused ever to leave again."[73]

The commentary to the ballad notes, "This surely cannot be the world of mortals," but the ballad is also clearly ambivalent about Liu and Ruan being seduced by the city's electric lights, just as they were, in the *locus classicus* of the story, by the "magical peaches" they discovered after getting lost during a search for medicinal plants. After finding the peaches the two were subsequently seduced by two beautiful women and lost track of time for ten generations.[74] The foreign settlements presented a similar opportunity and threat. The question the ballad and novel thus raise is: Was there any way out?

The Shanghai County Seat as Wulingyuan

The food culture and rituals of the Shanghai demimonde defined some of the terms according to which men and women asserted their authority and experienced city life in the foreign settlements, but it did not have a monopoly on the way that Shanghai residents experienced their relationship to the city through food. As discussed previously, regional restaurants, as oases of native-place taste, provided Shanghai's sojourners with a sense of home in a foreign city, both in the settlements and in the county seat. Moreover, even for the leading men and women of the Shanghai demimonde, comfort foods were found not in the dinner party paradise of the settlements, but in more mundane, albeit no less meaningful, fare. *Sing-song Girls*, for example, is replete with simple meals of congee that lovers eat after retiring to a private room after a dinner party. This is the food with which courtesans and patrons nourish one another, to help each other recover from sickness, or simply to recover from pure physical exhaustion. These meals also register the depth of an interpersonal relationship that will outlive the ups and downs of demimonde fashions.

The denizens of the demimonde, however, also looked outside the settlements to the food culture of the county seat, where they found equally, if not more, evocative foods. One such item of Shanghai comfort food were the vegetable rice-flour dumplings (*caiyuanzi*) that were sold in a small, one-bay shop front on Sanpailou Street, in the Shanghai County Seat, and that were prepared according to the "pure" (*su*) standards required of Buddhist vegetarian cookery. The shop, as longtime Shanghai resident Liu Yanong fondly recalled, was run by a Widow Xu and her mother, and the widow's son worked as the waiter. In addition to their vegetable dumplings, Widow Xu's family sold sweetened bean paste dumplings, as well as a delicious fresh pork dumpling. The latter was made with pork "nine parts lean and one part fat . . . cut into fine strips and then coarsely ground, taking care that the cuts are clean and the meat does not disintegrate." To this ground pork was then added "sun-warmed soy sauce, a smidgen of sesame oil, and a bit of finely diced scallion and ginger." These ingredients, Liu notes, added flavor, held the filling together while boiling, and prevented the filling from getting tough. Liu knew the recipe because he used to spy on the proprietors on his way to middle school.[75]

That was also how Liu obtained the recipe for the same shop's vegetable dumplings, which he reports were craved by the "old gourmets from the foreign settlements and the big spenders from the courtesan houses." For these men, "the distance [from the settlements to Sanpailou Street] didn't matter, [for] as soon as the sun began to set, they would send a servant out to vie for those dumplings." Being based in the settlements did have its disadvantages, however, for the dumplings "would sell out in fifteen minutes, and they wouldn't make a second batch, so late-comers would leave disappointed." The main ingredient was bok choy (*dacai*), "from which the veins of the leaf and core were removed, leaving only the truly tender leaves"—one *jin* of vegetable yielded barely half as much of leaves. The leaves were dropped in boiling water just long enough for the water to return to the boil, so that they would retain their crisp green appearance. After draining, the leaves were finely chopped and squeezed dry in a cloth. The proprietors then added ground sea salt and "a generous amount" of the best quality sesame oil. For the dumpling skin, the key ingredient was glutinous rice that had been ground into flour with water. This gave the cooked skin the lustrous appearance of nephrite, and it made the dumpling "so slick that the skin didn't stick to the teeth." Despite the shop's location in the former county seat and humble décor—it didn't even have a sign front—word of its dumplings spread far and wide, for they had "a taste that pleased everyone, and young and old knew about the Sanpailou Street rice-flower dumplings."

More commonly invoked as a refuge from the foreign settlements was the culture and history of the Shanghai honey nectar peach. This local peach variety attracted the attention of virtually all chroniclers of late Qing Shanghai, even otherwise unrepentant boosters of the foreign settlements such as Ge Yuanxu. As noted earlier, Ge claimed in the preface to his Shanghai travelogue only to record material pertaining to life in the settlements, but he made at least one exception to this rule when he described the peach orchards of Huangniqiang:

> The best honey nectar peaches are those grown at Huangniqiang, in the west-ern part of the city. The fruit is large with a flat top. Juicy and sweet, it melts in the mouth, and for that it is named. [The peaches] are off-white in color and patterned with a pale red hue commonly known as "goose feather follicles." Unfortunately, if picked before fully ripening, they are not even as good as those grown elsewhere, even if they are very big and [of the] fine [variety]. Taking a stroll in the western suburbs after Qing-Ming, [there are also] peach trees ar-rayed in rows and rosy clouds dazzle the eyes, [the view] is not inferior to the scenery of Wulingyuan.[76]

Ge's description of the peaches and orchards of Shanghai echoes earlier sources, from which he borrows much of his language and imagery, including his reference to Wulingyuan. When read in its historical context, however, the allusion to Wulingyuan gave new meanings to this ideal as a metaphor for Shanghai.

Wulingyuan, which Tao Qian depicts in the prose preface to the lyric poem "Peach Blossom Spring," is a land that time forgot encountered by chance one day by a fisherman of Wuling, who during the Taiyuan reign period (376–97) of the Jin lost track of the distance he had covered while following the course of a stream. "All at once he came upon a grove of blossoming peach trees, which lined either bank for hundreds of paces. No tree of any other kind stood amongst them, but there were fragrant flowers, delicate and lovely to the eye, and the air was filled with drifting peachbloom."[77] At the end of the grove, the fisherman finds a spring, and then a hill with a small opening. Working his way through the opening, he comes out the other side onto an isolated community of people living in complete harmony, who tell him that they had come there "fleeing from the troubles of the age of Qin [221–207 B.C.]," and who are surprised to learn how much time had passed, "for they had never even heard of the Han, let alone its successors the Wei and the Jin." Concerned that their paradise will not outlast its discovery by outsiders, the inhabitants implore the fisherman to keep their community a secret. The fisherman betrays their request and upon his return home describes what he found to his magistrate, but the search party sent out in search of Wulingyuan is unable to locate it. The precise site of this lost utopia became a source of endless discussion and debate, which one late-Qing Shanghai source joined by rehearsing one of the earliest and most conventional answers—a southwest corner of the Taoyuan hills, in Wuling County, Hunan Province.[78] For other Shanghai residents, however, the exact location was less important than the power of the idea of a society where, as Tao Qian put it, "Imposing buildings stood among rich fields and pleasant ponds all set with mulberry and willow. Linking paths led everywhere, and the fowls and dogs of one farm could be heard from the next. People were coming and going and working in the fields. Both the men and women dressed in exactly the same manner as people outside; white-haired elders and tufted children alike were cheerful and contented."

Ge's representation of Shanghai's peach orchards as a Wulingyuan represents a turning point not merely in the representation of Shanghai peach orchards, but of the representation of Shanghai more generally. Ge was not the first in Shanghai to invoke Wulingyuan in his discussion of Shanghai peaches, but he and his contemporaries did so in a distinctly new way. Earlier writers who invoked Wulingyuan with reference to Shanghai's peach orchards, such as the seventeenth-century local literatus Ye Mengzhu, did so as part of a broader representational strategy that emphasized Shanghai's emergence as a place that could be compared with other famous sites from Chinese history. Moreover, they referred to spaces that had given a new definition to the city. Ge and others, by contrast, made the connection with a tinge of regret, and to represent an aspect of urban space that was not so much coming into being but disappearing. For they lived and wrote at a time when Shanghai's honey nectar peaches were no longer widely grown in the places that had once made them famous. Huangniqiang was the last of the major peach orchards that lay inside the city limits—it was an important peach orchard that dates back to at least the time that Chu Hua wrote his *Treatise on the Honey Nectar Peach*—which may very well explain the eagerness with which city residents sought to pick the fruit from its trees. Peaches were also widely planted to the southwest of the city, where they had become such a prominent feature of the landscape that they were featured on the map of Shanghai included in William Charles Milne's mid-century *Life in China* (see Figure 2.2).[79] But the growing profile of peach orchards that were located outside of the county seat suggested a larger shift in the profile of the city. Shanghai was now home to many "imposing buildings," but the "rich fields and pleasant ponds" that had once been a source of local pride were moving farther and farther away from the city limits. For Ge, the blossoms at least remained a symbol of promise; others, however, complained that the quality of Shanghai's peaches was going into decline.

The decline of honey nectar peach cultivation in Shanghai was widely noted. The 1872 *Shanghai County Gazetteer* proudly included the honey nectar peach in its catalogue of Shanghai fruits, but it also observed that "few peaches" were growing in the locations that had once made them famous. It adds, "In recent years . . . only to the southwest toward the villages do the orchards have trees numbering in the tens of thousands."[80] Significantly, as peach cultivation moved farther away from its more renowned sites, city residents complained that Shanghai's peaches did not taste as good as before. As Shanghai native Mao Xianglin noted in his *Record of Leftover Ink*:

> A true variety has been planted in the west of the city, but when grown in other places the taste is inferior. Recently, tens of *li* have been planted outside the south gate, where everybody grows peaches for a living. The color and appearance is glorious, but the flavor lags far behind. Today, the peaches that merchants sell are all south gate peaches, and the true variety is hard to come by.[81]

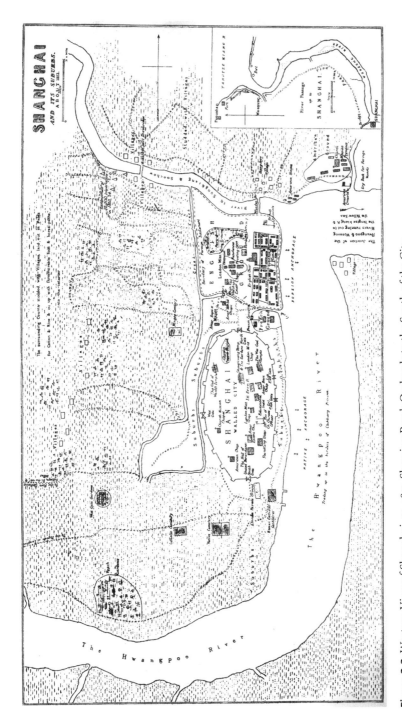

Figure 2.2 Western View of Shanghai, ca. 1853, Showing Peach Orchards to the South of the City

SOURCE: *All About Shanghai: A Standard Guidebook* (Shanghai, 1934). Courtesy of Oxford University Press.

Wang Tao echoed Mao, cribbing much of his own discussion of Shanghai's peaches from Mao's *Record*. However, Wang also noted, "Every year when the fruit is ripe, the orchards are closed by official order, and all the officials cash in on this to make a profit by raising the price and selling them to the people at 100 *qian* per peach. The poor and the gluttonous [alike] are not easily able to eat their fill."[82] The situation only grew more bleak over time. As Shanghai native Li Weiqing (1881–?) noted in his 1907 *Shanghai Local Gazetteer* (Shanghai xiangtu-zhi): "Dew Fragrance Garden was the famous garden of Mr. Gu and in the past produced honey nectar peaches. Today, however, the fine variety has been lost, and the former site no longer exists. All that is left is the imagination."[83]

That imagination was fuelled not by the image of Penglai, but by that of a receding Wulingyuan. It was receding in a literal sense: peach cultivation was moving outside the city walls, and even the blossoms that Ge Yuanxu praises are located in the western suburbs. It was also receding in a figurative sense. Originally conceived of as an allegory of escape from the corruption and infighting that plagued the Jin court, Wulingyuan now read as a poignant counterpoint to the rapid development and uncertainty of settlement life, and the apparent corruption, exemplified by gluttonous civil officials, of the county seat. None who equated Shanghai's peach orchards with this mythical utopia went so far as to suggest that the city would have been better off had it become isolated and cut off from the outside world. But it is clear that images of the past provided the idea of an escape from the city. For all that the new city of the foreign settlements offered, Shanghai's "discovery"—not only by the West, but also by the Qing government that upgraded Shanghai's political status— meant that the city itself was also being lost. Wulingyuan had only survived as a place, after all, for not having been discovered. Like the fisherman who left Wulingyuan voluntarily and then became "homesick" when he could not find his way back, Shanghai had also embarked on a journey from which there was, so it seemed, no return. Comparisons with Wulingyuan thus no longer communicated Shanghai's status as a place in the realm worthy of association with famous places from Chinese history; instead, references to Wulingyuan now provided a means of identification with Shanghai's own missing gardens, and with the city's past.

Penglai was an enticing image to project onto Shanghai, but Shanghai ultimately reflected back a pale version of Penglai. Penglai was, as many represented Shanghai, a sensuous place full of sensuous women, but it was also supposed to be an uncorrupted place, free both of peasants and struggling commoners such as Simplicity and Second Treasure, and free of people seeking to take advantage of them. As an image of Shanghai, therefore, it presented at best a divisive idea of the city, one that had a validity only for those city residents for whom Shanghai was all fantasy and no fear.

Wulingyuan, by contrast, offered an idea of Shanghai that appealed to residents with very different relationships to the city's history, natives and newcomers. Shanghai natives such as Mao Xianglin, Zhang Chunhua, and Li Weiqing were all clearly concerned about the transformations unfolding in Shanghai after the Treaty of Nanjing, and all were committed to their hometown and its cultural heritage. Mao was an important contributor to the 1872 *Shanghai County Gazetteer.* Zhang's *Folksongs of Shanghai Seasons* (Husheng suishi quge) compiled details about Shanghai folk culture into 120 items of carefully crafted verse. Li, a great-grandson of Li Linsong, the chief editor of the 1816 edition of the *Shanghai County Gazetteer* (Jiaqing Shanghai xianzhi), built on his family's tradition of local history writing by publishing his own *Shanghai Local Gazetteer* for young students in the Shanghai area. Li felt that they needed a new kind of textbook, one that emphasized local customs, after the Qing government terminated the traditional civil service examination.

The idea of Wulingyuan also appealed to newcomers to Shanghai such as Wang Tao and Ge Yuanxu. The foreign settlements in Shanghai provided both men with an opportunity to create new lives for themselves. Wang first visited Shanghai after failing in his first attempt to earn the rank of *juren* in the Qing civil service examination, and he soon found work there as the Chinese editor of the London Missionary Society's Mission Press. Ge worked in Shanghai as a medical doctor. The lives of both men, however, were also fundamentally transformed by the Taiping Rebellion, which destroyed their home regions and made return impossible. By recasting Dew Fragrance Garden through the idea of the Wulingyuan rural idyll, all five men found a shared resource for characterizing and transcending the problems of their day. Thus, in an idea of the old Shanghai, rather than in the idea of the new, residents of the city found a common cause.

3 From Modernity to Tradition

Western Food in Late Qing and Early Republican Shanghai

AS EVENING APPROACHED on June 12, 1899, a fire broke out on Fourth Avenue, the main entertainment and cultural artery of Shanghai's International Settlement. The source of the fire was a faulty match that reportedly exploded in the hand of an apprentice in the Tianlu Publishing House. The apprentice struck the match to light a kerosene lamp and then released it in a panic, dropping the match inside the lamp's well. The kerosene ignited with a bang, and Tianlu's employees hastened to extinguish the flames by smothering them with cotton quilts. The fire spread too quickly, however, and soon Tianlu's books were burning, and the publishing house employees were running for their lives. Before the fire was finally extinguished, it had spread through forty-six buildings, and another six suffered extensive water damage. Twenty-nine businesses were in ruins or damaged, with property losses estimated at 100,000 *taels* (*liang*), and merchandise losses amounting to another 80,000.[1]

Among the most badly damaged business operations were Chinese-owned Western restaurants, known as *fancaiguan*, that had come to dominate Shanghai's high-end restaurant scene during the previous decade. Western food culture came to Shanghai in as many forms as there were Westerners, but from the Chinese perspective, Western food in Shanghai meant largely some variety of English or French food, at least until the rapid growth of the Russian community in Shanghai after the Russian Revolution. The Chinese residents of Shanghai learned about foreign foodways in the city through several venues—retail shops that sold imported foods, gardens in which foreigners grew unfamiliar varieties of fruits and vegetables, municipal slaughterhouses and dairies that produced the foreign population's supply of beef and milk, brothels for Western prostitutes, and Western-run restaurants and hotels that catered largely, if not exclusively, to non-Chinese customers. Westerners established these spaces to shore up a sense of their own hometown, or national, culture, and to carve out spheres of material life as boundaries between the city's Western and Chinese populations. Chinese, however, quickly remade these spaces into vehicles for exploring and engaging in Western material culture. Chinese entrepreneurs, mostly of Cantonese origin, opened Chinese-style Western restaurants, known as *fancaiguan*, and these establishments created a late Qing craze for Western food. When the fire broke out on Fourth Avenue, the street had as many *fancaiguan* as it did restaurants serving all varieties of regional Chinese food combined.

The late Qing craze for Western food remade the idea and image of Shanghai, albeit not always in ways that made city residents proud. Certainly, Shanghai's Western restaurants became an important component of the idea of Shanghai as a progressively Westernized and "modern" city, such that visitors to Shanghai felt that their trip was not complete without having dined in a *fancaiguan*. However, many Chinese objected to eating beef, an important item in the Western food repertoire, but one that was not common to Chinese diets, on the grounds that cattle were a friend of humankind and should not be slaughtered for human consumption. Others were critical of the "Chineseness" of the Western food that Chinese entrepreneurs and customers made popular and complained that Chinese were no more successful at appreciating Western food than they were at carrying out genuine Western-style reforms of the Qing economy, military, or bureaucracy.

The Cantonese control of the *fancaiguan* market also raised concerns among the city's Jiangsu and Zhejiang cultural elites, who were wary of the growing influence of Cantonese entrepreneurs in the city's commercial and cultural life more generally. Commentators on the Fourth Avenue fire were struck by a pattern apparent in the direction taken by the fire, which seemed to have been guided by a combination of local pride and cultural chauvinism. As one article in the tabloid *Entertainment* (Youxi bao) noted, under the headline "Fire God Eats Western Food":

> The Xinghualou, a Cantonese restaurant, has caught fire several times. This time [the fire] spread to two Western restaurants, the Xinghuachun and Jinguchun. While [the Suzhou restaurant] Jufengyuan was slightly damaged, its [business]

was not at all impaired. A cynic remarked: "Shanghai's Fire God must think that Cantonese are putting on airs. In the past, he only ate Cantonese restaurants. Now he is gradually imitating the West and likes to eat Western food. Chinese food is not to his liking, and so Jufengyuan was left intact.[2]

Significantly, the article does not read the burning of the restaurants as an act of divine intervention that promised to quell the craze for Western food. Rather, it reads the fire as an indication of just how influential the craze had become and of how much the idea of the city was changing. Even Shanghai's Fire God had forsaken the varieties of regional Chinese cuisine that the Jiangsu and Zhejiang image makers of the city had identified as a core component of Shanghai's restaurant world and of Chinese cookery more generally.

The fire came at a turning point in the history of Western food in Shanghai and in the history of the customers who, more than any other sector of the urban population, represented the connection between Cantonese and Western culture and sustained the craze for Western food: Shanghai's courtesans. The Cantonese-Western connection originated in the pre–Opium War Canton System, which until 1842 had restricted Western trade to Guangzhou and provided a context for cross-cultural exchange between Western and Cantonese merchants. Even after Shanghai opened to foreign settlement and became the center of Western trade in China, Cantonese merchants maintained important links to Western merchants, because most of Shanghai's compradores (Chinese merchants who worked as intermediaries between foreign traders and the China market) hailed from Guangdong. Shanghai's courtesans also played a decisive role in disseminating Western material culture in Shanghai; in particular, their role was to soften the blow of Westernization that swept the city during the closing decades of the nineteenth century. Courtesans were regular patrons of shops selling Western and Cantonese goods (*Yang Guang huopu*) and made their goods fashionable features of urban material culture. "As the embodiment of the *fanhua* [glamour] of entertainment and the easy life," Catherine Yeh notes, courtesans "ensured that the Westernized cityscape and its installations were non-threatening as well as fashionable, fascinating, and valued."[3]

So closely was Western food linked to the image of the Shanghai courtesan that when reformist elites began to criticize courtesan culture during the closing years of the Qing, they also radically transformed the image of Western food. Western food remained closely associated with women, but now with new ideas about women at home and as homemakers. A precedent for this link may be found relatively early in Shanghai's treaty port history, in the city's first Chinese-language Western cookbook, American missionary Martha Foster Crawford's 1866 *Zao Yangfan shu* (Western Cookery), which was reissued in 1909.[4] Turn-of-the-century Chinese social reformers, concerned equally with providing new forms of education for women and with eradicating courtesan culture, embraced this link and made Western food preparation an important component of an evolving home economics curriculum. Their hope was to reconstitute the foundation of society by rearticulating a role for educated women in the home. Significantly, they drew the intellectual framework for their Western-style curriculum from canonical Confucian texts, in particular the *Great Learning*, which for two millennia was the *locus classicus* of the idea that the basis of a well-ordered state lay in a well-ordered family. The history of Western food in Shanghai from the late Qing to the early Republican periods was thus marked by a double process of domestication: first, through the creation of the Chinese- (or Cantonese-) style Western material culture of the *fancaiguan* that symbolized an idea of the "modern," and second, by the ironic re-inscription of Western food as a component of a "traditional" way of running a Chinese home.

Drawing Boundaries

Chinese first encountered Western food not in the restaurants that drove the late Qing craze, but in spaces that foreigners designed to help remake Shanghai in a Western image. Foreigners deemed such spaces essential to the maintenance of their own native place cultures and authority in Shanghai, where the Chinese population, even in the foreign settlements, far outnumbered that of the foreign population (see Table 3.1). Foreigners obtained some of the distance they sought from Chinese through forms of political and social exclusion. No Chinese sat on the Shanghai Municipal Council, the governing body of the International Settlement, until 1926. Chinese were prohibited from joining prestigious social organizations, such as the Shanghai Race Club or the Club House, which one long-term resident described as "the Exchange of the place, where business is discussed over a friendly glass of sherry."[5] During the last two decades of the nineteenth century, Chinese elites pushed for greater inclusion in the city's Western-dominated political and cultural institutions, but Westerners pushed back, sometimes redrawing boundaries with even greater clarity than before, as with the tightening of restrictions on Chinese admission to Huangpu Park.[6] The culture of everyday life was a key component of this process, which

Table 3.1 Foreign and Chinese Population
in the International Settlement

Year	Foreign Population	Chinese Population
1855	243	20,243
1865	2,297	92,884
1870	1,666	76,713
1876	1,673	97,335
1880	2,197	110,009
1885	3,673	129,338
1890	3,821	171,950
1895	4,684	246,679
1900	6,774	352,050

SOURCE: Zou Yiren, *Jiu Shanghai renkou bianqian de yanjiu*
(Shanghai: Shanghai renmin chubanshe, 1980).

made the retail shops, gardens, home and work places, and restaurants and wine shops from which Westerners obtained their food an important arena for the drawing and re-drawing of boundaries.[7]

Early foreign arrivals in Shanghai ate together, whether at home, at work, or aboard ship. Thus, in the days before Western restaurants and hotels, the "stranger is under the necessity of quartering on some of the residents," among whom, the visiting physician B. L. Ball was happy to find, "generosity and hospitality seem never to be wanting."[8] *The Times* special correspondent George Wingrove Cooke was invited during his stay in Shanghai aboard the opium-trading Dent and Company's boat, the Emily Jane, for "some well-cooled sautern, a joint of capital Shanghai mutton, and a successfully concocted ice pudding."[9] Unmarried male employees of foreign firms took their meals in their mercantile establishments, where Cooke noted, there was "no lack of good dishes or of pleasant iced drinks," and "where the junior partner, with his *employés* of silk-inspector and tea-taster, and book-keeper and clerks, holds a separate mess."[10]

Food was an important component of foreign efforts to shore up a sense of native culture and an identity as civilized people. Writing of the English in China in general, Robert Bickers notes that they "ate their domestic cuisine, reproducing as far as possible the tastes of their home with Chinese or imported ingredients, and they mostly found Chinese food disgusting."[11] Describing the "character of the foreign merchant in China," with special reference to the

English community in Shanghai, William Medhurst, the city's most prominent missionary, noted several aspects of English culture that merchants in Shanghai brought with them:

> His habits are very much what they are at home. He builds himself a mansion in the handsomest style that his firm or himself can afford. . . . For his business requirements throughout the day the Shanghae resident generally keeps a Norwich car, brougham, or some other convenient kind of vehicle. . . . For evening exercise, if a subordinate, he goes to cricket or rackets, or bowls, or takes a gallop on a pet pony, or trots out his dog-cart of phaeton. If a head of a house or a married man, he drives out some more pretentious vehicle with a pair of Cape, Australian, or California horses; nearly everybody drives or rides, and he must be a struggling creature who cannot muster an animal or vehicle of some kind.

Food, Medhurst added, was an especially important part of this repertoire, for "After the evening airing comes dinner, and it is at this meal that the foreign resident in China concentrates his efforts to forget that he is an exile from home."[12] Charles Dyce, reflecting at the beginning of the twentieth century on his thirty years of residence in Shanghai, confirmed Medhurst's observations about the important role that food culture played in demarcating differences between Western and Chinese culture: "We were different from them; we ate strong flesh of cows and sheep, which they avoid; and they looked upon our violent games as perhaps necessary to work off the effects of beef and mutton. 'Belong foreign man custom,' they would say, as they turned to their diet of rice and fish and cabbage."[13] Indeed, the desire to eat imported foods seems to have trumped the financial motivations for which many English went to China in the first place: "The chief expenses occurred in what was known as the store counter, that is to say pepper and salt, oil and vinegar, sauces, and all the accessories. All these things had to be sent out from England, and the cost was very high. One [man] . . . was nearly ruined by anchovy sauce, and another one said that the consumption of English ham was turning his hair gray."[14]

Boundaries, however, were not absolute, for what it meant to be English or civilized, and the ways in which food maintained or marked that state of being were not so straightforward. Some local products had to be eaten, in which case the eater's own discernment became the arbiter of differences between Western and Chinese products. Dyce thus describes the oysters of Ningbo as "excellent, though not so good as our own natives," although he allowed that the "small *Bamboo* oyster" of Fuzhou was "quite unlike that of any other oyster, and is to my taste delicious. On account of their small size a great many can be eaten. Yum-yum."[15] He was equally impressed by the "bamboo oyster" cultivation process, by which oysters fastened and grew on bamboo rods placed upright in the beds. Westerners who settled in Shanghai after having spent many years in southern China had also clearly made some of the foodways of southern China a part of their own diets. Thus the complaint lodged in the 1867 guidebook, *Treaty Ports of China and Japan*, "In fruit, Shanghai is very deficient. Oranges, plantains, and lychees are unknown."[16]

To some, moreover, what passed for English food in China was a potential source of embarrassment. Cooke, for example, wondered what it meant to say that one ate like an "Englishman," expressing his dismay at the diets of the English in China by imagining how Chinese must have viewed them:

> An Englishman's mode of feeding is, says John Chinaman, the nearest approach to that of the savages of Formosa. He does the chief work of the slaughter-house upon his dinner-table, and he remits the principle work of the kitchen to his stomach. . . . Sedentary and dyspeptic men of every race will think with the Chinese, that legs, shoulders, loins, heads, limbs, directly suggestive of the living animal, are common only to the banquet of an Englishman and a beast of prey. "Plain wholesome food" means a slice of red flesh and a crudely prepared vegetable, and requires animal heat, intensified by labour and exercise, to digest and assimilate it. It is the food of man in a state of nature.

Cooke's observations testify to a propensity among the English in China to hold on to a particular image of English food, even as English food was changing back home. Explaining these changes, Cooke notes that, back in London, "People's occupations do not prepare them to 'eat like a hunter,' [and] civilization is invading the kitchen." The idea that one should not eat like a hunter constituted a new and still emerging notion of civilization that overseas travel to places like Shanghai threatened to undermine; thus, "housewives say that 'travel and the clubs have spoiled the men.'" Cooke concurred with the housewives, noting that there was no evidence of the new form of civilization evident among the English in China, "where the natives see and are taught English cookery in its worst possible form. In Hong Kong and Shanghai, a dinner-table at the summer season is a melancholy spectacle of spoiled food. The creatures to be eaten were necessarily killed the same day, and the tough tissues are as hard as death has stiffened them."[17] This "worst possible form" of Western food would deter some Chinese from eating it, but it would not deter all Chinese from adapting new items of food and manners of eating and making them into a new way of life in Shanghai.

Crossing Boundaries

Although the foreign residents of Shanghai drew and redrew cultural boundaries with food, Chinese in Shanghai found many opportunities for crossing these boundaries. Westerners were able to resist Chinese demands for greater inclusion in political institutions and social clubs, but the boundary between China and the West that food demarcated was more porous, and food culture provided Chinese city residents with an opportunity to blur the very boundary between foreign and Chinese that the foreigners sought to erect. One of the ways that Chinese did this was by patronizing Western retail shops, which appeared immediately after foreigners began to settle in the city and were themselves a key component of the recreation of foreign foodways in Shanghai. Edward Hall, a shop operated by a baker of the same name, opened on the corner of Fourth Avenue and Sichuan Road in 1843. The following year, P. F. Richards & Co. opened on the same street, a block and a half to the west. A list of goods sold at the latter that ran in the *North-China Herald* of July 25, 1851, indicates that P. F. Richards was by then already well-stocked with staples of English diets, including orange marmalade, cheddar and stilton cheese, mustard, oatmeal, cocoa powder, and oil of Bergamot, as well as French olives and Turkish figs.[18] Writing of the International Settlement two decades later, Medhurst notes, "There are foreign shops on the spot which abound in delicacies of all kinds, supplied to them wholesale by Fortnum & Mason, Cross & Blackwell, and other larger grocery establishments of this country [England]." The supply of foreign wine and beer was so ample that "wines of superior quality are as a rule placed on the table; malt liquors abound in every variety." Medhurst concluded, "As far as the material is concerned, the table of the foreign merchant, need not suffer much in comparison with the board of any well-to-do gentleman at home."[19]

Exactly when Chinese first began to patronize these shops is not clear, but they evidently found the shops to be valuable sources of novelty, lifestyle accoutrements, and specialty food items that they offered to other Chinese as gifts to accrue cultural capital. In his *Miscellaneous Notes on Travel in Shanghai*, Ge Yuanxu marveled at the "Holland water" sold in the foreign settlements, along with lemonade, as a summertime refreshment, explaining to his readers that it was "made by using a machine to trap water and air in a bottle." The pressure, he added, caused a small "explosion" when the bottle was opened, and so he warned inexperienced customers to be careful not to "get splashed in the face."[20] Compradores were regular customers at such foreign goods shops, as were courtesans, both of whom relied on their association with the West to enhance their status in the city.[21] By virtue of their foreign identity, the food items sold in such stores carried a cultural cachet that made them especially good gifts. The late-Qing courtesan novel *Sing-song Girls of Shanghai* suggests that foreign goods struck some Chinese as a more valuable alternative to commonly exchanged Chinese fruits. Thus, after Simplicity Zhao fails to ascertain the intentions of Nature Shi toward his sister, Second Treasure, by offering him a basket of fresh peaches and litchis, Simplicity's mother reconsiders their options and takes a trip to "the foreign store Hall and Holtz to buy various imported candies, biscuits, and fruit."[22]

The Chinese in Shanghai also encountered Western food culture in the produce gardens that foreigners planted to maintain control of the source of their food supply. Health concerns were paramount among the foreign residents of Shanghai, where clean water was scarce, dysentery common, and the next outbreak of cholera believed to be never far around the corner. Foreigners felt that some of the foodstuffs sold in Chinese markets were perfectly safe, and even of exceptional quality, but they feared others were dangerous. As *Treaty Ports of China and Japan* explained, "The mutton and game of the Shanghai markets are celebrated throughout China, but in other respects the table is ill-supplied. The method of cultivation of vegetables by sprinkling them with liquid manure is such as to render them unsafe article of diet."[23] This problem was initially solved through the development of kitchen gardens, as at the house of the American Dr. Hall, who, as one relieved traveler through Shanghai reported, had a "large and pretty garden" where "many vegetables and flowers are growing."[24] Later, the foreign community cultivated vegetables in larger plots of land located in the more sparsely populated areas to the north of the city. Wang Tao visited these gardens and described some of the more novel and notable crops in his 1870 *Miscellaneous Notes from the Seaside* (Yingruan zaji):

> Beyond the Northern Suburbs are mostly vegetable plots for Westerners. There is one variety I do not know the name of. It is shaped like rape, but the leaves are slightly larger. It has an appealing fresh green color and is unusually crisp and tender. In wintertime it is blanched in boiling water and put in pickling brine, after which it can be eaten. The flavor is rather sweet and refreshing.[25]

Clearly, men like Wang were taking note of and sampling the vegetables that Westerners introduced to the city. Wang's associate Li Renshu was apparently "extremely fond" of this particular vegetable and reportedly remarked of it: "This superior product from a foreign land (*yifang*) is not something that carnivores can appreciate." Significantly, Li's remarks suggest that even at this early stage in the history of Western food in Shanghai, Chinese were asserting an ability to appreciate items of Western food culture even better than the meat-eating Westerners.[26]

Wang's observations also indicate that what "foreign" foods meant to a Jiangsu native like himself did not necessarily mean Western (or that "Western" did not necessarily mean non-Chinese) and could include even Cantonese foodstuffs. Of water spinach (*Ipomoea aquatica*, a semi-aquatic tropical plant grown as a leaf vegetable), he noted, "Water spinach also comes from a foreign territory (*yiyu*). The stalks are fat and the leaves tender; it is combined with shredded pork and is a flavor unto itself. The sprouts emerge in summer and the plant is tough by fall. On water spinach see the *Prospect of the Plants of the South*, by Ji Han of the Jin. It must be a plant from the Five Ridges."[27]

As discussed in Chapter One, the *Prospect of the Plants of the South* is a record of the flora of Southeast Asia, inclusive of the Lingnan region. Its author was a native of Zhi County, in today's Anhui Province, who served in a number of posts in northern and southern China in the early fourth century.[28] The Five Ridges lie along the border between present-day Hunan and Jiangxi to the north and the Lingnan ("south of the ridges") regions of Guangdong and Guangxi. On the one hand, Wang's observations provide additional evidence of Westerners having incorporated southern Chinese foodstuffs—vegetables as well as the tropical fruits noted earlier—into their diets. On the other, it is clear that Wang associated this product of southern China with the West, suggesting that, for him at least, the water spinach Ji Han described as "a strange vegetable of the south" was still a stand-in for the foreign some fifteen centuries after Guangdong had become an administrative unit of the Jin.[29]

Chinese gained additional exposure to Western food in foreigners' homes and places of work. The wealthiest foreign residents of Shanghai did not do their own cooking, and this "usually meant teaching Chinese cooks approximations of familiar dishes."[30] For wealthy foreign merchants, this did not necessarily entail violating the boundary around the Westernized spaces in which they sought to live their lives, for "one may live in China for years, and be perfectly satisfied all the while with the style and skill with which his viands are served up, without ever making the acquaintance of his *chef de cuisine*."[31] The buildings that housed foreign mercantile establishments, moreover, were built so that "the kitchen and servants' quarters were always quite apart in a building behind." The situation was somewhat different, however, for unmarried foreign men and men of lesser means, who were not able to maintain such a firm boundary and even found that they had to cross a new one. As Dyce notes, "Amongst the other accomplishments required of a young bachelor in China was a knowledge of house-keeping. Not that he wished to learn this eminently feminine branch of art, but he was obliged to do so. Nearly all the women in the open ports were married . . . . The bachelors were therefore driven to the mercies of the houseboy, and had to run the mess themselves."[32]

It is not clear if these Chinese "*chefs de cuisine*" and "boys" were as concerned as the English with cross-cultural boundary maintenance, but they were clearly drawn to the entrepreneurial opportunities the Western presence provided. As Medhurst noted of the Chinese operation of kitchens in Western homes,

> The kitchen is . . . presided over by a man, who has from two to four mates under him, the real artists in most cases. . . . The fact is that a good cook will often serve half a dozen establishments, receiving wages from each, and each employer congratulating himself upon the possession of an admirable artist, whilst all the while the man is simply educating a number of mates and apprentices, who, in the course of time, become chefs in their turn. They cook, of course, in the best English and French styles. I have seen dinners and banquets laid out in China that would do credit to home tables.[33]

A similar apprenticeship system would later provide Shanghai's Chinese-owned Western restaurants with its corps of professional chefs.[34]

Chinese also slowly began to patronize Western-owned restaurants in the foreign settlements. There were no such establishments in Shanghai when Chinese first moved into the foreign settlements in great numbers, in the wake of the Small Swords Uprising, but Chinese took note of the earliest Western restaurants soon after they opened and began to develop ideas about the kinds of restaurants that Westerners created and the distinguishing features of Western cuisine. Among the earliest Western restaurants in Shanghai were Richard's (located near the northern ramp to Wills Bridge, which crossed Suzhou Creek where it joined the Huangpu River), and Smith's Bar (opened by a former employee of Richard's at No. 11 Guangdong Road, before relocating to Fourth Avenue in October, 1872).[35] These were most likely the "foreign restaurants" (*waiguo fandian*) that Ge Yuanxu described in his *Miscellaneous Notes,* which contains the earliest Chinese description of Western restaurants in a Shanghai city guide:

> Foreign restaurants are places where foreigners banquet and have opened in such places as outer Hongkou. Billiards and cards can be played there as one pleases. A formal banquet requires a set number of people and must be reserved in advance; the price is three *mei* of foreign silver per person. A casual meal may be taken at any time, with any number of people; the price is one *mei* of foreign silver per person. The cost of wine is extra. Food items at a banquet generally emphasize individual flavors (*duo qu zhuan wei*); the roast mutton and snacks are especially good. Chinese also go in their leisure time.[36]

Ge clearly viewed these establishments as places for formal and informal dining, and as places of leisure as well as eating, which made them in form not so different from the restaurants that served regional Chinese cuisine. It was the food that most distinguished the foreign restaurants from their Chinese counterparts.

Ge apparently enjoyed eating at these establishments, but the "individual flavors" and the manner in which they were served earned Western food a special term in Shanghai: *dacai.* The term *dacai* originated with a small number of Chinese men who gained their initial exposure to Western food by patronizing Western prostitutes, who beginning in the 1860s worked out of brothels north of the Yangjingbang Creek (these brothels were originally established for foreign sailors, but Chinese also patronized them occasionally). *Dacai* was a literal description of "big slabs of food" that were usually served cold and that "had to be handled with a fork and knife."[37] Later in Shanghai's history, the term *dacai* came to mean something like "major cuisine," in contrast to the more "minor" Chinese cuisine, and connoted an inferiority complex among Chinese that was produced by Shanghai's semicolonial status.[38] But the origin of this term as a literal description of the appearance of Western food is borne out by several bodies of literature, including evidence from late-Qing visual culture.

A good example from visual culture is the entry on Yipinxiang, one of the most popular Chinese-run Western restaurants in the city, in the 1884 illustrated guide *Shanghai's Famous Sites, Illustrated and Explained* (Shenjiang mingsheng tushuo) (see Figure 3.1). The illustration is a Chinese depiction of a Chinese-owned Western restaurant, rather than of a Western-owned restaurant, so it reveals both the kinds of dishes that Chinese entrepreneurs created to replicate

Figure 3.1 "Taking a Friend to Eat Western Food at Yipinxiang"

SOURCE: Xiangguotoutuo, *Shenjiang mingsheng tushuo* (Shanghai: Guankeshouzhai, 1884). Courtesy of the C. V. Starr East Asian Library, Columbia University.

the offerings of Western food restaurants, as well as the views that Chinese held of these dishes. The "explanation" begins by noting that, "For the most part, [Western food] prizes particular flavors (*zhuanwei*), like steak, pork chops, roasted chicken, and roast mutton."[39] The accompanying illustration depicts a baffled customer trying to slice a piece of meat. He is holding a knife in one hand and the meat up in the air with the other. Two wine glasses and several items of serving ware sit on the table, but neither customer has a plate, as if the big slabs of meat were meant to be eaten with a knife out of one's hands. Chinese had clearly begun to gain some familiarity with Western food culture, but they were still not always sure just what to make of it, let alone how to eat it.

The depiction of Western food in *Shanghai's Famous Sites* sharply contrasts with the same guide's depiction of the food served in the Suzhou cuisine restaurant Jufengyuan (see Figure 3.2). In the Jufengyuan illustration, three male restaurant customers are being entertained by two courtesans, one playing a musical instrument, the other holding an opium pipe. These two articles of refined leisure and pleasure stand in stark contrast to the knife in the Yipinxiang image. The text describing the food at the Jufengyuan builds on this contrast by listing the dishes for which the restaurant was famous: duck broth, mutton stew, monkey lips, and elephant brain. Although Western food consisted of plain cuts of meat, the Suzhou dishes were prepared either by a slow and labored cooking process or the highly selective use of delicate animal parts.

The Rise of the *Fancaiguan* and the Stink of Beef

Restaurants such as Yipinxiang, which differed from the "foreign restaurants" Ge Yuanxu described by virtue of their Chinese ownership and largely Chinese clientele, proliferated in Shanghai during the last two decades of the nineteenth century. There were still none in the city as of Ge's writing in 1876, but Huang Shiquan's 1883 *Record of Dream Images of Shanghai* indicates that the earliest establishments had already made a strong first impression: "The *fancaidian* that have opened recently, like Yijiachun and Yipinxiang, have such extravagant decorations and attentive service that they almost surpass the Suzhou and Tianjin establishments."[40] Yipinxiang was the most talked about *fancaiguan* in Shanghai. It is not clear if Yipinxiang was the very first to open in the city, but it is generally credited with eventually originating the practice of preparing Western food specifically for "Chinese taste."[41] There were reportedly ten such establishments by the middle of the 1880s and double that number a decade later. The several hundred *fancaiguan* advertisements that appeared in the short-

Figure 3.2 "Drinking with Famous Courtesans at Jufengyuan"

SOURCE: Xiangguotoutuo, *Shenjiang mingsheng tushuo* (Shanghai: Guankeshouzhai, 1884). Courtesy of the C. V. Starr East Asian Library, Columbia University.

lived turn-of-the-century tabloid *Entertainment* made *fancaiguan* among the most heavily advertised commercial institutions of the time. Business was also quite lucrative. Many advertisements announced a restaurant's post-renovation reopening, others a restaurant's expansion into adjacent buildings.⁴² All establishments boasted, in set phrases that reappeared from one advertisement to the next, of "elegant décor," chefs "skilled in the preparation of English and French cooking," and "attentive service." The flow of customers was so great that restaurants apparently could not expand quickly enough. One commentator compared the crowding inside Shanghai's *fancaiguan* to the situation in the city outdoors, where land was scarce and expensive.⁴³

Little is known about the *fancaiguan* proprietors, but indications are that the industry was dominated by Cantonese entrepreneurs. Some establishments, such as the Xinghualou, served both Cantonese food and Western food. In other establishments, the Cantonese connection is evident in the restaurant's name, such as the Lingnanlou, named after the broader Lingnan region that encompasses Guangdong and Guangxi. Many of Shanghai's *fancaiguan* chefs came to Shanghai from Hong Kong, and restaurants boasted of this in their advertisements.⁴⁴ The Shanghai guidebook literature also clearly associated *fancaiguan* with the Cantonese presence in the city.⁴⁵

The term *fancaiguan* itself also suggests a Cantonese connection. "*Caiguan*" simply means restaurant, but the term *fan* is much more complicated. *Fan*, as Endymion Wilkinson notes, has "been in use since the Zhou to mean foreign or feudatory," and "has been written with several alternative characters: fan 蕃 (luxuriant), fan 番 (foreign, barbarian), fan 藩 (protecting, feudatory)."⁴⁶ As "foreign," it is one of the six most common terms Chinese have used to refer to non-Chinese peoples. The other five include the "four barbarians" (*siyi*)—*yi*, *rong*, *di*, and *man*—as well as *hu*. Of these six, only *hu*, *man*, *yi*, and *fan* were in common use during Qing times, each referring to distinct geographic regions and to the peoples who inhabited them. *Hu* referred to northern populations, such as the Khitan, Jurchen, Tangut, Mongol, and even Manchu peoples, and conjured a history of often-violent conflict and conquest. *Man*, in contrast, referred to the indigenous peoples of the south, who rarely presented a comparable military threat, and has a more patronizing than antagonistic tone. *Yi*, often translated as "barbarian," referred in late imperial times to autonomous states, such as Japan (Dongyi) or England (Yingyi), that Chinese recognized as legitimate, if lesser, political entities. *Fan*, which by some accounts is the most neutral of these terms, encompassed a wide range of peoples to the south, sometimes the same indigenous peoples referred to as *man*, but also foreign traders who, like the Westerners in Shanghai, approached China from the south and settled there for trade. The earliest traders to whom Chinese attached this term were the *fanke* or *fanmin* from Arabia, Persia, and Africa, who lived in quarters or streets known as *fanfang* or *fanxiang*, largely in Guangzhou during the Tang and Quanzhou during the Song and Yuan. Until the nineteenth century, Chinese did not generally apply the term *fan* to Europeans or North Americans, who were known in Ming and early-Qing times as *Xiyangren*, or peoples of the Western (or Atlantic) Ocean.[47] By the early nineteenth century, however, *fan* had come into use as a designation for Europeans and North Americans in southern China and was also applied to foodstuffs that entered China through the south, such as *fanqie*, the "foreign eggplant," or tomato. The *fan* moniker also distinguished the point of entry into China of these products, as products that entered from a northern region were so signified by the term "*hu*," as in *hujiao*, or black pepper.

What the term *fancai* meant as a designation of cuisine—foreign cuisine or barbarian cuisine—is another, and more difficult, question. To help sort this question out, it will be helpful to consider Lydia Liu's recent examination of the similar term "*yi*." Liu's analysis shows that the common translation of "*yi*" as "barbarian," in the derogatory sense, is highly problematic, because this rendition, which entered wide circulation in English in the mid-nineteenth century, does not necessarily capture the term's intended meaning. Instead, Liu shows that the *yi*/barbarian rendition reflects British anxiety about being so designated in official communications with the Qing empire.[48] Does the same hold for "*fan*," so famously associated, in English, with the term *fangui*? Today, this term is most commonly translated as "foreign devil," but according to one English language source that was written on the eve of the Opium War, *fangui* "literally signifies 'barbarian wanderer' or 'outlandish demon.'"[49] Should *fancaiguan*, therefore, be translated as "foreign cuisine restaurant," "barbarian cuisine restaurant," or perhaps even as "outlandish cuisine restaurant," recognizing that "outlandish" means both "of or belonging to a foreign country," and "going beyond what is considered normal or acceptable; outrageous, extravagant," as well as "far removed from civilization," in a derogatory sense.[50]

On the one hand, just as Liu has identified more neutral uses of *yi*, so do such terms in the Cantonese language as "*fan-kan*" (foreign soap) and "*fan-bing*" (cheese cake), like *fanqie* (tomato), suggest that *fan* might be best rendered in neutral terms.[51] On the other hand, the same early-nineteenth-century

English lexicon that Liu uses to identify a neutral sense of *yiren* describes *yiren* as a "more respectable term" than *fanren*, suggesting that *fanren* was the more derogatory of the two.[52] The use of *fan* as an alternate designation for the so-called "*man*" peoples, including the indigenous peoples of Taiwan, further suggests a more derogatory reading. In this broader context, *fan* operated as part of a wider discourse on acculturation, with the terms "*shengfan*" (raw *fan*) and "*shufan*" (cooked *fan*) designating different degrees of conformity among non-Chinese peoples to some notion of Chinese culture.[53] Cuisine, as an act of culture on raw materials, would thus have carried very different connotations than did mere foodstuffs. Still, it is equally clear that Chinese clearly distinguished the English from the "*man*" and did not expect the former to become "cooked." This was, indeed, why they called the English "*yi*" in official discourse, until the term was banned in 1858. Undoubtedly the ban on *yi* also provided a context for the wider proliferation of the term *fan*, especially in Shanghai, where the ban would have been well known, but where the term *fan* does not seem to have been used with regard to foreigners in Shanghai until the proliferation of Cantonese-owned *fancaiguan* in the late 1870s and early 1880s. Recall that, before the emergence of the Cantonese-owned *fancaiguan*, Ge Yuanxu described the foreign-owned restaurants as, simply, "foreign restaurants" (*waiguo fandian*).

It seems, therefore, that there is no one clear way to translate the term. Yet, if we accept this impasse and resist the temptation to seek an English term commensurate with *fan*, as Liu suggests we do for *yi*, it becomes possible instead to explore the ways in which the Chinese in Shanghai who patronized *fancaiguan* throve on these very paradoxes. Although the term *fancai* was not necessarily derogatory, it clearly suggested something much more "outlandish" than just "foreign," and even something remarkably "uncivilized," albeit not necessarily in a bad way.

This multivalence is perhaps most evident in early Chinese accounts of the taste and smell of Western food, which to many presented a formidable barrier. Many Chinese found the smell of Western food at best unpleasant, at worst nauseating. Huang Shiquan, for example, wrote, "Western food is all cooked over an open flame, [and consists of] items like beef, mutton, chicken, and duck. If [the taste] isn't sour and spicy, then it is rank and gamy (*xingshan*)." The shortcomings were attributed to several factors. First, the dishes were too meat-centered for Huang's liking. More importantly, the culinary technique by which they were prepared failed to transform the meat from a raw to a properly cooked state. *Xing* refers to an intrinsic, undesirable quality of freshly killed meat that in Chinese cookery is overcome through the use of cooking wine and seasonings like ginger that "expel" (*qu*) it. The choice of ingredients was also a deterring factor. Chicken and duck were commonly used in Chinese cooking, but mutton was more rare, especially in Huang's native Jiangsu Province. *Shan*, which literally means "the smell of sheep," was long associated with the food culture of non-Chinese peoples of the northern steppe regions, for whom mutton was an important foodstuff. Now it seemed as if the smell of sheep encroached upon Chinese borders not only from the north, but also from the south.[54]

Yet significantly, some of these strange smells and flavors were not so much eliminated from Chinese-run Western restaurants as made into pleasures in their own right. Huang noted that "Fops and dandies are always vying to eat exotic things (*yiwei*) and relish talking about them," suggesting that some consumers made the act of eating unpleasant-tasting Western food into a daring, even competitive, act of one-upmanship. The Yipinxiang entry in *Shanghai's Famous Sights* made this point more explicitly. Whereas the illustration highlighted the use of knives at the table, the explanation drew attention to aspects of Western food that were not so easily represented visually, its taste and smell: "[Western food] prizes particular flavors, such as steak, pork chops, roasted chicken, [and] roasted mutton, only the smell is so rank and rancid (*xingsao*), it is almost unbearable to get close to it." Here again the food is described as "rank" (*xing*), but now also as *sao*, which, in addition to meaning "rancid," also refers to the unpleasant smell of perspiration (*saoqi*). Remarkably, these were the very qualities in which some consumers took pleasure. The same author complained, "After I had my first taste of sliced meat, I felt like Junmo eating land crabs: I couldn't hold back the nausea and wanted to vomit," but he added, "those who are fond of gamy tastes consider it to be as sweet as sugar."[55]

Of the two "gamy" meats served in *fancaiguan*, beef raised special questions and concerns. Beef-eating required crossing an emotional and moral boundary, as well as a physiological one, because many Chinese considered cattle, so valuable for agricultural labor, a friend of humankind. Beef was eaten in early China, but its desirability derived in part, as Ying-shih Yü has noted, because "the ox was such a useful animal that the government occasionally prohibited its slaughter."[56] Such prohibitions became increasingly common with the spread of Buddhism in China during the Tang (618–907), from which time beef-eating went into a sharp decline.[57] Indigenous Chinese notions of cosmic retribution, mixed with the Buddhist concept of karma, identified the slaughter of cattle for human consumption as a cosmic transgression, whereas abstinence from beef-eating earned karmic merit. This was, in any event, how Chinese in Shanghai, such as Wang Tao, understood the origins of the prohibition. Wang traced it to a story included in the Tang collection of miracle tales, *Reports from the Palace Room* (Xuanshi zhi), which recounts how a young girl escapes misfortune after abstaining from eating beef.[58] The general prohibition seems not to have been strictly followed in Shanghai, even before the treaty port years, but the foreign presence clearly contributed to a rise in beef-eating, and even lent a certain legitimacy to those who sought to capitalize on the trend. This trend concerned many city residents, including Wang himself, who remarked, "People in Shanghai have no inhibitions about eating beef. There are shameless butchers everywhere. No one can stop them. Since the arrival of the Westerners, people who eat beef have increased in number. They are brazenly open about it, and they even display beef in the marketplace."[59]

What do such trends and the voices of their detractors tell us about the impact of this aspect of Western food on Shanghai eating habits during this time? Ye Xiaoqing states that the spread of beef-eating in Shanghai represents "the decline of agriculture-based traditions and belief," that opposition to beef-eating was a preserve of the "traditional gentry," and that "by the late nineteenth century eating beef was accepted as if it had always been so."[60] Vocal criticism of beef-eating does indeed seem to have died down by the early twentieth century, but Ye's use of "traditional gentry" encompasses a wide range of social types, including Wang Tao, editorialists for the *Shenbao* (Shanghai's leading daily newspaper), writers and artists affiliated with the popular illustrated magazine *Dianshizhai Pictorial* (Dianshizhai huabao), and the writer and entertainment entrepreneur Li Boyuan, who toward the end of the century mocked the ingenious justifications offered for beef-eating in Shanghai in his satirical novel, *A Brief History of Enlightenment* (Wenming xiaoshi). When one character in the novel is taken to task for eating beef, he defends himself by arguing, "The oxen of Shanghai are different from those in China proper. There, the oxen plough the fields and exert themselves for the good of man, and so people cannot bear to kill them and eat them. The foreigners in Shanghai, however, rear cattle and make them fat, so that they can kill them for their meat. So they are called edible oxen, and eating them cannot be considered wrong."[61]

It may thus be even more productive to view these men not only as "traditional gentry," but as concerned and self-conscious image makers of a new

Soups	Entrees	Desserts
Cream Soup	Fish Roulade	Butter Pudding
Teal (freshwater duck) Soup	Fried Fish (all varieties)	Cream Pudding
Asparagus in Beef Broth	Red-braised Fish	Almond Pudding
Asparagus in Chicken Soup	Braised Chicken with	Banana Pudding
Fish Soup	Black Mushrooms	Brandy Pudding
Tomato Soup	Braised Chicken with	
Almond Soup	White Mushrooms	
Oxtail Soup	Rolled Chicken Breast	
Goose-head Soup	Canard au Vin	
Beef Cream Soup	Braised Squab with Greens	
Abalone Soup	Braised Squab with Green Beans	
Scrambled Egg Soup	Quail Eggs in White Sauce	
Quail Egg Soup	Quail Eggs in Red Sauce	
	Quail Eggs with English Ham	
	Broiled Beefsteak	
	Roast Beef	
	Braised Mutton Chop	
	Grilled Mutton Chop	
	Shrimp Balls in White Sauce	

Figure 3.3 Menu of the Lingnanlou *Fancaiguan*
SOURCE: *Shanghai zhinan* (Shanghai: Shangwu yinshuguan, 1909).

Shanghai. For some, eating beef may have represented a positive commitment to Western-style cultural reform. But as the 1885 *Dianshizhai Pictorial* image, "Shrinking from Fear to Warrant Pity," indicates, others were clearly ambivalent about the spread of beef-eating and about defining the city as a place that lay outside the boundaries, figuratively and literally, of a Chinese moral universe. The image depicts a "country fellow" leading an ox to the foreign slaughter-houses in Hongkou. When he reaches the edge of the foreign settlements, he is stopped by a Chinese policemen. The ox then kneels down and begs for release. The commentary reads, "To be slaughtered for no reason—even though an ox is not the master of his own destiny, can it be unaware of this [injustice]?"[62] Shanghai, the image suggests, could yet become a place of moral justice, by shoring up such a moral frontier. Such ambivalence about the spread of beef-eating, moreover, seems to have had at least some impact on *fancaiguan* menus, such as that of the Lingnanlou (see Figure 3.3), which as late as the early twentieth century did not figure beef as prominently as one might expect, or even as prominently as other meats.

Material Culture, Courtesans, and the Taming of the West

By minimizing the presence of beef on restaurant menus and by making the "rank" smell of beef and mutton into a cult pleasure, restaurateurs and customers contributed significantly to the late-Qing craze. But equally, if not more important, was the material culture of the *fancaiguan*. The food received mixed reviews, but all chroniclers of *fancaiguan* were impressed by the characteristic features of the restaurants' décor, which distinguished *fancaiguan* from restaurants serving regional Chinese cuisine. Huang Shiquan disliked the food but was impressed by their "extravagant" interior design; Chi Zhicheng describes the architecture and the utensils as "ornate and glimmering"; a third guidebook emphasized the "elegance and cleanliness" of *fancaiguan*.[63] A fourth noted, with direct reference to Yipinxiang: "The knives and forks are bright as snow. The rooms are elegant and cool. The cups and plates so fine and bright. Foreign flowers and foreign fruits are all so new."[64] *Fancaiguan*, which were among the earliest Chinese establishments to install electric lighting, were clearly an important component of the Penglai image of Shanghai.

The importance of this material culture is especially evident in the history of visual representations of *fancaiguan*, and of Yipinxiang in particular, which over time developed a distinct iconography that shaped ideas about what constituted core elements of Western material culture. Early images of Yipinxiang, such as the image from *Shanghai's Famous Sites* discussed earlier, lacked a distinct iconography, and represent *fancaiguan* as a kind of borderland. What mattered there was the foreignness of the food, which sets it off from more familiar forms of Chinese cuisine. A similar attempt to negotiate the terms of a Chinese-Western boundary is evident in a second image that was published the same year in the *Dianshizhai Pictorial*. Indeed, in this image, titled "Catching a Glimpse of a Whole Leopard," nothing except the placard with the name of the restaurant in the top-right corner, and perhaps the lanterns, indicates that this is not a Chinese restaurant interior. Moreover, the Chinese-ness of the interior is crucial to the main action of the illustration, which depicts a group of Chinese customers viewing a leopard in a cage. As the text at the top of the image explains, the proprietor of Yipinxiang put exotic animals on display in his establishment, including pythons (pictures of which hang on the wall behind the cage), and more recently a leopard.[65] This was apparently "for the customers' enjoyment," but the description of the leopard also suggests that, at this point in Shanghai's history, engagement with the West, even in a *fancaiguan*, was still quite tentative:

> It is said that the leopard is not even ten months old but is already as big as a rabid dog, and its roar is as loud as a hog's. It crouches in the cage and eats raw beef, consuming several pounds in an instant. It has the disposition of a cat,

and if you throw it a ball, it plays without stopping, [but] when facing people it stares them down ferociously. Since it is like this when it is still only young, it will surely grow up to be as fierce as a tiger. The newspaper reports that this is what those who have witnessed it say. These people are fortunate to see the whole thing, which can not be compared with looking through a pipe and only seeing one spot.[66]

The leopard is clearly a stand-in for the West, and the scenario surrounding the leopard a metaphor of a contained encounter with the West. The leopard is described as young but powerful, a combination of traits that many Chinese saw in Western countries. It eats beef and, when left to its own devices, works out its aggression through play (recall Dyce's impressions, noted previously, that Chinese viewed British sports as "perhaps necessary to work off the effects of beef and mutton"). But when face to face with Chinese, the leopard is serious, even ferocious. Only by caging the leopard for his customers, in the confines of a conventional Chinese interior, is the proprietor to provide Chinese in Shanghai with a safe, "full glimpse" of the leopard and, thereby, of the West.

Later images of Yipinxiang, which depict Chinese eating Western food with skill and grace, are notable for the prominence they give to objects of Western material culture. This material culture is drawn into sharp relief through a comparison of images of Yipinxiang and the Suzhou cuisine Jufengyuan published in the 1898 *Illustrated Guide to Shanghai Entertainment*. The dining room of the Jufengyuan (see Figure 3.4) is framed by a large screen to the right and latticed wood paneling to the left. Chinese lanterns, graced with calligraphy and motifs from Chinese painting, are suspended from the ceiling. Teapots sit on a side table, and the main dinner table is set with chopsticks and appetizer plates before the guests even take their seats. The table is round; the chairs Chinese. In contrast, the dining room in the *Illustrated Guide*'s representation of the Yipinxiang (see Figure 3.5) is dominated by Victorian forms. It has bare walls that help set off the various "glittering" objects in the room. In place of the Chinese lantern is a gas lantern of blown glass bulbs attached to curved metal arms. The wall to the left has a fireplace, the mantle of which is decorated with a European-style clock, decorative bottles, and vases holding fresh flowers. The balcony is framed by a window with stitch-and-ball detailing. The table is curved at the edges but largely rectangular in form, so that the diners sit directly across from one another. The table also has turned details on the

Figure 3.4 The Jufengyuan Restaurant

SOURCE: Hushang youxizhu, *Haishang youxi tushuo* (Shanghai, 1898).

四馬路
一品香
喫大菜

Figure 3.5 The Yipinxiang *Fancaiguan*

SOURCE: Hushang youxizhu, *Haishang youxi tushuo* (Shanghai, 1898).

legs, is covered with a tablecloth, and is set with forks and knives. The chairs are cushioned, and each guest has his or her own serving of food. In the absence of photographic evidence of the Yipinxiang interior, it is impossible to confirm that this is a faithful rendition. It is clear, however, that this became *the* iconography of Western food in Shanghai. Indeed, the *Illustrated Guide*'s image of Yipinxiang is itself a redrawing of an earlier image of courtesans enjoying a meal of Western food, drawn by the *Dianshizhai Pictorial* illustrator Wu Youru (see Figure 3.6). This earlier image is not clearly set in Yipinxiang, but the interior is identical. Even the time on the clock is the same.[67] As discussed later, the exact same template would later be used for negative depictions of Western food in Shanghai.

It is hard to determine precisely how this material culture, and thereby the *fancaiguan*, became fashionable and familiar in Shanghai. The motifs themselves seem to have been borrowed from Western-owned establishments in the city, as suggested by Ge Yuanxu's early observations of "foreign wine houses,"

Figure 3.6 Courtesans Dining on Western Food
SOURCE: Wu Youru, *Wu Youru huabao* (orig. Shanghai, 1908; reprint, Shanghai: Shanghai guji shudian, 1983).

which also had a "glittering" décor.[68] But who orchestrated the borrowing? Catherine Yeh, whose *Shanghai Love* makes a strong case for the role of the courtesan as trend-setter, notes, "From pictures of Western-style restaurants of the time, one can easily see where the courtesans got their ideas," suggesting that, in this regard at least, the courtesans were not so much trendsetters as trend-followers.[69] But even if restaurateurs set the template, courtesans took this template in new directions, by appropriating the *fancaiguan* image of the West and making it a part of the Shanghai courtesan's signature style. Early on in the history of the foreign settlements, when courtesan patrons accorded high status to courtesans of Suzhou origins, even courtesans who hailed from other regions initially cultivated a Suzhou style. But by the 1880s, courtesans had begun to incorporate Western and Cantonese motifs into their style, furnishing their rooms with the very same objects that distinguished *fancaiguan* from regional Chinese restaurants.[70] If late-Qing courtesan fiction may be taken as a reliable indicator, some brothels even contained their own Western food dining rooms, which resembled the interiors of *fancaiguan*. In *Sing-song Girls*, the house of the courtesan Bright Pearl has one such dining room: "With its whitewashed walls, white curtains, an iron bed, and mirrors, it looked like a crystal palace."[71]

Late-Qing sources also suggest that men's relationship to *fancaiguan* was often mediated by courtesans. Men certainly patronized these establishments, and as the Yipinxiang image from *Shanghai's Famous Sites* suggests, they might even go by themselves. But absent the company of courtesans, they are clearly out of their element, in contrast to the Yipinxiang image from the *Illustrated Guide*, where they sit comfortably across the table from their female companions. And although male courtesan patrons may have been the ones who actually purchased many of the Western items that courtesans used to model their rooms after *fancaiguan*—including the *si-po-ling pao-tuo-mo-sha-fa* (spring-bottom sofa) and *di-ling tui-bo-er* (dinner table)—these men often did so under a courtesan's instruction, and thus engaged with the material culture through courtesan tutelage.[72]

The traditional frames of reference through which men often discussed Western food further suggest that, on their own, men's enthusiasm for Western food was somewhat more equivocal than that of courtesans. When Chi Chi-zheng described his own experiences "dipping a finger" in the food served at *xiaoyeguan* and *fancaiguan*, he borrowed the phrase from the *Zuozhuan*, a canonical commentary of the history classic, the *Spring and Autumn Annals*. The allusion is to Zi Gong, an officer of the State of Zheng. Zi Gong, having been rebuffed at a banquet held by Duke Ling of Zheng, transgressed table manners and "dipped his finger into a dish, tasted the turtle, and went out, which so enraged the duke that he wished to kill him."[73] The term suggests that men like Chi were more self-conscious than were courtesans of the possibility that eating Western food constituted a kind of symbolic transgression. Whereas for courtesans eating Western food involved the creation of a new kind of persona and cultural profile, for men it often involved imitating an old one. Indeed, "imitating Zi Gong" became a euphemism among men for eating Western food.[74]

Print and visual materials also generally represent courtesans as more dexterous than men at eating Western food. In *Sing-song Girls*, when Script Li, a "high-ranking official and man of great wealth," attends a dinner party in Bright Pearl's Western dining room, it is Bright Pearl who "bone[s the fish] for Script Li with her fork and knife."[75] Compare also the Yipinxiang image of men in *Shanghai's Famous Sites* with the Wu Youru illustration of courtesans enjoying a Western-style meal without the company of men (Figures 3.1 and 3.6). The woman seated at the far left skillfully wields a fork and knife even as her maid offers her a water pipe. The woman sitting directly across the table, who has already finished her meal, has gingerly rested her used flatware on the edge of the cleaned plate. The composure of the women is especially striking in light of the labored descriptions of how to eat Western food that circulated in texts for men. The rituals of eating Western food may have provided some relief from the constraints of Chinese banqueting. As Chi explained, "Each customer is served an individual portion, and each portion is of an individual dish, so there's no need to vie for [food] or yield [food] to others, because every customer gets his own portion." But detailed explanations of how to wield a fork, knife, and spoon also indicate that eating Western food was not necessarily a casual, or easy affair. One example included the following bits of advice:

> When eating [soup], the left hand holds the bowl, the right hand the spoon. When using the knife, it is essential to cut with the right hand. Hold the fork in the left hand, and eat with the fork. When done eating, place the spoon on the right side of the bowl facing upward; the knife on right side [of the plate] facing inward; the fork on the right side facing downward. If you wish to add butter or jam to the bread, you may pick it up with the knife.[76]

Those who learned and followed these rules successfully earned a badge of social respectability, but those who failed were subject to humiliation.[77]

With the passing of time, however, came higher levels of skill and comfort, which, combined with the increasingly familiar features of *fancaiguan* décor, made the *fancaiguan* into a relatively naturalized feature of the Shanghai cityscape. *Fancaiguan* are reported to have appeared in "all major cities and commercial ports . . . during the Guangxu reign period [1875–1908], and by the time of the Xuantong [1908–11] were especially prosperous," but only in Shanghai did *fancaiguan* become a defining component of the idea of the city.[78] Early in the history of these establishments, Shanghai District Magistrate Mo Xiangzhi invited distinguished visitors to Shanghai out to Western restaurants to sample "foreign dishes" (*yizhuan*).[79] What started out as a novelty, however, quickly became the norm. Recalling the time of his youth in "The Shanghai of My Childhood" (Ertong shidai de Shanghai), Bao Tianxiao (1875–1973) explains, "At the time, when people from the interior came to Shanghai for fun, there were two things that they had to do: the first was to eat Western food, the second was to ride in a horse drawn carriage."[80] Even visitors to China from other East Asian countries made sure to eat in *fancaiguan* while in Shanghai. Indeed, the image of Shanghai as a place to eat Western food became so powerful that one historical novel published in the early twentieth century anachronistically included scenes in Western restaurants set in times when they did not yet exist.[81]

The association of Shanghai with Western food culture cemented Shanghai's status as the vanguard of China's engagement with foreign culture. This idea received its most articulate formulation in an editorial published toward the end of the century in the tabloid *Entertainment*, which eloquently described Shanghai's *fancaiguan* as the end point of a historical process that had been unfolding for millennia, and that therefore had always been a part of Chinese culture. The editorial began by noting that a pursuit of novelty had always been a driving force in the development of a refined sense of taste, "from [the time when primitive people] ate birds and beasts uncooked to the present day." Over the years, food connoisseurs identified the most "refined of foodstuffs; for example, taking only the feet of the chicken, the lips of the ape, the paw of the bear, the wing-tip of the wild duck." This passion, the author added, "inspired Chinese to look outside their borders and to incorporate the foodstuffs of other peoples and places into their diets," for "just because a person may be Chinese, it doesn't mean that he doesn't consider foreign [foodstuffs] delicious. For example, the piper betle of the Southern Barbarians (*nanyi*), the cheese and hami melon of the Northern Barbarians (*beirong*), and the giant dates from Persia are all documented in the history books, and the food treatises that have made a record of them have praised them for being delicious." In the past, however, there were barriers to a fully developed Chinese appreciation of non-Chinese foodstuffs, for "in ancient times, when China and foreign lands were cut off [from one another] and communication was not possible, there were few who could describe their taste."

Present-day Shanghai, by contrast, presented a new kind of open environment that created expanded possibilities for eating and cross-cultural exchange:

> Today . . . China and foreign lands breathe the same air, and Chinese and barbarians cohabitate. The residents of treaty ports are especially accustomed to Westerners and imitate many aspects [of their life]. When it comes to customs of food and drink, they are even more passionate. Indeed, they consider the Westerners' carefully prepared roasts to be far more fragrant and clean than [the food of] China, [and that the difference between the two is] greater than that between Heaven and earth. This is why in Shanghai *fancaiguan* are as numerous as the trees in a forest. In imitation of the West, they are built in Western-style buildings, and they even use Western ingredients. When famous officials and rich merchants, royal princes, and even famous prostitutes from the courtesan houses and pretty young girls go on an outing in carriages—indeed all who drive pass by the doors [of these establishments]—they take their seats together, willing to taste a foreign flavor. As a result, the seats fill up and horse-drawn carriages block the door, while sandalwood clappers and beautiful voices [can be heard] night and day.[82]

Fancaiguan, the editorial argued, were not only beacons of a new stage of civilization, but also cultural institutions that fulfilled latent tendencies of early Chinese food culture. The only possible deterrent to the popularity of these establishments was, the author speculated, bad weather, which made for unpleasant carriage rides, or hard financial times, which indeed seems to have led to a slow down in business in early spring 1899.[83]

The *Fancaiguan* as a Social Problem

To many of Shanghai's leading image makers, *fancaiguan* were powerful emblems of the city's accomplishments; to others, they symbolized everything that was wrong with the place. Shanghai itself inspired such conflicting views, sometimes even in the same person. Even guidebook writers who had positive things to say about the *fancaiguan* phenomenon voiced concerns about the restaurants' clientele that hint of burgeoning social anxieties. Already during the early phases of the craze, Huang Shiquan described the typical patrons of *fancaiguan* as the "non-office-holding sons and younger brothers of the nobility" (*guiyou zidi*).[84] Chi Zhicheng, writing a decade later, noted that *fancaiguan* were places to which "young dandies and pot-bellied wealthy merchants frequently take concubines and family members in pursuit of foreign flavors."[85] Li Boyuan, the founder and lead writer for *Entertainment* and other Shanghai tabloids, also sounded an alarm, noting of the city's entertainment entrepreneurs and consumers, "They are unaware that the stage full of singing and dancing is but a place of bitter tears; that the tasty meats and delicious wines are but poison."[86] Overall, the *fancaiguan* phenomenon inspired two waves of criticism, one that grew out of the same cultural atmosphere that produced the craze, and a second, slightly later wave that grew out of a distinct historical process that dovetailed with urban food culture in Shanghai in unexpected ways.

The first of these two waves struck at a turning point in Sino-foreign relations. The year 1895 marked the Qing's humiliating defeat in the Sino-Japanese War and the signing of the Treaty of Shimonoseki, which stripped the Qing of Taiwan, the Penghu Islands, and suzerainty over Korea, and almost cost it the entire Liaodong peninsula. The subsequent "scramble for concessions" by France, Russia, and Germany led to a rapid deterioration of Sino-foreign relations on the eve of the anti-foreign Boxer Uprising. The Boxer Protocols, formulated after the Boxers' resounding defeat, granted foreign powers the right to station troops on Qing soil, confirming fears among Chinese that national sovereignty was at stake. These events transpired in the empire's northeast, but reverberations were felt in Shanghai, where nationalism soon infused Sino-foreign relations, and where local events played their own part. On May 13, 1898, the Ningbo community boycotted the goods and services of Westerners in Shanghai in reaction to efforts to move the Ningbo cemetery outside the boundaries of the French Concession, making for the "first political strike against a foreign power in the history of modern China."[87]

The new social and political context inspired outspoken criticism of Japan and the Western powers, but also of the previous decades of Qing reform efforts, which the defeat by Japan revealed to many to have been too superficial. Cultural chauvinists took issue with the apparent denigration of Chinese cuisine relative to that of the West and reasserted the superiority of Chinese cuisine. One writer countered the suggestion that Chinese food lacked distinction by pointing out that its repertoire contained more than eight hundred dishes, whereas Euro-American cooking only three hundred, and Japanese cuisine only five hundred.[88] A critical posture, however, did not necessarily mean a rejection of Western food culture per se. Several months after one *Entertainment* editorial described Shanghai's *fancaiguan* as the be-all and end-all of food culture in China, a second bemoaned their soporific effects, arguing that their "Chineseness," rather than their "Westernness," deterred rather than advanced China's emergence on the world stage.[89]

Remarkably, although the author of the second *Entertainment* column argued that China and Chinese needed to do a better job at Westernizing, he couched his argument in Confucian rhetoric. The article came with an innocent-sounding title, "*Fancaiguan* Should Pay Attention to Cooking," but it took a serious, even doctrinaire, position. The Confucian standpoint of the argument was marked in the opening lines of the essay, which contained a string of suggestive allusions to the *Doctrine of the Mean* and the *Analects*:

> The Master [Confucius] said: "There is no body but eats and drinks, but there are few who can distinguish flavors." If you eat something good but do not taste it, then the eating is crude. If the ingredients are not fine, then the cooking can not be great. The "Xiangdang" [chapter of the *Analects*] says: "His food he does not mind being of choice quality, his mincemeat he does not mind being cut fine." Choice quality and fine cutting are the source of taste. The commentary says: "Eating choice quality can cultivate the person, cooking crudely can harm the person."[90]

The *Doctrine of the Mean* entered the Confucian canon as a chapter of the classic *Book of Rites* and later became one of the "four books" (*sishu*) that defined the core of neo-Confucian orthodoxy. It depicts the "Way" (*Dao*) as a heavenly mandate to be abided by rulers and ruled, and the study of this mandate as a means for achieving virtue, or power. The problem is that few actually abide the Way, a problem that Confucius is shown to explain in the *Doctrine of the Mean* as follows: "The Master Said, 'I know how it is that the path of the mean is not walked in:—The knowing go beyond it, and the stupid do not come up to it. I know how it is that the path of the mean is not understood:—The men of talents and virtue go beyond it, and the worthless do not come up to it.'"[91] The prescription from the *Analects*, part of a larger code outlined there for the "gentleman courtier and householder," drove the point home.[92] Obtaining the mean required due diligence in all aspects of life, even eating, and cooking.

The bulk of the *Entertainment* editorial builds on this core idea through a critique of the Chinese-style Western food sold in Shanghai's *fancaiguan*. First, the author establishes that cooking in the West, like proper cooking anywhere, requires that one obtains the Mean: "When one examines the preparation of *fancai* by Westerners, it requires careful selection [of ingredients], cleanliness, freshness, and richness. Roasting, broiling, boiling, and seasoning all have a good technique. It doesn't matter if the meat is raw or the fish cured, it is essential to obtain the [proper] flavor and then do no more." Shanghai's *fancaiguan*, the author argued, failed in this regard, both by going "beyond it," and by "not coming up to it." Looked at from the outside, the restaurants appeared to be a great success: "The décor is refined, the utensils are elegant, and business thrives; [Western restaurants] are even doing better than Suzhou, Anhui, and Tianjin restaurants." Underneath the façade, however, lay a more fundamental problem: "Although the food is called Western food, it is really just Chinese food, with the only difference being a fork and knife exchanged for chopsticks and a spoon." Indeed, some of the food was apparently so unpalatable as to be "hard to get down," and so Chinese that "One wonders if it is really worthy of being called Western food. This is why Shanghai has no less than tens of Western restaurants but Westerners rarely patronize them."

From the author's point of view, much more than just taste was at stake—or, rather, that matters of taste were not to be considered minor issues. The editorial attributed the failure of Chinese to compete with Westerners to a broader Chinese misunderstanding of what made the West wealthy and powerful:

> Today, people who try to fix what is wrong with [Chinese] business do not hesitate to advise imitating the West in pursuit of wealth and power. Now, Westerners have a deep understanding of Chinese taste, and so their opium, rolled cigarettes, and medicine all sell well here and cater to our desires. Chinese merchants seek wealth and power by imitating Western ways, [but] as for the details of what Westerners eat and drink, they do not discern what makes it worth craving. Moreover, they have also lost a sense of what Chinese people crave. This is why I pity Western restaurants and I pity Chinese merchants.[93]

Seen in this light, *fancaiguan* were not a measure of successful Westernization, but of failed Westernization, and of the failures of Shanghai and China more generally.

The *fancaiguan* craze continued unabated for a good decade longer, but even to more equivocal observers, it seemed to be assuming an increasingly debased form. The emphasis of the critique thus shifted from the superficiality of *fancaiguan* to the threats they posed to social order. Chen Dingshan captured this state of affairs in his memoir, *Old Tales of Shanghai* (Chunshen jiuwen). Chen describes the Fourth Avenue neighborhood as the place to go on New Year's Eve to "get lucky." Late at night, after most of the area's restaurants had closed their doors, the Wanjiachun, Lingnanlou, and Yijiachun *fancaiguan*, all located at the Medhurst Circle intersection on Fourth Avenue, were still open, and one could see the "red sleeves [courtesans] hanging in the doorways and the brown fur coats [patrons] leaning up against the railings, congratulating one another from across the street." Combined with the "boom of firecrackers set off by children downstairs," and the "rumbling of horse-drawn carriages," it made for what Chen calls, somewhat favorably, a "bustling scene." But a short distance away near the Hu Family Residence, where the Yizhixiang *fancaiguan* was located, seductively dressed streetwalkers alternately "stormed passing carriages" and "seduced idlers who had gathered in groups to create disturbances." The painter Pu Hua (1834–1911), who Chen notes was an Yizhixian regular, could apparently only make it home each night after giving the "pheasants" who swarmed him in the street a token coin from his purse.[94]

Chen reports that the Yizhixiang neighborhood was so sketchy that "women from respectable families rarely passed through," but other sources indicate that married women were drawn to the *fancaiguan* phenomenon, and that their participation in the craze raised additional concerns. Courtesans enjoyed a degree of mobility and public visibility generally denied to the wives of their patrons, at least in principle. Western restaurants, however, seem to have been one space in which it was possible for a man to appear and entertain in public with his wife. As one guidebook put it, "Even though it is possible to call for a courtesan to encourage drinking and sing and play instruments, it is also possible to bring one's spouse (*juan*) along. Those who eat [here] also get to sample this aspect of Western customs."[95] This possibility of public conjugal sociability initially resonated with some conventional Chinese frames of reference. Thus, Ge Yuanxu, writing of Shanghai's foreign-owned wine houses, was struck by the presence of the foreign women who served the wine and likened them to Zhuo Wenjun (150–115 B.C.), the most famous wine shop proprietress in Chinese history.[96] Having been divorced from her first husband at the age of seventeen, Zhuo eloped with the poet Sima Xiangru and later returned with him to her hometown, where the two opened and operated a wine shop together and later went down in history as a shining example of conjugal bliss.[97] By the end of the century, however, the apparent goings-on in *fancaiguan* had begun to raise concern about the behavior of married women in Shanghai, prompting social commentators to use Western restaurants as the setting for stories about marital infidelity.

One such story, published in 1897 in the *Dianshizhai Pictorial,* bore the title "Becoming Laughingstocks for Trading Wives." The laughingstocks in question were two men who unwittingly exchanged wives, each taking the other man's wife as a lover. They discovered the fiasco only when they ended up, on the very same night, at Yipinxiang, where both men went in search of a place to pursue their illicit relationships. Because the two parties were seated in separate rooms, neither man realized what was going on at first. But when a third man acquainted with both discovers the "exchange," the truth comes out. When first confronted by the third man, one of the two laughingstocks "shamelessly" claims to be in the company of his own wife, but then the second man overhears the commotion and comes over to investigate. When "both men saw their wives, they cowered in shame and were very embarrassed." The story has a comical, almost slapstick, tone, but its setting in Yipinxiang reveals common conceptions and concerns about what transpired inside these establishments, and the ends to which city residents were putting them. Western food itself is irrelevant to the story, but a *fancaiguan* is the perfect setting for a tale about men trying to pass off other women as their wives, and about their wives being willing, if unsuspecting, participants in the infidelity.

These concerns about wives emerged in concert with a new late-nineteenth-century critique of Shanghai's courtesans. This critique reflected, in part, a "shifting self-assessment" of Shanghai's literati. These men had styled themselves as the courtesans' most valuable patrons in the 1860s, 1870s, and 1880s, but by the end of the nineteenth century they felt that their "values and privileged standing were under threat" by a "crass commercialization" that was sweeping the city.[98] One courtesan in particular, Hu Baoyu, bore the brunt of this critique. Although Hu was apparently actually of Suzhou origin, she consciously cultivated a Cantonese style, traveling to Guangzhou and returning to Shanghai with Cantonese furniture, and openly fraternizing with "salt water sisters" (*xianshuimei*), Cantonese prostitutes who took Westerners as patrons. Hu flaunted her own liaisons with Western patrons, as well as those with leading actors from the Shanghai stage, actors being an ever-present irritant for literati patrons. Her behavior made her the subject of several critical literary

Figure 3.7 Hu Baoyu in Yipinxiang, from *Jiuwei hu* (Nine-tailed fox)

SOURCE: Menghuaguanzhu Jiang Yinxiang, *Jiuwei hu* (orig. Shanghai: Shanghai jiaotong tushuguan, 1918), reprinted in *Zhongguo jindai xiaoshuo daxi* (Nanchang: Baihuazhou wenyi chubanshe, 1991).

representations, including Wu Jianren's 1897 novel *Hu Baoyu* (Hu Baoyu) and the early-Republican *Nine-Tailed Fox* (Jiuwei hu). These novels, which articulated the "conflicting experiences of the city's commercial might and decadence," were themselves an important component of a turn of the century denigration and vulgarization of the courtesan image.[99]

Fancaiguan were important backdrops for this critique, which the illustrators of these novels incorporated into iconic images of Western food culture. Figure 3.7, for example, a representation of Hu Baoyu's "rendezvous with an opera singer," appeared in *Nine-Tailed Fox*. The illustration is a redrawing of Wu Youru's earlier depiction of courtesans eating Western food in the company of their maids (Figure 3.6), which had itself already served as a template for yet another image of courtesans and patrons enjoying a meal at Yipinxiang (Figure 3.5). In the *Nine-Tailed Fox* version, however, Hu sits not in the company of other courtesans, nor of respectable literati patrons, and she lacks the grace and poise that characterized the courtesans in the original. Instead, Hu Baoyu sits opposite the opera singer Huang Yueshan, wooing him, with one eye open and one eye closed, out in Yipinxiang on the inaugural eve of their love affair.[100] The courtesan culture that had once helped make Western food culture a feature of Shanghai urban life and a positive component of the idea of the city now made Western food into a marker of Shanghai life out of balance.

The Re-Domestification of Western Food as Tradition

The second wave of the reevaluation of Western food culture, which unfolded during the closing decades of the Qing period, dovetailed with the denigration of the image of the courtesan in print culture. This second wave grew out of a separate social and political context—the education reform movement of the late nineteenth and early twentieth centuries. This reform movement sought to create the first public education institutions for women in China, and in this regard, it anticipated some of the demands that intellectuals would soon make during the New Culture Movement in favor of establishing equal opportunities for men and women. The late-Qing movement, however, was much more conservative in character and must be understood at least in part as a response to the apparent dissolution of social order that Shanghai's courtesan culture typified. The reformers hoped that, by creating a new public profile for women's education, they would be able to provide women with the skills necessary for raising a family. In the interests of this reform program, they circulated images of respectable women that could compete with the image of the courtesan as a symbol of city life. The movement drew much of its inspiration from long-standing family ideals, but it also incorporated certain aspects of Western education, including food culture, into its curriculum for women's education. By the end of the movement, women would remain closely associated with Western food culture in Shanghai, but less as consumers and more as homemakers skilled in Western cookery and knowledgeable about the health benefits of Western foods.

For centuries in China, there had been schools for boys and men to help them prepare for the national civil service examinations, but women's education during the late imperial period took place largely at home, where fathers and mothers instructed their daughters in a wide range of skills, arts, and knowledge, from poetry and the classics to medicine, embroidery, and cooking.[101] Courtesans, by contrast, whose patrons expected them to be skilled in poetry, music, and performance, received much of their education in courtesan halls, although some certainly also drew on an education received at home. Christian missionaries and gentry reformers established schools for women in the mid- and late-nineteenth century, but the Qing rulers did not grant these efforts formal sanction until the beginning of the twentieth century. In 1907, Qing officials approved of schooling women in a curriculum of family affairs (*jiashi*) and household governance (*jiazheng*) to "assist their husbands" and "correct their sons."[102] Officials and gentry reformers had slightly different sets of concerns: the former viewed women's education as a means to promote obedience and loyalty, but the latter sought to "[divest] the lower classes of their 'backward' customs . . . and equip them with skills necessary for China to compete economically on the international stage."[103] These differences aside, the highly visible courtesan culture of the foreign settlements convinced both groups of the need to provide women with new kinds of educational opportunities.

Qing officials had not previously given much political consideration to the entertainment culture of the foreign settlements. This was partly because it developed in a territory over which they did not exercise political control. But neither officials nor gentry actually considered courtesan culture to constitute a social problem—indeed, they were both important constituencies of courtesan patrons. By the beginning of the twentieth century, however, prominent and outspoken intellectuals had identified the status of women in China as a barrier to political reform and nation-building, and they equated courtesan culture with prostitution.[104] In this new intellectual and political context, the foreign location and the extravagance of Shanghai's courtesan culture inspired political and social reformers to develop new ideas about the role of women and Western food culture in society.

There was no consensus reached among the various parties to the discourse on women's education in the early twentieth century, but reformers did not initially envision women's education as a route to professional life outside of the home. Zheng Guanying (1842–1923) urged that women be schooled in the performance of household tasks, such as embroidery, cooking, and budgeting, while Liang Qichao (1873–1929) argued that women should be educated in ways that would leave them morally fit for the task of raising future citizens and talented enough to become "producers" instead of simply "consumers" of wealth.[105] Wu Rulun (1840–1903), a prominent late Qing educator, helped channel these ideas into a tangible curriculum when he published *Home Governance* (Jiazhengxue), a translation from Japanese of the imperial household educator Shimoda Utako's 1893 two-volume work of the same name, *Kaseigaku*, with Shanghai's Society for Renewal (Zuoxinshe) publishing house.[106] On the one hand, *Home Governance* represented a new model of Westernization for food culture in Shanghai because Shimoda developed the format and content of her text by consulting Western models. Wu himself explained that the book represented what was "originally a branch of Western learning." On the other hand, Wu's preface to the Chinese translation indicates that he saw his reform efforts as ultimately conservative in nature, remarking, "The ancients who governed all under heaven first had to order their homes, [for] the home is the root of the kingdom."[107] This idea was a well-worn maxim from the *Great Learning*, a text that, like the *Doctrine of the Mean* cited in the *Entertainment* critique of Shanghai's *fancaiguan*, was counted among the "four books" that defined the heart of neo-Confucian orthodoxy.[108]

The general idea that a well-governed kingdom relied on a well-governed home thus had a long history in Chinese thought and letters, but Wu and Shimoda drew a novel connection between the welfare of the state and the nutritional quality of the food that people ate at home. As Shimoda herself wrote,

> If the home is ordered, the commandery and county will be calm. If the commandery and county are calm ... the kingdom will be ordered. Therefore, a kingdom's virtue and education springs from the virtue and education of the home. A kingdom's wealth is rooted in the home's economics. The citizen's health is based on home hygiene. . . . If all homes are effectively governed, then even if it was desired that the kingdom not be [well-] governed, it would not be possible.[109]

In addition to issuing such platitudes, Shimoda's text also contained one of the earliest systematic presentations of the principles of Western, or biomedical, nutrition in Chinese that was written for a lay audience. *Home Governance* thus helped define the parameters of a biomedical discourse that linked household diets to national salvation and national health. It began a process by which a specialized biomedical vocabulary was popularized as a branch of knowledge deemed especially important for women, on the pretext that women, as homemakers, were responsible for raising healthy families. Such concerns about national health were especially salient after the Sino-Japanese War, which suggested to many Chinese that Chinese bodies were weak compared with those of Westerners and Japanese. These links provided guiding principles for a new kind of commercial cookbook that, by putting forth competing representations of women as producers and homemakers, challenged reigning representations of women as urban consumers and entertainers.

Published collections of recipes were relatively rare in China before the twentieth century; commercially marketed collections, which were widespread during the Republican period, were probably unknown, except as minor components of much larger texts.[110] In both periods, however, cookbooks contained both recipes and representations of cultural values, and it seems that early-Republican cookbooks were modeled on Qing texts, such as Li Hua'nan's (*jinshi*, 1743) *Record of Xing Garden* (Xingyuan lu). What made Li's recipe collection a model of cultural values was not so much the content of the recipes, but the way in which Li's son, Li Tiaoyuan (1734–?), justified their publication. Tiaoyuan published the cookbook, which consisted of recipes that his father collected during a term in office in Zhejiang, as a tribute to his father's filial piety. As Li explained, "When my father was a student, he ate coarse foods, like vegetables and stews, without seeking comfort or repletion. However, when he served his . . . parents, he insisted on preparing delicacies."[111] The cookbook's recipes for delicacies and more common dishes derived their value from their link to Li's father's moral rectitude.[112]

Texts such as the *Record of Xing Garden* provided models for early-twentieth-century cookbook writers, who turned the format into a vehicle for the dissemination of cultural values and knowledge for women. There is no record of cookbooks written by or published for women specifically until the very end of the Qing. Recipes did circulate, however, in a realm of oral transmission among women, in the same manner as did knowledge regarding the arts of embroidery and other forms of "women's work" (*nügong*). Cooking was also valued as a publicly recognized skill, especially in southern China.[113] In the wake of campaigns for women's educational reform at the end of the Qing dynasty, however, many subjects of *nügong* were written down into instructional manuals, and cookbooks written by and for women were published in considerable numbers for the first time. The earliest of the cookbooks is Zeng Yi's (fl. 1890) *Home Cooking* (Zhongkui lu), first published in 1907.[114] Zeng's cookbook resembled the *Record of Xing Garden* in its use of the cookbook format for propagating normative cultural values. However, Zeng's particular emphasis on normative values for women distinguished her work and set new parameters for cookbook writing that shaped the circulation of recipes during the closing years of the Qing and the early Republican period.

Zeng signaled her emphasis on women by putting the term *zhongkui* in the title of her book. The term refers specifically to the handling of matters pertaining to food and drink in the home by women, and by extension the term came to mean, simply, "wife." Zeng elaborated on this idea in her preface, noting, "In the past, duckweed and pondweed were eulogized in the 'Guofeng,' and stews and soups were cooked by the new wife. Of all the virtuous and beautiful women of the past, not one was not skilled in cooking. Thus, all women should practice [cooking] prior to getting married."[115]

The passage contains two allusions. The eulogizing of duckweed and pondweed refers to the poem "Caiping," from the *Book of Odes*, and describes the picking of certain plants by women for food and ceremonial offerings.[116] The second allusion, to custom rather than classic, refers to the expectation that a new wife would prepare a meal for her in-laws on the third day of her marriage.[117] Zeng's cookbook thus reiterated long-standing ideals in a new form. Significantly, her recipes were largely for prepared foods, such as smoked meats and sauces, that were commonly sold on the marketplace, a focus that suggests the degree to which reformers sought to extricate women's participation in food culture from commercial activity.

Zeng limited the culinary repertoire of her *Home Cooking* to Chinese food, but her work provided a template for redefining Western food culture as a woman's responsibility in the home, rather than, as it had been known and represented earlier in Shanghai's history, as a form of entertainment to be undertaken in restaurants and courtesan houses. Shanghai's leading women's magazine, the *Ladies Journal* (Funü zazhi), ran a food and cooking column named after Zeng's book. Two new lengthy cookbooks appeared in 1917—Li Gong'er's *Family Recipes* (Jiating shipu) and Lu Shouqian's *Fundamentals of Cooking* (Pengren yiban)—and new titles were published at an average of more than one per year for the duration of the Republican period.[118] Recipes also appeared regularly in magazine columns, home economics texts, and as chapters in "daily life" (*richang shenghuo*) encyclopedias. Western recipes sometimes appear as an add-on to these collections—as something that women as homemakers should know in addition to the basic Chinese recipes—but several single-volume collections of Western cookery also appeared during these years, such as Li Gong'er's 1923 *Secrets of Western Cookery* (Xican pengren mijue).[119] Even cookbooks that lacked Western recipes communicated ideas about Western food culture in the form of nutritional charts and guidelines.

The two main messages that the authors of these texts sought to communicate were clear. The first message was stated perhaps most clearly in the 1918 *Precious Mirror for Household Affairs* (Jiashi shixi baojian), which noted, "The custom for banqueting in the West is for the housewife to prepare all of the dishes with her own hands, in order adequately to express her respect [for the guests]."[120] The second message, as stated in an article published in *Women's Times* (Funü shibao), was that eating was not for entertainment, but for health:

> People who write about eating have always attended to that which tastes good, without taking into consideration its potential benefit or harm to the body. That is, they mistakenly consider food only in terms of enjoyment. . . . It is essential to know the chemical properties of all foodstuffs, which must correspond to those of the human body, or be able to be absorbed into our body, to nourish our body's development. Then it can be called eating. Otherwise, even though it might consist of [the activity of] eating, it is no different than . . . stabbing oneself with a spear.[121]

The long history of dietetics in China provided many examples of how to eat in a healthy manner.[122] For these reformers, however, only Western food culture seems to have provided a viable framework and body of knowledge for discussing such issues.[123] Thus Lu Shouqian's *Fundamentals of Cooking* opened with a discussion of digestion and metabolism and closed with a "foodstuffs analysis chart" that provided the protein, fat, carbohydrate, fiber, and mineral content of basic foods. Lu included this material, she noted, "with the hope that all women take [from this] the essence, and thereby increase their knowledge of household affairs, and facilitate attaining the key to health. Therefore, it will not only be in the area of cooking that insights are obtained."[124]

These books and articles contained normative images of women and their engagement with Western food that differ markedly from the late-nineteenth-century images of Shanghai courtesans and Western food. Images of courtesans placed women prominently in urban settings, identifying them clearly as figures of the city, whether walking around the city streets, or riding in carriages on their way to meet with clients, often at *fancaiguan*.[125] As Figure 3.8 indicates, the cookbook images, by contrast, depict women inside the home, and as producers rather than consumers. The exception to this rule came in the form of images of the items women would need to purchase to cook, rather than eat, Western food, or descriptions of how to shop in a discerning manner. Thus, whereas courtesans were known to send their patrons out to purchase spring-bottom sofas and Western-style dinner tables, the new cookery literature provided shopping lists of such items as the *su-si guo* (sauce pan), *ercengguo* (double-boiler), *pai-ai ming* (pie pan), *bu-ding mo* (pudding mold), and *sai-li mo* (salad mold), and tips for how to pick out ingredients.[126] Strikingly, one text offered advice for purchasing beef that urged women to be careful to purchase only beef raised specifically as "genuine cattle beef" and not the product of slaughtered old agricultural oxen.[127]

The new literature also contained detailed instructions for holding Western banquets in the home. Such instructions had not circulated in print for courtesans, who learned how to eat Western food on the job, although instructions were, as discussed earlier, important for men. Now authors wrote these instructions specifically for women, modifying them to identify a place for the wife of the host among dinner party guests: "For a Western banquet the husband and wife sit at the two ends of the table and the guests sit on the two sides. The wife of the guest of honor sits to the right of the host, while the male guest of honor sits to the left of the wife. The wife of the secondary guest sits to the host's left, and the male secondary guest sits to the right of the host's wife."[128] This seating arrangement was completely different from that which prevailed among courtesans and their patrons during the late-Qing *fancaiguan* craze, when the dominant image of Western food was one of courtesans and patrons dining across the table from one another.

The commodity culture that developed in Shanghai during the Republican period, about which more will be said in the next two chapters, only heightened the sense of urgency with which reformers reiterated a connection between women and Western food in the home. The purveyors of nutritious Western food products pursued vigorous advertising campaigns depicting women as the providers of such items for their families.[129] For example, one advertisement for the Swiss import Ovalmaltine, a beverage made from wheat, milk, and

歐美家庭新食譜

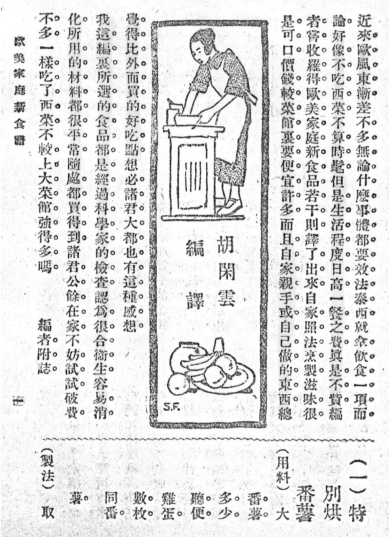

近來歐風東漸差不多無論什麼事體都要效法泰西就拿飲食一項而論妤像不吃西菜不算時髦但是生活程度日高一餐之費眞是不贊編者嘗收羅得歐美家庭新食品若干則譯了出來自家照法烹製滋味很是可口價錢較菜館裏要便宜許多而且自家親手或自己做的東西總覺得比外面買的好吃點想必諸君大都也有這種感想我這編裏所選的食品都是經過科學家的檢查認爲很合衛生容易消化所用的材料都很平常隨處都買得到諸君公餘在家不妨試試破費不多一樣吃了西菜不較上大菜館強得多嗎

編者附誌

胡閑雲 編譯

S.F.

歐美家庭新食譜

（一）特別烘番薯大

（用料）
番薯。多少。聽便。
雞蛋。數枚。同番薯。

（製法）取薯。

Figure 3.8 Euro-American Family Cookbook, from *Jiating* (*Home Companion*)

SOURCE: *Jiating*, Issue 4 (1923).

eggs, referred to the product as the "four season supplement" and "a family's best enriching and supplementing beverage." The advertisement contained a picture of a family embodying the traditional Chinese family ideal of having three generations under one roof. The grandfather, wearing a Chinese cap and gown, is helping the youngest boy drink a hot glass of the beverage, while the grandmother looks at them fondly, holding a cup of her own. The daughter sips her glass carefully at the table next to her father, who also holds a glass, while another son clamors for a glass from his mother. Significantly, the mother is dressed in a fashionable cheongsam, suggesting that broader urban trends in material culture could be followed, provided women did not lose sight of their purported role in the home.[130] Women thus remained important symbols of Western food in Shanghai, but less as consumers, and more as homemakers knowledgeable about the benefits of Western food. During the early twentieth century, images of women gradually disappear from mainstream representations of the Western restaurant scene, only to reappear in images of home.[131]

4 "Where the Five Directions Come Together"

Regional Foodways, the Nation, and
Consumer Culture in Republican Shanghai

ON SEPTEMBER 26, 1911, on the eve of the Nationalist Revolution that overthrew the ruling Qing dynasty, Shanghai's *Shibao* newspaper published the celebratory "Song of Shanghai's Famous Foodstuffs" (Shanghai zhuming shipin ge).[1] The lyrics identified the famous foodstuffs available in the city and named the shops and vendors where the finest preparation of each item could be purchased. There were the mutton noodles of Xiandelou, and the Western food of Yijiachun; Jinhua ham at Wanyouquan, and the dried "southern goods" of Shaowansheng; Cantonese midnight snacks at Xinghualou, and Suzhou-style stewed pork at Lugaojian. Liang Village chestnuts (from the Fangshang district of Beijing) could be found on every street corner, and Shaoxing wine was best at Yanmaoyuan and Wangbaohe. Even if, as the lyricist allowed, Shanghai's soup dumplings were still only second best to those prepared at Suzhou's Lidingxing dumpling house, readers of the song would have taken comfort in knowing that the city was also home to its own special variety of grilled pork buns, *xiaomantou*. Shanghai, the song indicated, had come a long way from the days when it could still be called a minor city "in a corner by the sea," as Wang Tao had dubbed Shanghai in his guidebooks to the Shanghai demimonde. Indeed, the song was a celebration of Shanghai's definitive status as a city "where the five directions come together" (*wufang zachu*).

The "Song of Shanghai's Famous Foodstuffs" testified to the transformation of Shanghai during the second half of the nineteenth century, during which time the city became a meeting place of people and things from all over the Chinese realm and from several parts of the wider world. Shanghai had a long history of interregional trade before becoming an international treaty port in 1842. Its reputation as a place famous for distinctive foods, however, derived from local crops and products. Ming and Qing city residents, as discussed in Chapter One, had not considered the decidedly local dimension of Shanghai's pre-treaty-port specialty foods as constitutive of a provincial status. But from the standpoint of the beginning of the twentieth century, Shanghai was now a part of a very different kind of world. No longer did the city derive its cosmopolitan status from a link to a cosmos that conferred on the city and its soil a set of distinct "topographical advantages." Shanghai's advantages were now understood to be its favorable geographic location at the mouth of the Yangtze River, which linked the city to the country's interior and to the wider transoceanic world. During the nineteenth century, new commercial opportunities made possible by this location, among other more incidental factors, had attracted merchants from all over the country and from many different parts of the world. All had brought with them the specialty foods and foodways of their native places, endowing the city with an especially diverse urban food culture. New modes of transportation facilitated this process, turning Shanghai into a national and international culinary marketplace, where foods from afar, as Ge Yuanxu noted in his Shanghai travelogue, could be "eaten out of season."[2]

Shanghai's status as a diverse culinary marketplace was especially evident in the city's restaurant industry. Before Shanghai became a treaty port, it had a small number of restaurants that catered to local palates and to the native-place taste preferences of sojourning merchants. During the second half of the nineteenth century, however, the city became famous for its cosmopolitan restaurant industry. The city's Western restaurants further cemented Shanghai's status as the forerunner of culinary internationalism in China. Not all city residents were proud of what these Western restaurants revealed about urban culture, but the early reference to Western food in the first stanza of the "Song of Shanghai's Famous Foodstuffs" indicates that Western food remained, as of 1911, an important component of the idea of Shanghai. The lone mention of Yijiachun, however, also hints at the burgeoning interest in the varieties of regional Chinese foodways and specialty foodstuffs that would soon eclipse the late-Qing craze for Western food. Indeed, this interest in varieties of regional Chinese foods would dominate Republican-era discourse on food culture in the city. The song itself even struck a strident nationalist tone when it claimed that China's Tai Feng canned goods were superior to products imported from abroad.

Several factors animated this renewed appreciation of regional Chinese food culture, including political fragmentation on local and national levels, the intensification of the consumer commodity culture that had developed in Shanghai during the late Qing, and the apparent Westernization of Shanghai intellectual and cultural life. Chinese exercised very little consistent formal political power in Shanghai during the early Republican period.[3] Chinese political influence in the foreign settlements also waned considerably during these years.[4] Shanghai did not have a powerful Chinese-run municipal government with a reasonable chance of maintaining order and providing social services until after the Northern Expedition (1926–28). This joint Nationalist and Communist Party military campaign to unite China brought Chiang Kai-shek's Guangdong-based Nationalist Party to power in the new national capital in nearby Nanjing. The Northern Expedition also paved the way for the establishment of the new Municipal Government of Greater Shanghai. Even that government, however, presided over only parts of the city, while the rest remained under foreign jurisdiction.

The city's commodity culture also became more pervasive and extensive during the Republican period, creating markets for food culture but also problems that animated public discourse on food in new ways. The rising cost of living became a daily concern and topic of public conversation. Even the price of rice, arguably the city's most inelastic commodity, had few controls. City residents had begun tracking rice prices during the closing decades of the Qing, posting prices regularly in the city's leading newspaper, *Shenbao*.[5] Urban guidebooks, a twentieth-century analogue of the travelogues of the late nineteenth century, increasingly identified not just the many wonders of the city, but also how much life in the city cost, and how much more it cost now than before. There was a pervasive sense that all forms of food—staples, specialty products, and even regional restaurant fare—which were ideally the building blocks of community, were instead on the verge of becoming nothing more than commodities. Various government agencies in Republican Shanghai put forth solutions to these problems, but a powerful state agency would not confront the problem that Shanghai's consumer society raised for food culture in a systematic way until the founding of the People's Republic of China in 1949. Meanwhile, city residents were left largely on their own to develop distinct consumer strategies.

Intellectually and culturally, the city was also Westernizing in significant ways. The Revolution of 1911 had promised to replace China's traditional imperial political system with a constitutional republic based on Western models of political organization. But the political vacuum that followed the fall of the Qing dynasty raised for many the question of how such a new political entity could be constituted. The iconoclastic New Culture Movement that rejected the Confucian tradition in favor of Western models of science and democracy promised to create a new culture for China that could support a new kind of political system. And even though the Treaty of Versailles (1920) and the May 30th Incident (1925) dampened unrestrained Chinese enthusiasm for Western thought and culture, foreign models of cultural and political reform remained more influential than the many varieties of neo-traditionalist alternatives, even those, such as the New Life Movement, that received strenuous government support. Moreover, Western material culture in Shanghai seemed to have become more pervasive than ever—in deco architecture and home décor, men's and women's fashions, and new modes of transportation, such as automobiles and electric trams. Trends in art, literature, music, and cinema unfolded in a close dialogue with Western models. Food discourses of a non-culinary nature, as in the field of nutrition, also took a decisive Western turn. Building on the foundation established by late-Qing reformers, the new state endorsed Western medicine, and even incorporated biomedical nutritional categories into its studies of the city's food problems. Even though Chinese engagement with Western ideology, material culture, art, and medicine often produced work with a distinctive local style, these local elaborations still read as a form of "Westernization" to onlookers.

The culinary front, by contrast, was another matter. The Republican period in Shanghai witnessed an unprecedented use of regional Chinese food culture for shoring up a sense of national unity and culture relative to the West. Shanghai underwent a regional Chinese cuisine renaissance that began in the very early years of the Republican period and lasted through the Nanjing Decade (1928–37). The city's already diverse restaurant industry became even more diverse. More importantly, city residents put regional food culture to powerful new uses, to address problems arising from the city's consumer culture, and to reckon with the forms of political fragmentation taking place at local and national levels. City residents did not all agree about what it meant to be Chinese, let alone Chinese and living in foreign settlements, but food clearly provided important anchors of cultural continuity.

Discourse on food as regional and national culture in Republican Shanghai thus provides many clues to the range of solutions that different constituencies of the urban community generated in response to the problems of the day. Commercial guidebooks, for example, detailed the rich diversity of food culture that Shanghai's purveyors of regional food provided. City residents related their own observations and experiences of urban food culture in personal essays, attributing quite different, often incompatible, meanings to the varieties of regional Chinese culture available in the city. Some celebrated the city, others criticized it, and yet others waxed poetic about ideal olden days. Consumer guidebooks, such as Wang Dingjiu's *Keys to Shanghai* (Shanghai menjing) and *Shanghai Advisor* (Shanghai guwen), built on all of these models and offered two kinds of solutions.[6] First, Wang's writings on food provided both an introduction and overview of the city's many different kinds of regional restaurants, as well as a template for integrating China's many regional cultures into a coherent framework. Second, Wang also provided his readers with a consumer strategy for navigating the commodification of regional food culture that he and other city residents both celebrated and bemoaned.

A Renaissance of Regional Food Consciousness

The renaissance in regional Chinese food consciousness during the early years of the Republic of China is evident in commercial guidebooks, memoir literature, and popular verse such as the "Song of Famous Shanghai Foodstuffs." The song celebrated the foodstuffs that had become famous in the city during the late Qing, but the renaissance also consisted of new developments in Shanghai food culture, and in restaurant culture in particular, during the first decade of the Republican period. During this decade, the city's regional restaurant industry became even more diverse than it had been during the closing decades of the Qing.

This growing diversity was especially evident to natives of the city, for whom the new developments made even the city's former culinary diversity seem to pale in comparison. According to Liu Yanong, whose childhood memories of the Sanpailou dumpling shop were discussed in Chapter Two, during the closing years of the Qing, "Other than Shanghai restaurants, there were only Beijing, Suzhou, Anhui, and Ningbo establishments; Sichuanese, Hunanese, Fujianese, and Cantonese [restaurants] were not yet in fashion." However, things changed soon thereafter, and "with each passing day, the tastes of each province became available."[7] Writer and editor Yan Duhe (Yan Zhen, 1889–1968) made a similar observation, offering in addition an explanation for the change:

> In the past there were only four kinds of restaurants in Shanghai: Suzhou . . . Beijing, Cantonese, and Zhenjiang. Since the Revolution, notables, politicians,

and ministers of the previous dynasty have all settled here, and as a result there was a great wave of epicureanism. The former restaurants were clearly incapable of satisfying the appetites of such people, and so Fujian and Sichuan restaurants stepped in and flourished. Now Fujian and Sichuan cuisine prospers more and more with each passing day and have taken tables away from Beijing and Suzhou cuisine.[8]

Although Yan and Liu held slightly different perspectives on the outstanding features of the restaurant industry before the Revolution of 1911, they agreed that the industry had became increasingly diverse and that customers new and old were eager for fresh and different regional styles of cooking.

The diversification and renewed interest in regional Chinese cooking styles in Shanghai is also registered in different editions of the Commercial Press' *Guide to Shanghai* (Shanghai zhinan), the most important of the city's early-twentieth-century commercial directories. The first edition, published in 1909, in the wake of the late-Qing Western food craze, characterized the city's restaurant industry in the following terms: "The restaurants in Shanghai are as numerous as the trees in a forest. Although the dishes [they serve] are varied, they may be divided simply into Chinese and Western styles. Whether one speaks of Chinese or Western [restaurants], they differ in name, differ in price, and also differ in terms of the taste in which they excel."[9]

The 1909 *Guide* acknowledged that both the Chinese and Western restaurant sectors were diverse. It even attributed a regional provenance, albeit in small print, to each of the Chinese restaurants for which it provided an address. The bulk of the entry, however, consisted of a transcription of the menus of only two restaurants, the Cantonese Xinghualou, and the Lingnanlou *fancaiguan*, suggesting that the impulse to illustrate differences between Chinese and Western-style foodways eclipsed any interest in clearly identifying the ways in which Chinese cooking styles "differ in terms of the taste in which they excel." In contrast, the 1912 edition highlighted the regional character of the city's food offerings, beginning its entry on restaurants as follows: "Restaurants are divided into Beijing restaurants, Nanjing restaurants, Suzhou restaurants, Zhenjiang-Yangzhou restaurants, Anhui restaurants, Ningbo restaurants, Guangdong restaurants, Fujian restaurants, Sichuan restaurants, and Sectarian [*Jiaomen*, or Muslim] restaurants. For fresh seafood, the most frequented are Fujian, Guangdong, and Ningbo restaurants. In terms of price, Sichuan and Fujian restaurants are the most expensive, while Beijing and

Anhui restaurants are the cheapest."[10] The 1912 edition thus noted that different sectors of the city's restaurant industry specialized in certain kinds of dishes, such as seafood, or even Halal cooking.

These two editions of the *Guide to Shanghai* also register the beginning of a shift in what might be called the commodification of restaurant food. In its discussion of the Chinese restaurant sector, the 1909 *Guide* emphasized different grades of banquets, which it noted ranged in price from one to ten *yuan*, and indicated how many plates and food items came with each grade.[11] The 1909 edition thus clearly identified the banquet grade as the primary object for distinguishing restaurant food offerings.[12] This emphasis on banquet grades contrasts with the emphasis of the 1912 edition, which shifts the focus from differences in banquet price grades to those of regional style, indicating that city residents had begun to associate high and low prices not so much with the banquet grades typical of all restaurants, but with different kinds of cuisine. The 1912 edition further highlighted the regional character of other kinds of food service venues, such as Cantonese night markets and *fandian*—smaller, less-expensive restaurants that served either Suzhou, Sichuan, Shandong, or Tianjin styles of cooking.[13] In a few short years, the guide had shifted its emphasis from the banquet as the primary commodity form of food to regional cuisine itself.

The 1912 guide also devoted far more space to its description of regional Chinese cuisine than it did to Western food. This contrasts starkly with the 1909 guide, which allocated roughly the same amount of space to each branch of the industry. After noting that the Western restaurant branch was itself divided into Chinese-, Western-, and Japanese-run sectors, the 1912 guide provided only a short explanation of the structure of the Western meal, emphasizing the rituals of eating rather than the food itself (the 1909 edition had provided, in contrast, a detailed list of the food offerings of the Lingnanlou *fancaiguan*). The 1912 guide also provided a lengthy and meticulous overview of even the city's low-end Chinese food offerings, as illustrated by the following description of Shanghai's noodle shops:

> Noodle shops sell fish noodles, vinegar fish noodles, pork noodles, shrimp noodles, ham noodles, turkey noodles, *guomian* noodles, *mantou*, and soup dumplings. The best is Qicuilou on Jixiang Street. The best mutton noodles are at Xiandelou and Siruchun on Shandong Street. Pure noodles are best at Liuluxuan at the City God Temple in the walled city. Fried noodle shops have fried noodles, fried rice cake, fried rice noodles, and soup noodles. Wonton shops

have wontons, boiled dumplings, *shaomai*, spring rolls, soup dumplings, and rice-flour dumplings. The best are Siruchun, Jinshuitian, Sishixin, and Juxing-chun on Fuzhou Road.[14]

In addition to these year-round foods, the 1912 edition further noted a number of the city's lower-end, seasonal Chinese specialties, such as the summertime dishes of lotus root and candied taro. It provided yet more tips for punctuating different times of the day with appropriate regional snack foods: Zhenji-ang-Yangzhou restaurants specialized in noodles and sweet and sour cakes and breads for breakfast; Cantonese tea shops offered steamed dumplings, boiled dumplings, and *shaomai* in the afternoon; and Cantonese midnight snack shops served sweetened almond soup (*xingrencha*) and lotus seed por-ridge at night.[15]

The amount of detail city guides provided continued to grow during the Republican period. A little more than a decade later, the 1925 *Shanghai Precious Mirror* (Shanghai baojian), for example, provided such detailed listings of res-taurant offerings that it had to organize the material into charts. It listed the names of forty-one dishes served at the city's Sichuan restaurants, and forty-three served at Fujian restaurants, including regular offerings and seasonal specialties from spring, summer, autumn, and winter. Even the shorter lists provided for the Cantonese and Anhui branches, which contained eighteen and fifteen items respectively, provided enough details for readers to develop a coherent idea of the characteristics and flavors of each regional cuisine and learn the names of the more famous dishes of each.[16] The names of the dishes listed in the *Precious Mirror*'s charts were reprinted in many other Shanghai guides and publications, including the 1926 enlarged and revised edition of the Commercial Press' *Guide to Shanghai* and the 1928 daily-life handbook *Common Knowledge* (Changshi daquan). This repetition makes it hard to trace changes in the food offerings of these restaurants over time, but it provided a degree of continuity to the textual representation of Chinese regional cuisine in Shanghai, and it helped make the city's regional restaurant offerings into "common knowledge."[17]

Commercial guidebooks also continued to identify the value that city residents placed on different varieties of regional cuisine. The *Precious Mirror* listed more dishes for some sectors of the restaurant trade than others, and these differences reflected the relative status and cost of each branch of the industry. The *Precious Mirror* noted that Sichuan restaurants were remarkable for their "refined cooking" and "vast scale," whereas Fujian cuisine was "equally matched with Sichuan cuisine; the cooking is superb, and the average person enjoys eating it." In contrast, Cantonese food did not fare so well—at least not "authentic Cantonese food," which, unlike Cantonese night market food, the guidebook suggested, "the people of other provinces do not like to eat."[18] Thus, according to the *Precious Mirror*, some regional branches of the industry had a universal appeal, but others struck non-fellow provincials as having a decidedly more limited audience.

Regional Food Culture and the City: Three Views

During the early years of the Republican period, the diverse regional food offerings that urban guidebooks described and celebrated became a distinguishing feature of the idea of Shanghai as a place. Not surprisingly, therefore, regional food culture was also key to the way Shanghai residents experienced the city. Three distinctive essays on food culture published in Shanghai during these years provide examples of the different ways that individuals expressed their relationship to the city. Yan Duhe's "Comparison of Shanghai Restaurants," published in 1923, illustrates the efforts of an urban elite to gain and communicate a sense of mastery over the city. Ye Shengtao's "Lotus Root and Water Shield," published the same year, suggests that less affluent city residents, who could not afford to eat in the expensive restaurants that Yan frequented, might express their relationship to the city by writing about regional foodstuffs. Ye's essay also illustrates that, for newcomers to the city, regional food culture continued to function as a repository of native-place sentiment, even as other city residents, like Yan, took great pleasure in exploring the food culture of non-fellow provincials. Finally, Chen Boxi's entries on Shanghai food culture in his 1924 *Compendium of Shanghai Anecdotes* illustrate that, as Shanghai underwent rapid social change, food culture emerged as an important arena for shoring up a sense of local cultural continuity.

Yan Duhe, Culinary Flaneur

Yan Duhe was one of the most enthusiastic observers of Shanghai food culture during the early Republican period. Born in 1888 into a relatively illustrious family (he was the grandnephew of a Hanlin academician), Yan was well-placed to take advantage of Shanghai's high-end restaurant culture. His native place was in Tongxiang, Zhejiang Province, approximately 130 kilometers to Shanghai's southwest, but he was born in Shanghai, where his early education in the

Chinese classics earned him a *xiucai* degree by the age of fifteen. Yan then entered the Munitions Academy of the Jiangnan Arsenal and eventually took up English and science at the Interpreters' College, becoming equally well-versed in Chinese and Western scholarly traditions.[19]

Yan belonged to a sizable cohort of urban elite men who dined in a wide variety of restaurants, and who considered their knowledge of the differences among the regional branches of the restaurant industry to be a measure of urban savoir faire. Banqueting was a long-standing feature of Chinese food culture, and when restaurant culture blossomed in Shanghai during the second half of the nineteenth century, the art of hosting banquets became a key component of elite status. As discussed in previous chapters, the ability to pull together impromptu dinner parties was essential for navigating the late-nineteenth-century Shanghai demimonde, both to establish commercial relationships with other male patrons, and for presenting oneself as a man worthy of being loved by the city's most sought-after courtesans. What was new to Shanghai banquet culture in the early Republican period was the way that men such as Yan took advantage of the proliferation of regional cuisine in Shanghai to demonstrate their understanding of Shanghai's ever-changing urban landscape. Men like Yan created new badges of distinction, by making it important to know what kind of food to eat on what occasion and where to eat it.

Even though elite status now demanded that one eat widely across native-place lines, individuals of course still had personal regional food preferences. It is striking, however, just how closely Yan's personal preferences correlated with the ranking of regional cooking styles in Shanghai guidebooks:

> If I were to state my preferences generally, then Sichuan cuisine would rank highest, Fujian cuisine second, and Beijing cuisine after that. Suzhou and Zhenjiang cuisine are common in comparison and do not stand out. Cantonese cuisine is only for snacking on: a serving of night market fare, or a bowl of congee with duck, eaten occasionally when hungry at night, also has a distinctive flavor. But for banquet fare I do not dare commend it, although a Cantonese person eating it might consider it first rate. Thus, outstanding and base [aspects] of cuisine must be addressed on a regional basis, otherwise it wouldn't be fair.[20]

Yan's remarks indicate, on the one hand, that regular restaurant-goers sampled the cuisine of different parts of China, and developed a working sense of a hierarchy of regional cuisine. Conversely, although there might be limits to what non-fellow provincials could appreciate, it was nonetheless important to identify unique dishes that distinguished even the weaker branches of the industry. Among these dishes, Yan counted the shark's fin prepared in certain Suzhou restaurants, which he claimed were the only establishments in the entire city where this item was prepared appropriately (despite the otherwise "common" character of this sector more generally), and the cured and molded pork shank with julienne of pressed tofu served in Zhenjiang restaurants, for which he would endure even the "bad habits" of Zhenjiang waiters.[21]

Distinction came from being a discerning and persevering eater, as well as from knowing where and when to each in what establishment. During the early years of the Republic, Sichuan restaurants were the city's most exclusive, a distinction they first earned in 1912. As Yan notes, "The pioneer of Sichuan cuisine in Shanghai was Zuiou, where the food was delicious and the price unusually high. During the first and second year of the Republic, if you didn't banquet at Zuiou, you couldn't be considered a wealthy person."[22] Zuiou's exclusiveness may have done wonders for the image of its customers, but the high prices were also the restaurant's undoing, for it was unable to attract enough customers to stay in business. Still, six new Sichuan restaurants followed in Zuiou's wake, and each made an effort to become the next most important place to eat. Douyichu did so well on Hankou Road as a one-bay shop front operation specializing in snack food that it eventually expanded into a three-bay restaurant with a garden for outdoor seating in summertime. Such seating was rare, if not unprecedented, in Shanghai, but from Yan's perspective, it came at a cost, for "from the standpoint of the cooking, [the larger operation] wasn't as good as its Hankou Road days." That left either Taolechun for snacks; Meili, where "it helps if you have an insider invite you, for if you're an unfamiliar customer, the food is only so-so"; the Dayalou, a former Zhenjiang cuisine restaurant that changed its regional suit to cash in on the Sichuan cuisine cachet; or the Xiuxian Villa, the reigning Sichuan restaurant at the time of Yan's writing, where the cooking "adopted an original approach" and developed an unusual dish of winter melon and cream.[23]

Yan further demonstrated his mastery of the regional restaurant industry by explaining how restaurants acquired their names, who ate where, and how to order different kinds of regional fare. Fujian establishments, like those serving Sichuan fare, were relative newcomers to the Shanghai restaurant scene, but they also established themselves quickly. The pioneering Xiaoyoutian, or "Little Piece of Heaven," took its name from a line in a poem written by the educator, artist, and Daoist Li Meian (Li Ruiqing, 1867–1920), and the choice set an industry precedent. The Bieyoutian, or "Another Piece of Heaven," opened next, when a constituent of the Xiaoyoutian broke off and established the "other" (*bie*) "youtian" restaurant. Then came Zhongyoutian, or "Chinese Piece of Heaven," the cramped, latecomer to the scene, which nonetheless managed to steal a fair share of Xiaoyoutian business. Japanese residents in Shanghai were especially fond of Fujian cooking, and Zhongyoutian opened up on North Sichuan Road, considerably closer to the Japanese community than Xiaoyoutian. Yan knew this because he lived nearby and was a Zhongyoutian regular himself. As a frequent Fujian restaurant-goer, Yan also understood how important it was to order only set menus in Fujian establishments. Assuring his readers that "any experienced eater is sure to know that I'm not mistaken in this regard," he complained about having had to sit through a Xiaoyoutian meal for which his incompetent host had ordered five or six dishes à la carte. The meal was quite expensive, but none of the dishes was a specialty, and none was worth eating.[24]

Beijing restaurants, Yan reported, were somewhat less subject to trends than were Sichuan and Fujian establishments. This meant two things: first, that a place like Yaxuyuan, the Beijing establishment with the "oldest credentials" could "still attract its regular customers," and second, that choosing a Beijing restaurant was less about going to the newest establishment than about finding the place the served the best kind of Beijing food the restaurant-goer wanted to eat: "Snacks are best at the Yuebinglou. For banquet fare, Tongxinglou is recommended as inexpensive and delicious." Still, these establishments were important places to be seen at, and business at the Tongxinglou was apparently so good that, "When the evening lanterns are lit, the dandies and fops all show up, and the latecomers often regret missing out." Beijing restaurants were also haunts for the city's actors, "who banqueted at the Huibinlou nine times out of ten." It was therefore in the interest of would-be patrons to dine there in the company of a theater world companion, for the Huibinlou practiced subtle discrimination against customers it perceived as outsiders, and without an inside connection, the meal would "inevitably be substandard."[25]

Yan's mastery of Shanghai's regional restaurant scene included knowing about the more prestigious branches and establishments of the industry, and about how to make judicious and enterprising use of those sectors that he considered to be less remarkable. Suzhou restaurants, he explained, were appropriate for certain conventional purposes, since "their banquet prices were inexpensive and the interiors spacious; so when people have a wedding to celebrate or are hosting a big banquet with tens of tables, they usually enjoy going to one of these."[26] Suzhou and Zhenjiang restaurants both had a few special dishes, as noted earlier, but the latter were apparently not hospitable to non-Zhenjiang fellow-provincials. Shi Jiqun, the managing editor of *Red Magazine* (Hong zazhi), the magazine in which Yan published his restaurant musings, made this point by interjecting his own opinion on Shanghai restaurant food into Yan's essay. Shi was especially fond of Zhenjiang pork shank and steamed buns, but found the attitude of the waiters so off-putting that he stopped going out for Zhenjiang food. The problem, according to Yan, was that the waiters in Zhenjiang restaurants were notorious for their "bad temperament" (*xiqi*). Yan's solution for the determined eater—to work in a little Zhenjiang dialect, which would earn the quality of service granted to regulars—suggests that Zhenjiang restaurateurs were more protective of their native place constituencies than were those of restaurants serving other regional cuisines. Why this would have been the case is not clear, but their reluctance to serve non-fellow provincials suggests that they were reluctant participants in the commodity culture of Shanghai's regional restaurant industry and would have been happier serving only fellow Zhenjiang sojourners in Shanghai.

For Cantonese cuisine, Yan was less determined to make such efforts, although he remained eager to establish his credentials as a discriminating eater by explaining what was wrong with Cantonese restaurant fare, deriding small and large Cantonese establishments alike. The former, which seemed to be located "everywhere," served food that was so cheap it was "almost not worth recording," and the latter were "so indistinguishable that it was impossible to determine which [establishment] was better and which worse." He did make an exception, however, for the Xinghualou, which he explained had the "oldest credentials," suggesting that the age of an establishment in and of itself could be an important component of a restaurant's value. Yan attributed the lack of appeal of Cantonese restaurants to what he considered to be the main defect of Cantonese cooking: "It's for looking at but not for eating," for even though it was "colorful in appearance, no matter what the dish is, there's only one flavor, and it makes for an uninspiring meal." Rumor had it, however, that there was a new Cantonese restaurant worth trying, Weiya, at the intersection of North Sichuan Road and Chongming Road, in the heart of the city's largest Cantonese community. It was small, but friends had recommended it to him several times; he just hadn't eaten there yet himself.

Yan's essay sheds light on an elite man's engagement with the commodification of regional cuisine in the city. The *Guide to Shanghai* and the *Shanghai*

Precious Mirror celebrated the rich variety of regional Chinese food available in Shanghai and provided their readers with clues to the value placed on each variety of regional cuisine. Yan's essay contributed to that process by glorifying the act of eating, the art of being seen eating, and the importance of making it known to all that one was good at eating. Yan knew where to eat, what to order, and what accounted for the quality of food, and although he could be quite critical in his assessments of certain branches of the industry, he was also concerned to present an image of himself as a "fair" judge of good and bad. The *Shanghai Precious Mirror* may have observed that Cantonese restaurant food was not popular among non-fellow provincials, but Yan took such observations one step further, by making the ability to issue such judgments, and to issue them fairly, a badge of personal distinction and character.

Not all readers, however, agreed with the judgments Yan made in this public record of his insight and experience. Taking issue with Yan's derisive comments about Suzhou restaurants, Shi Jiqun objected that, "Duhe's remarks seem biased toward the north part of the city. Considering what I know, Nanshi still has the Dapulou and the Dajilou, where the cooking is still not bad."[27] Shi thus established his own credentials as an experienced eater, by identifying a blind spot in Yan's perspective on the urban landscape. According to Shi, Yan unnecessarily favored establishments in the more prosperous International Settlement, and thereby lost sight of opportunities for fine dining in parts of the city that a status-conscious figure might overlook, but that a true gourmet would know about.

Ye Shengtao, Culinary Nostalgia as Cultural Critique

In his wistful but piercing essay on his favorite hometown foodstuffs, "Lotus Root and Water Shield" (Ou yu chuncai), Ye Shengtao made explicit what remained only implicit in Shi's interjection into Yan's essay. Although urban elites such as Yan took advantage of Shanghai's diverse restaurant industry for the pleasures, prestige, and sense of self it might provide for the city's more affluent residents, less wealthy individuals like Ye elaborated an image of a pure regional food culture to criticize aspects of the city's consumer culture that underlay the restaurant industry that Yan celebrated. Ye, whose father was a landlord's bookkeeper, was born in 1894 into a considerably less illustrious family than was Yan. Although Ye eventually emerged as a major May Fourth intellectual, editor, and educator, he struggled financially through much of the 1920s.[28] A man of many talents, he is best known as a participant in two key May Fourth institutions—

the New Tide Society, a Beijing University student organization, and the Association for Literary Studies, which Ye cofounded with Mao Dun (1896–1981) and Zhang Zhenduo (1898–1958) to advocate for realism and reject art for art's sake. In 1930, Ye became the editor of Kaiming Press, the most important publisher of textbooks during the second half of the Republican period. However, Ye's writing career reflects an equally strong commitment to more obviously "traditional" forms of Chinese culture. He published classical Chinese novels in *Saturday Magazine* (Libailiu), and he wrote widely about daily life and local customs.[29] This interest in local customs infused Ye's writings about food.

Ye's schooling and professional obligations demanded a peripatetic lifestyle, and his travels raised his awareness about the distinctiveness of regional cultures in China. He first came to Shanghai in 1915 to teach at the Commercial Press' Shanggong Primary School. Then, from 1917 to 1922, in between trips to Beijing during the early days of the May Fourth Movement, he taught high school in Luzhi Township on the outskirts of Suzhou, before finally settling in Shanghai as an editor for the Commercial Press. From Shanghai, Ye would write most longingly for Suzhou culture, as in his 1935 essay "Guojie," in which he regretted that his children, having grown up in Shanghai, were unable to understand the importance of the title term to Suzhou people of his father's and uncle's generation. For the elders, "*guojie*" was a special way of referring to "ancestor worship" (*jizu*); to his children, however, it meant little more than what it meant to other Chinese, an occasion when "people buy a lot of food and wine and everybody has a big meal for the holiday."[30] The essay registers Ye's fear that long-term residency away from one's native place eroded native-place culture and sentiment.

Ye had previously discussed the hazards of leaving one's native place in "Lotus Root and Water Shield." Written and published the same year as Yan Duhe's "Comparison of Shanghai Restaurants," Ye's essay, through a nostalgic representation of the food culture of his native Suzhou, cast a dark eye on the city that Yan's essay celebrated. "Lotus Root and Water Shield" indicates that Shanghai food culture not only inspired enthusiasm but also induced a hunger for certain specialty foodstuffs that were not easily obtained in the city. By writing about the two foodstuffs that most typified the food culture of his native place, Ye identified a number of social problems particular to Shanghai and brought to light some of the difficulties sojourners of modest means faced in the city.

Although Yan described the food culture of Shanghai itself, Ye's experience with Suzhou food culture in Shanghai drew him out of the city. Ye related this experience in a remarkably "Proustian" manner. Describing a rare opportunity to eat lotus root in Shanghai, he notes: "Nibbling on a thin slice of lotus root while drinking with friends, I suddenly missed my home town." The taste of the lotus root conjured scenes from Ye's childhood, especially of the village men and women who harvested the lotus roots and brought them into town to sell. The men were "the picture of health," with "bulging bare arms and calves" and "tall, erect torsos"; the women—barefoot and dressed in short, ramie skirts, their heads wrapped in white scarves with a green flower print—also had a "unique kind of healthy and graceful bearing." These men and women, he recalled, walked by his house daily, "shouldering buckets filled with long, fresh, and tender jade-colored roots," which they "washed carefully in the pools where the lotus root grows, along the banks of the small, winding river outside the city." The cleanliness of the roots indicated just how seriously they took their work, for they treated the roots as if they were "delicacies to be presented for a tasting" or "subject matter for an early morning still-life." Stopping to rest en route to town, the harvesters might "gnaw on an overripe root or a relatively withered seed," but they saved the best for passers-by—a young girl in a red shirt or a "white-haired grandpa"—who stopped to make a purchase. And so the "mild sweet flavor was carried into every household, day in and day out, until deep into autumn, when leaves had fallen."[31]

The image of the fallen leaves of late autumn, which marked the end of the lotus root season back home, reminded Ye of Shanghai, which he describes in the next part of the essay, contrasting the city with his home town:

> Here in Shanghai, lotus root is practically a delicacy. It is probably shipped in from my home town, only not in large quantities, so naturally those toadying teahouse proprietors who cater to wealthy young dandies and pot-bellied merchants make off with the bulk of it, while the remainder goes to the larger fruit stands, where it sits between Jinshan apples and mangos from Luzon, awaiting the highest bidder. True, they're sold on the streets too, but those roots are as thin as the arms and legs of beggars, and they taste as bitter as an unripe persimmon . . . . And so except for this one time, we had no lotus root to eat this year. This root wasn't one that we bought; our neighbors gave it to us to eat. Only they didn't buy it either; a relative from home brought it to them.[32]

With the focus turned to Shanghai, Ye's essay becomes an exercise in contrasts. Back home the lotus root is fully integrated into the structure of daily life and the rhythms of nature, but in Shanghai it is a commodity, and out of Ye's reach, because of scarcity, social stratification, and marketing strategies. Instead of the muscular, healthy, and virtuous harvesters who sell the root back home, Shanghai has conniving teahouse owners who sell the cream of the crop not to young girls and old men by the side of the road, but to dandies and pot-bellied merchants. Even the street peddlers in Shanghai offer Ye no consolation, for their product is withered, whereas in Suzhou the roots are as shapely as the male harvesters' well-toned limbs. Consolation comes only from networks of friends and relatives, who draw him back into the moral economy of his hometown and make it possible to obtain a root worth eating.

Such networks also made it possible for Ye to eat another favorite hometown food, water shield, which was also hard to come by in Shanghai. Significantly, Ye resumes his essay by returning to the cycle of seasons, which are marked in his memory by harvest time:

> Thinking of lotus root reminds me of water shield. Back home in the springtime we ate water shield practically every day. Water shield has no taste of its own and relies for its flavor on a good soup. Its tender green coloring endow it with a rich poetic potential, and this flavorless flavor is truly intoxicating. There were always one or two boats (the kind without sails) resting by the docks along the waterways, their cabins full of water shield harvested from Lake Tai. It being that easy to obtain, of course you could eat a bowl every day. Things are different here in Shanghai, where it is hard to find water shield without going to a restaurant. Naturally, we don't eat in restaurants. On one or two occasions we've been the beneficiaries of a friend's banquet, but it wasn't when water shield was in season, so we hadn't eaten any yet this year. Most recently though, Boxiang's relatives visited from Hangzhou and brought him some bottled West Lake water shield. He gave me a bottle, and I can finally say that I have eaten in season (*changxin*).[33]

Like the lotus root, water shield was also a fixture of daily life back home, but once again in Shanghai it has become a luxury good, and Ye must rely on extra-urban social networks, in this case those of his Commercial Press colleague Wang Boxiang, to feel at home again, and in touch with the cycle of nature that produces food. Like Yan's efforts to distinguish himself through his mastery of the Shanghai restaurant world, Ye's essay was also a socially significant act, for his writings made food culture into metonyms of the regional culture that produced them.

The importance that Ye attributes to "eating in season" also draws into relief the value of food culture for the construction of chronotopes, defined in the introduction as notions of place characterized by a temporal rhythm. In Yan's "Comparison," the passing of time in Shanghai is marked by the coming and going of new and fashionable restaurants. By contrast, the men and women of Ye's Suzhou live in a cyclically reoccurring state of nature: their morning walks past Ye's front door are regular and seasonal, so unlike the frenzied and rapid pace of Shanghai city life. Moreover, each chronotope carried within it its own vision of society. The care with which the lotus root harvesters clean the roots indicates that, though simple, they are honest and devoted cultivators, and that they have an integrity manifested in their commitment to a social contract with their customers in town. Foodstuffs, the harvesters know, provide not merely sustenance, but also an aesthetic experience that commands respect. Tired and thirsty after a long day's work, the harvesters frugally reinvigorate themselves with damaged goods they dare not pass off on to their customers, while the local residents, male and female, young and old, make their purchases in turn, uniting each household in town in a common gustatory cause. Ye's Suzhou is thus a model of a good society, in contrast to Yan's Shanghai, which is out of sync with the needs of everyday people.

Chen Boxi's "Old Shanghai"

Ye acknowledges that he did not usually eat in restaurants, but even frequent restaurant-goers, such as Chen Boxi, sought a sense of cultural continuity outside of the trends of the city's high-end restaurants. The details of Chen's birth and education are not known, but he was a long-term Shanghai resident who worked in newspaper circles, including a stint as an editor of the *Zhonghua xinbao* newspaper, and he was especially knowledgeable about Shanghai history and geography.[34] Significantly, Chen's remarks about Shanghai foodways in his 1924 *Compendium of Shanghai Anecdotes* indicate that the quest for a constant, recurring food culture did not require a turn to the foodways of another place, or of another place's time. Shanghai's own past also provided such food for thought.

The "Seasonal Customs" (*Suishi fengsu*) entry in Chen's *Compendium* clearly bears out this signifying potential of local food culture. Structured like a gazetteer entry on local customs, the entry reviews the main dates of the Chinese lunar-solar calendar and records, among other customs, unique Shanghai festival foodways. The entry begins on New Year's Day, when "each family offers congratulations over rich soup and fried glutinous rice cakes with leafy greens." The God of Wealth is welcomed on the fifth day of the year, with a banquet held for this occasion the night before. The centerpiece of this meal is a fresh fish known as the "ingot fish," which is delivered the day before by "fish vendors who use a red rope to secure the fins and go from door to door," a practice referred to as "delivering the ingot." Chen also mentions the Lantern Festival, on the fifteenth, a day marked by eating rice-flour dumplings; the custom of eating "wealth-come-smoothly" wontons on the sixteenth; and then the taking down of the lanterns on the twenty-third, which was punctuated by eating rice-flour cakes. He explains that this is "in contrast to the eating of rice-flour dumplings when the lanterns are lit, and so there is the expression 'rice-flour dumplings when the lanterns go up and cakes when the lanterns come down.'"[35]

Like Ye Shengtao's discussion of lotus root, the *Compendium*'s account of Shanghai's New Year's celebrations links food culture to the cycle of the seasons. It further contrasts this pattern of continuity in foodways with tangible signs of change in other forms of celebration, noting:

> Each of the customs I have related above are customs that have prevailed in Shanghai from olden times. In the Shanghai where the five directions come together, the situation in the foreign settlements and former county seat is different, and it is not possible to consider one as the example [of all]. For example, seeking the limelight in an automobile, watching the horse races at Jiangwan, playing at the amusement park, burning incense at the Rainbow Temple and City God Temple: such [new activities] appear in an endless stream year after year.[36]

Incense-burning aside, each of Chen's examples bespoke a particularly Shanghai way of life. Shanghai had more automobiles than any other Chinese city, automobiles having evolved into symbols of power and prestige soon after their first appearance in 1901. The Shanghai racecourse and polo grounds had been an urban spectacle since the 1880s, and Huang Chujiu's Great World amusement park, which opened in 1917, was an everyday playground for city residents and a must-see destination for visitors to the city.[37] These activities, therefore, were ways of celebrating the New Year that bespoke of a distinctive Shanghai lifestyle, even if they had not "prevailed in Shanghai from olden times." Yet Chen notes no such changes to New Year's food culture, suggesting that food functioned as a cultural anchor that made it possible to shore up a sense of tradition during a festival that otherwise allowed celebrants to find new ways of marking the occasion.

The continuity Chen observes in festival foodways stood in stark contrast to other local customs that he saw as having faded by the time of his writing. For example, although it was still the custom in the Shanghai countryside to eat "waist-support cakes" (*chengyao gao*) on the second day of the second month to ward off lumbago in the coming year, flower lanterns were apparently no longer hung up during the Festival of the Goddess of the Hundred Flowers, celebrated on the fifteenth day. As Chen put it, "Since the Tongzhi [1861–1875] and Guangxu reigns, folk culture has withered, and the lantern festival has been discontinued." It therefore comforted Chen to know that he could still expect the fermented glutinous rice, plum, cherry, and spiral shelled mollusk vendors to appear on the day of the Summer Equinox, and that it was still considered mandatory on that day for the proprietors of handicraft shops to treat their employees to a banquet of yellow croaker, salted egg, amaranth, and broad beans. Even these customs were under threat of being commodified, however. As Chen explained with regard to the Summer Equinox handicraft shop banquet: "The amaranth was considered especially important, so if there was none, it would have to be made up for in cash." Still, even if, as the Dragon Boat Festival (the fifth day of the fifth month) approached, the city's Daoist monks and nuns "only made their annual rounds delivering talismans as a pretext for soliciting alms," at least the city's brothels still followed the time-honored practice, at the same time of year, of honoring their regular clients with a private meal.[38] Time and again in his account of Shanghai's seasonal customs, Chen registers such patterns of continuity in foodways amid examples of cultural deterioration and social change.

Regional Food Culture and the Nation

Yan, Ye, and Chen each found value in regional food culture in early Republican Shanghai, but their writings about this culture produced three very different images of the city: Yan's was a land of opportunity, Ye's was a society in a state of decline, and Chen's was a city undergoing rapid change, albeit not without holding on to some of its cultural traditions. One man whose writings reconciled some of these tensions was the guidebook writer Wang Dingjiu, whose two Shanghai guidebooks, *Keys to Shanghai* and *Shanghai Advisor*, are the richest guides to Shanghai commercial and consumer life of the 1930s.

The social and political context in which Wang wrote was slightly different from that animating the writings of Yan, Ye, and Chen. By the time of Wang's writing, the Northern Expedition and the political institutions of the Nanjing Decade had brought to Shanghai a new cohort of wealthy and powerful merchants, militarists, and political figures, as well as a municipal government that represented the interests of the Nationalist Party. This influx of wealth and power sent Shanghai into yet another new era of material and cultural prosperity, but it also fed the consumer trends that many in Shanghai found troubling. For the first time in decades, Shanghai's municipal government answered to a national government that had a reasonable chance of fulfilling its promise to unify the country. Yet, many city residents were equally troubled by the visions of nation and state that the Nationalist Party pursued. This ambivalent context provided a new environment for constructing ideas of the local, the nation, and consumer culture through regional food culture.

Rich in detail, anecdote, cautionary tales, and tricks of every trade, Wang Dingjiu's Shanghai guidebooks disclosed to their readers a vast panorama of material culture, urban leisure, and social relationships. His description of Shanghai regional food culture provided a template for integrating different regional chronotopes into a vision of national history and culture. His tips for navigating the city's treacherous commodity culture provided a set of strategies for mitigating some of the more baleful effects of the commodification of regional food culture. Wang's national template is described in this section; his consumer strategies in the next.

The prospect of national unification affected Shanghai's regional food culture in an important new way: the signifying potential of regional food culture became more closely linked to the idea of the nation. This development is readily apparent in Wang's discussion of regional restaurants in his Shanghai guidebooks, which represent the city's restaurant industry as a microcosm of Chinese regional culture, history, and geography. Wang divides the food chapters of each book into regional food styles and begins each section with a succinct phrase about the region to be discussed, followed by a more elaborate discussion of the cuisine and the best places in the city to dine on it. For example, writing of the Zhenjiang branch of the industry, he begins, "Zhenjiang was known as Jingkou in former times. It was a place of strategic importance, and after the provincial government moved there, it became a provincial capital and has become more and more prosperous each day."[39] Of Wuxi, Wang notes, "Wuxi's industry is very developed, and it is the port of origin of rice and bean thread noodles. For this reason, it is a prosperous city and is on the route from Beijing to Shanghai. It is acclaimed as 'Little Shanghai.'" In Wang's hands, each branch of the restaurant industry became a symbol of regional culture and the region's contribution to a national history.

This linking of regional history to national history is most dramatically illustrated by Nanjing Decade developments in the Cantonese branch of the regional restaurant industry and in Wang's depiction of these developments. Noting a remarkable turnaround from the previous few decades, all Shanghai guidebooks from the Nanjing Decade uniformly agree that Cantonese restaurants were the most expensive and fashionable establishments in the city. As indicated earlier, non-Cantonese residents of Shanghai had previously held a relatively low opinion of high-end Cantonese restaurants (as distinct from *xiaoyeguan*, which enjoyed a wide popularity during the late Qing). As the *Shanghai Precious Mirror* put it only one year before the Northern Expedition: "People from provinces other than Guangdong do not like to eat authentic Cantonese food; therefore, Cantonese food is very rarely used for banqueting."[40] Consequently, Shanghai's finer Cantonese restaurants remained on or near North Sichuan Road, "clustered off in a corner [of the city]," as one commentator noted, "where the average person hardly gave them a thought."[41]

New and old establishments worked hard to change this reputation. The Xinya Cantonese Cuisine Restaurant (Xinya Yuecaiguan), which advertised its regional character in its name, was one of the newcomers. Its proprietor, Cai Jianqin, hailed from Nanhai, Guangdong Province. He came to Shanghai in September 1926, shortly after the Northern Expedition Revolutionary Army had captured Hankou and set out toward Shanghai. Cai first opened the small, one-bay shop front Xinya Teahouse, employing only ten or so workers. One year later, he started serving food on the second floor, and then soon started planning for a move to Nanjing Road, where he expanded his operation into a three-bay shop front downstairs beneath an eight-bay dining room upstairs.[42] The Xinghualou, one of the oldest Cantonese restaurants in the city, also remade itself during these years. Renovations undertaken in 1927 made this industry veteran into a new seven-bay, four-story restaurant, and the following year, it launched sales of Cantonese-style moon cakes, attaching poetic names to new varieties of this popular snack food and taking over a sector of the regional food market previously dominated by the Jinfang Bakery.

Wang Dingjiu attributed the sudden popularity of Cantonese cuisine to the "tendency of Shanghai people to act like a swarm of bees," but he also noted that the new prestige accorded to high-end Cantonese cuisine represented more than just a passing food fashion.[43] First, the post-Northern Expedition

high-end Cantonese restaurant reflected the new class and power structure of Shanghai society during the Nanjing Decade. Cantonese restaurants
represented the rising commercial power of Cantonese merchants in the city.
As Wang explained, "Shanghai's commercial power is divided into two cliques
(*bang*), the Ningbo and the Cantonese," the difference between the two being
that the Ningbo influence was dispersed, "such that every retail shop and every
residence has a Ningbo occupant," whereas the Cantonese style of influence
was "imposing"—"their businesses don't begrudge large capital [investment]
and they excel in decoration."[44] The imposing new restaurants charged such
high prices that, to Wang and others, the banqueting common to high-end
Cantonese restaurants reflected the "wanton extravagance of modern society"
and its "pursuit of luxury." Even near the bottom end of the Cantonese restaurant price-scale, it was not unusual for a "common, informal meal" to cost
at least two to three *yuan*, and the price was more than forty to fifty *yuan* per
item for the seafood or tonics typical of *haute* Cantonese cuisine, more than
twice the average monthly earnings of a factory worker.[45] Indeed, as Wang observed, the class and power structure that lay behind these prices gave new
meaning to the old saying, "A wealthy family's banquet [costs as much as] a
poor man's grain for half the year," for "only the big heads of the military and
government and wealthy merchants" could afford such meals, while "a poor
man could not even imagine it in a lifetime."[46] The most expensive Cantonese
banquets cost as much as a thousand *yuan* per table, and "mid-priced" tables
could run anywhere from three to six hundred. Guidebook writer Xiao Jianqing's *Shanghai Common Knowledge* (Shanghai changshi) confirmed Wang's
observations, noting that banquet prices ranged from a low of seven or eight
yuan to as much as several hundred for dishes of shark's fin, swallow's nest, and
snake. The cost of a banquet soared even higher when finished with litchi- or
green plum-infused wines.[47]

The powerful new consumer base for Cantonese food enhanced the value
of Cantonese cuisine and forced a reassessment of the taste of Cantonese food.
One guidebook noted that the "best cuisines" in Shanghai restaurants were
"Beijing, Suzhou, Cantonese, Sichuan, and Fujian," adding that although "Beijing, Suzhou, Sichuan, and Fujian cuisine excels in quality (*yi zhi shang*)," Cantonese food "excels in taste (*yi wei shang*); the cooking is done in the proper way
(*defa*), and the presentation is elegant and clean."[48] Nothing could have been
further from Yan Duhe's suggestion that Cantonese food was only good for
looking at, and that shark's fin was only cooked appropriately in Suzhou res-

taurants. The conspicuous patronage of Cantonese restaurants by Shanghai's wealthier European and American residents enhanced the cuisine's prestige, and the assessment of Cantonese cuisine by Japanese during this decade was also quite high: apparently, a team of Japanese chefs sent to Shanghai during these years to research Chinese cooking determined that Cantonese cuisine was the best in the world.[49] This assessment too reflected some change from the past because during the previous decade, Fujian cuisine had attracted the attention of Japanese in Shanghai.

In addition to reflecting the new power structure of Shanghai, Cantonese restaurants also conveyed a new vision of a viable future for Chinese politics and culture. In this regard, the symbolism of high-end Cantonese restaurant décor was more important than the taste of Cantonese cuisine. Even though these establishments exhibited the political-economic contradictions of Nanjing Decade Shanghai, they also put forth a vision of Chinese culture that could compete with Western culture: "In the eating industry today, the decoration of Cantonese restaurants is the most luxurious; it outdoes even that of Western restaurants." The design, in fact, reached entirely new cross-cultural heights: "Each table and chair is an antique Chinese style [modified] by an elegant Western touch. Each chopstick and spoon is uncommonly and elegantly detailed. The walls are perfectly decorated, and upon entering [it feels like being inside] nothing less than a palace. So going to a Cantonese restaurant provides not only gastronomic pleasure; it is simply the perfect place for the body and mind."[50]

Restaurants facilitated the experience of such perfection by decorating their private dining rooms according to culturally evocative motifs. For example, the Guifei Parlor was named for the famous Tang concubine, Yang Guifei, famous for her love of litchi, a Cantonese specialty food.[51] The splendor of these environments indicated that Chinese restaurants more than measured up to Western restaurants in scale, design, and comfort. The idea that only Western restaurants could count as "aristocrat-modern" (*guizu modenghua*) was, as Wang put it, a thing "of the past."[52] It was no wonder then, as Wang summed it up, reiterating a connection between political and cultural developments, that "Western food restaurants have lost their luster en masse and Beiping [Beijing] cuisine restaurants have all been affected. For this reason Cantonese restaurants deserve [to be considered] the Revolutionary Army of the restaurant industry."[53] This was a Revolutionary Army that did more than wipe out China's warlords; it also signified the power of a Chinese regime that could stand up to Western power and culture.

Though Wang depicted Cantonese restaurants as establishments that provided a clear vision of a future in which Chinese culture had transcended Western culture, he depicted other regional restaurants in Shanghai as emblematic of different aspects of the Chinese past, as if they now provided a regional prehistory for the future of China that the Cantonese branch of the industry represented best. The signifying potential of restaurants was closely related to décor, and the décor of high-end Cantonese restaurants set them off from other, once-popular Chinese regional cuisines and marked a transition from the chapter of Shanghai's restaurant history that had begun in the wake of the Revolution of 1911. The Fujian cuisine Xiaoyoutian was still in business in the late 1920s, but now it and the other Fujian establishments struck customers as having fallen behind the times. Wang referred to them as "old-time establishments" (*laozihao*), but in a way that carried a pejorative connotation, noting that "they don't concern themselves with décor, and so the setting recalls the days of the early Republic." For Wang, the equation of Fujian style with faded elegance was clear: "Inside the décor is completely Fujian style, and marked by primitive simplicity through and through, while the bowls and plates are also in the old style."[54]

As was the case with Cantonese restaurants, the new evaluation of the appearance of Fujian restaurants also affected perceptions of the quality of Fujian cookery. Whereas the 1925 *Precious Mirror* referred to Fujian cooking as "superb" and popular among non-fellow provincials, it had become provincial by 1931:

> Because Fujian is adjacent to the ocean, its cuisine is dominated by seafood, and Fujian recipes are very unique. This no doubt suits the appetite of the fellow-provincial, but non-fellow provincials with a weak constitution will find that it is truly a case of deliciousness up front followed by nausea afterwards. The fishiness and shrimpiness is really quite foul. For this reason, Fujian restaurants have very few customers who are not fellow-provincials.[55]

In previous years, Wang suggests, Fujian establishments had modified their recipes to appeal to a wider audience, "but in recent years, they have become complacent and conservative, and have fallen behind in the ranks."[56]

Not all non-fellow provincials took such a dim view of Fujian cuisine, yet like Wang, they too linked its qualities to the Fujian region's broader history. Lin Yin-feng, who describes herself as a "true Cantonese," observed, "Fukienese are the sailors of China, so it is natural that sea-food is their specialty. They can steam Samli fish so that the memory of it makes my mouth water—such delicate flavour, and such tender meat, words fail me! . . . Any kind of sea-food becomes a poem under a Fukienese cook's deft touch."[57] This historical association of Fujian with seafaring was not lost on Wang himself, although he located it not in a high art of Fujian cookery but, instead, in the more everyday Fujian fare that could be found at the small restaurants that dotted the docks of the Huangpu river in the far south of the city near Gaochang Temple:

> Originally, the dock area was a naval headquarters and stopping point for many of our country's naval boats. Because all of our country's sailors, from the bottom to the top of the ranks, are from Fujian, Fujian restaurants opened up there. . . . And because the location abuts the ocean, it is easy to catch fish and shrimp. When the sailors on board are idle, they cast their nets and . . . later sell [their haul] to the restaurants for a low price. . . . Generally speaking, each of the restaurants has a chef or two who worked as a private chef to naval commanders, so their cooking skills are superb. . . . From the outside these places look truly cheap and dirty, and a lot of lowlife do crawl in to eat there, but if you want inexpensive and delicious Fujian fare . . . there's no other place in Shanghai like it.[58]

Significantly, for Wang and Lin alike, Fujian cuisine could be best enjoyed and appreciated when viewed in the larger context of Fujian culture and Fujian's contribution to Chinese history.

Wang did not single out Fujian restaurants for their ability to evoke a period of the Chinese past. As suggested previously, the Beijing cuisine sector of the restaurant industry, referred to during this period by the city's new name, Beiping, also took a hit from the Cantonese cuisine sector, although at least one Beijing restaurant, the venerable Tongxinglou, followed the Cantonese sector's lead and underwent a major renovation in the late 1920s. The Tongxinglou's updated décor and its prime location partially explained the enduring popularity of Beijing cuisine during the Nanjing Decade. Another likely factor was Beijing restaurants' relatively reasonable prices, for a full banquet could be had for as little as seven or eight *yuan*.[59] But these factors did not explain the entire appeal of Beijing restaurants. Wang and other commentators singled out the finer establishments for one additional key aspect of their service. As one journalist writing a food column in *Livelihood Weekly* (Rensheng xunkan) explained,

> What makes dining on Beiping food so satisfying is that the service is so attentive and amiable. When the host [of a banquet] and guests enter and exit, there are always three or four attendants dressed in green cheongsams and black

gowns greeting and seeing off [the customers]. Even though [the finer Beiping establishments] all prepare excellent food, they still generally rely on their conscientious service."[60]

The draw of the food and polite service was not understood generically, however, but as a legacy of Beijing's history. As Wang observed, "Beiping was a capital city for many generations, and the daily life of food and drink [there] is naturally out of the common run." Significantly, the polite service found at Beijing restaurants provided customers with a vicarious experience of the ancient capital city's former glory, for "when the waiters speak to the customers, they still use the customs of old officialdom and love to flatter their customers until they are satisfied."[61] This historical significance of Beijing cuisine was only reinforced by the new term with which it was designated after the relocation of the national capital from Beijing to Nanjing. Beijing cuisine (*Beijing cai*)— literally "Northern Capital cuisine"—became *Beiping* cuisine—or "Northern Peace cuisine"—carrying within its own name a recognition of the legitimacy of the new Nanjing regime, whose Cantonese-based "Revolutionary Army" had performed the work of pacifying the country.

Restaurateurs themselves made these associations between time and place the very pretext upon which they developed their décor and food offerings. One of the clearest examples of such entrepreneurship comes from the Wuxi branch of the restaurant industry. High-end Wuxi cuisine was not widely available in Shanghai and was generally served only in a small number of Zhenjiang and Suzhou restaurants. The cuisine was famously sweet and known for a small number of inexpensive specialty dishes, such as steamed pork with rice noodles. This "street food," however, as Wang called it, "paled in comparison to the region's flagship 'riverboat cuisine' (*chuancai*)," a high-end Wuxi specialty that had become popular in Wuxi toward the end of the nineteenth century. "Riverboat cuisine," Wang explained, "was a by-product of Wuxi's natural environment; the city "had picturesque scenery, and such sites as the Huishan Hills, Turtle Head Isle, and Plum Garden Park were famous near and far, and so . . . on fine days in the spring and fall tourists went there in great numbers."[62]

The tourists went for the sites, but also for the high-class courtesans who developed the area's natural resources into a specialized cuisine. Wang summarized the tradition as follows:

> Wuxi is a water-port located near Lake Tai, where the mountains are brilliant and the water clear. In former times there were lantern boats resembling the

gaily-painted pleasure boats [that once lined] the banks of the Qinhuai River in Nanjing, with courtesans aboard to entertain the travelers. . . . While some sing songs and play instruments to keep the guests company . . . [others] prepare a banquet . . . drawing most of the ingredients from the river.[63]

A day's companionship, which Wang priced at a whopping 240 *yuan* per person, came with two meals taken aboard ship, prepared in a kitchen installed at the bow: "The taste was completely different from on land. The fish and shrimp all hit the wok while still alive, and the customers can insist that the chef clean and gut the fish before their eyes." Although the practice had thrived in Wuxi for decades, making the term "riverboat cuisine" synonymous with Wuxi cuisine in some circles, the Nationalist Party's ban on prostitution a few years earlier had brought an end to the custom, and tourists there "feel that great changes have taken place in the land."

Riverboat cuisine came to Shanghai shortly after the ban, when the advertiser-turned-restaurateur Zhou Minggang sought to recreate this lost world of Wuxi courtesan history and culture as a Shanghai commodity. Zhou first secured his niche in the Shanghai restaurant world with the Wuxi Congee Shop. No poor man's porridge house, the Wuxi Congee Shop was modeled after high-end Cantonese restaurants, and its menu boasted fifty-some varieties of congee that Zhou had a hand in inventing. Business was good, but to keep the customers coming Zhou added a riverboat cuisine section, which prepared the classic "freshly killed" items, as well as other specialty Wuxi dishes, such as sweet eel and Wuxi gluten. Zhou sold prix fixe riverboat cuisine menus for forty to fifty *yuan*, but to attract even more customers he sold some items à la carte, and others in a pre-cooked set menu format that consisted of a serving of rice with cooked vegetables and meat on top. The à la carte items went for one or two *yuan* each, the set menu for under five *jiao*.

Zhou's business strategy made a once-exclusive food culture into a mass commodity, and at first earned Wang's praise.[64] Detractions, however, came a few years later:

[The new strategy] made it possible for your average fame-seeking drooling epicure to enjoy a quick bite, and business wasn't bad. But riverboat cuisine served this way lacked the beautiful female companions urging the customers to drink and was devoid of the attractive scenery. Moreover, by the time the Wuxi specialty products had passed through all the necessary hands in transit, the flavor was inferior to real riverboat cuisine.[65]

The sweet eel, which was supposed to be firm and crispy, was especially difficult to prepare. The recipe called for fresh Wuxi eels cleaned in spring water from Mt. Huiquan, without which the dish could not obtain the proper consistency.

As these examples indicate, Wang Dingjiu's Nanjing Decade guides to Shanghai food culture provided one solution to the problem of political fragmentation and the Republican era quest for a national identity. Although some city residents clung to the idea that their regional culture presented a more viable alternative for China's future than other regional cultures, guidebook writers such as Wang took up the challenge of integrating such claims into a coherent, national framework by bundling the chronotopes embodied in the regional food culture available in the city into a workable, if provisional, patchwork. Shanghai regional restaurants in the 1920s and 1930s evoked a sense of place and made sense of the recent unfolding of Chinese history. A meal in the "Beiping" restaurant Tongxinglou evoked the former Qing dynasty and historical capital. Eating in the Fujian Xiaoyoutian might carry a customer back to the early Republican period, whereas the smaller Fujian establishments by the waterfront called to mind Fujian's place in the long history of Chinese seafaring. Wuxi riverboat cuisine provided customers with an opportunity to wax poetic about the long history and culture of literati-courtesan relations that dated back to the late Ming, but that had been brought to an abrupt end, most recently, by the Nationalist Party's ban on prostitution. The Nationalist government itself, and its importance to Chinese history, was represented by the Cantonese branch of the restaurant industry. This was Wang's "Revolutionary Army," which evoked a Tang-dynasty pedigree for Cantonese food and culture and provided a vision of China's future as a country that was equal to the West. Shanghai food culture provided a rich body of material that city residents could draw on to begin to imagine how many different local histories might fit together into a coherent whole.

"The Real Thing at the Right Price"

One might reasonably ask how meaningful such an analysis of Shanghai food culture was to everyday city residents. On the one hand, Wang's analyses of Shanghai's restaurants provided an internally coherent vision of national culture. On the other, these were often very expensive restaurants, and many of the meals that Wang describes were affordable to only a small sector of the population. Moreover, some of the branches, such as the Cantonese branch, represented not only the prospects of national unity, but also the problems of Shanghai's commodity culture itself. Indeed, Wang's vision of the way regional food culture fit into a national whole was beholden to the very commodity culture that underlay the value system according to which branches of the regional restaurant industry acquired their place in his vision of Chinese history.

Yet Wang's guidebooks also offered a means of diagnosing these problems and of negotiating the demands they placed on everyday consumers. His guidebook is as replete with assessments of the price of food and tips for finding affordable versions of regional fare as it is with discussions of the food's regional distinctiveness and historical significance. Moreover, as suggested by his discussion of the everyday Fujian fare available near Gaochang Temple, he was careful to guide his readers toward varieties and items of regional food culture that gave them a chance of getting "good food at a cheap price" (*jialian wumei*), as well as "the real thing at the right price" (*huozhen jiashi*). The Gaochang Temple Fujian restaurants were less expensive than the higher-end Fujian establishments, and the food was better and more authentic, caught and cooked as it was by Fujian sailors and navy chefs. Wang's tips for getting "the real thing at the right price" provided a consumer strategy for reckoning with a commodity culture that made food cost more than it was, in the minds of some, really worth.

Wang tailored his tips to the specific character of Shanghai's commodity culture, the characteristics of which he analyzed in the preface to *Keys to Shanghai*. After suggesting that Shanghai, the "port of the East," rivals London, New York, Paris, and Berlin, Wang provides a blistering critique of the commercial culture that had characterized Shanghai since the onset of the Nanjing Decade:

> Oh the folly of gentlemen in Shanghai! The ease with which, regardless of the subject, they pay attention only to surfaces (*biao*) without penetrating to the essence (*shi*)! Whenever they have one little insight, based on what really amounts to little more than a crude knowledge of surface residue, they consider themselves experts, even though they have not even sought to get a foot in the door, or probed around on the inside. It is no wonder that Shanghainese are always going on and on about those Bund-side suckers being as common as river carp.
>
> Respectable men, women, and officials have seen enough, and they have clamored for this book to be written. They know that, though I am still young, I

have a prior familiarity with the shapes and colors [of life] "behind the curtains," and that I know where the keys lie. With the power of pen and ink, I make this book a reference to gentlemen who wish to take up residence in Shanghai. It has taken three full months of time: during daylight hours I cast about gathering information; at night, I hunched over my desk to write. Because I wanted to verify every single detail, I didn't begrudge [the need] to spend time and money sampling things [myself]. Therefore, every word and sentence is spoken from experience. I, for one, do not deign to scratch at itchy feet through shoes or engage in the vapid discourse of novelists.[66]

Clearly, Wang viewed Shanghai as a city where true essences lay buried beneath superficial surfaces. This was a world structured by a metaphysics of surface and depth, fiction and nonfiction, ignorance and knowledge. Wang's "Key to Eating" provided the key to getting behind the "curtain" and obtaining real value.

Finding real value meant learning how to look "behind the curtain." This was not, however, an easy task, because the curtain was an ever-shifting phenomenon. As Wang wrote with regard to the city's Western restaurants, "Those who wish to eat their fill naturally demand the real product at the right price, but Shanghainese are vainglorious and pursue décor at the expense of taste. Therefore, the cooking at fancy Western restaurants is not as delicious as is that at smaller establishments. And so, if you are looking for an honest meal, it's better to try the delicious inexpensive fare at a small restaurant."[67] Still, a trip to even some of the city's least expensive *fandian*, or small food shops, revealed just how arbitrary was the relationship between price and value. At *fandian*, which Wang describes as "the type of place to resolve the average person's eating needs," a meal could be had for as little as 200 *wen*, and even be paid for in Chinese copper coins, rather than the silver currency generally used in the foreign settlements.[68] Many *fandian* consisted of little more than a countertop piled high with dishes facing out onto the street. Some *fandian*, however, were somewhat more complex in structure:

The price of *fandian* food is all very cheap and most of the patrons are your average country bumpkins, or our noble working friends in short pants. In order to attract a more upscale clientele, *fandian* have installed upstairs seating. Although there is nothing but a simple board separating the two areas, the price is wildly different, because downstairs the cost is calculated in copper, and upstairs is it figured in foreign currency. In this way alone the cost differential is two-thirds [cheaper downstairs]. But on top of that, the same food that costs six *min* downstairs will require six *fen* upstairs. Moreover, where the food costs more, the bowls are small, and where the price is lower, the bowls are large. This is entirely for the benefit of the workers. But really, the downstairs area is simply too filthy, and any respectable person would find it unbearable to eat there.[69]

Evidently, even inexpensive *fandian* reflected the class structure and commodity culture of Shanghai society.

Such paradoxes inspired Wang to search for bargains in even the more expensive sectors of the regional restaurant industry. One type of common restaurant offering that was less expensive than banquet food was the *hecai*, or set-meal. Though inexpensive, this offering was available at most restaurants that sold banquet food. At a typical Beijing restaurant, a *hecai* might cost as little as one *yuan*, and although there were also hecai offerings that cost as much as four or five *yuan*, a one-*yuan hecai* included two cold dishes, two stir-frys, and a soup—"enough for two," as Wang notes. Such meals, which could also be ordered by price instead of by name, were much easier to order than banquet food, the dishes of which were often graced by regionally specific or ornamental names that obscured the actual food items in question. Ordering by price was thus also a good strategy for the uninitiated in a particular regional cooking style: "If you don't know how to order, or if it's your first time in a Beijing restaurant and you don't know the names of dishes, the best thing to do is order a one- or two-*yuan hecai*."[70] The least expensive *hecai* were sold in Anhui restaurants, where for only half a *yuan* one could get a meal of two stir-frys and a soup, "already enough to feed two people with small appetites."[71] The older model of ordering by price was thus a partial solution to the new industry criteria that attributed a different value to cuisine types.

Many Cantonese establishments catered to this price level too. Some offered an item called "Company Style" Western food, which Wang described as a "mock-Western-style *hecai*." Meals at such establishments ranged in price from one-*yuan*-twenty to three or four *yuan*, and here too, "you can order based on how much money you want to spend." The *hecai* for one-*yuan*-twenty at Qingyise even included a portion of shark's fin. Cantonese *xiaoyeguan* were also a source of inexpensive meals, and "one of the cheapest types of *hecai*."[72] Although some *xiaoyeguan* were more expensive than others, a typical *xiaoyeguan hecai* could cost as little as three *jiao* and still include one cold dish and one hot dish. Wang also describes wintertime *xiaoyeguan* meals that could be had for half a *yuan*, one *yuan*, or one and a half *yuan*. The menu of each was replete "with items like shrimp, pork kidney, eggs, sliced fish, cuttlefish, and spinach. Everything is fresh. When you are ready to eat, you cook your own food in the middle of the pot. This way of eating is not expensive, and it's quite a lot of fun."[73]

Eating in this price range, finally, drew customers into regional food cultures that did not enjoy a high reputation during the Nanjing Decade, such as Anhui cooking and local Shanghai fare. Significantly, even these cuisines evoked a sense of regional history. Anhui restaurants, as discussed in Chapter Two, had a long history in Shanghai. They prospered initially in the vicinity of the former county seat, and by the late nineteenth century had begun to establish a small presence in the foreign settlements, drawing a nod from the city's late Qing guidebook writers. Anhui restaurants also seem to have prospered in the foreign settlements in the very early twentieth century, as the names and address of seventeen Anhui establishments are recorded in the 1909 *Guide to Shanghai*.[74] But the fortunes of Anhui merchants dwindled soon thereafter, as the result of natural disasters back home and the collapse of the imperial salt monopoly, upon which Anhui merchants depended heavily for their wealth. The reputation of their restaurants fell accordingly. Wang remarks, somewhat disparagingly, that Anhui restaurants were "everywhere," numbering "more than five hundred" and located "on every single street."[75] During the Nanjing Decade, Anhui cooking was best known for big portions and low prices, and Anhui establishments were patronized largely by fellow-provincials or the urban poor, whose status in Shanghai society represented the commercial status of Anhui merchants in China more generally. The location of Anhui restaurants near pawnshops, a sector of the urban economy that Anhui natives continued to dominate, only reinforced their generally negative impression. Still, Wang notes that even Anhui establishments had their merits, for in addition to the stews and "rich and heavy" dishes for which Anhui cuisine was best known, Anhui establishments also sold affordable breakfasts and famously large bowls of noodles: one order of fish-tail noodles, ham and chicken noodles, or shrimp noodles was apparently enough for two or three.

One item of local Shanghai cooking—vegetable rice (*caifan*)—also provided a regionally specific food bargain that shed light on the history of the city that played host to this national banquet. Invoking a metaphor from Shanghai's movie culture, and playing up his image of Shanghai as a city where true essences were buried beneath superficial surfaces, Wang called vegetable rice the "minor star of Shanghai's restaurants circles." The dish was prepared by adding a local variety of salted pork and a small portion of sautéed greens to a pot of rice. When cooked together, the rice absorbed the salt and fat of the pork. It was a simple dish, Wang noted, but it "actually had an incredible taste." Vegetable rice was originally an item of everyday home cookery, but by Wang's time, it also constituted a separate sector of the restaurant industry.

Legend attributed the origin of this branch of the industry to a "down and out opium addict and gambler with a passion for eating."[76] Realizing that there were no appropriate foods for the addicts and gamblers in the vicinity of opium dens, this industry pioneer "regained a sense of his former self" and pulled together a sum of money to set up a food stall that specialized in vegetable rice. Business took off, and many other small proprietors soon followed suit. The latecomers even upgraded the offerings by adding side dishes of pork chops, stewed meats, and chicken feet. Over time, *caifan* vendors and "the proprietors of opium and gambling dens developed a mutually beneficial relationship," linking the idea of local Shanghai cooking to some of the least salubrious aspects of the city's history.[77] It was a reputation for which the city and its food culture would pay dearly, in political rather than commercial capital, in the years to come.

5 Serve the People
Socialist Transformations of Shanghai Food Culture

IN EARLY MAY 1949, a young People's Liberation Army (PLA) recruit from the slums of Shanghai's Hongkou district requested a short leave from his post to meet his girlfriend for dinner at the sumptuous International Hotel. The girlfriend, whom the young recruit had met during a recent hunger strike, was a talented violinist scheduled to perform that night in celebration of the city's recent "liberation" by the Communists. To the recruit's surprise, his trip to the restaurant caused a rift among the leadership of the PLA units charged with patrolling the city's fashionable Nanjing Road, where the PLA, fresh from the countryside, saw its main task as fending off the "counterrevolutionary" forces that threatened to turn back the revolutionary tide. At the heart of the rift was a tension in what the Chinese Communist Party identified as a revolutionary dialectic between austerity, which the party identified as a prerequisite for the development of a revolutionary will, and the promise of prosperity, the good life that the revolution was to provide, eventually, for all. The party's awareness of this tension was especially acute in Shanghai. Just two months earlier, Mao Zedong had formally announced that "the centre of gravity of the party's work has shifted from the village to the city," and he warned of the "peril of the 'sugar-coated bullets' of the bourgeoisie, which could wound or destroy unwary cadres."[1]

The rift among PLA leaders set off by the young recruit's actions is the inciting incident of the early 1960s fictional stage play and later feature film, *On Guard Beneath the Neon Lights* (Nihongdengxia de shaobin), of which the young recruit is the protagonist.[2] The central questions *On Guard* raised pertained to what it meant to be a member of the revolutionary forces and to how far authorities could push a revolutionary line defined by austerity before it risked alienating its constituency. The Third Platoon Leader, who granted the young recruit permission to take leave for the meal, defended his actions on the grounds that "one must be flexible and make allowances when leading soldiers from Shanghai. The big-stick policy [used in the countryside] won't do."[3] When disciplined by the Company Commander upon his return from the meal, the young recruit offered in his own defense: "Of course I want to help the revolution. But don't I have the right to go to the International Hotel?" The Company Commander disagreed, replying: "All right! Go to the International Hotel, and to the coffee bars, dance-halls, and other such places. But remember, if you do, you'll not be fit to wear that uniform of yours!" Flabbergasted, the young recruit strips off of his uniform and terminates his relationship with the army, insisting, "Now that the country is liberated, I can go any place and still help the revolution."[4]

The Company Commander's hard-line position grew out of his revolutionary experience in the countryside and is embodied in *On Guard* in the character of the Third Platoon Leader's wife, a model peasant who carried grain to soldiers at the front. When even she briefly considers leaving Shanghai—after she realizes that her husband is embarrassed by the smell of the hard-boiled eggs she leaves in his pockets, and by the stains they leave on his uniform—the Company Commander realizes just what a threat the environment of Shanghai poses to revolutionary will. The Old Mess Officer pleads with the Company Commander and the unit's Political Instructor to convince her to stay, reminding them of the moral economy the PLA has built with the Chinese peasantry and of the risk represented by her departure: "The peasants fed us with their grain, and carried our things in their wagons to help us cross the Yangtze and come to Shanghai. Are we going to let her go back with tear-filled eyes? What will her fellow-villagers think when they find out what's happened?"[5] The peasant woman stays in Shanghai, but significantly, it is the young recruit himself who emerges as the principal hero of the play—he rescues his kidnapped sister after she is lured into a trap by a local gang boss on the pretense of a dinner engagement in a fancy hotel—suggesting that hard-line austerity is not the only recipe for virtuous behavior, even if fancy hotels were, in fact, a source of danger. Notably, when the young hero reenlists and prepares to leave for Korea to help in the mounting war effort there, the Third Platoon Leader's peasant wife, true to form, brings him apples from her hometown to help sustain him on his long journey, and all is well.[6]

On Guard condenses into dramatic tension a series of political and cultural lessons learned over a period spanning roughly thirty years, the last two decades of the Republican period and the first decade of the People's Republic of China; this chapter charts the history of that learning process. The lessons pertained to what it meant to eat, and of what food culture should look like, in a socialist society.

As discussed in earlier chapters of this book, city residents already had a politically charged relationship to food, but the Chinese Communist Party (CCP) sought to redefine the terms according to which food could have a political meaning. From the standpoint of the CCP, the primary relationship that one could have to food culture was a revolutionary relationship, according to the terms of which food was, first and foremost, the basis of a moral economy of mutual aid. Food was to become a luxury good only after the material conditions of society were such that all members of society had enough food to meet their basic needs, and that food luxuries could be enjoyed by all. What the CCP learned, however, was that even poor city residents like the young recruit were eager to enjoy the fruits of the revolution, and thereby, forms of food culture of which they had been deprived in pre-revolutionary Shanghai. Significantly, even the Third Platoon Leader's peasant wife, on whose actions the hard-liners in *On Guard* modeled their ideas regarding the social and political significance of food, is aware that food has an emotional significance and value that is not limited to its importance as sustenance. Thus, she provides the young recruit with the apples of her hometown, to help him maintain a connection to his comrades while off in a foreign land.

The longer history shaping these lessons began in the Republican period, in the wake of demographic changes in Shanghai that created large pockets of poverty in the city, swelling the ranks of the city's hungry and malnourished residents. The number of hungry city residents grew even larger during the economic crises brought on by Japan's occupation of Shanghai (1937–45) and the years of civil war between the CCP and the Nationalist Party (1945–49). Early CCP organizers were aware of the problem of hunger in the city at the time of the party's founding there in 1921. However, the CCP was not able to maintain a strong presence in Shanghai after the collapse of the First United Front, which ended in 1927 when the Nationalists turned violently on the Communists and Shanghai labor unions, decimating the unions and driving

Communist organizers underground. During the next two decades, the CCP, working largely out of base areas in the countryside, developed distinctive policies on the problem of hunger and of how to solve it. These policies, which the party formulated to facilitate close ties with peasant communities, included rural models of mutual aid and strict party discipline that prohibited party members and soldiers from living off the fruits of peasant labor.

Meanwhile, in the absence of a strong CCP presence in Shanghai, left-wing writers and activists in the city circulated new kinds of images about urban food culture. The process of developing these new images of Shanghai food culture was not a smooth or rapid one, but by the end of the Republican period, the idea of Shanghai as a land of plenty had become not only increasingly implausible, it was also politically suspect. According to the new images, Shanghai was not a place to be celebrated for its culinary diversity, but one where many went hungry, where the rich squandered valuable resources on extravagant and wasteful banquets, and where the time was ripe for revolutionary change. Some writers and activists identified rural foodways as a more ideal form of food culture than that which prevailed in the city. These critics drew attention to the growing disparities between the diets of the city's rich and poor, and argued that industrialization and modern technologies of food processing had left the urban poor chronically malnourished. Others, however, found ways of valorizing even the diets of the urban poor, suggesting that only those who scraped by on meager fare could develop a revolutionary will sufficient to change society for the better. These activists and writers, many of whom would later join the CCP, anticipated and shaped the party's plans to remake Shanghai food culture. Their writings also foreshadowed some of the contradictions in the revolutionary dialectic noted earlier.

These contradictions played out in an unprecedented context of municipal state power, for the early years of the People's Republic of China (PRC) witnessed a new role played by state agencies in both the organization and representation of food and city life. Previously, state organs and agencies had played only shadowy or sporadic roles in shaping urban food culture. As will be discussed later, during the Nanjing Decade, even the left-leaning Bureau of Social Affairs of the Municipal Government of Greater Shanghai adopted relatively conservative or consumer-based approaches to solving the problem of hunger in the city. This meant that city residents were often left largely on their own to develop strategies for navigating what became, during the first half of the twentieth century, an increasingly precarious market in food and foodstuffs. Thus, as discussed in Chapter Four, guidebook writers such as Wang Dingjiu developed consumer strategies to help everyday city residents navigate the mysterious price structure of the restaurant industry. In contrast, government agencies of the PRC set out to transform the entirety of urban food culture. They sought to do this by controlling the main industries underlying the distribution and consumption of food, and by redefining the terms according to which food culture could be represented.

The Decline of Shanghai Living Standards

When PLA soldiers entered the city in May 1949, they found a city in shambles. Years of rising and then record-breaking inflation, food shortages, and political violence had destroyed the urban economy and left most city residents skeptical that the Nationalist Party had the capacity or political integrity to restore order. As a result, even ambivalent observers of the Communist march into Shanghai were impressed by the behavior of the occupying PLA troops. One of the most noted differences between the Communist and Nationalist soldiers was their respective attitude toward food. One man recalled watching that Communist soldiers "refused to accept any gifts. He watched women street-sellers offer some of them rice cakes and tea. They refused with a smile and a bow."[7] In contrast, Nationalist troops holed up in Broadway Mansions apparently only agreed to surrender to their, by then inevitable, defeat after being treated to a "slap-up Chinese dinner . . . . Broadway mansion with its restaurants had an excellent chef and the [Nationalist] troops sat down to a sumptuous meal, after which their officers handed each man a red armband to be worn when leaving the building."[8] How had it come about that the residents of Shanghai, a city famous for its commercial capitalism and home to China's most sizable and comfortable middle class, welcomed Communist troops into their city, and viewed them as the political organization that was most capable of restoring a semblance of order to city life?[9]

Shanghai's demography changed markedly during the Republican period, yielding a sizable middle class, as well as increasingly vocal and visible clusters of hungry city residents. Already at the beginning of the twentieth century, Shanghai was home to a considerable number of skilled and unskilled workers who found the cost of living so high that they had begun to organize offensive strikes for wage increases.[10] Even a small wage increase made a big difference in the average worker's diet because food accounted for more than 50 percent of the average working household's expenditures.[11] Moreover, whereas migrants to Shanghai during the second half of the nineteenth century consisted mostly of "well-off merchants, absentee landlords, frustrated bureaucrats and literati, skilled workers, and adventurers," most newcomers during the first three decades of the twentieth century came from rural areas and were much poorer than their predecessors.[12] Many of the new migrants sought work in factories but just as often ended up working as rickshaw pullers, night soil carriers, and prostitutes. They settled in the slums of Yaoshuilong and other shantytown communities that cropped up in factory neighborhoods.[13] Those lucky enough to get a steady factory job might find just enough to eat in the workplace fare that some factories provided for their workers. Others prepared monotonous meals of rice with scant side dishes in makeshift shantytown kitchens. One social survey of 305 working families conducted in the 1930s found that the average family of 4.6 members annually consumed more than twelve hundred pounds of rice, but only eleven pounds of pork, the most heavily consumed meat.[14]

Despite these developments, ideas about Shanghai food culture were initially quite slow to change. Indeed, the idea that Shanghai presented a richer food culture than other places remained largely intact through the first two decades of the twentieth century. Thus, while factory owners in Shanghai resisted workers' demands for wage increases, wealthy city residents worked hard to raise money to help the hungry in other parts of China. Severe drought in 1919, for example, led to two years of famine in the northern provinces of Hebei, Shandong, Henan, Shanxi, and Shaanxi. With no focused relief campaign forthcoming from the national government in Beijing, prominent Shanghai merchants formed the United Famine Relief Drive to raise money to aid the famine-stricken. In March 1921, the Relief Drive held a "starvation procession" featuring a collection of tableaux that illustrated what one local paper called the "condition of the hungry millions in the famine areas." Among the scenes depicted were those of "refugees eating the bark of the trees to appease hunger; the rich man who stands unmoved at the sight of famine sufferings; the thunder god ready to kill by lightening; [and] rice smugglers."[15] The procession drew attention to the crisis in the north and raised a significant amount of relief aid, but it also conveyed the idea that hunger was an episodic problem that, for the time being, lay strictly in the north, and that the chronic hunger animating workers' demands for wage increases was not equally worthy of sympathy or concern.

Mounting inflation, however, soon began to affect the living standards of all city residents and helped focus attention on the problem of chronic hunger within the city. By the early 1920s, even "middle class" families were feeling the pressures of inflation. The 1924 study *Food Economics* (Shipin jingjixue), for example, profiled four professional households, headed, respectively, by a government ministry official, a scholar, a doctor, and a primary school teacher. These families were all part of what the author called "middle society" (*zhongliu shehui*), and all were feeling the strains of the rising cost of living. Compared with the urban poor, these families seem to have lived in relative comfort and eaten fairly well. The government official's family of three, for example, spent only one-third of household income on food: 12 *yuan* per month on rice, and almost twice that amount, 20.5 *yuan* on non-staple foods (including fuel)—roughly one-half on fish, pork, and vegetables, the other half divided equally among condiments, a daily catty of wine, and one or two more luxurious meals of chicken, duck, or mutton. Yet the official, a graduate of China's prestigious Beiyang Naval Academy, complained of difficulties maintaining the appearances of a "gentleman" (*shenshi*) on his monthly salary of eighty *yuan*, an amount that was more than twice the total monthly income of the average factory-working family.[16]

Inflation prompted concerns about how to make ends meet, as well as a wave of nostalgia for earlier times with lower prices. Newspapers filled with stories and personal anecdotes about the challenges of making ends meet in the city. Local historians published price lists of goods from different periods of the city's past, remarking, "Shanghainese at the beginning of the Qing passed their days with incredible ease," and "the cost of living was so much lower during the early years after Shanghai was opened as a treaty port that residents today have no way of imagining it."[17] Everything seemed to be more expensive than before, but rice was the item of food about which city residents talked the most. The high price of rice became such an important component of the idea of Shanghai that Chen Wuwo opened his 1928 *Record of Things Seen and Heard over Thirty Years in Old Shanghai*, an anecdotal history of the city that comprised more than five hundred entries, with an entry on the price of rice, as if this were now the first thing one needed to know about the city.[18]

There were few comprehensive solutions implemented to reign in inflation and solve the city's mounting food problems during these years, but the organization that came closest to doing so was the Bureau of Social Affairs (BSA). The BSA was a branch of the Municipal Government of Greater Shanghai, the administrative body of the Chinese-governed jurisdictions of the city from 1927–37, and the first viable Chinese form of government in Shanghai since the fall of the Qing in 1911.

Because the price of rice was of concern to almost all city residents, public discourse about rice was central to debates about the state of urban food culture and to efforts to solve Shanghai's food problems. The BSA, recognizing the importance of rice to city life, conducted the first systematic and comprehensive statistical study of rice prices in the city's history. The study attributed the high and widely fluctuating price of rice to "unscrupulous merchants" (*jianshang*), who, the BSA suggested, took advantage of all city residents by capitalizing on periodic shortages caused by disturbances in the international and domestic political climate. Thus, the BSA identified notable rice price spikes following the Great War and in the wake of the outbreak of civil disturbances in China.[19] The BSA's solution to the city's rice price problem was to establish fixed prices in times of scarcity, to protect, indeed to restore, what it called the *minshi*, or the "people's food."

The idea of the *minshi* had been an abiding concern of Confucians throughout most of China's imperial history. For more than two millennia, Confucians argued that states derived their authority from their ability to provision the people.[20] Late imperial states, and the Qing in particular, safeguarded the empire's food supply through an extensive granary system that dispersed grain to the needy for free or sold it at subsidized rates to offset high prices in times of scarcity.[21] Authorities established granaries in Shanghai during the Kangxi (1661–1722) and Yongzheng (1723–35) reign periods, the heyday of the late imperial state granary system, and these granaries operated through most of the nineteenth century. In 1881, however, local gentry in Shanghai argued that "policy should accord with local circumstances," and that it was easier for them to "collect money" (*jikuan*) and then buy rice in times of need than it was to "collect grain" (*jigu*) to have on hand for distribution.[22] Collecting money became the law of the land until the fall of the Qing. Provincial authorities then assumed this same approach during the Republican period. It was not, however, a failsafe solution. By 1924, the Shanghai County Special Accounting Office had exceeded its goal of raising 100,000 *yuan* of reserve cash for purchasing grain. But in August of that year, when war broke out between the military governors of Jiangsu and Zhejiang provinces, He Fenglin, then Defense Commissioner of Shanghai, siphoned off the entire amount for military purposes.[23]

Five years later, in fall 1929, drought and pestilence brought bad harvests to most of rice-growing China, presenting the BSA with a food supply crisis and an opportunity to assert its political and moral authority.[24] The BSA did this by re-invoking the principles and rhetoric of *minshi*. By spring 1930, Shanghai residents faced the highest rice prices on record in the city's history, and the BSA established a Rice Price-Fixing Committee to register and fix a price for all rice entering the city. The process did not go as smoothly as the committee hoped. The city's rice supply entered the city by riverboats, and rice boat operators in the employ of Changshu rice merchants (one of several parties to the Shanghai rice trade) engaged in passive resistance for several weeks by lingering downstream and refusing to unload their cargo. Then, on June 27, this passive resistance turned to "mob gathering and blackmailing" (*juzhong yaoxia*), when, in direct opposition to the BSA's measures, a Changshu rice merchant collected a crowd on the docks at one of the city's two main rice markets. Still, the crowd dispersed after the BSA called in the police, and by the middle of July, the committee had brought prices under control. And the BSA took advantage of this incident to wage a publicity campaign to discredit the Changshu Rice Merchants Guild, posting notices around the city relating the ways in which "Changshu rice merchants endangered the *minshi* by surrounding public servants and obstructing public works." To salvage its tarnished reputation, the Changshu guild took out advertisements in local newspapers acknowledging that the BSA's price limits were, indeed, designed "to maintain the *minshi*."[25]

The acknowledgement of duplicity by the Changshu guild helped bolster support for the BSA's understanding of and solution for Shanghai's food problems and created a semblance of public consensus to counter dissenting opinions from other quarters of the city. The BSA maintained that it had restored urban order by controlling the price of rice, but not all city residents were likely to have been persuaded by the idea that restoring order fully solved the city's food problems. Indeed, others insisted that urban life remained fundamentally out of balance, that urban diets were now inferior to those of the past, and that the diets of many urban residents paled in comparison even with those that prevailed in ostensibly more "backward" rural areas.

Among the more notable dissenters were labor activists and sympathizers, such as the historian Tang Hai. Tang had already conducted his own analyses of Shanghai's food problems. His study identified rice price spikes that did not figure into the BSA study and further drew into relief the way that rising prices fed a growing tension between laborers and capitalists. "Because prices are high," he observed, "[workers] demand that factory owners raise wages, but from the factory owners' point of view, if wages are increased, costs also increase, and [they] therefore raise prices, resulting in a spiraling pursuit and workers' wage struggles."[26] Tang also attributed inflation not simply to unscrupulous merchants, but also to social contradictions growing out of foreign imperialism and China's transformation from an agrarian to an industrial society. "Thirty or forty years ago," he argued, "China was still a [country of] ancient customs based on agriculture. Therefore, all goods were very inexpensive. Later, owing to the flooding of [markets] by foreign goods, and the loss of economic rights [to foreigners], China gradually inclined toward industrialization, and prices have shot up accordingly."[27] Tang did not argue that China should revert to some form of preindustrial national agricultural economy, but he did insist that the living standards problem in Shanghai called not simply for defending the "people's food" from occasional market distortions brought about by a small sector of society; rather, it required a rethinking of the implications of the entire urban experience.

Activists and writers such as Tang Hai were not politically positioned to implement urban policy, so they focused their energies on documenting the problems of urban life or the virtues of more rural ways. Indeed, during the 1920s and 1930s, the meager diet of the urban poor gradually evolved into a well-worn theme of left-wing literature. Among the most important examples of this literature is Xia Yan's exposé on the living and working conditions of young female contract-laborers (*baoshengong*). Food, Xia Yan reported, was one of the many promises labor contractors had used to lure young rural women to factory work in Shanghai, promising them and their families that they would "live in Western style houses and eat dishes of meat and fish."[28] The popular term for the labor system, *baofan* (guaranteed rice), derived from the contract parents signed stipulating that the contractors take responsibility for providing the young women with food.[29] As Xia Yan discovered, however, as a result of low wages and poor factory provisions, "*guaranteed* rice" often meant little more than "guaranteed *rice*." Echoing Tang Hai's favorable assessment of agriculture before industrialization, Xia Yan noted that many contract laborers from the countryside actually ate better back home in the countryside than they did in Shanghai, where the young women got by on only "two servings of congee and one of rice [per day], congee for breakfast and dinner, plain rice for lunch." Even the congee, he noted, was "not anything like what is commonly meant [by the word]." Instead of consisting of a rich rice porridge, it contained "a tiny portion of rice, burnt pot scrapings, broken rice, and a large portion of the tofu dregs that people in the countryside use to feed pigs!"[30] Whereas a decade earlier Shanghai had compared favorably with rural areas in its food culture, now ideas about traditional rural diets provided a benchmark for criticizing the ways of the city.

Nutritional researchers in Shanghai confirmed these new dim views of Shanghai diets. According to one study of Shanghai factory workers in the mid-1930s, "Of nearly two thousand . . . apprentices in small workshops in Shanghai, 70% showed at least one deficiency sign."[31] Nutritional research into the quality of diets in Shanghai had begun in the early 1920s, largely as an academic enterprise (nutritional research departments were routine components of biomedical teaching and research institutions, which were established in Shanghai and other parts of China during these years). However, the researchers soon found themselves embroiled in social issues, because there was considerable disagreement over the causes of poor urban diets. The main disagreement, reflecting differences of opinion in the field of research nutrition more generally, pertained to the weight to be attached to poverty on the one hand, or to an ignorance of nutritional values on the other.[32]

A 1937 research trip to the Shanghai countryside for a study of rural diets helped clarify the dispute and find a middle ground. As one key report on the findings of the study noted, comparing Shanghai explicitly with a rural area:

> Several visits have been made to a rural area for close examination of the clinical conditions of the inhabitants. The results of these observations are in striking contrast with those of the city in the almost complete absence of gross signs of deficiency and in the better general state of health and well-being. In this locality, comparatively difficult of access and more than two hundred and fifty miles away from Shanghai, it was interesting to find that scarcely a household had not contributed to or in some way was affected by labour demands in Shanghai. In general the conclusion was that there is little to teach the Chinese countryman in the utilization of his resources and much to be learned from his empirical methods. This is in contrast with conditions in the city where modern conditions of transport and marketing have been found to vitiate traditional customs in so far as the food value of the manufactured product is concerned.[33]

The heart of the problem was that Shanghai workers preferred to eat polished rice, despite its nutritional deficiencies, because it was a symbol of urban status and prosperity—indeed, it was one of the ways that urban workers distinguished themselves from the farmers of rural communities. Polished rice was also eaten in rural areas, but technological advances in Shanghai rice-husking technology produced a much more highly polished product.[34] Yet Shanghai workers were not making up for the resulting loss of nutrients, because they were not complementing the highly polished rice with adequate supplementary foods. The overall message of the report was that Shanghai had become a place that corrupted "traditional customs," and that it was time for the city to learn from the country.

The BSA, to the dismay of the labor activists, found considerable policy and political value in such scientific findings. Having conducted its own nutritional analyses of workers' diets, it concluded that the working poor were not malnourished because they were poor and underpaid, but because, by choosing to eating polished white rice instead of healthier foods, they were not allocating their financial resources adequately. Accordingly, the BSA recommended what amounted to a cultural solution to the problem of malnutrition—that working families reform their consumer habits—rather than a political-economic solution that addressed structural wage issues and capital-labor relations.[35] By shying away from the class-struggle rhetoric that left-wing writers used to discuss the living conditions and poor diets of Shanghai workers, the BSA's analyses of Shanghai working family diets thus complemented the comparatively conservative *minshi* rhetoric that underlay its investigation into the city's rice price problems.

The Shanghai Food Supply During Wartime

Even the limited efforts of the BSA to intervene in Shanghai's food problems, however, were ultimately curtailed by Japan's invasion of south China. Japanese forces occupied Shanghai in two phases, taking the Chinese jurisdictions in August 1937, and then the International Settlement and French Concession a little over four years later, after the bombing of Pearl Harbor. The initial impact of the occupation on material life in the city was mixed. Early in the occupation, the International and French Settlements were flooded with refugees from the Chinese jurisdictions, and shantytowns appeared in great numbers along the city's periphery. Although some commodities, such as rice, had to be brought to the city from new areas, the city's economy was not immediately affected by the occupation. Basic and luxury goods remained available, and inflation was relatively slow to appear. According to some accounts, foreign settlement Shanghai actually witnessed an initial period of prosperity, evident in the tremendous growth of, among other things, the city's restaurant industry.[36] As one contemporary observer remarked, "Life among the Americans and British seemed to follow pretty much the pre-'37 pattern, though with rather more dining and dancing than before and certainly more drinking."[37] Life was not so cheerful for all city residents, however, for "the war, far from leveling off inequalities between the rich and poor, increased the disparity and intensified the stratification."[38] Moreover, the period of initial prosperity did not last for long. According to Eleanor Hinder, former Chief of the Industrial and Social Division of the Shanghai Municipal Council (SMC), by August 1939, two years into the occupation, cost of living index figures were double what they were in 1936.[39]

Among the many items affected by inflation was rice.[40] The Japanese army and occupation forces had blocked the waterways through which Shanghai's rice was brought to market from the interior. The SMC averted immediate disaster by placing orders for rice from Saigon.[41] Hostilities also gradually subsided in Shanghai's neighboring provinces, making it possible for rice to enter the city "in fair quantities." By early 1940, however, the Japanese military was siphoning off local rice for its own use, and after Japan gained control of northern Indo-China, it "naturally came into possession of a weapon with which to force 'cooperation' upon Occupied China. Straightaway she used it, in precisely the same way Germany used food as a weapon in Occupied Europe."[42] Prices soon rose rapidly, and the SMC established its own Rice Price-Fixing Committee. The committee slowed the rate of inflation, but in December 1941, in the wake of the Japanese bombing of Pearl Harbor, Japanese forces occupied the entire city, and by early in the following year, prices were again climbing at unprecedented rates.

The rapid rise in the cost of living during the second phase of the occupation was partially the result of the depreciation of the Chinese national currency, and partially because of shrinking supplies and the growth of the black market in rice. The currency crisis resulted from the introduction of the new Central Reserve Bank (CRB) currency by the collaborationist Chinese regime in Nanjing (the official central government of China had relocated to Chongqing and had lost control over the economy of the Shanghai region). After the new currency was issued, Hinder notes,

> Chinese National Currency depreciated day by day till two national currency notes were equal to one Central Reserve Bank note issued by Nanking Chinese authorities. Prices then naturally rose in terms of Chinese National Currency. [When, in June 1942] it was announced by the financial authorities that Central Reserve Bank notes would be henceforth the only legal currency,

most shopkeepers merely altered the enhanced National Currency prices un-changed into prices expressed in Central Reserve Bank notes, automatically doubling them.[43]

This inflationary situation was then exacerbated by new restrictions on the sale of rice issued by the Japanese occupation authorities. In July 1942, the Japanese authorities approved a plan to issue rice ration tickets for local rice.[44] Four hundred rice shops, which opened at 9 A.M. each morning to long lines, were licensed to sell 1.5 *sheng* (roughly 2.7 lbs.) of rice per week to ration card holders, for CRB $4.20. As Poshek Fu points out, because one adult consumed an average of .88 lb. of rice per day, one ration provided enough for only three days. People thus turned to other sources, and as a result, by January of the fol-lowing year, the black market "accounted for 70 percent of rice consumption in Shanghai." Black market prices were much higher than in the licensed rice shops and rose from $170 CRB per picul in December 1941 to $1,200 in Febru-ary 1943. In an effort to reign in the black market, Japanese authorities lifted its ban on unlicensed rice trafficking in March 1943. The price dropped temporar-ily back down to $700 CRB, only to rise yet again to unprecedented heights. On one day alone, July 6, 1944, it jumped from "CRB $6,800 in the morning to $8,000 in the afternoon and to $10,000 by nighttime." By the end of the year, it was nearing $50,000, and in May 1945, "with U.S. B-29s bombing Shanghai, it had reached the all-time high of $1,000,000 (over against rationed rice which sold for $6,500)."[45]

The challenges of the occupation period brought widespread hunger, and introduced the powerful idea that the city's food problems had been brought about by the Japanese occupation forces and their collaborators. The identifi-cation of these two new factors shifted attention away from more generally un-scrupulous merchants, workers who misallocated their financial resources, or idealized images of rural foodways. Thus it was believed that, with the coming of the end of the war, the problem would go away, and city residents expected the post-war Nationalist regime to be able to bring inflation under control and restore a semblance of order to urban life.

However, as is well known, economic conditions in the city scarcely im-proved with Japan's defeat, and during the next four years, city residents only grew increasingly frustrated with the Nationalist government's inability to curb inflation. Inflation took a toll on nearly all aspects of city life and ad-ministration and ultimately "alienated large segments of the Chinese people, especially the intellectuals, who blamed the government for mismanagement and irresponsibility."[46] In autumn and winter 1948, butter reportedly cost 750,000 *yuan* per pound, eggs 10,000 *yuan* each, and chicken 200,000 *yuan* per pound. Food itself had become a valuable form of currency, with the wealthy paying their servants in rice and barter becoming the rule of the day. One foreign import-export operator related how he obtained some "urgently needed supplies from a Chinese merchant by 'paying' with some cases of tinned sardines worth £4,000." As one insider's account of the "fall of Shanghai" put it, "Inflation was not only a human tragedy, it was a political tragedy which played into the hands of Communist sympathizers, for it was the workers who suffered—the very people on whom the economy depended . . . . What hope had any government of retaining their loyalty, if they starved while corrupt officials made fortunes."[47] When word began to spread in Shanghai, in April 1949, that the Chinese Communist Party had crossed the Yangtze and was heading toward Shanghai, many were hopeful that Shanghai's food problems might be solved, once and for all.

Food and Liberation

For several months after the PLA entered the city, order-keeping was its and the CCP's main order of business, both within the city limits and in its agricultural hinterland. This priority decisively shaped the CCP's early approach to solving the city's food problems and underlined its early successes. One of the CCP's first priorities was to monitor all forms of movement in and out of the city, a task that aided the CCP's efforts to supervise the shipment of food supplies. Moreover, the party took a much more comprehensive approach than the BSA had ever considered taking to gaining control of the city's rice supply.

A comparison of the CCP's approach with that of the BSA helps draw the magnitude of its intervention into relief. First, it will be helpful to have a better understanding of the Shanghai rice trade. Rice changed hands six times from the point of production to its sale in rice shops in Shanghai. It was grown by rice farmers, who sold their product in bulk to traveling rice merchants known as *mike*. This peasant-*mike* transaction, however, was not direct, but mediated by either "inland" rice merchants (*neidi mihang*) or rice huskers (*michang*). After purchasing their rice, the traveling rice merchants, generally organized into *bang*, or groups based on native place (the Changshu, Wuxi, Kunshan, Qingpu, and Luli *bang* dominated the Shanghai trade) shipped it, usually by boat, to Shanghai. Once in Shanghai, the *bang* would then entrust their rice to "distributors" (*jingshoushang*), intermediaries between the traveling rice merchants and urban-based rice merchants (*mihang*). The distributors would take samples and assess the volume of cargo and then try to find a rice merchant buyer. Eventually, a meeting among all three parties would be held to set a price, and after a deal was struck and the rice was unloaded, the urban rice merchants would then sell and distribute their rice to individual rice shops (*midian*), where it was finally sold to the urban consumer.[48]

The BSA policies had required professional registration for most of the parties to the Shanghai rice trade, but the Bureau itself actively sought only to control the behavior of one party, the traveling rice merchants (*mike*). Although the BSA successfully asserted its authority over this sector of the rice trade during the rice price crisis of 1930, a more comprehensive system that sought to influence the actions of all parties to the trade might have prevented the problem from becoming so severe in the first place. Moreover, the complex exchange network had left the city's rice supply vulnerable to Japanese control and black market profiteering during wartime. The CCP was thus determined to control production, transport, distribution, and prices.

The precise process by which the party gained control over this six-stage process is not clear, because the archival records on the Shanghai food supply between 1949 and 1951 remain sealed. What is clear, however, is that the party's more comprehensive focus anticipated its eventual efforts to nationalize agricultural production. It also reflected the party's sense that, given the state of economic disarray at the time of its arrival in Shanghai, order-keeping, at almost any cost, was a key priority for the city.

This prioritization of order-keeping was perhaps most evident in the way that the CCP carried out land reform in the Shanghai hinterland. Indeed, in the countryside surrounding Shanghai, the party's policies for land reform, generally the second major step in the consolidation of power in rural areas, were "fairly moderate."[49] In theory, and in some parts of China, land reform was a violent process. It was designed to put into practice Mao's observation, "A revolution is not like inviting people to dinner . . . . A revolution is an uprising, an act of violence whereby one class overthrows another."[50] Land reform was key to the process of social leveling that redistributed land from landholders to landless peasants, but also a part of the process by which "poor peasants," who were "alone capable of carrying out the work of destruction," could carry out that destruction. Their degree of poverty, and thereby revolutionary potential, distinguished them from "rich peasants," who had "surplus money and grain," and from "middle peasants," who "do not have any surplus money and rice" but are still "able to assure themselves of clothing, food, and shelter every year."[51] Experience had taught the party, however, that land reform, if conducted too swiftly, produced a disorderly process that Shanghai could ill afford.

Land reform in the Shanghai countryside began in June 1950.[52] Significantly, the only landholders hit hard by the campaign were those classified as "rich peasants of a semi-landlord type." The party requisitioned without compensation land that agricultural households in this category rented out, but even they were "allowed to keep fields that they had previously worked with hired labour." There was, on the whole, less change in the way that crops were planted, grown, and harvested than in the way that they were distributed, which "increasingly resembled industry more than agriculture." The government also purchased additional land previously owned by private groups, "family meetings, temples, churches, schools and urban industrialists and merchants," and "distributed [it] only on the basis of 'state-owned land use certificates.'" When land reform was declared complete, just after the 1951 spring planting, officials emphasized its "technological benefits" more than its political gains.[53]

The party complemented these rural measures with austerity campaigns in the city designed to reduce dependency on scarce commodities and reign in extravagance and undesirable consumer practices. Some of these campaigns appealed to all city residents; thus, "People were urged to eat an ounce less of rice a day, or to eat gruel twice a week instead of rice."[54] Others focused more closely on certain sectors of the urban economy. An August 1949 proclamation made it illegal for brothels to, among other things, "host large banquets."[55] Soon thereafter, prostitution was declared illegal, and before long, the city's brothels closed down. Because restaurants provided food for brothel banquets and were often the site of assignations between prostitutes and clients, there was a sharp decline in restaurant business, further easing strains on the city's food supply. Political stability gradually created conditions for improved harvests of food grains in the countryside, and urban incomes rose moderately during these years, at least until 1953, providing for a slightly larger "market basket" for the average working family.[56]

Restaurants also attracted some more focused attention from the party organization in Shanghai because they posed two threats to its authority in the city. On the one hand, restaurants were the "sugar-coated bullets" that tempted even young PLA recruits, as suggested by *On Guard*. On the other hand, they were potential bases for counterrevolutionary activity. That restaurants might

present the latter danger was a lesson the party likely drew from its own successful effort to establish an underground Shanghai party organization in the
city's Meilongzhen Restaurant, beginning in 1945.[57] One restaurant that drew
particular scrutiny was the Beijing cuisine Kaifu Restaurant, which the party
identified as having once been an important meeting ground for capitalists,
Japanese militarists, and Nationalist Party officials. Gao Zhisheng, the Kaifu
manager from 1945 to 1951, learned this lesson the hard way. On April 21, 1951,
Gao was "rounded up," along with 8,358 others citywide, on the first night of
the Campaign to Achieve Unity of Thought and Action (*Tongyi xingdong*).[58]
Gao was detained for two months of political study and released only after the
authorities were satisfied that his consciousness had been raised.

It is not clear how many other restaurateurs the party targeted during the
campaign, but a record of the party's concerns survives in Gao's self-criticism.
The self-criticism illustrates what kind of transformation party members had
in mind and in store for the restaurant world and members of the restaurant
industry:

> I was arrested late at night on April 27 (arrested on account of being a counter-
> revolutionary). At the time I was dumbfounded. How could somebody like
> me—somebody who after leaving school (at age nineteen) worked in film and
> theater circles (for twenty-one years), and then at Kaifu Restaurant (for six
> years), and who, moreover, did not participate in any organizations, cliques, or
> reactionary political parties . . . and who considered himself to abide by the law,
> know his place, and not do anything bad—[how could somebody like me] be
> said to be a counterrevolutionary element? . . . I [eventually] realized that I was
> indeed guilty. Before Liberation, 60 percent of Kaifu Restaurant's customers
> consisted of reactionary soldiers, puppet police, and puppet air force and navy
> [figures]. Because I was the manager, I was in regular contact with them, and so
> I became acquainted with many of them, in the way a proprietor gets to knows
> his customers. After Liberation, a small portion of these reactionary political
> party figures frequently ate at Kaifu. At the time I had forgotten my standpoint,
> I had forgotten that I was of the People of the People's Government . . . [and]
> as before I was extremely polite and respectful in my attitude when welcoming
> [these customers]. From my subjective view point, this was just doing business:
> whoever came I should treat that way . . . . But it was precisely my tolerance of
> counterrevolutionary elements that demonstrates that I committed the grave
> counterrevolutionary crime of harboring evil-doers.[59]

The formulaic format of Gao's self-criticism is typical, but two features stand out in particular. First, as far as Gao knew, what he refers to as his "subjective" viewpoint, being a restaurateur was about providing service to anyone, for a customer was a customer, plain and simple. What he learned, however, was that, viewed from the "non-subjective" viewpoint of the "People," customers differed depending on their relationship to the political process. Second, Gao's failure to recognize this difference made him no different from the various "counterrevolutionaries" who patronized Kaifu. Future restaurant managers, as Gao learned, would not be able to view their work as just "doing business," but would become participants in a political process. That political process yielded new images of urban food culture, new ways of organizing the city's restaurant industry, and new ideas regarding the role of a food service industry in a social ist society that was designed to "serve the people" and not their enemies.

Old-Shanghaiing Shanghai Food Culture

These new images of Shanghai food culture emerged from reports that party committees and government organizations produced on Shanghai's restaurant industry. The most important of these organizations was the Shanghai Food and Drink and Service Company (Yinshi fuwu gongsi), the umbrella organiza-tion for service industry trades in Shanghai. The company's reports grew out of a series of investigations that party authorities conducted to prepare restau-rants for their transformation from private enterprises into "joint state-private enterprises" (*gongsi yeying qiye*), the first stage of the socialist transformation of private business after the Five Anti Campaign of 1952, which focused largely on heavy industry. The reports shed valuable light on the process by which the Communist Party "Old-Shanghaied" Republican-era Shanghai food culture, converting prior left-wing criticisms of Shanghai food culture into officially sanctioned images of the city's past.

These left-wing images, some examples of which have been discussed ear-lier, lay crucial groundwork for the government's longer-term goal of creating a new food culture for the city. Yet, although many of the left-wing writings of the Republican period provided diagnoses of the problems with urban food culture, not all of them provided valuable models for constructing a new urban food culture. The CCP certainly did not want to revert Shanghai into the rural image that Tang Hai had noted as a better day for Chinese foodways. Indeed, the CCP's long-term plan for Shanghai was to transform it from a center of commercial capitalism into the most important industrial city in all of China. The party was also realistic about not expecting Shanghai's urban workers to modify their diets to conform to the more whole-grain-based rural diets that nutritional researchers identified as the source of healthier living. Instead, for constructing a new urban food culture, the party built on a third line of argumentation that made the diets of the urban poor into a symbol of revolutionary potential. At the same time, it also hedged its bets on a growth in agricultural output that would soon provide ever richer and more abundant supplies of food.

Among the most notable left-wing precedents for this idea was Ding Ling's novella "Shanghai, 1930." Although many left-wing writers, as noted earlier, depicted Republican-era urban diets as a problem, writers such as Ding Ling developed their accounts of urban food culture into some surprising new directions, redefining elite urban diets as backward, and the diets of the urban poor into a model of a future, good society. The purpose of such literature was to provide its readership with models for cultivating and hardening revolutionary will, so that individuals could promote and participate in processes of progressive social change in the absence of a government body committed to doing so.

This aspect of Ding Ling's writing is evident in both halves of "Shanghai." In the first half of the novella, Ruoquan, an earnest left-wing writer, visits his psychologically ailing mentor, Zibin, in the company of Meilin, Zibin's reluctant girlfriend, and his own girlfriend, Xiaoyun. Even before they visit, Meilin complains that doing so will be "useless," because with Zibin, "all you can talk about is food, drink, or entertainment."[60] Ruoquan persuades Meilin to try anyway, and the scene of their visit is punctuated by talk of food, and especially of those foods that marked "regressive" and "progressive" behavior:

> The maid brought in a mound of candy and fruit. Zibin ate the most. He picked up a famous chocolate, praised it highly, and urged his guests to help themselves. "Meilin just loves this. Right, Meilin?" he looked at her.
>
> "Sure she likes it," Xiaoyun thought to herself. "But you were the one who instilled this taste in her because it shows class. If she only liked *dabing* and *youtiao*, you probably wouldn't be so happy to put her on display."
>
> Actually, what Meilin retorted was, "No I don't like it any more. I'm tired of it. Yours is the taste that never changes."[61]

The scene registers the powerful class and political markings of food—chocolate as bourgeois and Western, *youtiao* and *dabing* as Chinese and proletarian—and of the struggle to define one or the other as progressive. It notes, on the one hand, the way in which the morally bankrupt Zibin has sought to "instill" these markings in Meilin, to make her seem "modern." Yet, on the other hand, it registers Meilin's discomfort with being so marked, as well as her own understanding that these foods constitute a world that "never changes." Indeed, this very exchange anticipates the rest of the story line: Meilin soon appeals to Ruoquan for help, having decided that she wants to join the revolution and improve living conditions in the city, where "pot-bellied businessmen" live a stone's throw from workers whose "lives got harder with spring's arrival because rent and the price of grain were up."[62] Meilin, whose interpretation of the rice price inflation of 1930, it should be noted, differs markedly from that offered by the BSA, eventually leaves Zibin, who, for all his apparent overeating, slowly wastes away. She thus recognizes that urban diets need to be improved, but that, at the same time, only the diets of the urban poor provide one with a revolutionary potential to carry out that change.

Food operates similarly in the second story-line of the novella, which centers on the deteriorating relationship between an underground Communist Party organizer, Wang Wei, and his girlfriend, Mary, a fashionable "modern girl" who has just moved back to Shanghai. On the night of Mary's return, she suggests that they have dinner where Wang usually eats, but he realizes how much he has changed since they were last together: "Small, filthy, crowded restaurants flashed through his mind. Then he glanced at her outfit—the imported velvet coat with a fur collar, the neat gloves, and the shiny satin shoes—and bursts out laughing, 'We can't go to any of those places. Mary, lately I've been living in the style of the common people.'"[63]

Mary, it turns out, is fond of Cantonese cooking, so they hop in a rickshaw and head across town, Wang hoping that the four *yuan* in his pocket will cover the cost of a meal that is not too extravagant. Again food serves as mark of character, for the fashionable Mary is predictably fond of Cantonese food, the trendiest regional cuisine in Shanghai during the Nanjing Decade, and Wang notes that her eating habits mark her as a bad candidate for his newly austere life: "Every inch of her body testified to the fact that she was fit only for a happy life, nutritious food, and pure fresh air."[64] Mary was also fond of going to small Western food restaurants, but Wang was even less comfortable in those establishments, and their different attitudes toward food and eating out becomes the undoing of their relationship. Anxious to head off to organize political events, Wang "would become nervous because he could see the clock on the restaurant wall moving very quickly, and he didn't have a lot of time to keep her company."[65] Meanwhile, Mary keeps trying to drag Wang Wei off to try new restaurants and to purchase fruit in large department stores. Over time, the demands of Wang's political organizing prevent him from coming home for dinner, and Mary is left alone to eat by herself.

Like such left-wing literary accounts of the Republican period, the PRC state's early reports on Shanghai's restaurant industry also yielded both negative and positive images of Shanghai food culture. The reports are replete, on the one hand, with negative and highly critical images of Shanghai's high-end restaurant culture, which they evaluated alongside the least salubrious aspects of Shanghai's entertainment culture and organized crime. But they also contained numerous positive images of Shanghai's "mass" food culture. Moreover, they register the party's earliest understanding of ongoing trends in the transformation of Shanghai's consumer base from a high-end to lower-end market. The party was encouraged to see already taking place many of the changes that it planned to implement through the transition to joint state-private ownership.

The reports' negative and positive images defined the new terms of food politics in the city. On the negative side were Shanghai's high-end restaurants. Party reports grouped these establishments together with other forms of urban leisure, and restaurant owners together with notorious figures of the Shanghai underworld and "collaborators" from the Japanese occupation period. They thus contain many references to figures such as Xie Baosheng, who in addition to being Shanghai's police chief during the occupation period was also the owner of a bath house, a hotel, and a dance hall, and Huang Jinrong, the criminal boss and racketeer, who owned the Dalu and Zhongyang Hotels.[66] The reports castigated these men for lording over an industry that had a "slave-like management structure" and that gave employees no freedom, no job security, and no social status.[67] A second component of the negative image of Old Shanghai put forth in these reports pertained to the city's status as an "adventurer's paradise."[68] The reports described the city as a veritable "brothel district for living a life of luxury and dissipation" and associated the city's high-end restaurants with less reputable branches of the entertainment and service industry, condemning the men who ran and patronized these establishments. "Those imposing hotels, extravagant restaurants, debauched coffee shops and bars," one report noted, "are all places where 'upper class' gentlemen spend freely, seek pleasure, show off their wealth, and waste away. . . . The bureaucrat-compradors, the despotic landlords, opportunistic unscrupulous merchants, foreign devils—all day they led a life of debauchery, flirted and made merry, [committing] rape and murder: no evil was not committed."[69]

The reports took some comfort, however, in certain ongoing trends. Party investigators were pleased to discover that, even before the transition to joint state-private enterprise, the components of Shanghai food culture that the party found most problematic were already showing signs of disappearing. The high-end Chinese restaurant sector had been one of the most volatile sectors of Shanghai's broader food industry, having been "distorted" by social trends and recent history. Regional restaurants, party investigators noted, numbered some three hundred before the outbreak of the Second Sino-Japanese War, but during the war, the number shot up to more than 1,500, only to drop to 778 by 1955. Of those that remained in 1955, the investigators reported that the smaller establishments were doing fairly well because "the working people were their main customers," but the mid-sized and larger establishments, "which in the past had served a small parasitic class and specialized in ostentatious-ness and extravagance," had lost much of their customer base. The Western restaurant branch suffered similarly, in business and in reputation. Reports counted two hundred such establishments before and after the occupation period, noting that they served a clientele consisting largely of "foreigners, bureaucrat com-pradors, opportunistic merchants, clerks in foreign businesses, and 'A-Fei' dancing girls." But by 1955, only sixty-seven remained, and of these, only ten served "authentic" Western food, to "foreigners, art and literature workers, and people in the medical profession." The others now sold Chinese food.[70]

Other branches of the food and drink industry fared better in government investigators' assessments, indicating that there were components of "Old Shanghai" food culture that the party was eager to see continue into the present and eager to support. The party found that the city's "bakeries and snack food shops," for example, initially suffered a drop-off in business after 1949 because the bulk of their business came from festival and family celebrations, and businesses and private consumers alike were now spending less on holiday celebrations, weddings, and funerals. But these shops apparently adapted quite quickly to Shanghai's changing consumer base, and their business recovered soon after they started to provide more "mass" (*dazhong*) food items, such as soy milk, rice balls, and fermented glutinous rice dumplings. The "noodle and dumpling shops" had an even easier transition. They had always served relatively simple fare, such as Yangchun noodles, wontons, and boiled rice-flour dumplings (*tangtuan*). Although investigators found that their "skill [level] was conservative and backwards," and that members of the industry had a "rural outlook," this was not a liability: "Because their prices are relatively low and their business hours long, they are able to meet the needs of the average working people." Other establishments that continued to do a good business were congee shops, which had a similar clientele and prospered in the lower-income neighborhoods of the Tilan and Zhabei districts, as did shops specializing in fried wheat cakes (*youbing*). Finally, government investigators found that one sector of the food industry—the food vendor (*tanfan*) sector—had grown substantially during the early years of the PRC. Food vendors numbered 4,448 in 1945, 7,145 in 1949, and 22,949 by 1955, a pattern of growth for which investigators offered a straightforward explanation: "Food vendors meet the needs of the working people." The proliferation of food vendors reflected both changing mechanisms of supply and demand, as well as party policy. They represented the component of Shanghai's food culture that the party initially encouraged most, on the grounds that they were run by everyday people—83.4 percent were "husband and wife" operations—and for everyday people.[71]

The business histories of food vendors were also amenable to a kind of storytelling that emphasized the success stories of everyday people struggling through the trials and tribulations of Shanghai's recent history. One subject of such storytelling was a certain Zhang Yuanding, a native of Zhang Village in Ma'an Town, in Shaoxing, Zhejiang Province. Zhang started working in a dye shop in nearby Jiading in 1937, but when the shop was taken over by Japanese in 1939, he made his way to Shanghai. He first found work in a lumberyard, where he acquired the nickname "Old Shaoxing." Soon, however, he went into business for himself, when he realized that there was more money to be made by purchasing and cooking left-over cuts of chicken—heads, wings, and other miscellaneous parts—and selling them after dark on the streets and, secretly, to lodgers in small hotels. Business was good enough for Zhang's son and mother to join him in Shanghai early in 1940. The son, aged only sixteen at the time, earned the name Xiao Shaoxing (Little, or "the younger," Shaoxing). In 1943, the father moved the business to a street stall on today's Yunnan Road, near the intersection of Ninghai East Road, and they continued their hotel business on the side.[72]

After the war, the street food business picked up, and the father-son team expanded down the street, where they started to sell poached chicken and chicken congee. Their poached chicken was apparently unremarkable, however, until the son picked up a cooking tip from a customer visiting from Hangzhou, who advised him to submerge the chicken in cold water after poaching. The technique produced a chicken that had "snappy skin and tender meat," and before long, "Xiao Shaoxing" was the most popular stall in the neighborhood. Xiao Shaoxing and its story were tailor-made for the changes that party officials had in mind for the city's restaurant industry. In 1959, party officials incorporated the business into the Yunnan Road cooperative canteen and designated the original stall a branch canteen.[73]

Despite the prevalence of this negative and positive imagery in party reports on Shanghai's restaurants, the state's interest in the industry, and in industry reform, was not simply ideological or political. It was equally concerned with finding ways of supporting sectors of the urban economy that were faltering well before any direct state intervention in its operations. Shanghai's service industry revenue increased considerably from 1952 to 1953, but revenue decreased by almost 25 percent the following year. Business for the Western Food and Coffee Shop branch of the industry dropped 50 percent, and business for the Chinese Restaurant branch dropped more than 40 percent.[74] According to one report, 669 of 873 Chinese restaurants were losing money, and the majority of Western restaurants and "take-out" (*chufang*) establishments, the latter of which had once done a brisk business catering to brothels, were also in the red.[75] The drop in business had reduced cash flow in some establishments to such an extent that many were not able to stock their kitchens. The Indian Curry Shop and the Shengxin and Sanliujiu restaurants started borrowing money from employees to purchase supplies. Other establishments required that customers pay for their meals first, after which the managers sent employees out to buy the necessary ingredients. Yet other establishments bought prepared food on credit from food stalls and then resold it to their customers. This created situations that on more than one occasion led to brawls between restaurant workers and food stall operators, because many restaurants were not able, or simply refused, to honor their debts.[76]

There were, from the state's perspective, pros and cons to these broad trends. On the one hand, the investigators attributed the trends to changes in the composition of Shanghai society that the party was encouraging. Thus, reflecting on the causes of this problem, one report explained, with evident pride:

Following the reorganizing of economy and society, the old service target has disappeared. The service target of the trades experiencing difficulty were mostly: (1) imperialists; (2) reactionary bureaucrats; (3) comprador capitalists, opportunistic merchants, and dancing girls; (4) mobile consumers like guest merchants from other cities and [extra-local] wholesalers; [and] (5) market traders, [local] wholesalers, and middlemen. For example, the Imperial Coffee House was the meeting place for opportunistic rubber, cotton, and tobacco merchants; the Indian Curry House used to serve the prostitutes of Huile Alley; the Xueyuan Laozhengxing served the Xianle and other cabarets, cabaret customers, and dancing girls.[77]

On the other hand, however, the drop-off in business had serious social consequences. Employees at a number of the city's largest establishments, the investigators found, "live in straightened circumstances and make it through the days by pawning clothing and [other] articles." A certain Cai Qingyun of the Indian Curry House apparently "sold his three-year-old daughter" in desperation; many others turned to selling blood to get by.[78] The state's hands were also tied by its initial reliance on a corps of restaurant managers who had been trained in a management climate that made them good at "putting on a show" and "going in for ostentation and extravagance," but not always so good at responding to the "change in the social climate away from the phenomenon of splurging on food and drink." There also was very little capital for the state to work with because most high-end restaurants had apparently "squandered all of their capital on construction, tables, chairs, bowls, and stoves, and so mobile capital was very low."[79]

Recognizing these problems even before the state did, some high-end restaurant owners had begun to seek new kinds of customers. They, like the party investigators after them, realized that establishments selling "mass" food items were able to maintain a stable business and even do more business than in the past, and they tried to adapt accordingly. For example, the Bailaohui Restaurant, "to meet the needs of the working masses in neighboring factories, added mass food items, changed its menu, adjusted the portion sizes of its dishes, changed its business hours, [and] listens to feedback from the masses."[80] Liuhexin Restaurant "in the past served only capitalists, but because their target had disappeared they took the initiative to lower the price of their set meals, add varieties, speed up service, and [reorient] their service to the workers and cadres at neighboring offices and industries." The Xiyang Western Restaurant, once a meeting place for rubber merchants, reinvented itself as a purveyor of vegetable rice (*caifan*), an inexpensive staple of Shanghai cookery.[81] Xinya and Xinghualou, among the more successful high-end Cantonese restaurants during the Nanjing Decade, each added a "mass dining hall" and a "snack division" to serve workers and cadres. The criteria for what made for a successful restaurant had changed so much that Xinya now deserved recognition for its successful efforts to cut costs on fuel, water and electricity, soap, and staff meals.[82] The state, having taken stock of the restaurant industry, planned to support such trends and, ultimately, rebuild the industry from the bottom up, to create a restaurant industry that catered to the needs of everyday city residents and the urban poor.

Between Austerity and Prosperity

The state was determined to create an urban food culture that would "serve the people," but it faced a set of economic and ideological challenges. The state's plans for developing a sound socialist service industry geared toward "mass" consumers depended on steady economic growth. One phrase that appears repeatedly in reports preparing for the transition to joint ownership was the following: "During the years 1955 to 1957, in the wake of the rise of purchasing power, restaurants industry business will probably rise, but it is estimated that during 1955, because a portion of the old consumer target is disappearing before the new is there to take its place, business will drop a tenth from 1954."[83] Reports containing this phrase did not clarify just what the "new" consumer target would be, but they intimated that a new population with resources to eat in restaurants would be one of the fruits of economic reform. Reports of just six months later, however, were considerably less sanguine. This was not because they doubted that a new consumer target with purchasing power would eventually emerge, but because of the difficulties restaurants in Shanghai continued to face obtaining raw materials.[84]

These were real problems reflecting real food shortages in the city, and they demanded dramatic solutions. Despite improved levels of agriculture production in the Shanghai hinterland, the city faced a grain deficit between 1949 and 1957, and it was forced to begin rationing food grains in August 1955. The rationing of edible oils had begun even earlier, in 1953, and pork rations were implemented in November of 1956.[85] The food shortages meant that the number of shops selling even some of the most "mass"-oriented of foods, such as *youbing*, was expected to decline. One solution called for expanding the boundaries of Shanghai, a policy carried out in 1958. The idea was that the "incorporation of a large and rich agricultural area would reduce external dependence for basic commodities and, by increasing the municipal authorities' control over agricultural production, supply and distribution, facilitate planning."[86] Ten previously independent counties in the greater Shanghai region were incorporated into Shanghai Municipality that year, and the policy was moderately successful at ameliorating the city's food supply problems, providing greater supplies of grain, vegetables, and pork.

Yet, although there were few food supply crises in the city during the next decade, the worker's paradise that the party had promised to all never materialized. In addition to encouraging commercial food vendors to increase their offerings of affordable "mass" foods, the party also created a vast network of communal canteens to complement the workplace cafeterias in which many city residents ate. But the poor quality of the food became a source of common complaint, and so many continued to supplement these state-provided provisions with home-cooked meals. Supplies at local food markets, however, remained limited, and these markets thus became yet one more arena where the city's enduring food problems were evident to all. Indeed, in her memoir of her Shanghai childhood, Wang Zheng refers to Shanghai's food markets as a "battlefield":

> Even with all the kinds of coupons that rationed food equally for city dwellers, the quality and quantity of everyone's meals were not equal. If a housewife could manage to be first in line in the market, the best cut of pork would be hers. Otherwise, she might have to purchase a piece of lousy meat from pig breast with her half a jin monthly ration. Vegetables and fish were not rationed, but sold on a first-come first-served basis. The markets did not usually open until 7:00 A.M., but many housewives began to lining [sic] up as early as 4:00 A.M.[87]

For Wang's mother, who "ran from line to line every morning" on her formerly bound feet, "getting enough food was a major part of her life. She had eight children and a husband (a picky one) to feed."[88]

Although party officials were aware of the challenges that everyday city residents still faced at putting food on the table, it was also becoming increasingly aware of ideological challenges regarding the city's food supply. First, party investigators insisted that reforming the restaurant industry and other food providers like workplace cafeterias and communal kitchens required finding solutions to economic problems and developing techniques for "consciousness raising." For example, though party reports approved of and sought to facilitate ongoing changes in the restaurant industry, they questioned the motives of those implementing these changes, by calling their political consciousness into question. In particular, they faulted industry reformers for adopting the general attitude that "improving business management work was simply [a measure] to mitigate difficulties." They voiced the additional concern that "once difficulties were vaguely mitigated, the work to improve business management would stop."[89] Failure to convince all food suppliers to adopt more than a "purely economic viewpoint" might jeopardize the party's ability to provide a genuinely socialist service industry for Shanghai.

One solution to these economic and ideological problems came from the economic ideologies taking shape in China on the eve of the Great Leap Forward (1958–60). The Great Leap was a program for rapid economic development that identified ideology and revolutionary will as the foundation for material prosperity. Its policies demanded optimism about the future, despite, even because of, the widespread poverty that still characterized much of China in the mid-1950s. As Mao put it, "Poor people want change, want to do things, want revolution. A blank sheet of paper has no blotches, and so the newest and most beautiful words can be written on it, the newest and most beautiful pictures can be painted on it."[90] Poverty, in short, provided the starting point for a "yearned-for future."

It was in an ideological context shaped by Mao's "poor and blank" thesis that the Food and Drink Company attributed to restaurants a certain future status in an emerging four-fold classification of service industries in Shanghai. It identified sectors of the food service industry selling inexpensive foods, such as congee shops, as "needed by vast numbers of the People, beneficial for production and commodity circulation, still currently sustainable, and temporarily irreplaceable." Restaurants, however, it grouped with hotels, Western-style suit shops, designers, wash and dye shops, and bath houses, deeming them, more ambiguously, "high-end-consumer oriented, at some distance from the average [person's] purchasing power, but for which, from a long-term perspective, there is still need." It also classified restaurants alongside hair-stylists, mechanized sewing shops, and a portion of Western-style suit shops, designers, photographers, and wash and dye shops, into another category, that of "over-supplied in Shanghai while lacking in other parts of the country." The overlap is significant. Although the Food and Drink Company recognized a temporary glut of restaurants in Shanghai, it remained convinced that the rise of purchasing power would one day provide enough customers to sustain that sector of the economy. Moreover, it also anticipated that purchasing power would be rising all over the country, and that Shanghai's surplus would become a valuable resource for meeting the broader consumer demand for restaurants that would follow nationwide. Thus, the Food and Drink Company did not locate the restaurant sector, as it did advertising, transshipment and news agencies, caterers, tailors, and inns, among "those intermediary in character and unnecessary given shifts in the social atmosphere."[91] Despite the economic difficulties of the present, the government recognized there was definitely a place for a more high-end variety of food provider in Shanghai's future.

The Shanghai government put this optimism to work by turning its attention to the resources at its disposal, Shanghai's rich history of regional food culture. Ideological considerations aside, party investigators were probably relieved to find that even if Shanghai, like the rest of the country, had not become as wealthy in material terms as had been hoped, from the standpoint of regional food culture, the city was neither poor nor blank. Party organizations in Shanghai had not paid too much attention thus far to the regional character of food in Shanghai, largely because the regional character of food had not fit neatly into the class emphasis of early government reports on Shanghai's food problems. Party policy was by no means hostile to the idea that food culture had a significant regional dimension, but early industry investigators did not have a clear place for the regional significance of food culture in their particular politicized view of food and identity. In contrast, reports from the mid-1950s through the early 1960s are preoccupied with identifying local specialty foods in Shanghai, and with finding ways of perpetuating the many regional restaurants that had once made Shanghai a center of culinary cosmopolitanism.

Party officials may have first become aware of the magnitude of local interest in regional specialty foodstuffs in 1954. That year word got out that a farmer named Liu Sigen, in neighboring Xinzhuang Village, had carried out successful grafts on ten peach trees in the peach orchards of Xinzhuang's Luchang Temple. The grafts came from old peach trees in nearby Huajing, Longhua Township, and were reportedly of the treasured honey nectar variety. Longhua had been a site of honey nectar peach cultivation since the late nineteenth century. Even though Shanghai residents deemed the Longhua product a pale version of the peach that had once been grown in Shanghai, farmers there had continued to grow the fruit. But Longhua peach cultivation went into decline in the early 1930s, and the few orchards that remained at the time of the outbreak of the Second Sino-Japanese War were reportedly destroyed during wartime.[92] Locals greeted Liu's effort to revitalize peach cultivation with excitement, and the party quickly picked up on this development. The year after Liu grafted his trees, a *Liberation Daily* news story noted, "The masses all report that the honey nectar peach is of very good quality" and proposed that "the loss of the Longhua honey nectar peach be prevented, and production of the honey nectar peach be restored."[93] Liu's trees apparently produced a delicious peach and came to be known on the Shanghai market as the Luchang Peach. Conveniently, the expansion of Shanghai's borders in 1958 incorporated Xinzhuang into Shanghai Municipality, effectively making the Luchang peach a Shanghai honey nectar peach (laboratory testing would later confirm that the Luchang peaches were, indeed, heirloom varieties of the Gu family peaches).[94]

The revival of local peach cultivation heightened party awareness of aspects of food culture that had not fit so neatly into the Manichean distinctions that early party reports drew between "mass" food culture and the city's "decadent" high-end restaurants of the Republican period: the local or regional character of food. Significantly, the party found a way of linking this character of food to its idea of the "masses." As the *Liberation Daily* news article indicates, the party now recognized that the "masses" themselves had an interest in local specialty foods. It was the "masses," after all, who had revived local peach cultivation of their own initiative. And it was to the "masses" that the party could now turn for further guidance about how to develop regional food culture. The challenge lay in figuring out how to provide specialty foods with a "mass" character.

The solutions that party officials generated for preserving and developing Shanghai's regional food cultures called for new ways of assessing the labor of food production. During the first half of the 1950s, the party had been so concerned with identifying a "mass" consumer base for Shanghai food culture that it had, remarkably, largely overlooked the labor that went into preparing food. That would soon change, as officials began to formulate policies for training chefs, and new frameworks for celebrating their accomplishments as model workers. This new focus on the labor of the chef dovetailed in important ways with the policies and ideology of the Great Leap, which emphasized the potential for human beings to transform nature. The result of party policies regarding Shanghai food culture would be a revitalization of the local snack food culture of the neighborhood of Shanghai's City God Temple, Chenghuangmiao, and of the idea of Shanghai as a place that was home to a regionally diverse restaurant industry.

Speaking the Five Flavors

Having devoted several years and much ink to criticizing the high-end food culture of "Old Shanghai," and especially that of the foreign settlements, the party first turned its attention to a sector of Shanghai's specialty food culture that they were able to describe in politically unimpeachable terms, the food-stuffs in the neighborhood of the City God Temple. This neighborhood had been a defining feature of the former county seat for centuries, and so it had a long history to which many Shanghai residents felt a strong attachment. More-over, it was located in a part of Shanghai not commonly associated with the ideologically derided culture of Old Shanghai. Finally, the foodstuffs for which the temple neighborhood had become famous had the virtue of being relatively inexpensive, and made from relatively inexpensive ingredients. Thus, they were affordable to the masses, and they could be prepared even in a time of relative food scarcity. As one report explained:

> Chenghuangmiao has a lot of specialty foods and snacks with a rich tradition of unique characteristics. . . . Some, like fermented glutinous rice dumplings, have a history of over one hundred years, and are famous near and far. Moreover, [these items] are delicious and inexpensive . . . costing as little as three *fen*, with the most expensive costing only three *jiao*, like the three *fen* fragrant and flaky "crab-shell" cakes from Xudeji . . . and the three *jiao* eight-treasure rice from Gushunxing . . . and the three *jiao* Nanxiang pork dumplings from Changxin-glou, with a thin skin and fatty stuffing, and which have a history of more than fifty years. . . . In addition, the sweet congee, noodles with scallion-infused oil and dried shrimp, deep-fried squid, savory vegetable crisps, and wheat gluten with tofu skin are all relatively famous products. Maintaining and carrying on the characteristic features of these famous foods and making these foods more available is what the Party wants; it is also what the great masses want.[95]

The idea was sound; the only question that remained was how best to support food culture of the City God Temple neighborhood.

When the Food and Drink Company first took an active interest in the City God Temple, in the late 1950s, it was already an important urban market place and "leisure space for the city's working people," receiving more than fifty thou-sand visitors per day, twice that number on Sundays, and often more on holi-days. It boasted sixteen food shops that served sixty-two specialty food items to twelve thousand customers daily (again, double that number on Sundays).[96] But the quality of the food sold there was faltering. One reason for this was a short-fall of ingredients, such as lard, which was a key ingredient in eight-treasure rice. A second reason was the aging of the city's corps of chefs, which threatened to break off transmission of the knowledge of specialty food production.

Party investigators had first become aware of the aging of the city chefs during the transition to joint state-private ownership. The political transformation and economic difficulties of restaurants during the early years of the PRC had brought a temporary halt to the recruitment of new chefs. Historically, young chefs had learned their trade through an apprenticeship system, training with a recognized master of a particular regional cuisine for three years, before taking work in a new environment or, in establishments that were large enough to require a team of chefs, continuing on in a subordinate position. However, the financial crises that many high-end restaurants faced during the civil war years and the early years of the PRC had made it impractical for restaurant chefs to take on new apprentices. Thus, as one government study observed, "Since Liberation [these sectors] have basically not absorbed new personnel."[97] As a result, of the twenty-six "famous chefs" (*mingchu*) in Huangpu District, thirteen were ill, and 85 percent of the talented chefs and pastry chefs citywide were older than age forty-six. The situation was further exacerbated by the reassignment of personnel for industrial and agricultural production.[98] Thus, in a city that had once been famous for its restaurants, the restaurant industry was becoming characterized by a "low skill level, with only fifty chefs widely regarded as highly skilled." The city's shrinking corps of professional chefs, combined with the shortfalls in ingredients, meant that specialty foods were not being prepared in the same ways that they had been in the past.

The party came up with several solutions for these problems, two of which will be discussed here (others will be discussed in the following section). One solution was to streamline the distribution of ingredients and the food offerings of each City God Temple food establishment, to guarantee that the supply of food items met the needs of as many customers as possible. New policies dictated that each vendor would specialize in only one item; thus, Nanxiang pork dumplings were to be sold only at Changxinglou, Shanghai-style spring rolls only at Songyunlou, and "crystal dumplings" only at Guihuating. There were also new regulations mandating smaller portions, six dumplings instead of ten per order, and that extra supplies be delivered to prepare for the increase in business on Sundays.[99] Policy went so far as to dictate the quantity of ingredients that were to be contained in each item, so that the skin of a *xiaolong* pork dumpling was to weigh exactly 2.5 grams and contain 2.5 grams of pork filling.[100] The measures were minor, but they testify to the Food and Drink Company's determination that regional specialty foods be made available to as wide an audience as possible.

A second solution was to "mobilize" the employees and chefs of the City God Temple neighborhood's specialty food shops. This solution was designed to help chefs remember forgotten preparations and to "excavate snack foods that were on the verge of being lost," like sweet tofu, Chinese chive and egg fritters, garden pea soup, pickled wheat gluten, pickled river snails, stinky pressed tofu, and fish dumpling soup. The chive and egg fritters had apparently not been made for thirty years. Older workers thus participated in informal "memory-discussion" sessions, during which they discussed cooking techniques and their memories of the taste of different items. They were then invited back for follow-up meetings to taste samples of specialty foods prepared according to their instructions.[101] A second report elaborated on how this process worked and the gains that it yielded:

> In order to develop and enhance famous dishes and food items . . . we adopted excavation, interview, view-and-emulate, exchange, heart-to-heart, and compare-and-assess methods. Under the leadership of the Party, we held a series of meetings to exchange experiences regarding product quality, as well as symposia on different cooking techniques and cooking demonstrations. . . . And in so doing we broke through the shop barrier, expanded the horizons of food varieties, enriched and raised the skill level of employees, and studiously manifested the Party's demand—"What others have, we have more of; what others don't have, we also have"—finally turning Chenghuangmiao snacks into a feast for the eyes, [a place of] so many beautiful things that one can not take them all in.[102]

These "memory-discussion" sessions were a trademark feature of Maoist revolutionary practice. They were an activity that people most associated with the "speaking bitterness" (*suku*) campaigns of the land reform period. During land reform, the party had encouraged poor peasants to speak out in public forums about the abuses they had suffered over the years at the hands of landlords. The objective was to take the results of oral history and put them into revolutionary practice to change society for the better. The Food and Drink Company officials who designed the City God Temple food shop sessions did not orchestrate these sessions to elicit bitterness, however, but to recover the wider range of tastes and flavors that distinguished Shanghai specialty foods. The past, the party was now indicating, did not have to be only bitter, but could also be spicy, sour, salty, and even sweet. The party had made culinary nostalgia into a form of revolutionary praxis.

The City God Temple food shop measures focused largely on recovering and developing distinctive Shanghai foodstuffs for a "mass" consumer base. The focus on Shanghai foods was itself significant because it provided Shanghai's "masses" with a distinctly Shanghainese food culture. Officials also recognized, however, that nonnative Shanghainese, as well as Shanghai's Muslim Hui population, still had preferences for the foodstuffs of their native places, or special food needs that needed to be catered to. Thus, as the final report on work at Chenghuangmiao proudly reported: "Out of consideration for the needs of minority nationalities, we have added at Chenghuangmiao a Halal dining hall and Cantonese snacks, providing beef soup, beef pot stickers, sweetened almond soup, and sesame porridge."[103]

Top Chef

The revitalization and streamlining of the local specialty food offerings in the neighborhood of the City God Temple was only one of two major party interventions into the city's regional food culture. The second major intervention was the party's efforts to restore Shanghai's faltering high-end regional restaurant industry. It is hard to know exactly what the party's motivations were in undertaking this latter enterprise, since few city residents could afford to eat in them. Yet, there was some demand, and even expectation, that the party maintain at least some of these establishments. Undoubtedly, there were official allowances made for a small number of high-end regional cuisine restaurants to cater to the food preferences of local political elites, and also to serve nonlocal or national political elites, who when visiting Shanghai on official business expected to be able to sample the many cuisines that had given Shanghai a reputation as a food-lover's paradise. Such officials were, after all, the main patrons of these restaurants during the late 1950s and early 1960s, and anecdotal evidence suggests that officials ate quite well even during the years of the famine that followed the Great Leap Forward. At the same time, it was not entirely ideologically inconsistent for the party to maintain these restaurants in anticipation of more prosperous days, by which point larger numbers of city residents would presumably be able to dine in them. Whatever the party's motives were, it undertook this work by strategically identifying restaurants not as places of consumption, but as places of production. To do this, they focused considerable attention on the training of chefs and on documenting their many talents. In so doing, they made high-end restaurant chefs into a kind of model socialist worker.

To maintain the city's regionally diverse restaurants government officials in Shanghai instructed all sectors of the food and service industry to undertake recruitment drives and establish trade and training schools. For the first time in the city's history, professional chefs would be trained in a culinary school system, and a state-sponsored system at that. The Shanghai Food and Drink Company created several tiers of cooking institutes and called on local chefs from the city's best restaurants to draft the schools' curricula and train new chefs in classroom settings. The chefs were also put to work writing education manuals and compiling cookbooks. Among the new educational institutes were the Huangpu District Food and Drink Trades Middle School and the Shanghai Food and Drink Trades Class for Advanced Training in Culinary Technique. A third, the Shanghai Food and Drink Trades Culinary Technique Teaching and Research Group, combined teaching and research into cooking technique and culinary pedagogy, and a fourth, the Shanghai Food and Drink Trades Culinary Technique Research Group, focused specifically on research into the various regional cuisines of China. Leading chefs from Shanghai restaurants filled posts in all of these institutes. Among the texts drafted for classroom use were surveys and introductions to culinary technique, and recipe collections of a general and focused nature. Recipe collections included a comprehensive *Famous Dishes of Shanghai* (Zhongguo mingcaipu), as well as textbooks on Cantonese, Sichuan, Shanghai, Russian, and Western cookery, and treatments of particular kinds of foods and ingredients, such as snack foods, fowl, aquatic products, and cold plates.[104]

It is not clear how eager chefs were to participate in such institutions, which required them to disclose trade secrets in a state-controlled environment, but party authorities provided powerful incentives for participation that helped raise the public and professional profile of chefs. Among the most important of these incentives was an accreditation system for ranking chefs. Already in 1956, thirteen Shanghai chefs participated in an accreditation exam for the rank of "Top Chef" (*Gaoji chushi*). To earn this rank, examinees had to demonstrate the following set of skills: a mastery of techniques particular to a regional cooking style, such as the dry-sauté (*ganchao*) and dry-roasting (*ganshao*) of Sichuan cooking; an ability to prepare famous dishes; an ability to organize banquets; knowledge of the history of a regional cuisine; an ability to innovate and invent new dishes within the framework of a regional cooking style; and knowledge of raw ingredients.[105] The thirteen chefs were tested in one of four cuisine groups, Cantonese, Sichuan, Beijing, and Western.[106] Their evaluation consisted of a written exam followed by an oral presentation and cooking performance held at the Sino-Soviet Friendship Mansion (Zhong-Su youhao daxia). Among the judges for the event were Shen Jingsi, a renowned local gourmet, and Dong Zhujun, the proprietress of the most popular Sichuan restaurant of the Republican era, the Jinjiang Restaurant. Dong was by now a powerful figure in Shanghai politics, and her presence was emblematic of the opportunities for social advancement that the party was holding out for restaurant industry members. In 1951, her restaurant was incorporated into the Jinjiang Hotel complex, of which she was the first director. The new complex had been established on the site of the former Cathay Mansions, a luxurious hotel and residential compound built in 1929.[107]

The top chef exam received wide coverage in local newspapers. The news coverage highlighted the chefs' breadth of knowledge of regional Chinese cooking traditions and also noted that, during the cooking demonstrations and chef presentations, the question of the political status of chefs in China and overseas generated a lively discussion. Unfortunately, the accounts do not specify the substance or conclusions of this conversation.[108] We do know, however, that eleven of the thirteen earned the rank of top chef and were subsequently posted to restaurants located in major hotels: the Jinjiang Hotel, the Peace Hotel, the International Hotel, and Shanghai Mansions. Complementing the reportage was one article contributed by (or at last attributed to) a participating chef, Xiao Langchu.[109]

The assignment of these chefs to leading hotels helped the hotels develop their own reputations as purveyors of regional specialty foods. In 1961, the International Hotel had a team of ten experts in Beijing cuisine, Shanghai Mansions had sixteen in Yangzhou cuisine, and the Jinjiang Hotel had four in Sichuan (as well as one in Cantonese). The Peace Hotel had a wider mix of chefs, including Cantonese and Western food chefs, but still had a focus on Shanghai cuisine. This division of regional culinary labor seems to have been intentional. A report on the training of chefs for these hotels urged them to "work hard to accommodate to the tastes of customers and to provide dishes of varying taste," but it also added that they "should not add chefs trained in each regional style in order to accommodate tastes." Instead, to prepare for the need to cook the cuisine of a region in which a hotel did not specialize, hotels were instructed to train existing chefs to cook other cuisines on an "ad-hoc" (*kechuan*) basis.[110]

The Food and Drink Company reported that the first few years of cooking school training were a resounding success. One report, from 1960, noted that

Shanghai now had forty fully staffed regional cuisine restaurants that served upward of five thousand different dishes, and that "all of the traditional specialty dishes and cooking skills that were on the verge of being lost have basically been restored."[111] It also noted the establishment of several new educational institutions for training future chefs, including three middle schools, twelve vocational middle schools, two advanced study classes, one training center, and one practice kitchen. By 1960, the new training institutions had trained 2,100 new chefs. Many of these went to work in regional restaurants. Others were assigned to cafeterias attached to other urban institutions and even communal kitchens, to help diversify their food offerings.

The overall message of the report represented a remarkable turnaround from the kinds of messages about Shanghai's food culture that the same office had communicated in the early 1950s. It is perhaps not surprising that the Food and Drink Company would emphasize the accomplishments of its own office, but it is significant that it now considered these kinds of developments to be notable accomplishments. Indeed, the Food and Drink Company was starting to sound more and more like those who had celebrated Shanghai's food culture in earlier periods: "Chinese cooking has a long history and tradition and is one of China's treasured cultural inheritances. . . . Shanghai is a major city where specialty dishes from the country's various regions are gathered together."[112] The old reputation of the city also prevailed in the new national capital. In 1964, the State Council, the Guowuyuan, sent forty-nine chefs and hotel managers from Beijing to Shanghai for a six-month training session. Eighteen chefs went to the Jinjiang Hotel for training in Sichuan and Cantonese cooking; eighteen to Shanghai Mansions for training in Yangzhou cooking; eight to the Peace Hotel for Shanghai, Sichuan, and "Asian" cooking, and four more to the Overseas Chinese Hotel for Fujian and Cantonese. Remarkably, the State Council also sent fourteen chefs to the International Hotel for training in Beijing cooking, suggesting that Shanghai might have become a better place to learn Beijing cookery than even Beijing itself.[113] Party officials in the Food and Drink Company seem to have had good reason to be proud of their own efforts and of the chefs with whom they worked closely to perpetuate Shanghai's high-end restaurant culture.

Nowhere is this pride more evident than in the personnel files that the Food and Drink Company compiled for the city's leading chefs in 1963. These files reveal the value that officials placed on each of the different regional cuisines represented in Shanghai restaurants and hotels, local understandings about what distinguished each cooking style, and how officials sought to promote their presence in Shanghai and help them innovate in the future. The files contain detailed records of each chef's professional history, regional or culinary specialty, and special skills, as well as short narratives that identified each chef's record of innovation in his or her area of expertise and commitment to teaching. For example, the file of Beijing cuisine chef Tan Tingdong, a forty-three-year industry veteran who had been cooking professionally since the age of seventeen, described his basic skills as follows:

> He has a complete mastery of Beijing cuisine cooking techniques. He is an expert in the various [dishes] for banquets and snacks, and is skilled at deep-frying, stir-frying followed by thickening, sautéing over very high heat, stir-frying, steaming to finish in sauce, sautéing to finish in sauce, pan-frying, and roasting. The famous Beijing dishes that are his specialties include deep-fried chicken tenderloin, sliced fish in wine sauce, deep-fried "crispy pairs," pan-fried sliced chicken, pork tripe with nine turns, and steamed and sauced bear's paw, among which his sliced fish in wine sauce is especially notable. It has a pleasing appearance and an appetizing taste; the fish is tender, and the sauce thickens without visible thickening.[114]

Tan's file also stressed his record of innovations, noting that he "has conducted thorough research on technique . . . and carries on and develops Beijing style cooking, creating quite a few new dishes." One dish that he created with his co-chefs at Shanghai's Yanyunlou restaurant was the restaurant's signature Yanyun Chicken, for which cubes of chicken were first deep-fried and then stewed.

The name of Tan's restaurant and its signature dish hints at the way that, under party patronage, regional restaurants and cuisine continued to signify the broader regional history and cultural characteristics of the place from which the cuisine originated. Yanyun referred to the so-called "Sixteen Prefectures," a stretch of territory near Beijing that, one millennium earlier, the Later Jin (936–47) had ceded to the Khitan Liao Kingdom (907–1125), and that did not become a part of a Chinese ruled territory until the fall of the Yuan dynasty in 1368.[115] The continued integration of this territory with China proper under Ming and Qing rule suggested, on the one hand, that they were properly a part of China. But on the other hand, that the territory had changed hands so many times during its history suggested equally that its status as a part of China was uncertain. One can thus imagine that, at the time of the restaurant's establishment, in 1936, with warlords laying claim to the capital and Japan preparing to head south from its Manchukuo stronghold just to the north, the Yanyunlou restaurant conjured the northern city's then uncertain fate. However, by the early 1960s, Beijing, the Yanyun territories, and, indeed, all of the northeast territories had been firmly consolidated into the body politic of the People's Republic. For those who were familiar with the twists and turns of this regional history, Yanyun Chicken, having been lifted out of the deep fryer and returned to the saucepan, was no doubt a metaphorically suggestive, and perhaps even reassuring, dish. Other files make such cultural and regional associations more directly, such as the file praising Cantonese chef Feng Pei for being able to prepare "ingredients particular to Cantonese cooking, like seal, pangolin, and palm civet," and for being "one of the few chefs in Shanghai truly skilled at butchering snake." To help perpetuate this aspect of Cantonese cookery in Shanghai, Feng took a special trip in 1959 to source and purchase snake for Shanghai's restaurants.[116]

The personnel files, finally, reveal that party officials focused their attention on those aspects of chefs' work that could be identified as having a connection to the needs of building a new socialist society. This aspect of the files is not readily apparent because the bulk of each file contains a level of detail that suggests more of an interest in food than in building a new society. For example, the file of the Sichuan cuisine chef He Qikun notes,

> His skill in seasoning is outstanding. He excels at preparing such Sichuan flavors as "strange flavor," "hot and sour," "hot and numbing," "salty and numbing," and "hot oil." For example, his "fish flavor" perfectly balances sweet, sour, and spicy and is rich in litchi notes. His "*gongbao*," prepared by deep-frying red chili and Sichuan peppercorn and then removing them [from the wok], has the unique effect of "tasting spicy without looking spicy, and tasting numbing without looking numbing."[117]

What are we to make of such precise and labored descriptions of chefs' talents? On the one hand, they might be taken to reflect the extent to which party officials had forsaken the ideology of austerity on which the party had risen to power. This is a point that other components of the files seem to bear out. Thus, like his Cantonese cuisine colleague Feng Pei, Yu Hong is also praised for his ability to cook foods that few in Shanghai could even have imagined eating—"elephant trunk, monkey brain, monkey lips, bear's paw, deer fetus, swallow's nest, pangolin, shark's fin, and abalone"—if not because of the high cost and relative scarcity of these ingredients, then because these were foods in which only the most eccentric of gourmets had a genuine interest.[118]

Yet, on the other hand, the files also betray a profound respect for the artisanship of chefs, for their ability to use their talents to ameliorate social relations, and also for their exercise of mastery over the physical world. Thus, the file for Beijing cuisine chef Ning Songtao praises his skill at expelling the gamy taste from mutton, "so that when southerners go to his restaurant and eat mutton they do not notice any gamy taste." It further praises him for his ability to cater to the needs of minority nationalities, by modifying Beijing cuisine dishes to suit Hui dietary needs. Finally, it places great emphasis on his ability to work with his hands, as in this explanation of his *daofa*, or knife technique:

> He can julienne pork on top of a sheet of silk . . . without damaging the silk or leaving a trace of pork on the blade, and he can cut ginger into slices as thin and transparent as the wings of a cicada. . . . He is familiar with the bone structure of pigs and sheep and the connective tissue of each cut of meat, and when he butchers an entire pig or sheep, he not only works fast and produces a clean cut of meat, but his placement of the knife is precise, so that the meat is left intact and the carcass properly divided.[119]

One cannot read this description of Chef Ning's *daofa* without thinking of the depiction of the talents of Cook Ding in the early-Daoist classic, the *Zhuangzi*. In this hilarious but profound send-up of the Confucian valorization of mental over manual labor, Cook Ding impresses the Lord Wenhui with his ability to carve up an ox. When asked the secret of his success, Ding replies, "What I care about is the Way. . . . I go along with the natural makeup, strike in the big hollows, guide the knife through the big openings, and follow things as they are. So I never touch the smallest ligament or tendon, much less a main joint."[120] Yet there is an important and crucial difference between the *Zhuangzi*'s representation of Cook Ding's talents and the personnel files' depiction of Chef Ning's abilities. Cook Ding's talents lie in his ability to become one with nature and abide by the Way. Chef Ning's, in contrast, lie in his mastery over and ability to transform nature, a key component of Maoist economic ideology since the years leading up to the Great Leap. By celebrating the labor and talents of Shanghai's leading chefs as exemplary workers, party officials in the Food and Drink Company found a way of identifying their patronage of high-end cuisine as being perhaps not entirely inconsistent with the demands of the party's economic ideology and with revolutionary practice.

Restaurants and the Cultural Revolution

The party's effort to reconcile the tension in the revolutionary dialectic between austerity and prosperity in this manner was not, however, convincing to all. In 1966, two years after the Food and Drink Company compiled its chefs' profiles, its effort to promote and perpetuate Shanghai's diverse regional restaurant industry came to an abrupt end. The new political climate created by the tumultuous Cultural Revolution (1966–76) once again redefined high-end restaurants as corrupt, bourgeois institutions. To this idea, Cultural Revolution discourse added the additional observation that high-end restaurants constituted a component of the new bureaucratized apparatus of state elites that Mao himself identified as the greatest inhibitor of the development of socialism in China. All high-end restaurants quickly shut down, and although most eventually reopened and remained in business during the Cultural Revolution decade, all were reduced to serving the same few basic items of everyday Shanghai fare.

Typical in this regard was the fate of the Yangzhou cuisine Mo Youcai's Kitchen. This restaurant, which in its early years might be better characterized as a high-end cafeteria, was named after a highly respected chef of Yangzhou cookery, Mo Youcai. During the late Republican period, Mo, along with his three sons, had worked in a semi-private capacity for the managers of Shanghai's leading banks, preparing food for banquets that the bankers hosted in their homes. In June 1950, shortly after the establishment of the People's Republic, the father-son team acted on the suggestion of silk industrialist Rong Yinren, as well as other members of Shanghai's silk industry, and opened a "members-only" restaurant, in June 1950, in the United Club (Lianhe julebu). The membership of the club was composed largely of silk industry leaders, and it was located on the third floor of the Bank of China building on Ningbo Road. With only one dining room and a seating capacity of fifty, Mo Youcai's Kitchen was not an especially large operation, but it was initially quite exclusive, and served anywhere from ten to twenty different dishes per day to industry insiders. After the transition to joint state-private ownership, Mo Youcai's clientele expanded to include high officials and began to take in business off the street. It soon became famous outside of Shanghai, and high-ranking party members from around the country, including Dong Biwu, Chen Yi, Li Fuchun, and Chen Shutong, would eat there while in Shanghai so that they could sample its delicious Yangzhou cooking. In 1966, however, it was labeled a "black shop that serves cow demons and snake spirits" (class enemies) and remained closed until 1970. That year, it reopened as a restaurant for the "masses," serving every-day Shanghai fare.[121]

Chefs who worked at other high-end restaurants during these years report a similar pattern. Meilongzhen, once a high-end Yangzhou restaurant that had changed its repertoire to Sichuan cuisine to cater to wealthy returnees from the wartime capital in Chongqing, now drew its principle customer base from delivery truck drivers, whose trucks lined Nanjing West Road during the noon hour each day. It no longer served Yangzhou or Sichuan cuisine, however, and for nearly ten years its menu consisted of three dishes of inexpensive Shanghai fare: tofu and shredded pork soup, stir-fried baby bok choy, and vegetable rice. Chefs working at the Xinya Cantonese Restaurant, which was renamed "Red Flag Restaurant," served the same three items.[122] Cultural Revolution politics had thus restructured Shanghai's restaurant industry to accord with a new vision of a proletarian China, and restaurants ceased serving as vehicles for the appreciation of the country's diverse regional cultures. As discussed in the Epilogue, however, the new Shanghainese inflection of the Meilongzhen, Red Flag Restaurant, and Yangzhou Restaurant menus during these years was not itself without a certain cultural and historical significance.

Epilogue:
Shanghai Cuisine Past and Present

Between *Benbangcai* and *Haipaicai*

SHANGHAI HAS DEFINED ITSELF as a locus of regional food culture and consciousness, from the time of the city's emergence as a place of note during the Ming through the twentieth century. Culinary nostalgia, the recollection or purposive evocation of another time and place through food, provided city residents with a framework for understanding and identifying the importance of Shanghai as a place. Culinary nostalgia also helped city residents make sense of and define their relationship to the city, to other parts of China, and to the world beyond.

Culinary nostalgia took many different forms in each period of Shanghai's history, but as this book shows, some forms of culinary nostalgia were so pervasive that they constituted a central component of urban culture and identity. During Ming and Qing times, city residents located the region's agricultural accomplishments, and peach growing in particular, within a broader history of Chinese horticulture and food writing. In so doing, they created an image of Shanghai as a garden city that recalled culturally and politically significant gardens and orchards of the Chinese past. The second half of the nineteenth century, which marked Shanghai's transformation into an international treaty port, brought many newcomers to the city. These newcomers created and patronized regional restaurants that served the foods of, and evoked the cultures of, their home regions. But the newcomers also sympathized with city natives who mourned the fading of Shanghai's garden culture, and the idealized society it represented, that accompanied the rapid growth and transformation of the city during the second half of the nineteenth century. The introduction of Western food culture to Shanghai during the closing decades of the nineteenth century provided a new framework for representing Shanghai culture: first as China's most "modern" and cosmopolitan city, and then as a place in need of a restoration of "traditional" Chinese family structures. During the Republican period, a renaissance of regional Chinese food provided city residents with a template for imagining a national Chinese culinary heritage. After the founding of the People's Republic of China in 1949, even the Chinese Communist Party, which came to power with a mission to make Shanghai into a model of socialist industrial development, became a patron of the city's culinary history, especially the distinctive historical foodstuffs of the neighborhood of the City God Temple and the accomplishments of Shanghai's most experienced and brilliant professional chefs.

The post-Mao period (1976–present), and especially the last two decades of Shanghai's history, has witnessed developments that warrant additional attention. The first of these is the renewed importance that Shanghai residents attribute to Shanghai cuisine, a variety of local cooking that is commonly sold in two kinds of restaurants: everyday family-style (*jiachang*) restaurants, and more elaborate, high-end Old Shanghai theme restaurants that evoke the city's imagined heyday of the 1930s. The second development is the adoption of the term *Haipai* ("Shanghai faction") to designate Shanghai food culture more generally. Historically, this term referred to aspects of Shanghai cultural production in the arenas of theatre, visual arts, and literature, but never to food culture. Its recent use with regard to *food* brings a new meaning to the term and a new idea about the city itself. This rising consciousness, really a new ideology of regional pride, illuminates patterns of continuity in change in the history of culinary nostalgia in Shanghai, and in food history in China more generally.

"Old Shanghai" Revisited

Although I have devoted much space to the history of Shanghai's specialty foodstuffs and the various regional cuisines served in Shanghai's many restaurants, I have thus far said little about the meanings attached to Shanghai cuisine itself. This is because unlike Shanghai's specialty foodstuffs, like the Shanghai honey nectar peach, which city residents made into a symbol of the city as far back as the Ming period, Shanghai cuisine rarely figured into dominant constructions of the idea of the city before the post-Mao reform period. There were, of course, many restaurants in the city that served local Shanghai fare. By the early twentieth century, this style of cooking had come to be known as *benbangcai*.

"*Ben*" in this context means "local," whereas "*bang*," which might be translated as "group," is one of the terms by which city residents historically distinguished native place units in Shanghai.[1] *Benbangcai* thus might be translated as "local cuisine," but it has also clearly meant something more like "our people's food," and the term has helped Shanghai natives set off local Shanghai cuisine from the many other regional Chinese cuisines that appeared in the city beginning in the mid-to-late nineteenth century. *Benbangcai* was sold in almost all of the city's neighborhoods, generally in small food shops, or *fandian*, although a small number of large establishments selling *benbangcai* were popular. Yet, although many of the city's nonlocal regional cuisines acquired a broader prestige among non-fellow provincials and connoted a broader cultural significance for many city residents, *benbangcai* rarely constituted a central component of the city's identity as a center of food culture. To be sure, local cuisine mattered to many city residents. Indeed, the Chinese Communist Party's recognition of its importance led them to seek systematically to revitalize the Shanghai foods of the neighborhood of the City God Temple. However, recent developments in the city's history reveal the historical significance of *benbangcai* much more clearly than would be possible by focusing on local cuisine in the late Qing, Republican, or Maoist periods of Shanghai's history separately.

During the past two decades, local Shanghai cuisine has become the most popular and widely discussed regional cuisine in the city. Shanghai cuisine is still sometimes referred to as *benbangcai*, but now an equally common term is *Shanghaicai*, a shift that suggests that the meaning of local cuisine now derives less from what distinguishes it from other regional cuisines and more from its direct connection to the city itself. This variety of cuisine is quite popular and is sold today in two kinds of restaurants: family-style restaurants and 1930s-style Old Shanghai theme restaurants. These restaurants constitute two dimensions of a new food trend in Shanghai that has been shaped and animated by broader social processes. These include reform period economic policies, and ideologies that have changed the structure of Shanghai society and reevaluated Shanghai's historical contributions to the development of the Chinese economy and Chinese history more generally. Also significant has been a nationwide wave of nostalgia that has been especially acute in Shanghai, and which has inspired a renaissance of interest in Shanghai cultural production of the past.

Early post-Mao economic reform policies in Shanghai had a relatively limited impact on city life. The country's earliest economic reforms were rural in focus. And although there were also a number of important urban initiatives,

Shanghai was not among the relatively small number of urban areas identified as key to the reorientation of China's economy.[2] Shanghai did receive some foreign investment beginning in 1984, and a limited number of "new forms and types of employment were grafted onto the existing system."[3] Moreover, as in many other Chinese cities, living standards in Shanghai rose gradually during the 1980s, providing many city residents with often small but growing amounts of spending money. Yet on the whole, during the 1980s, Shanghai's "relative pre-eminence in the Chinese economy declined."[4] This pattern did not begin to change until the early 1990s. The year 1990 marked the designation of Pudong, located across the Huangpu River from the downtown Shanghai Bund, as a "focal point of the country's opening and reform drive." Then, early in 1992 Deng Xiaoping took his famous "southern tour," during which he was "widely reported to have said that Shanghai should 'seize the opportunity,' have 'more courage' and 'take faster steps' in reform."[5] Shanghai soon become the jewel in the crown of China's promise of economic development, and before long, the city was awash in money. These developments inspired new patterns of commercial growth and spending in the city, including a revitalization of the city's restaurant industry and restaurant culture.

Although the city's restaurant industry grew much more rapidly during the second phase of the reform period than it did during the first, it had shown some signs of growth even during the first phase. Restaurants were among the earliest of new commercial enterprises established in cities during the early years of economic reform, the policies of which provided new guidelines for private business management and ownership. Many of these restaurants, owned and operated by *getihu*, or small-scale entrepreneurs, were modest establishments and amounted to little more than street side or shop-front food vendors who catered to workers commuting between their homes and workplaces. Although small in size, their numbers grew quite rapidly. There was clearly a growing demand for eating venues that provided convenient alternatives to the workplace cafeterias in which most city residents ate their meals and for transient workers who lacked facilities for cooking at home. These vendors also offered a new kind of space for casual gathering and conversation outside of the workplace or home. Most simply sold noodles, wontons, and inexpensive everyday fare, but some introduced regional specialties to their menus. At the same time, larger state-run establishments also began to reassume the regionalist orientation for which they had become famous. Typical in this regard was the Yangzhou restaurant, which grew out of the former Mo

Youcai's Kitchen. As discussed in Chapter Five, during the Cultural Revolution, this once high-end Yangzhou cuisine establishment had been reduced to selling little more than vegetable rice, sautéed baby bok choy, and tofu soup with shredded pork—basic everyday Shanghai fare. In 1978, however, after being relocated and renamed the Yangzhou Restaurant, it begin to complement these Cultural Revolution "mass" offerings with a small number of specialty Yangzhou dishes. Soon it was offering set-price Yangzhou cuisine menus for special occasions such as weddings.[6]

In the wake of Deng Xiaoping's "southern tour," however, the restaurant industry really began to take off. The 1990s brought city residents and newcomers to Shanghai many new opportunities for employment and increasingly large amounts of disposable income, much of which went into restaurant meals. Each year seemed to bring a new regional food craze to Shanghai, ranging from Sichuan hotpot to Cantonese cuisine restaurants specializing in "live and kicking" (*shengmeng*) seafood. Many of these trends played out in new private enterprises, but business also picked up in many state-run establishments, a number of which, such as the Xinya Cantonese Restaurant and Xiao Shaoxing, developed into complex business enterprises housed in new multistory buildings with several distinct tiers and styles of dining rooms. Recognizing the growing market for regional specialty cuisine, some restaurant managers adopted commercial strategies that had prevailed during the Republican period to draw attention to their sector of the industry. The Yangzhou Restaurant, for example, developed a special "Dream of the Red Chamber" banquet menu that recreated famous dishes from the eighteenth-century novel of the same name.[7] This revitalized marketplace in culinary nostalgia also inspired the creation of new restaurants that evoked more recent history. Beidahuang, or Great North Wasteland, located in Shanghai's Hongkou district, specialized in the cuisine of northeast China, in particular that of Heilongjiang, a province to which many of Shanghai's youth had been sent during the Cultural Revolution.

These special menus and restaurants were part of a broader trend that achieved its most elaborate articulation in a new kind of Shanghai restaurant: the Old Shanghai theme restaurant. Among the more notable of these establishments was the "1930s Restaurant" (Sanshiniandai dafandian), which a news column published at the time of its opening described as follows:

> The dining room is decorated in 1930s style, in the color and flavor of the past
> (*guse guxiang*). The dining rooms are adorned with 1930s movie star posters,

and the background music is songs from movies of the 1930s. The restaurant also holds 1930s modern (*modeng*) hairstyle demonstrations, and every Saturday afternoon there is a free 1930s culture lecture series, including 1930s movie appreciation; famous 1930s residences; 1930s tea shops and *pingtan* [a Suzhou style of storytelling and ballad singing popular in 1930s Shanghai]; 1930s coffee shops and Western restaurants; 1930s farces, oil painting, Shanghainese theater and entertainment circles; and 1930s hair styles and clothing.[8]

The menu, the article failed to mention, was laden with many dishes of standard Shanghai fare: eight-treasure duck, fresh and salted pork soup, red-braised pork shoulder, sticky eel, and sweetened lotus root with osmanthus. Among the other Old Shanghai theme restaurants created during these years were Henry, Big Fan, and 1931, as well as such establishments as the Xi Family Garden that operate out of famous mansions and villas that, in the 1930s, had belonged to some of the city's most influential political figures and financiers. Such Old Shanghai theme restaurants have made headlines and attracted large pools of customers not only in Shanghai, but also in Hong Kong (Yé Shanghai, named for a popular 1930s song), New York (Old Shanghai Restaurant), and San Francisco (Shanghai 1930s). These Old Shanghai theme restaurants indicate that Old Shanghai nostalgia is thus both a local and an international phenomenon. Moreover, as the news article indicates, they point to the seemingly paradoxical manner by which this wave of Shanghai nostalgia evokes a "color and flavor of the past" that is able to connote a sense of the "modern."

These restaurants, which began to appear in Shanghai in the mid-1990s and continue to open today, were a logical outcome of the new emphasis being placed, during the second phase of the reform period, on Shanghai's historical contribution to the development of China's economy. The Chinese Communist Party's eventual promotion of a "socialist market economy," its repudiation of Maoist-era austerity, and its promotion of Shanghai as a front line of China's future economic, commercial, and even cultural development has fostered an unprecedented wave of nostalgia among Shanghai city residents for the city's Republican-era past. As Zhang Xudong has noted in his study of Shanghai's post-Mao nostalgia, the "sense that 'something is over' has created a window of opportunity to redefine the Chinese modern by reconstellating the past in terms of a future nurtured in a global context of ideology."[9] For decades considered a den of iniquity and injustice that exhibited all of the social, cultural, and political ills of what Mao termed China's "semi-feudal, semi-colonial" condition, Shanghai's past has now been rehabilitated. Looking backward, Shanghai residents have begun to note with pride the role that they too consider the city to have once played in the development of China's twentieth-century industry, finance, and culture, a role many consider Shanghai now able to play once again.

For many city residents, an idea of Shanghai's 1930s is the starting point for this reconstellation. As Rose Rong, proprietor of the Old Shanghai theme restaurant 1931 puts it: "The 1930's [sic] in Shanghai stand out as a time of peace, prosperity and culture. . . . It was a time when the different cultures harmonized instead of clashed. We try to recreate that 30's [sic] atmosphere completely; food, music, decor, because it's a time we are proud of, a time we like to remember."[10] It is worth pointing out, however, that as recreations of high-end 1930s Shanghai restaurants, one thing that the Old Shanghai theme restaurants seem to have gotten wrong, in a certain important sense, is the food. As the discussion of Republican-era restaurants in Chapter Four of this book indicates, the cuisine of choice in Shanghai's 1930s high-end restaurants was not Shanghainese food, but Cantonese.

Less anachronistic in their commodification of Shanghai food culture are the many "family-style" restaurants that have also spread across the city, and in far greater numbers than have Old Shanghai theme restaurants. These restaurants point to another important reform period development in Shanghai. Alongside the Old Shanghai euphoria noted earlier, the economic reform period has also witnessed the emergence of ambivalent feelings about social and economic change, as well as less uniformly enthusiastic statements about the Shanghai present and the city's 1930s than those offered by Old Shanghai boosters like Rong. Significantly, city residents express nostalgia not only for the 1930s, but also for what are sometimes seen as the more stable days of the Maoist period. At the very least, there is a recognition that both Maoist and post-Maoist forms of economic organization bring both benefits and risks. As Ban Wang notes in his study of nostalgia in reform-era Shanghai: "No sooner does the city get a chance to revive its auratic past than it is endangered by a new commercialization and money-grabbing."[11] It is thus perhaps not surprising that in addition to the glitzy Old Shanghai theme restaurants that celebrate the 1930s and the economic reforms, the 1990s also witnessed a rapid proliferation of much more modest, 1930s-aura-free, family-style restaurants. The menus in the two kinds of establishments are not notably different, but the atmosphere in the family-style establishments is generally unassuming. For customers, the difference is between establishments such as the "1930s Restaurant" that focus on selling an idea of the city and restaurants that focus on selling familiar and comforting foods. To apply the terms introduced at the beginning of this book, the Old Shanghai theme restaurants constitute an example of reflective culinary nostalgia and provide an opportunity to reflect upon a possible world, whereas family-style restaurants constitute an example of restorative culinary nostalgia and an arena for shoring up a sense of cultural continuity in a period of rapid change.

Excitement and ambivalence about the economic reforms are evident in the many articulations of nostalgia that became pervasive during the 1990s. On the one hand, there is a marked fascination with the 1930s. During the second half of the 1990s, bookstores and book stands throughout the city were piled high with old and new books on practically all aspects of this and slightly earlier periods of the city's history. There were reprints of classic anecdotal accounts of Shanghai's past, such as Chen Wuwo's *Record of Things Seen and Heard over Thirty Years in Old Shanghai* and Yu Muxia's 1935 *Shanghai Tidbits* (Shanghai linzhao); new books bearing such titles as *Old Shanghai: Years Gone Bye* (Lao Shanghai: yishi de shiguang); and more focused historical accounts of old universities, old architecture, old postcards, old movies and movie stars, and old fashions.[12] Also common were reprints of early-twentieth-century and Republican-era "Shanghai faction" (*Haipai*) literature that had been unavailable for more than fifty years.[13] On the other hand, there was also no shortage of books addressing some of the less salubrious aspects of the city's past and even a certain longing for the Maoist period. Books bearing titles like *Old Shanghai: Not Just Romantic Stories* (Lao Shanghai: bujinjin shi fenghua xueyue de gushi) are full of checkered reminiscences of the 1930s: about the problems of living in a city overrun with gangsters, the social problems caused by widespread gambling, drug abuse, prostitution, and hunger.[14] Alongside these, moreover, were collections of personal essays recalling the days of the ration system, noting both the deprivations the system reflected and caused and the various strategies that people found for living with it.[15] These works are all part of the broader wave of Mao nostalgia that arose during the reform period.[16] The simultaneous emergence of these two forms of nostalgia indicates that it is not obvious to all that the 1930s constituted a better time than the 1950s and early 1960s.

As Zhang and Wang note, few developments attest better to this reform-era and Old Shanghai ambivalence than the renewed popularity of the writings of Zhang Ailing, one of the most significant Shanghai writers of the 1940s, and the success of Wang Anyi, one of the most widely read Shanghai novelists of the post-Mao period. Zhang Xudong's study of Shanghai nostalgia, which focuses on these two writers, adopts a critical stance toward advocates of the rosy image of the 1930s. As he notes, the rosy image of the 1930s "can be considered a sentimental Chinese response to a global ideology, whose singularity lies precisely in its homesick longing for a futurological utopia hinged on some earlier or more classical phase of world-capitalism, on something Shanghai was once or at least could have been." When seen in this light, he adds, "The current Zhang craze (and for Zhang's Shanghai) becomes a coercive ideological discourse" characterized by "free-market dogmatism and empathy with a bourgeois universal history."[17] Instead, Zhang suggests, the resonance of the past lies instead in the way that it also provides a mirror for the problems people face today. Thus, Zhang's analysis of Shanghai nostalgia suggests that Zhang Ailing has become popular again not because she provides an image of a perfect pre-socialist alternative to the Maoist period, but because she offers a familiar picture of the complexity of life in a capitalist world.

Building on Zhang's analysis, Ban Wang goes so far as to suggest that the "alienating effects" of socialist and capitalist modernization are "comparable."[18] He finds confirmation in the popular response to the remarkable story line of Wang Anyi's 1995 novel *Song of Everlasting Sorrow* (Changhen ge), which recounts the checkered fate of a movie starlet during the Republican, Maoist, and post-Mao periods. *Song of Everlasting Sorrow*, he concludes, provides "a good example of the way the nostalgia narrative [both] affirms a certain practice of the commodity form and critiques the unquestioned embrace of the market among liberals and postmodernists."[19] It is worth adding to these observations that Wang Anyi has carefully appropriated and critically inverted the meaning of one of the best-known poems in Chinese history, Bo Juyi's (772–846) "Song of Everlasting Sorrow." This poem romanticizes the love of the Tang Emperor Xuanzong for the concubine Yang Guifei, and in so doing effectively whitewashes the disruption of the An Lushan rebellion (755–63), which is widely recognized as eroding Tang power and social order at its zenith, resulting in a death toll that some sources estimate to have reached thirty-six million.[20] Wang clearly recognized that Old Shanghai nostalgics were trafficking in a similar kind of nostalgic amnesia and is criticizing this trend by turning the impulse of the poem on its head.

Zhang and Wang's respective insights into the relationship of nostalgia to the uncertainties of the new marketplace in things and ideas helps us understand the appeal and challenges of nostalgia restaurants. Let us consider first Beida-huang, the Cultural Revolution theme restaurant mentioned earlier. Despite all of the self-evident peculiarities of a Cultural Revolution theme restaurant, Beidahuang, like some other forms of Cultural Revolution and Maoist-era nostalgia, provides a de-politicized version of Maoist-era life, one that is packaged as a product that can be bought and sold on the marketplace. Yet, as others have observed about these establishments, they also provide a valuable environment for maintaining and establishing social relationships. Many former sent-down youth use them for getting back in touch with other sent-down youth whom they met in the countryside during the Cultural Revolution and with whom they have lost contact. Beidahuang's entrance boasted a large bulletin board on which customers could post their contact information to facilitate such reunions. These establishments also provide an environment for extending these social relationships in ways that help city residents find a sense of security amid the uncertainties of the reform period, whether with finding opportunities for work, marriage, or financial investment.

These two activities—the commodification of time and place, and the quest for stable social relationships outside of the newer and more pervasive forms of commodified daily life—reflect a symbolic split in the two kinds of Shanghai cuisine restaurants that became popular during the 1990s. Indeed, the longing for the familiar evident in the proliferation of family-style restaurants is a logical counterpart to the changes in urban life brought in the course of the "rediscovery" of Shanghai's prosperous past, and the numerous ongoing attempts to reinvent that prosperity in a manner suitable to current international economic norms. A desire for continuity thus lurks in the background even of some of the more bold celebrations of the 1930s. This is evident, for example, in the newspaper article heralding the opening of the "1930s Restaurant." "The 1930s," the article notes, "was an important historical period of Eastern and Western cultural contact, when not only *shikumen* and *xiaoyangfang* went up simultaneously, but also when Chinese and Western food influenced one another."[21] *Shikumen*, or "alleyway houses" also known as *lilong*, became the most common form of Shanghai housing during the late-nineteenth and early-twentieth centuries. They then remained a defining feature of the urban landscape through the Maoist period, during which time the city experienced very little city planning in areas where there was already significant housing. In the 1990s, however, entire blocks of *shikumen*, many of which were located in or near commercial districts, were torn down to make way for new and more commercially lucrative high rise office towers. The city government relocated many former *shiku-men* residents, not all willingly, to suburban residential communities that now dot Shanghai's periphery. Vast tracts of the city center are now unrecognizable to many lifetime city residents. Family-style Shanghai cuisine restaurants help recall the city's increasingly unfamiliar urban landscape.

Between *Bengbang* and *Haipai*

The city's many "family-style" Shanghai cuisine restaurants also provide arenas for shoring up a sense of local culture distinct from ongoing efforts to define Shanghai as a crossroads of regional Chinese and non-Chinese cuisine, and of Chinese and world history more generally. In the context of reform-era food culture, these efforts are most evident not in Old Shanghai theme restaurants (although they do engage in this activity to some extent), but in a new discourse about "*Haipaicai*," or Shanghai-faction cuisine. The term *Haipai* is not itself new; it dates to the late-nineteenth century, when critics coined it to describe trends in Shanghai theater, art, and literature that distinguished Shanghai cultural production from a Beijing (*Jingpai*, or "capital faction") style.[22] The term has only recently come to be applied to Shanghai food culture. Its recent use to describe food culture, however, endows the expression with connotations beyond its original meaning. The reform-era discourse on *Haipaicai* is itself part of an effort to construct a new image of Old Shanghai, an image that, remarkably, has no clear place for local Shanghai cuisine, or *benbangcai*.

Haipaicai is not a new term for *benbangcai*. According to the proponents of the new term, a mixed group that includes culinary professionals, government officials, and social and cultural critics within and outside of China, *Haipaicai* is the product of an attitude toward cooking that is characterized by innovation and adaptation, and by a kind of culinary combination that may be described as "fusion." Possibly the first formal use of the term came during a government-sponsored municipal exhibition of cooking skills in the mid-1980s. At this exhibition, the representatives of the state-owned restaurant Meilongzhen presented dishes identified as *Haipai* cooking. Other participants in the event greeted the designation with surprise and skepticism. The skeptics, as Chen Xiande and Lang Hong note in their account of the event, "thought that this old establishment was [simply] starting something new in order to be different and harbored motives of trying to please the public with claptrap."[23] It was also not clear exactly what the term meant. Meilongzhen, which first opened its doors in 1938, originally specialized in Yangzhou cuisine. The restaurant then modified its repertoire to capture a short-lived craze for Sichuan cooking in the 1940s that followed Shanghai returnees from the wartime capital in Chongqing. For more than two decades, Meilongzhen was then known to specialize in Sichuan cuisine and Yangzhou snack foods. During the Cultural Revolution, Meilongzhen, like other high-end Shanghai restaurants, served little more than inexpensive items of local Shanghai fare. But Meilongzhen's representatives' claim that it was a restaurant that specialized in *Haipai* cuisine was not based on its approach to cooking or serving these items.

Instead, the claim was based on the idea that its chefs had created a new variety of Sichuan and Yangzhou cookery that warranted the designation *Haipai*. Chen and Lang characterize this new variety as the outcome of a broader process of the "Shanghaiing" (*Haihua*) of Sichuan and Yangzhou cuisine that took place during the movement of Sichuan and Yangzhou cuisine to Shanghai:

> Sichuan, which lies in the upper Yangtze region, has unique climatic and geographic conditions that leave it rich in foodstuffs, such as poultry and fish and shellfish, as well as melons, fruits, vegetables, and bamboos that comprise the ingredients of Sichuan cooking. Moreover, because of the humid climate, the Sichuan people's penchant for spicy food has become an addiction. [Yet] Sichuan cuisine is not only hot, it also excels at seasoning, and so the sayings "the seven savors and eight flavors" (*sizi bawei*) and "to every dish its own style" (*yicai yige*) have attached to it. As for Yangzhou, situated in the lower Yangtze region, the climate there is warm and the rainfall abundant, and fish and shellfish and agricultural by-products are plentiful. Yangzhou cuisine excels in knife-work and colorful arrangements; moreover, there are noted changes [in its repertoire according to changes in] the seasons. After these two regional cuisines followed the Yangtze River to Shanghai, in the course of encountering some limitations in their reception [among non-fellow provincials] they were reformed. *Haipai* Sichuan cuisine, while retaining the "seven savors and eight flavors" and the "to every dish its own style" characteristics [of the original], nonetheless call for a lighter use of spicy [chili] and of numbing [Sichuan peppercorn]. *Haipai* Yangzhou cooking, for its part, demands that its flavors be even milder and the choice of ingredients even more meticulous. Meilongzhen, by exploring [new approaches] in this manner, has exhibited the genius of Shanghai people . . . digging deep into a repertoire of several hundred traditional dishes and inventing more than a hundred new dishes, becoming the standout of what may be called Shanghai's "Sichuan-Yangzhou" cuisine.[24]

Here, *Haipai* cuisine is characterized in two overlapping ways: by its modification of non-Shanghai cuisines to accommodate the taste preferences of Shanghai palates, and by an inventiveness that creates new dishes according to, and by combining in new ways, established models and principles.

Chen and Lang suggest that the innovations of the Meilongzhen chefs were part of a broader trend in Shanghai cooking. As they note, "The banner that Meilongzhen first waved, and which newly animated a process that had been building up over several decades, has its theoretical basis and its practical experience."[25] Chen and Lang's rhetoric about *Haipai*'s theoretical basis and practical experience seems to echo ongoing early reform-era ideology regarding the need to "seek truth from facts." This principle was a trademark of the reform era that came to be associated with the "pragmatic" approach to economic development promoted by Deng Xiaoping. Yet, the term *Haipaicai* was not mere rhetoric and ultimately resonated quite widely in the Shanghai restaurant world. As clarity about the meaning of the term emerged during the conference, other participants observed that the innovations were not the private preserve of Meilongzhen, and that other restaurants also engaged in such experimentation and adaptation. That chefs had historically approached their work in this way is also clear from the Food and Service Company's chefs' resumes compiled in the early 1960s, which register the very innovative qualities that party officials identified as a defining characteristic of Shanghai's leading chefs.

However, the timing of the coining of the term in the early 1990s coincided with a shift in the significance attributed to this approach to cooking. In the 1960s, party officials valued this approach for what it revealed about the talents of chefs as model workers with a remarkable capacity to transform nature into culture and smooth over social relationships. In the 1980s and 1990s, in contrast, advocates of this talent of Shanghai chefs described it as a much more pervasive and deeper aspect of Shanghai culture more generally. As Chen and Lang note, "*Haipai* cuisine is the crystallization of the collective wisdom of veterans of Shanghai food and drink circles with a breath of vision, of chefs, and all the Shanghai people."[26] This was, moreover, a form of culture particularly appropriate to the party's new image of Shanghai. The party no longer viewed the city as a paragon of the development of socialist industry and labor, but as a meeting place of world commerce and culture. As Zhu Gang, director of the Shanghai Culinary Association, argued at a separate meeting of the Shanghai Restaurant Association: "*Haipai* cuisine consists of a repertoire of dishes that perpetuates and develops the outstanding traditions of all of the [regional] cuisines [of China] and adopts the strong points of all Chinese and foreign dishes . . . to create dishes that retain each cuisine's special characteristics and are suitable for the palates of Chinese and foreign guests."[27]

One topic that is strikingly absent from this discourse on *Haipaicai* is a clear articulation of what local Shanghai cooking, or *benbangcai* is, and of what place it has in a city with a culinary identity defined according to the concept of *Haipaicai*. Indeed, local Shanghai cooking has a remarkably shadowy presence in the *Haipaicai* discourse. There is, as the passages cited suggest, an implicit idea that local Shanghai food culture has such a powerful hold on the palates of city residents that it has forced chefs who cook non-Shanghai cuisine to modify their repertoire accordingly. Yet, local Shanghai cuisine, which itself is thereby represented as *not* having the same qualities of adaptation, innovation, and fusion, is *not* identified by the *Haipaicai* discourse as definitive of urban culture more generally. This paradox reflects a tension in terms of ideas about the sources of the cultural identity of the city. At stake is what one means when one is talking about, and identifying a character to the culture of, Shanghai. Does the crucial element of Shanghai culture lie with locals, who have watched their city be transformed during the past century and a half by several waves of migration from all parts of China? Or do these migrants themselves, by virtue of the ways that they adapt to Shanghai and its multicultural environment, define the city's character and identity? Once we pose the question this way, we can begin to see the way that the *Haipaicai* discourse marginalizes a remarkably common component of urban culinary practice.

The deeper implication of the marginalization of local Shanghai cooking by the *Haipaicai* discourse may be seen by considering the slightly different uses to which the Taiwan historian Lu Yaodong has elaborated a similar notion of *Haipaicai*. Lu shares Chen and Lang's and Zhu's vision of *Haipaicai* as an adaptive, innovative, and combinatory approach to cooking. What distinguishes Lu's notion of *Haipaicai* from that of Chen, Lang, and Zhu is his sense that it is an oppositional cultural strategy. Lu identifies this oppositional aspect of *Haipaicai* by situating it more clearly in a broader context of Shanghai cultural production. For Lu "inventiveness" is an important component of *Haipai* culture in general. As he explains and demonstrates through numerous examples drawn from art, theater, and literature, *Haipai* referred to a kind of cultural inventiveness that self-consciously distinguished Shanghai culture from the more orthodox northern varieties that were especially prominent in

Beijing.[28] This cultural inventiveness, he argues, grew out of long-term trends in Chinese middlebrow urban culture, *shijing wenhua*, but it achieved its highest degree of elaboration and authority in late-Qing and early-Republican Shanghai. This culture, he adds, ended with the rise to power of the Chinese Communist Party in 1949. "Under political repression," he concludes, "Shanghai not only stagnated, but moreover the present was cut off from the past." He expresses some hope, however, that a new link to that past may be in the process of being forged: "In the past twenty or so years Shanghai has gradually been reborn, taking shape as a mighty economic force. This economic force is in the process of penetrating each level of society, and maybe it can shape a new *Haipai* culture."[29]

Yet, despite Lu's identification of *Haipai* as an oppositional culture, his account of Shanghai food culture shares with that of Chen, Lang, and Zhu the idea that Shanghai food culture is best characterized by the idea of *Haipai*, rather than by local cuisine itself. This is evident in Lu's own examples of *Haipaicai*. Lu traces the origins of *Haipaicai* to the Republican period. He notes that the appearance in Shanghai of many different varieties of regional cuisine led, on the one hand, to a conservative impulse. Thus many establishments posted the words "authentic" (*zhengzong*) at their front doors and sought to differentiate the qualities and flavors of their variety of cooking from others.[30] Yet, on the other hand, it is also evident that there was a pattern of mutual studying and borrowing and an adaptation of flavors to meet Shanghai tastes. As an example, Lu notes the effort of the Anhui branch of the restaurant industry to expand its shrinking consumer base by creating the dish known as "wonton duck" (*hundunya*). This innovative dish contained shrimp wontons cooked in a clay pot with duck, and the waiters served it with a side dish of pig's blood soup (*daxuetang*), a local Shanghai favorite. The Cantonese branch of the restaurant industry, Lu notes, also "had no choice but to appeal to the Shanghai penchant for river shrimp and so the Xinghualou invented a dish known as Xi Shi Shrimp." The name referred to the appearance of the dish, which was said to evoke the milky-white skin of Xi Shi, one of the four famous beauties of ancient China. But its *Haipai* character came from the way it succeeded at "combining fresh river shrimp with milk . . . keeping the original Cantonese characteristic of appearance, fragrance, and taste, but preparing it for a Shanghai palate."[31]

Lu's account of *Haipaicai* raises two issues. The first pertains to his characterization of *Haipaicai* as analogous to other forms of *Haipai* culture and as a form of culinary practice particular to Shanghai. In this regard, Lu has overlooked what, even in his own analysis, are two very different uses of the term *Haipai*. Indeed, Lu's discussion of *Haipai* opera, theater, and art, while noting their quality of inventiveness, does not represent them as exhibiting tendencies toward regional combination. If anything, the immediate inspiration in his discussion is not the various qualities of regional Chinese forms of culture, but art and culture associated with the Western colonial presence, such as literary modernism. It is thus not clear to what extent the developments in Republican era culinary culture can be identified as "*Haipai*," if the term is to retain the meaning it had for people during that time. Indeed, it is more likely that precisely because developments in culinary culture were *not* analogous to those taking place in other cultural arenas, urban food culture never figured in the protracted late-Qing or Republican-era debates about the differences between *Haipai* and *Jingpai* culture.

Even if we endow the term with new significance for the purpose of identifying trends in the approach to cooking among some Shanghai chefs of non-local cuisine, it is not clear that such a trend should be considered a unique element of Shanghai food culture. In fact, the uniqueness attributed to the innovative and combinatory tendencies of *Haipaicai* may be an artifice of historical shortsightedness. It is arguable that the kind of fusion, or "incorporating vigor" attributed to *Haipaicai* is not unique to the development of what now passes for *Haipai* cuisine. Chen Mengyin, writing in the *Singtao Daily News* (Xingdao ribao) in the 1950s, made strikingly similar observations about the development of Sichuan cuisine.

As Chen explains, what passes for Sichuan cuisine today only took shape relatively recently, probably no more than 250 years ago. The population of Sichuan diminished considerably during the mid-seventeenth-century Ming-Qing transition, first under the short-lived rule of the rapacious rebel leader Zhang Xianzhong (1606–47), and then even more when Zhang's Great Western Kingdom was extinguished by the Qing. The population was replenished during the next century with fresh migrants from the central plains and several southeast provinces. During this massive population relocation, Chen suggests, cuisine in Sichuan developed in a way that seems to be remarkably similar to the way that Zhu Gang characterizes the development of Shanghai *Haipai* cooking: "When [the migrants] arrived in Sichuan, at first the dishes they ate were the original hometown flavors, but as the days passed, they and the local Sichuan people came together and understood each other more profoundly." Sichuan, Chen notes, enjoyed relative peace and prosperity for the next two centuries, and Sichuan residents turned to food as a form of leisure and entertainment, during which time what we know today as Sichuan cuisine took shape. As Chen puts it, "Authentic Sichuan people and the migrants from various other provinces engaged in mutual exchanges of cooking techniques, building on each others' strengths and dispensing with the weaknesses. And so, the art of Sichuan cuisine encompasses (*jianyou*) the strengths of each province."[32]

The second issue that Lu's account of *Haipaicai* raises pertains to the way that Lu posits this style as definitive of Shanghai culinary culture more generally. Like Chen, Lang, and Zhu, Lu suggests that local tastes, having been originally shaped by the character of *benbangcai*, demanded that nonlocal cuisine be transformed, thus leading to the emergence of *Haipaicai*. Yet, Lu too fails to discuss the character, let alone the enduring appeal, of *benbangcai* itself. Thus, even though Lu invokes the idea of *Haipaicai* to a very different end than Chen, Lang, and Zhu, in Lu's analysis too, *Haipaicai* becomes the defining element of mainstream Shanghai food culture. In relation to *Haipaicai*, local Shanghai cuisine occupies, again, a marginal and shadowy presence. It is present, and even influential, but it is somehow not meaningful.

The reluctance of critics as diverse as Lu and Chen, Lang, and Zhu to identify local Shanghai cuisine as a defining element of urban culture is no doubt related to the convention of insisting that Shanghai culture is innovative, progressive, and forward looking. Yet, a closer examination of the history of Shanghai cuisine itself suggests that it has not changed markedly over the last century. We also find little evidence that people have wanted it to change. This study has hinted at such a history of continuity, noting a tension between older images of the city based on specialty food crops like the honey nectar peach and ever-changing fashions of the regional cuisine restaurant world. Such a tension also seems to have played out between Shanghai cuisine itself and the many varieties of nonlocal cuisine sold in the city. This tension dates back to the early history of the city's treaty port years, but it has recently become markedly more pronounced. As the image of Shanghai as a peach orchard paradise became increasingly untenable, local cuisine came to serve the symbolic role once played by specialty food items as the repository of a Shanghai tradition and an enduring object of nostalgia.

Benbangcai in Retrospect

Reconstructing the history of local Shanghai cuisine during the past 150 to 200 years is not easy. Direct and clear evidence of its character and importance appears much less frequently in the historical record than does that for other regional cuisines in the city. Following the historical reconstructions of Zhou Sanjin, a member of several Shanghai culinary associations and work units, it could be said that local Shanghai cuisine just before and after the designation of Shanghai as a treaty port was similar in style to the cuisines of nearby Suzhou and Wuxi.[33] This makes good sense, as Suzhou and Wuxi cuisine, like that of Shanghai, are often grouped under the broader rubric of Huaiyang cuisine. Still, cuisine in Shanghai also drew on local aquatic products, vegetables, and preparations of salted pork and soybean products in ways that gave its dishes some distinguishing characteristics.

Shanghai cuisine, Zhou notes, was available at three distinctive types of establishments. Small food shops that served inexpensive fare like stewed pork with tofu skin, tofu with salted pork, soybean and shredded pork soup, grass carp with bean or sweet potato sheet jelly, and eight-treasures in sweet chili sauce. Then there were mid-sized establishments that differed from small food shops less in their offerings and more in the scale of the buildings that housed them and the use of set menus, although the mid-sized establishments did also offer a few more luxurious entrees of shark's fin, swallow's nest, roast duck, and mandarin fish, a prized local freshwater fish variety. More expensive high-end establishments boasted much more elaborate menus, in the variety of preparations and cost of ingredients, and offered such items as red-braised shark's fin, sea cucumber in scallion oil, steamed shad, eight-treasure chicken (a chicken stuffed with the same eight-treasures in sweet chili sauce sold in small food shops), and yellow croaker soup with clams.[34] Many of these dishes and the cooking styles that define them, from both the lower and higher ends of the industry, can be found in Shanghai family-style restaurants today.

This pattern of continuity, as well as the impulse to maintain this continuity, can be traced in the somewhat limited record of Shanghai cuisine restaurants available in urban travelogues, memoirs, and guidebooks. Shanghai cuisine restaurants are, to a great extent, the "unmarked" restaurants of late-Qing Shanghai travelogues and commercial guides. That is, guidebooks and commercial directories provide a regional designation for restaurants serving the cuisine of other provinces, such as Anhui restaurants (*Huiguan*) or Tianjin restaurants (*Jinguan*), but restaurants serving local cuisine are designated simply as representing the *jiuguan* (or "restaurant") branch of the restaurant industry.[35] One important exception to this pattern is the brief account of the Taiheguan in Ge Yuanxu's *Miscellaneous Notes on Travel in Shanghai*. As mentioned in Chapter Two, Ge notes that this establishment was "owned by a Shanghainese" and served "both northern and southern cuisine." This description suggests that the proprietor adopted a kind of combinatory approach to designing the menu, but there is nothing in the historical record to indicate that this approach consisted of anything more than putting the dishes of more than one region on the same menu, so it is not possible to know if this combination also constituted the kind of adaptation that has recently been identified as typical of *Haipaicai*. The approach of the Taiheguan may have also been aimed more at non-Shanghai natives than at local Shanghainese, since it was located in the International Settlement, where nonnatives vastly outnumbered natives. Indeed, the restaurant's International Settlement location was precisely what made it worth mentioning in Ge's guide, which conceived of its audience as consisting largely of newcomers to Shanghai.

Some indirect evidence that seems to support a more skeptical approach to the idea that the northern-southern Taiheguan was a typical late-Qing Shanghai cuisine restaurant may be found in Liu Yanong's recollections regarding the Shanghai cuisine Renheguan several decades later, just after the fall of the Qing. Liu describes the Renheguan not as a hybrid establishment like the Taiheguan, but as a place that was distinguished from those serving other kinds of cuisine, and a place that represented a kind of long-standing local tradition:

> Fifty years ago, other than Shanghai restaurants, there were only Beijing, Suzhou, Anhui, and Ningbo Restaurants; Sichuan, Hunan, Fujian, and Cantonese [establishments] were not yet popular. Later, things changed with each passing day, and the taste of each province was available. Moreover, the latecomers surpassed [the early establishments]. [Still] the serving ware (*zhuanqi*) was no longer the same as before; as most [establishments] abandoned *gui* for *die* and completely lost their elegance. Only the Renheguan—an old-time Shanghainese restaurant located in front of the City God Temple at the Yamen gate, next the Huacao Hotel—did not change the old style and prepared and served food in dishes in a manner that preserved the ancient meaning (*guyi*).[36]

The passage depicts more than just restaurant trends in Shanghai in the early twentieth century, but also the way in which city residents read the Renheguan restaurant as a repository of "ancient" practices, and nonlocal regional cuisine restaurants as bearers of change and innovation. Food at the Renheguan, Liu notes, continued to be served on *gui*, a term that referred to the bamboo vessels used for storing grains, or bronze vessels for serving feasts, in antiquity. In contrast, the newer regional cuisine restaurants that sprang up in Shanghai's foreign settlements simply used *die*, or small porcelain plates, serving ware that, to Liu at least, had no historical significance. This suggests that, if anything, early Republican Shanghai cuisine restaurants sought to distinguish themselves from restaurants selling other regional cuisines by emphasizing that they did things the old-fashioned way.

The Zhengxingguan, a second and slightly less venerable Shanghai cuisine establishment than the Renheguan, displayed a different style of continuity. Established in 1862 as a small food shop, the restaurant soon expanded into a more formal operation. Signs bearing the restaurant's name, which was based on a combination of two characters from its owners' names, Zhu Zhengben and Cai Renxing, would eventually become a nearly ubiquitous feature of the Shanghai urban landscape.[37] The Zhengxingguan was so popular that it inspired numerous imitators, and by several counts there were as many as 120 Zhengxingguan's in the city by the 1920s, many boasting names that claimed both a Shanghai character and an "old" character, such as the Shanghai Old Zhengxing and the Great Shanghai Old Zhengxing.[38] To establish its credentials, the original operation changed its name to the Tongzhi Laozhengxing, or "The Old Zhengxing of the Tongzhi Era," associating itself with the Qing reign period that prevailed at the time of its founding. The Zhengxing phenomenon suggests that one important way that a new Shanghai cuisine restaurant established itself was by identifying with a preexisting, old-time establishment.

This pattern of Shanghai cuisine restaurants serving as markers of continuity in Shanghai history continued throughout the Republican period and was typical of more than just the Zhengxingguan and its imitators. Wang Dingjiu, whose writings on Shanghai's restaurants were discussed in Chapter Four, observed that Shanghai cuisine *fandian*, or food shops, were located throughout the city, "on every street and lane."[39] Wang, it may be recalled from Chapter Four, said the same thing about Anhui restaurants, but the ubiquity of the Shanghai cuisine restaurants meant something different than did that of the Anhui. When writing about Anhui restaurants, Wang had been disparaging, suggesting that the purveyors of this variety of regional cuisine, which had once been as famous and prominent as the Anhui merchant communities for whom the restaurants were originally created, had let the business go to pot. This was, after all, why they needed to innovate with new-fangled dishes like Wonton Duck. The ubiquity of Shanghai cuisine restaurants, in contrast, represented their ability to provide a kind of comfort and routine; indeed, Wang likens their food offerings to "convenient home cooking" (*jiachang bianfan*) and notes that they were accessible to the only sector of the Shanghai population that could be said to approximate an "average" city resident. Describing the patrons of the famous "Food Shop Alley" (*fandian nongtang*), a small street full of small restaurants serving local Shanghai fare located at the eastern end of Bathtub Alley, between Nanjing East Road and Jiujiang Road, Wang noted, "The customers in this alley are all clerks from the banks, native banks, companies, business, and other kinds of shops in the neighborhood of Nanjing Road. There are quite a few restaurants on or near Nanjing Road, but most are terribly expensive and only suitable for wealthy people of the 'aristocratic' classes to banquet in." Food Shop Alley establishments had an "everyday" feel to them that was reinforced by the comings and goings of regular customers—"Each restaurant has old customers that come rain or shine"—and regular offerings with set prices: every serving cost three *jiao*, plus an extra tip of three *fen*, and consisted of a bowl of the soup of the day, a dish of the customer's choice, and a bottomless bowl of rice. The names of the dishes were written on a blackboard and included red-braised beef, sliced pork with hearts of bok choy, scallion-braised carp, and yellow croaker sautéed in vinegar.[40]

Food Shop Alley became such a well-known lunch spot that it acquired a widely recognized social value and, for commoners and entrepreneurs alike, a history worth preserving. Shanghai native Yu Muxia, in his *Shanghai Tidbits*, bemoaned Food Shop Alley's loss to the Dalu shopping center, a massive commercial shopping complex built in the mid-1930s. Yu called Food Shop Alley a "thing of the past,"[41] but by 1939 the alley had been reconstructed in a new location, this time running north of Nanjing Road, in Charity Flourishes Alley (Cichang li).[42] As Wang explains, "The developer recognized that Food Shop Alley was convenient for everyday people who worked in foreign firms and businesses, and also that it had a long history, so after the construction [of the Dalu] was finished, a T-shaped alley was built in so that there would still be a Food Shop Alley."[43] Wang strikingly juxtaposes the urban innovations of Shanghai's new department stores with the essential, if mundane, restaurants of everyday life. Remarkably, even the commercial developers of the area recognized the need to maintain a semblance of continuity.

The family-style restaurants that are so popular in Shanghai today are the heirs of these earlier food shops and Shanghai cuisine restaurant cooking traditions, although their proliferation today may also be due to the historical importance that Shanghai's Food and Service Company placed on what it identified as historically significant local Shanghai food. As discussed in Chapter Five, the government officials charged with redefining the character of Shanghai food culture initially identified the "mass" food items of the Shanghai working class as symbols of revolutionary potential. The food served at small food shops in Food Shop Alley was clearly, in richness and quality, a step or two above the diets of Shanghai's urban poor. Moreover, Shanghai's workforce was by no means drawn strictly, or even largely, from a population of Shanghai natives. But over time, "mass" food in Shanghai clearly came to mean cheap local Shanghai fare. The party also focused considerable attention on the food culture of Shanghai's City God Temple, the sector of the city with the highest concentration of Shanghai natives. Even the menu served at Shanghai's higher end regional cuisine restaurants during the Cultural Revolution consisted of inexpensive everyday Shanghai fare, as if local Shanghai cuisine constituted the logical repertoire from which it was possible to draw a common urban denominator. That culinary common denominator now anchors Shanghai city residents as the city embarks on an uncertain yearned-for future.

Notes

Introduction

1. Svetlana Boym, *Future of Nostalgia*, 3.

2. The identification of rural folk culture as a source of national culture is of course not limited to the European Romantic tradition. On discourses of Japanese folk culture, for example, see Kim Brandt, *Kingdom of Beauty*.

3. For a genealogy of this critical perspective on nostalgia, with a focus on the term's disciplinary uses in medicine, psychiatry, criminology, and education, see Nauman Naqvi, "Nostalgic Subject," 4–51.

4. For an insightful examination of Chinese "nostalgiology," see Philip A. Kafalas, *In Limpid Dream*, 143–83.

5. This distinction is adapted from Boym, *Future of Nostalgia*, xviii, where it is applied to the history of nostalgia in Europe in general and Russian art and literature in particular.

6. Dore J. Levy, *Chinese Narrative Poetry*, 10–15.

7. James Legge, *Li Chi: Book of Rites*, 449–79; translation of *Guanzi* follows Allyn W. Rickett, *Guanzi: Political, Economic, and Philosophical Essays—A Study and Translation* (Princeton, NJ: Princeton University Press, 1985), 22, cited in Gang Yue, *Mouth That Begs*, 428. For an overview of this classical literature, with a focus on discourse regarding the state's responsibility to provision the people, see Yue, *Mouth That Begs*, 30–60.

8. Marcel Proust, *Remembrance of Things Past*, 48–51. For an anthropological elaboration on Proust, see David E. Sutton, *Remembrance of Repasts*.

9. *Mencius* 1A.3.3, translation by Legge, *Chinese Classics*, Vol. 2: 130–31.

10. Bryna Goodman, *Native Place, City, and Nation*, 7.

11. Levy, *Chinese Narrative Poetry*, 14.

12. Special thanks to Tobie Meyer-Fong for sharing her understanding of this issue with me.

13. Such imagery is common, for example, in People's Republic of China (PRC) propaganda posters. For a useful collection, see Anchee Min, Duo Duo, and Stefan Landsberger, *Chinese Propaganda Posters*.

14. Jennifer Hubbert, "Revolution IS a Dinner Party," 125–50.

15. Not addressed in the following review are several outstanding examples of scholarship on food in China and Chinese food overseas that address separate aspects of food history. For works in English, on food in early medieval and middle-period China, see David R. Knechtges, "Gradually Entering the Realm of Delight," 229–39; Stephen West, "Cilia, Scale and Bristle," 595–634; and West, "Playing with Food," 67–106; on food and religion, see Roel Sterckx, *Of Tripod and Palate*; on food and medicine, see Judith Farquhar, *Appetites*; on Western views of Chinese food, see J. A. G. Roberts, *China to Chinatown*; on the literary discourse of hunger, see Yue, *Mouth That Begs*, and David Der-wei Wang, "Three Hungry Women," 48–77; on the technology of food processing in China, see H. T. Huang, *Science and Civilisation in China*; and on the globalization of Chinese food, see David H. Y. Wu and Sidney C. H. Cheung, *Globalization of Chinese Food*.

16. Lin Yin-feng, "Some Notes on Chinese Food," 298–99.

17. On the concept of *terroir*, see Amy B. Trubek, *The Place of Taste*.

18. K. C. Chang, "Introduction," in *Food in Chinese Culture*, 11.

19. Kafalas, *In Limpid Dream*, 143.

20. Charles Hayford, "Review of *Food in Chinese Culture*," 738–40.

21. Chang, "Introduction," 20–21. Since Chang's writing, the dates for the Xia have been revised to ca. 21st–18th century B.C., and those for the Shang to ca. 1600–1045 B.C., although this does not affect Chang's point regarding the general time frame of the main stages of development.

22. Chang, "Introduction," 20.

23. Frederick W. Mote, "Yüan and Ming," 202; Schafer, "T'ang," 128; and Freeman, "Sung," 144; all cited in Hayford, "Review," 739.

24. In Chinese studies, such a line of inquiry has been most vigorously pursued for the Qing and Manchuria. For two reviews of this literature, see Evelyn Rawski, "Re-envisioning the Qing," 829–50; and Joanna Waley-Cohen, "The New Qing History," 193–206. For a rebuttal and reiteration of the nationalist perspective, see Ping-ti Ho, "In Defense of Sinicization," 123–55. The most important statement on the problem of the nation as a category of analysis for understanding history in the China region remains Prasenjit Duara, *Rescuing History from the Nation*.

25. Tejijiaodui, pseud. [Chen Mengyin], *Jinshan shijing*, 10–13.

26. Tejijiaodui, *Jinshan shijing*, 14.

27. Valerie Hansen, *Open Empire*. Just how much there is to gain from such re-

thinking of the geographical frameworks for understanding food history in China is evident in Paul D. Buell and E. N. Anderson's heroic translation and study of the 1330 food treatise *Yinshan zhengyao* (Essentials of eating and drinking). This treatise opens a window onto the complex processes through which Yuan court physicians interpreted Mongol foodways through Chinese medical frameworks. See Buell and Anderson, *Soup for the Qan*. On the importance of American food crops in late imperial China, see Ping-ti Ho, "Introduction of American Food Plants to China," 191–201.

28. See, for example, the discussions in Frederick Simoons, *Food in China*, 43–60; Zhang Zhou, "Shilun Zhongguo de 'caixi,'" 17–18; and Du Zhizhong, "Yetan Zhonguo de caixi," 9–10.

29. E. N. Anderson Jr. and Marja L. Anderson, "Modern China: South," esp. 353–54.

30. See, for example, Shizhe, "Shanghai de chi, si," 36.

31. Lu Yaodong, *Duda nengrong*, 48.

32. Jeffrey Alford and Naomi Duguid, *Hot Sour Salty Sweet*.

33. Other records of regional food culture include scattered references in Chinese classics and founding texts of Chinese political philosophy, early botanical and agricultural treatises, travel writing and belles-lettres, encyclopedias, and cookbooks. Differences in form and content among these genres are introduced in the body of the manuscript when relevant. Gazetteers are the focus of the discussion here, because in addition to being an important source of material for the present book, they were also, during the late imperial period, the main reference point for ideas about local history and culture.

34. For a more detailed list, see Endymion Wilkinson, *Chinese History*, 155, from which this sampling is drawn. On a separate genre of "topographical" and "institutional" gazetteers, see Timothy Brook, *Geographical Sources of Ming-Qing History*.

35. Timothy Brook, "Native Identity under Alien Rule," 236–37.

36. *Zhongguo fangzhi dacidian*, 68.

37. *Zhujing zhi* [Gazetteer of Zhujing], 12.

38. Translation by Knechtges, *Wen xuan, or Selections of Refined Literature*, 337–39.

39. *Jiajing Shanghai xianzhi* [Shanghai County gazetteer, Jiajing era] (hereafter *JJSHXZ*), 1.12a.

40. *Qianlong Shanghai xianzhi* [Shanghai County gazetteer, Qianlong era] (hereafter *QLSHXZ*), 4.49b. The 1750 Qianlong edition is cited here and throughout the present work in lieu of the 1683 Kangxi edition because the latter has not yet been reprinted and is less widely available than the former. The *wuchan* section in the two is identical. "Fine and coarse" and "*jun* and *lu*" follow Bernhard Karlgren, *Book of Documents*, 14–15.

41. Susan Daruvala, *Zhou Zuoren and an Alternative Chinese Response to Modernity*, 63.

42. Marta Hanson, "Robust Northerners and Delicate Southerners," 515–49; and Hanson, "Northern Purgatives, Southern Restoratives," 115–70.

43. On the emergence of the skeptical tradition, see John B. Henderson, *Development and Decline of Chinese Cosmology*.

44. *Zhongguo jingjizhi, Anhuisheng Ningguo, Jingxian*, 517.

45. Wang Zhenzhong, "Qing-Minguo shiqi Jiang-Zhe yidai de Huiguan yanjiu."

46. Edward H. Schafer, "T'ang," 137.

47. Schafer, "T'ang," 137.

48. Cited in Michael Freeman, "Sung," 175.

49. Freeman, "Sung," 175.

50. Mote, "Yüan and Ming," 244. Richard Belsky has recently questioned the extent to which Mote's observations about *huiguan* cooking staffs hold for Beijing *huiguan*. See his *Localities at the Center*, 110–13. Belsky's observations, however, do not call into question the larger point being made here about cuisine operating as a marker of the other.

51. On linear history in Republican China, see Duara, *Rescuing History from the Nation*.

52. See, for example, *Lidai shehui fengsu shiwu kao*, 98–120.

53. Duara, "Local Worlds," 13–16, 36–40. It is important not to overstate the "modern" novelty of the local as a historically significant formulation. The local mattered in imperial times and remains relevant today; what has changed, as noted earlier, are the terms according to which the local is articulated. As Ellen Neskar observes, the pantheon of worthies enshrined in Confucian temples in the Song varied significantly from place to place. Communities of scholars constructed place-based genealogies of literati learning to highlight the contributions that local worthies made to the transmission of the Way, or to draw special attention to more widely recognized figures who had passed through their home region. These genealogies often differed markedly from representations of the transmission in orthodox accounts. See Neskar, *Politics and Prayer*. Material artifacts, such as architecture, ruins, and tombs, provided yet another a template for articulating competing views of history in imperial China. Thus, on the one hand, as Jonathan Hay explains, the ruins of the Ming imperial palace and tomb in Nanjing "functioned as signs of the cosmological pattern of history" and represented the passing of the Mandate from Ming to Qing. But on the other hand, these ruins also contained the source of counter-histories, "signs of . . . interdynastic time—that vanquished limbo created by the process of continued mourning for the vanquished dynasty." This limbo is evident in the writings of locals who studied and wrote about ruins in ways that "reminded themselves and their audience of the Mandate's mutability, thus keeping history open, at least as a discourse." See his "Ming Palace and Tomb in Early Qing Jiangning," 20–21. Diana Lary has noted

an analogous process at work in Guangdong in the post-Mao period: "The leaders of Lingnan today are celebrating a past, a distant cultivated past that evolved independently of the North and was outside its direct influence." See Lary, "The Tomb of the King of Nanyue," 7.

54. Zhou Zuoren, "Mai tang" (Selling candy), 319–21.

55. On the question of Zhou's collaboration, see Lu Yan, "Beyond Politics in Wartime," 6–12.

56. Translation follows E. Wolff, *Chou Tso-Jen*, 94.

57. Daruvala, *Zhou Zuoren*, 81.

58. Mao Dun, *Midnight*, 29, 31–32.

59. Marie-Claire Bergère, "The Other China," 1–34; Rhoads Murphey, *Shanghai*.

60. See, for example, Leung Yuen-sang, *The Shanghai Taotai*; Paul Cohen, *Between Tradition and Modernity*; Rudolf G. Wagner, "Role of the Foreign Community," 423–43; Mary Bakus Rankin, *Early Chinese Revolutionaries*; Yen-P'ing Hao, *Compradore in Nineteenth Century China*; Parks Coble, *The Shanghai Capitalists and the Nationalist Government*; Emily Honig, *Sisters and Strangers*; Elizabeth Perry, *Shanghai on Strike*; S. A. Smith, *Like Cattle and Horses*; Christian Henriot, *Shanghai, 1927–1937*; Yingjin Zhang, *Cinema and Urban Culture in Shanghai*; Andrew Jones, *Yellow Music*; Leo Ou-fan Lee, *Shanghai Modern*; and Shu-mei Shih, *Lure of the Modern*.

61. Hanchao Lu, *Beyond the Neon Lights*.

62. Goodman, *Native Place, City, and Nation*.

63. Catherine Yeh, "Creating a Shanghai Identity," 107–23. As Yeh notes, Wang's mournful texts dwell on the "displacement . . . coming with exile" in the wake of the Taiping Rebellion, adding, "The literary effect is obvious, there is no visible break with traditional culture. Shanghai now provides the pleasures of the capitals of earlier times, while at the same time marking the displacement earlier coming with exile" (114).

64. The illustrated guide ran in the daily pictorial *Tuhua ribao*; Chen Boxi, *Shanghai yishi daguan* [Compendium of Shanghai anecdotes]; Chen Wuwo, *Lao Shanghai sanshinian jianwenlu* [Record of things seen and heard over thirty years in old Shanghai]. As Jeffery Wasserstrom notes, the rapid changes in Shanghai also prompted many foreign investigations into the city's past. See his "New Approaches to Old Shanghai," 263–79.

65. Poshek Fu, *Passivity, Resistance, and Collaboration*, 110–11.

66. Dorothy Solinger, *Chinese Business Under Socialism*.

67. On nostalgia in reform-era Shanghai, see Zhang Xudong, "Shanghai Nostalgia," 349–87; and Wang Ban, "Love at Last Sight," 669–94.

68. Linda Cooke Johnson, *Shanghai*, 38–39, 119–21.

69. William S. Atwell, "Ming China and the Emerging World Economy," 376–416.

70. Craig Clunas, *Superfluous Things*. See also Timothy Brook, *Confusions of Pleasure*.

71. Goodman, *Native Place, City, and Nation*, 22.

72. Xu Guozhen, *Shanghai shenghuo*, 38–39.

73. *Guangzhou zhinan* [Guide to Guangzhou], 242, 250.

74. This term is borrowed from Ann Anagnost's study of the much more purposefully wrought national monument theme-park Splendid China. See her "The Nation-scape," 585–606.

Chapter One

1. Robert Fortune, *Three Years' Wanderings*, 404.

2. Donald P. McCracken, *Gardens of Empire*, 138–39.

3. Lucile H. Brockway, *Science and Colonial Expansion*, 7–18; Richard Drayton, *Nature's Government*.

4. On Fortune's interests and writings, see Susan Schoenbauer Thurin, *Victorian Travelers*, 27–54.

5. Wolfram Eberhard, *Dictionary of Chinese Symbols*, 227. For a concise overview of peach symbolism, see also Frederick J. Simoons, *Food in China*, 217–20.

6. Edward H. Schafer, *Golden Peaches of Samarkand*, 1–2. On the Samarkand tribute peaches, see also Berthold Laufer, *Sino-Iranica*, 379. On Emperor Wu's encounter with the Queen Mother of the West, see Michael Loewe, *Ways to Paradise*, 115–26. On Tao Qian and the legend of the Peach Blossom Spring, see Chen Yinke, "Taohua yuan ji pangzheng," 183–93; see also James Robert Hightower, *The Poetry of T'ao Ch'ien*, 254–58.

7. The description came in a letter from the Society to Fortune, cited in Thurin, *Victorian Travelers*, 29.

8. Chu Hua, *Shumitao pu* [Treatise on the honey nectar peach].

9. See the discussion of Sima Xiangru's "Sir Fantasy," in Burton Watson, *Chinese Rhyme-prose*, 30.

10. Linda Cooke Johnson, *Shanghai*; and Hanchao Lu, "Arrested Development," 468–99.

11. Richard von Glahn, "Towns and Temples," 176–211; Timothy Brook, "Xu Guangqi in His Context," 72–98. The *haizou* designation appears, for example, in the title to Suzhou native Wang Tao's (1828–97) study of Shanghai courtesan culture, *Haizou yeyou lu*.

12. As Hanchao Lu points out, Shanghai, a county seat, was technically a "third-class" city, ranking in the administrative hierarchy behind Beijing, the metropolitan capital, and such "second-level" prefectural capitals as Nanjing, Guangzhou, and Suzhou. See his *Beyond the Neon Lights*, 26.

13. I am grateful to Tobie Meyer-Fong for helping me appreciate the scope of this phenomenon.

14. See, for example, Antonia Finnane, *Speaking of Yangzhou*, esp. 284–92.

15. William Rowe, "Introduction," 12.

16. John Meskill, *Gentlemanly Interests and Wealth*, 3.

17. By the end of the Ming, the broader Songjiang region in which Shanghai was located would be famous for a "Songjiang school" of painting, of which the most notable members were Dong Qichang and Chen Jiru. These painters, however, hailed from what was then nearby Huating County, which no longer contained Shanghai. And thus even though Huating is, today, a part of the Municipality of Shanghai, it would be anachronistic to consider them "Shanghai" artists. On the Songjiang school, see Zhu Xuchu, "Songjiang School of Painting," 52–55. Special thanks to Maggie Bickford for drawing this work to my attention.

18. The late imperial trend is addressed in Craig Clunas, *Fruitful Sites*. See also Finnane, *Speaking of Yangzhou*, 64–68, 188–203; and Joanna F. Handlin Smith, "Gardens in Ch'i Piao-chia's Social World," 55–81.

19. Scholars of garden history in China will thus note that the history of garden building in Shanghai reveals similarities with developments in other cities, but it also exhibits a least one notable countervailing trend. In his study of gardens in late Ming Suzhou, Clunas argues that the sixteenth and seventeenth centuries represent a turning point in the concept of the garden in China. Early Ming gardens, Clunas notes, were valued for both their aesthetic refinements and their productive potential, so much so that the Chinese term for garden, *yuan*, could just as accurately be translated as "orchard." During the second half of the Ming, however, evolving elite ideals inspired new kinds of social spaces, and *yuan* became redefined as nonproductive sites of repose and aesthetic refinement, as "pure objects of luxury." The new distinction was so strong, Clunas adds, that it created "two entirely separate discursive fields," driving a wedge between horticultural literatures and poetic representations of crops, which had previously been closely intertwined: "If onions have no place in gentlemen's gardens, poems now have no place in agronomic treatises." Clunas, *Fruitful Sites*, 22, 101, 89. Yet, as this study shows, there was no such uniform split between horticultural and aesthetic traditions in Shanghai, where city residents clung to the hybrid idea of the garden/orchard. Clunas, it should be noted, was not the first to make this observation about the orchard/garden shift. See the discussion in Smith, "Gardens in Ch'i Piao-chia's Social World," 58.

Determining precisely what accounts for this apparently different trajectory in the history of Shanghai gardens lies beyond the scope of this project. It may be, however, that we need to reconsider the idea of the garden/orchard distinction as a functional, or even symbolic, split for the late imperial period more generally, at least to the extent that the split is considered a manifestation of a more fundamental gentry/merchant split. Gardens may have constituted an important dimension of the hybrid *shishang* world that now appears to have animated trends in book publishing and sales, and which Kai-wing Chow reveals to have brought together arenas of activity commonly associated with literati, merchants, and businessmen. See Kai-wing Chow, *Publishing, Culture, and Power*. As purveyors of fruit, embroidery, inkstones, and preserved vegetables, the members of the Gu family that made Shanghai famous for the honey nectar peach were clearly local entrepreneurs as well as local gentry. Understanding the ways in which local notables engaged in such enterprises must await new discoveries of historical evidence regarding such families' finances.

20. Fortune, *Three Years' Wanderings*, 115.

21. von Glahn, "Towns and Temples," 178. For a detailed description of this process, see Johnson, *Shanghai*, 21–42.

22. It might be objected, along the lines discussed in note 16, that Southern Song Huating history should be considered distinct from the history of Shanghai because Shanghai eventually broke off from Huating, and Huating itself was only much later made into a district of the Municipality of Shanghai. Many accounts of Shanghai history do indeed anachronistically claim late imperial Huating history as a part of Shanghai's history. This is not the intention of the present work. Instead, the *Gazetteer of Yunjian* is discussed here because Shanghai residents in Ming and Qing times used it as a point of reference for identifying what was particular to the Shanghai component of the wider region after it split off from Huating, and so it helps establish the historical terrain against which Shanghai natives sought to distinguish themselves from neighboring regions and their earlier shared past.

23. Wang Qiyu and Luo Yousong, eds., *Shanghai difangzhi gaishu*, 27.

24. "Yunjian zhi xu," in *Shaoxi Yunjian zhi* (hereafter *SXYJZ*) [Gazetteer of Yunjian, Shaoxi era], 1a.

25. *SXYJZ*, 1.9a–b.

26. *SXYJZ*, 1.9b–10a.

27. *SXYJZ*, 1.9b.

28. *SXYJZ*, 1.9b–10a.

29. The description of Huating is from Lu Lin's *Bawang gushi* (Stories of the eight princes), cited in Richard B. Mather, *New Account of Tales*, 508.

30. Liu Yiqing, *Xishuo xinyu* [New account of tales of the world], 33.3; *Jinshu* [Jin History], 54.8b (Zhonghua edition, 1480).

31. Nanxiu Qian, *Spirit and Self in Medieval China*, 6.

32. Translation by Mather, *New Account of Tales*, 507.

33. Lu Ji's lament no doubt inspired the Tang poet and essayist Liu Yuxi (772–842) to write two poems about cranes in honor of a close friend who also left Huating for Luoyang, which the *Gazetteer of Yunjian* also cites in its celebration of Huating's cranes (*SXYJZ*, 1.9b), perhaps on the grounds that, as some claimed, Liu was a native of Wu.

34. Wu king He Lu's (r. 515–496 B.C.) assessment of Wu is cited in Michael Marmé, *Suzhou*, 41.

35. Liu Yiqing, *Shishuo xinyu*, 2.26, translation modified from Mather, *New Account of Tales*, 45.

36. *Jinshu*, 54.7a (Zhonghua edition, 1472–73).

37. Mather reads the text as Moxia, but confusingly explains that he does so following the Zhonghua edition of the *Jinshu*, which renders it as *weixia*. Much of the relevant commentarial tradition has been collected in Yu Jiaxi, *Shishuo xinyu jianshu*, 88–90.

38. Shi Zhecun, "Chungeng," 758–61.

39. Johnson, *Shanghai*, 25–26.

40. Johnson, *Shanghai*, 30.

41. S. A. M. Adshead, *Salt and Civilization*, 80.

42. Adshead, *Salt and Civilization*, 74.

43. This overview of the region's salt producing history follows Xiong Yuezhi, ed., *Shanghai tongshi*, Vol. 2, 102–109.

44. For an English translation and study, see Hans Ulrich Vogel, *Salt Production Techniques in Ancient China*.

45. Translation from Vogel, *Salt Production Techniques*, 111.

46. Brook, "Xu Guangqi," 74.

47. The literature on Shanghai cotton is extensive. For brief overviews with sources for additional reading, see Lu, "Arrested Development"; and Johnson, *Shanghai*, 43–65.

48. Lu, "Arrested Development," 485–87.

49. Mark Elvin, "Market Towns and Waterways," 445, 447.

50. Cited in Elvin, "Market Towns and Waterways," 458.

51. Elvin, "Market Towns and Waterways," 459.

52. Cited in Elvin, "Market Towns and Waterways," 447.

53. *Hongzhi Shanghai zhi* [Shanghai gazetteer, Hongzhi era], 3.12b–18b.

54. *Wanli Shanghai xianzhi* [Shanghai County gazetteer, Wanli era], 3.18a–22b.

55. *JJSHXZ*, 1.12a.

56. Brook, "Xu Guangqi," 77.

57. Brook, "Xu Guangqi," 79.

58. *JJSHXZ*, 1.13a–b. *Mencius* 1A.3.3; James Legge, *The Chinese Classics*, Vol. 2, 131.

59. *JJSHXZ*, 1.12a–13b.

60. *JJSHXZ*, 1.12b–13a.

61. *JJSHXZ*, 1.12a.

62. Translation after Mather, *New Account of Tales*, 213.

63. Clunas, *Fruitful Sites*.

64. Brook, "Xu Guangqi," 83–86.

65. The figure of eleven comes from the *Jiaqing Songjiang fuzhi*, 78.21b–28b (hereafter *JQSJFZ*). It is possible that more than eleven gardens were built but that some were not included in the registry of "residences and gardens" in the Shanghai gazetteers. On the politics of gazetteer inclusion, see Clunas, *Fruitful Sites*, 18–21.

66. For thumbnail histories of these gardens, see Xiong Yuezhi, ed., *Shanghai tongshi*, 165–69; and Chen Bohai, *Shanghai wenhua tongshi*, Vol. 1, 83–86.

67. Gu Bingquan, *Shanghai fengsu guji kao*, 130–31. For Gu Mingshi's official biography, see *Tongzhi Shanghai xianzhi* (hereafter *TZSHXZ*), 9.10a–b.

68. This sequence of events is related in all gazetteer entries on Dew Fragrance Garden. See, for example, *JQSJFZ*, 78.26b.

69. The longer version may be found in *JQSJFZ*, 78.26b–27a, and in *Gujin tushu jicheng*, as Zhu Chaqing, "Luxiangyuan ji," 703.117.14a–b; Shanghai gazetteers printed the shorter version, apparently following a copy kept in the Gu family genealogy.

70. *JQSJFZ*, 78.26b.

71. *JJSHXZ*, 10.58b.

72. On degree earning in Ming Shanghai, see Brook, "Xu Guangqi," 77.

73. *JQSJFZ*, 78.27a.

74. See, for example, *Jiaqing Shanghai xianzhi*, 7.59a.

75. Ye Mengzhu, *Yueshi bian*, 10.10a.

76. Zhang Suowang, *Yuegeng yulu* [Notes on reading and plowing], 5.19a. As Brook notes, Suowang was the younger brother of Zhang Suojing, one of six assistants to the editor, Zhang Zhixiang, who was from a different branch of the family ("Xu Guangqi," 80 and 91 note 53).

77. Ye Mengzhu, *Yueshi bian*, 10.9a. The reading here follows Ye's rendition of Lu Ji's encounter with Wang Rong; see note 37.

78. *Mingshi zhuan* commentary on *Shishuo xinyu*, 6.4, cited in Mather, *New Account of Tales*, 191.

79. The Southern Song *Gazetteer of Kuaiji* (Kuaiji zhi) places the honey nectar peach in the Xiaoshan Mountains, in the outskirts of Hangzhou, but Wu Zimu's 1274 *Record of the Splendors of the Capital City* (Mengliang lu), notes that the variety was available as a snack in the same city's tea and wine shops. *Kuaiji zhi*, 17.25b; *Mengliang lu*, 16.8b.

80. *Jiangnan tongzhi* [Comprehensive gazetteer of Jiangnan], 86.8b. The five prefectural gazetteer are for Suzhou, Songjiang, Zhenjiang, Shaoxing, and Shaowu, cited in *Gujin tushu jicheng*, 681.115.47a; 699.116.63a; 735.119.36b; 992.138.20b; 1093.146.7a.

81. Alfred Koehn, "Foreword," *Fragrance from a Chinese Garden*, np.

82. These passages are drawn from the original 30-*juan* version. Wang Xiangjin, *Qunfang pu* [Treatise on many fragrances], 2.2a–b.

83. See, for example, Zhang Yushu's *Yuding yunfu shiyi*, the 1720 supplement to his 1711 phrase-collection dictionary *Peiwen yunfu*, 19.6a–b; Yao Zhiyin's 1721 collection of Yuan and Ming era anecdotes, *Yuan Ming shileichao*, 35.9b; Chen Yuanlong's (1652–1736) encyclopedia, *Gezhi jingyuan*, 74.10a–b; and the 1747 *Qinding shoushi tongkao*, 63.7b.

84. *Jiaqing Daqing yitongzhi*, 85.14b. The *Chongzhen Songjiang fuzhi* is cited in *Gujin tushu jicheng*, 699.116.63a.

85. *Loutang zhi* [Gazetteer of Loutang], 61.

86. *QLSHXZ*, 5.50a.

87. *QLSHXZ*, 5.50a.

88. *QLSHXZ*, 5.50b–53a.

89. Johnson, *Shanghai*, 155, 161. Before the Ming ban, maritime shipping had been an important source of the city's wealth, the loss of which was offset only by the development of the cotton economy.

90. Johnson, *Shanghai*, 122–54.

91. James Chin Shih, *Chinese Rural Society*, 83.

92. Chu discusses his relationship to Shanghai's cotton merchants in his cotton treatise, cited in Shih, *Chinese Rural Society*, 83.

93. All three works are collected in Shanghai tongshe, *Shanghai zhanggu congshu*, Vol. 2.

94. The difficulties that the family faced as a result took their toll on family harmony. Rifts in the Gu family first emerged around Gu Huihai's younger half-brother (the two shared a father, Mingshi, but the younger brother was born to a concubine). First, the half-brother was arrested; then, after obtaining amnesty, he frittered away his share of the family estate. Before long, Huihai's share had also shrunk—perhaps too much was spent on "distinguishing himself from his contemporaries," as Ye Mengzhu put it, through his food, drink, and clothing. Huihai's son, Gu Bolu, died without issue. *Yueshi bian*, 10.9a.

95. Ye Mengzhu, *Yueshi bian*, 10.3a–b.

96. Chu Hua, *Shuimitao pu*, 1a.

97. For Li's official biography, see *TZSHXZ*, 21.41a–b.

98. *JQSJFZ*, 78.29a. Shen Fuxu, "Shanghai yuanlin goushen."

99. Translation modified after George Kao, *Chinese Wit and Humor*, 37. On interpretations of Yanzi's statement about plant metamorphosis in the Chinese botanical tradition, see Joseph Needham, *Science and Civilisation in China*, 103–16. I am grateful to Anne Reinhardt for pointing my way to the *Yanzi*.

100. Chu Hua, *Shuimitao pu*, 1a.

101. Chu Hua, *Shuimitao pu*, 1b–2a.

102. Chu Hua, *Shuimitao pu*, 1b–2a.

103. Chu Hua, *Shuimitao pu*, 2b.

104. Chu Hua, *Shuimitao pu*, 1b.

105. Chu Hua, *Shuimitao pu*, 2b–3b.

106. On Chen's patronage of women's poetry, see Ellen Widmer, *Beauty and the Book*.

107. On Yuan Mei's reputation as a gourmet, see Jonathan Spence, "Ch'ing," 272–76.

108. Chen Wenshu, "Xu" [Preface], 1a. As Needham notes, "It is singular that no medieval Chinese botanist wrote a monograph consecrated wholly to the peach" (*Science and Civilisation*, 423).

109. Schafer, *Golden Peaches*, 117–18.

110. Chen Wenshu, "Xu," 1a.

111. *Analects* 17.9, cited in Needham, *Science and Civilisation*, 440.

112. Needham, *Science and Civilisation*, 464.

113. For an English translation, see Hui-Lin Li, *Nan-fang ts'ao-mu chuang*.

114. In the former, a visitor to the Heir Apparent of the state of Chu seeks to "stimulate" the Heir Apparent into good health by describing seven scenes of pleasure, for which he enumerates the marvelous features of several hunting expeditions, gardens and forest groves, banquets, and amorous encounters. For an English translation and interpretation, see Hans H. Frankel, *Flowering Plum and the Palace Lady*, 186–211. In Zuo Si's rhapsodies fruits are among the many features and delicacies that make capital cities spectacular places. Of the capital of Shu, Zuo Si wrote, "In the orchards there are/Red apples and Loquats/Coolie orange, persimmons, date plums, and wild pears./Mountain peaches stand in neat clusters/Plums grow in orderly rows./All fruits burst from their pods/Sundry colors equal in splendor./The vermilion cherry is ripe in spring/The white apple bears fruit in summer." Translation by David R. Knechtges, *Wen xuan*, 353.

115. Paul Kroll, "Chang Chiu-ling," 208.

116. *Dongxian zhuan* [Biographies of grotto immortals], as cited in *Yuding peiwenzhai Guang qunfangpu*, 57.2b. Originally a work of ten *juan*, most of the *Dongxian zhuan* has been lost, although one *juan* of remnants has been preserved in the Daoist canon, as *juan* 110 of the Song compendium *Yunji qiqian* (Seven tablets in a cloudy satchel), compiled by Zhang Junfang (11th cent.).

117. See Donald Harper, "Flowers in T'ang Poetry," 139–53.

118. *Liangshu* [Liang history], 54.7a.

119. Guo Xian, *Dongming ji* [Record of caves of mystery], 2.1a–b.

120. Wang Guoliang, *Hanwu dongming ji yanjiu*, 58, note 9.

121. Special thanks to Dore Levy for sharing these insights from her ongoing research. See also Watson, *Chinese Rhyme-prose*, 29–51; Yves Hervouet, *Poète de cour sous les Han*; also Hervouet, *Chapitre 117 du Che-ki*; and Maggie Keswick, *Chinese Garden*, 45–51.

122. Liu Xin, *Xijing zaji* [Miscellaneous notes on the western capital], 1.7a.

123. On the size of the garden and the location of Penglai, see the discussion in Xiang Xinyang and Liu Keren, *Xijing zaji jiaozhu*, 49, notes 2 and 3, and 55, notes 56 and 57.

Chapter Two

1. The following account of the explosion is based on Mao Xianglin, *Moyu lu* [Record of leftover ink], 16–17. See also *TZSHXZ*, 11.30b–31a.

2. Catherine Yeh, *Shanghai Love*, 11.

3. Yeh, *Shanghai Love*, 14.

4. Wang Tao, *Haizou yeyou fulu*, 2.34a.

5. Zhang Chunhua, *Hucheng suishi quge* [Folksongs of Shanghai seasons], 906.

6. Rhoads Murphey, *Shanghai*, 59.

7. Leung Yuen-sang, *Shanghai Taotai*, 39–41.

8. Linda Cooke Johnson, *Shanghai*, 181.

9. Johnson, *Shanghai*, 180–181. On Cao Sheng's account, see also Arthur Waley, *Opium War through Chinese Eyes*, 186–96.

10. For maps of the various settlements and their expansion over time, see Leung, *Shanghai Taotai*, 52; and Hanchao Lu, *Beyond the Neon Lights*, 30.

11. N. B. Dennys, William Frederick Mayers, and Charles King, *Treaty Ports of China and Japan*, 355.

12. Dennys et al., *Treaty Ports of China and Japan*, 370–71.

13. On the jail and court system, see Mark Elvin, "Mixed Court of the International-al Settlement in Shanghai," 131–59; and Pär Cassel, "Excavating Extraterritoriality," 156–82. On public health measures, see Kerrie MacPherson, *Wilderness of Marshes*.

14. Johnson notes that total property damages were estimated to total $3,000,000 (*Shanghai*, 332). John Scarth, a British resident and first-hand observer of the Small Swords Uprising noted that the rebels "appropriated a good deal of property and shipped it off in Fokien junks." See his *Twelve Years in China*, 188.

15. Johnson, *Shanghai*, 334–35.

16. Leung, *Shanghai Taotai*, 87.

17. Robert Fortune, *Three Years' Wanderings*, 137–42.

18. George Wingrove Cooke, *China*, 98.

19. Dennys et al., *Treaty Ports*, 385.

20. The International Settlement's Mixed Court, on which a Qing appointee sat alongside a foreign assessor jointly to adjudicate cases involving Chinese defendants, was a frequent source of tension. So were urban development strategies, as when efforts to build a school, a hospital, and roads through a cemetery in the expanded French Concession led to a skirmish and riot that left seven Chinese dead and shops

and homes in the French settlement looted and destroyed. On legal tension, see Elvin, "Mixed Court." On the cemetery riots, see Susan Mann Jones, "Ningpo *Pang* and Financial Power at Shanghai," 158–69.

21. Catherine Yeh, "Representing the City," 166–202.

22. Ge Yuanxu, *Huyou zaji* [Miscellaneous notes on travel in Shanghai], 8.

23. Yeh, *Shanghai Love*, 97.

24. Ge Yuanxu, *Huyou zaji*, 41.

25. *TZSHXZ*, 8.6b–7b.

26. *TZSHXZ*, 8.6b.

27. *QLSHXZ*, 5.54a–55b.

28. Bryna Goodman, *Native Place, City, and Nation*.

29. For an overview of Shanghai guidebooks, see Yeh, *Shanghai Love*, 304–40.

30. In 1885, the Chinese population of the International Settlement numbered approximately 125,000. Of that number, 15 percent, or 15,814, were native Shanghainese. Of the remaining 85 percent, 41,304 hailed from Zhejiang Province, 39,604 from Jiangsu, and 21,013 from Guangdong, and smaller numbers came from Anhui (2,683), Zhili (1,911), Fujian (708), and Shandong (374). Zou Yiren, *Jiu Shanghai renkou bianqian de yanjiu*, Table 19, 112; Table 22, 114–15.

31. Wang Yi, *Xinghualou*, 8.

32. *Zhongguo mingcanguan*, 104.

33. Goodman, *Native Place, City, and Nation*, 7–8.

34. Wang Dingjiu, "Chi de menjing," in *Shanghai menjing* [Keys to Shanghai], 26. This process of cultural differentiation through cuisine in Shanghai is also briefly discussed in Lu Yaodong, *Duda nengrong*, 48.

35. Cited in Xiong Yuezhi, ed., *Shanghai tongshi*, Vol. 5, 156.

36. Huang Shiquan, *Songnan mengying lu* [Record of dream images of Shanghai], 127.

37. *Shanghai Huashang hangming buce* [Register of Chinese merchants in Shanghai], 112a–13b

38. Wang Tao, *Haizou yeyou fulu*, 2.34a.

39. Huang Shiquan, *Songnan mengying lu*, 126.

40. Chi Zhicheng, *Huyou mengying* [Dream images of a visit to Shanghai], 158.

41. Ge Yuanxu, *Huyou zaji*, 30–31.

42. Hushang youxizhu, *Haishang youxi tushuo* [Illustrated guide to Shanghai entertainment], 4.14b–15a.

43. On these links, see Brett Sheehan, "Urban Identity and Urban Networks," esp. 56–58.

44. Zhongguo Wannan Huicai yanjiusuo, "Huicai fayuan jixi kao."

45. On the Shanghai Cantonese community, see Song Zuanyou, *Guangdongren zai Shanghai*.

46. On the relatively "late" development of Cantonese restaurant culture, see Tejijiaodui, *Jinshan shijing*, 10–12.

47. Ge Yuanxu, *Huyou zaji*, 31.

48. Chi Zhicheng, *Huyou mengying*, 158.

49. *Tuhua ribao*, Vol. 3, 115.

50. Fortune described the dark city streets of the county seat in *Three Years' Wanderings*, 146. Before the creation of the foreign settlements, even Shanghai's courtesan houses were set up outside the walls of the city on lantern boats along the bank of the Huangpu River. See Christian Henriot, *Prostitution and Sexuality in Shanghai*, 203.

51. Chi Zhicheng, *Huyou mengying*, 158–59.

52. *Tuhua ribao*, Vol. 3, 115.

53. "Shanghai Phenomena" (Shanghai xianxiang) was the name of a popular series of illustrations of city life that ran in the *Tuhua ribao*. See note 49.

54. Goodman, *Native Place, City, and Nation*, 111–17.

55. Goodman, *Native Place, City, and Nation*, 159–62.

56. Leung, *Shanghai Taotai*, 131.

57. The discussion of these parties is based on Shanghai tongshe, *Shanghai yanjiu ziliao*, 540–42.

58. Fortune, *Three Years' Wanderings*, 54. Cooke also noted the crowds in such establishments: "We went through the Tea-gardens; so called because there are restaurants, in and about the premises, where the Chinese take tea and refreshments. These were full, as we passed them by. In some, I should think, there were a hundred persons, closely seated at little tables." See Cooke, *China*, 229.

59. For a concise overview of demimonde rituals, see Han Banqing, *Sing-song Girls of Shanghai*, 544–61.

60. Yeh, *Shanghai Love*, 111.

61. Han Banqing, *Sing-song Girls*, 363, 416.

62. The phrase "fantasies and fears" is adapted from Yeh's "fears and fantasies" (*Shanghai Love*, 254).

63. Han Banqing, *Sing-song Girls*, 3, note 2.

64. Han Banqing, *Sing-song Girls*, 2.

65. Han Banqing, *Sing-song Girls*, 8.

66. Han Banqing, *Sing-song Girls*, 13.

67. Han Banqing, *Sing-song Girls*, 22.

68. Han Banqing, *Sing-song Girls*, 245.

69. Han Banqing, *Sing-song Girls*, 248.

70. Han Banqing, *Sing-song Girls*, 308.

71. Han Banqing, *Sing-song Girls*, 312.

72. Yeh, *Shanghai Love*, 11–12.

73. Cited and translated in Yeh, *Shanghai Love*, 11–12. My interpretation of the ballad emphasizes that this equation is an illusion.

74. Yeh, *Shanghai Love*, 348–49, note 18.

75. Liu Yanong, *Shanghai xianhua*, 55–56.

76. Ge Yuanxu, *Huyou zaji*, 41.

77. Translation here and below follows Cyril Birch, *Anthology of Chinese Literature*, Vol. 1, 167–68.

78. *Tuhua ribao*, Vol. 7, 193.

79. William Charles Milne, *Life in China*.

80. *TZSHXZ*, 8.6b–7a.

81. Mao Xianglin, *Moyu lu*, 8–9.

82. Wang Tao, *Yingruan zaji* [Miscellaneous notes from the seaside], 18–19.

83. Li Weiqing, *Shanghai xiangtuzhi* [Shanghai local gazetteer], 76.

Chapter Three

1. "Simalu huochang xinwen," *Youxi bao*, No. 705 (1899), 2.

2. "Huoshen chi dacai" [Fire god eats Western food], *Youxi bao*, No. 705 (1899), 3.

3. Catherine Yeh, *Shanghai Love*, 26.

4. *Zao Yangfan shu.*

5. W. H. Medhurst, *Foreigner in Far Cathay*, 16.

6. Robert A. Bickers and Jeffrey N. Wasserstrom, "Shanghai's 'Dogs and Chinese Not Admitted' Sign," 445–47.

7. On this push and pull, see also Ye Xiaoqing "Shanghai before Nationalism," 33–52.

8. B. L. Ball, *Rambles in Eastern Asia*, 226.

9. G. Wingrove Cooke, *China*, 94–95.

10. Cooke, *China*, 220.

11. Robert Bickers, *Britain in China*, 102.

12. Medhurst, *Foreigner in Far Cathay*, 24–25.

13. Charles M. Dyce, *Personal Reminiscences of Thirty Years' Residence*, 99–100.

14. Dyce, *Personal Reminiscences*, 204–5.

15. Dyce, *Personal Reminiscences*, 205–6.

16. N. B. Dennys, William Frederick Mayers, and Charles King, *Treaty Ports of China and Japan*, 392.

17. Cooke, *China*, 236.

18. Cited in Hu Yuanjie, *Fuzhoulu wenhuajie*, 307–15.

19. Medhurst, *Foreigner in Far Cathay*, 25–26.

20. Ge Yuanxu, *Huyou zaji*, 40.

21. On courtesan patronage, see Yeh, *Shanghai Love*, 34–51.

22. Han Banqing, *Sing-song Girls of Shanghai*, 315, 317.

23. Even those who spoke more graciously of Chinese markets noted that they

were insufficient, such as Medhurst, who noted, "The native markets abound with fish, meat, poultry, and vegetables, and the foreigner's own carefully-kept poultry-yard, pigsty, dairy, and kitchen garden assist materially in supplying him with luxuries not procurable of the same quality amongst the Chinese" (*Foreigner in Far Cathay*, 25–26).

24. Ball, *Rambles in Eastern Asia*, 226.

25. Wang Tao, *Yingruan zaji*, 18.

26. Wang Tao, *Yingruan zaji*, 18.

27. Wang Tao, *Yingruan zaji*, 18.

28. Hui-Lin Li, *Nan-fang ts'ao-mu chuang*, 8–9.

29. Hui-Lin Li, *Nan-fang ts'ao-mu chuang*, 71. Hui-Lin Li, a Jiangsu native who studied biology at Yenching University and later Harvard (Ph.D. 1942), translates *yongcai* as "Chinese spinach," indicating just how much more clearly Chinese-Western lines were being drawn a century later.

30. Bickers, *Britain in China*, 102.

31. Medhurst, *Foreigner in Far Cathay*, 28.

32. Dyce, *Personal Reminiscences*, 200.

33. Medhurst, *Foreigner in Far Cathay*, 28–29.

34. "Fancai feisheng," in *Youxi bao*, No. 619, 3.

35. Hu, *Fuzhoulu wenhuajie*, 318.

36. Ge, *Huyou zaji*, 30.

37. Yeh, *Shanghai Love*, 121.

38. As longtime Shanghai resident Chen Dingshan (?1897–1987) recalled, writing from the standpoint of the mid-twentieth century, "Shanghainese don't call Western food (*xican*) 'Western food' (*xican*), they call it '*dacai*.' Residents of the foreign concessions have always had an inferiority complex, and so for all foreign things they add a '*da*' [big; major] in front of it." See Chen, *Chunshen jiuwen*, 189. Early in the history of Western food in Shanghai, however, when Chinese views of the foreign settlements were more sanguine, the more literal meaning of *dacai* predominated. The later meaning did not appear until the beginning of the twentieth century, when Chinese began to feel that Western food was becoming more significant to city residents than Chinese food, which might be referred to as "*xiaocai*," or minor cuisine. The distinction appears, for example, in "Xiao da cai jian," *Youxi bao*, No. 1774, 2. Only after the turn of the century was Western food identified, finally, as "Western" (*xi*), and at the time the term was not itself self-evident. The 1909 *Shanghai zhinan* defined it thus: "*Xishicai: Fancai*, commonly known as *dacai*" (8.6a).

39. Xiangguotoutuo, *Shenjiang mingsheng tushuo* [Shanghai's famous sites, illustrated and explained], 38a.

40. Huang Shiquan, *Songnan mengying lu*, 132.

41. One study of Fourth Avenue indicates that Yipinxiang opened in June, 1879, at No. 22 Fourth Avenue, but it is not clear on what evidence this is based (Hu, *Fuzhoulu*

wenhuajie, 318). Ye Xiaoqing, following Chen Dingshan (*Chunshen jiuwen*, 191), suggests that the first Western restaurant was Wanjiachun, and that Yipinxiang came later (Dianshizhai *Pictorial*, 109, note 151). It is not clear, however, if Chen's word is enough to settle the issue because he only places Yipinxiang at Tibet Road, where it later relocated. Still, it may only have been the fame of Yipinxiang that led writers to identify it as the first, as in the 1906 travelogue, *Huitu youli Shanghai zaji*, where it is said: "The first Chinese *fancaiguan* was Yipinxiang, which opened on Fourth Avenue" (7.10a–b).

42. Advertisements for Xinghuachun and Wanchangchun, among other *fancaiguan*, appear in virtually every third issue of *Youxi bao* published during the years 1897–1902.

43. "Fanguan chukai," *Youxi bao*, No. 783 (1899), 2.

44. See, for example, the advertisement for the Jinguchun in *Youxi bao*, No. 1047, 9.

45. Chi Zhicheng, *Huyou mengying*, 158.

46. Endymion Wilkinson, *Chinese History*, 725. See also John King Fairbank, *Chinese World Order*, 9–10.

47. Wilkinson, *Chinese History*, 729.

48. Lydia Liu, *Clash of Empires*, 40–46.

49. C. Toogood Downing, *Fan-Qui in China*, Vol. 1, v.

50. "Outlandish," *Oxford English Dictionary*.

51. Robert Morrison, *Vocabulary of the Canton Dialect*, np.

52. Robert Morrison, *Dictionary of the Chinese Language* (1815), cited in Liu, *Clash of Empires*, 41.

53. John Robert Shepherd, *Statecraft and Political Economy*, 362–94.

54. Ruth Rogaski notes a similar Chinese-Western olfactory boarder in place in the northern treaty port city of Tianjin. See her *Hygienic Modernity*, 84.

55. The allusion refers to Cai Xiang (1012–67), whose courtesy name was Junmo.

56. Ying-shih Yü, "Han," 74. Evidence of beef eating in early China comes from bamboo slips bearing the names of dishes found in the Han Mawangdui tomb (K. C. Chang, "Ancient China," 58). Frederick J. Simoons provides a quick summary of trends in the history of the beef taboo (*Food in China*, 303–305). For a full-length study, see Vincent Goossaert, *L'Interdit de Bœuf en Chine*, or the short summary in English, "The Beef Taboo and the Sacrificial Structure of Late Imperial Chinese Society," 237–48.

57. In the Song, Freeman notes, "beef is not mentioned explicitly in the lists of dishes made for banquets or by restaurants" ("Sung," 164). Writing of the Yuan and Ming, Mote notes, "Many persons, probably under Buddhist influence, avoided beef, and many found both beef and mutton too malodorous to eat" ("Yuan and Ming," 201).

58. Wang Tao, *Yingruan zaji*, 23.

59. Translation follows Ye Xiaoqing, *Dianshizhai Pictorial*, 217.

60. Ye, *Dianshizhai Pictorial*, 217–20.

61. Cited in Ye, *Dianshizhai Pictorial*, 219.

62. Translation follows Ye, *Dianshizhai Pictorial*, 217.

63. Huang Shiquan, *Songnan mengying lu*, 126; Chi Zhicheng, *Huyou mengying*, 158; *Huitu youli Shanghai zaji*, 7.10a–b.

64. *Haishang youxi tushuo*, cited in Ye, *Dianshizhai Pictorial*, 61.

65. The proprietor may have hit on this idea from the example set by a foreign merchant who ran a business operation in the French Concession, and who had taken in a "distressed Singapore tiger, whose roaring attracts a crowd of Chinese around his gates" (Cooke, *China*, 221).

66. *Dianshizhai huabao*, Bing 37a.

67. Special thanks to Deborah Cohen for noticing this detail.

68. Ge Yuanxu, *Huyou zaji*, 30.

69. Yeh, *Shanghai Love*, 36.

70. Yeh, *Shanghai Love*, 34.

71. Han Banqing, *Sing-song Girls*, 149.

72. Yeh, *Shanghai Love*, 44.

73. James Legge, *Chinese Classics*, Vol. 5, 296.

74. It also appears, for example, in the text describing the Yipinxiang in *Shanghai's Famous Sites*, discussed earlier (*Shenjiang mingsheng tushuo*, 38a–b).

75. Han Banqing, *Sing-song Girls*, 152.

76. Xu Ke, *Qingbai leichao*, 6270. The logic of seating also had to be learned, and adopted to a range of situations: "The male and female hosts must sit at opposite ends of the table, while the guests sit on either side. The guest of honor sits to the right of the female host; the second most honored guest sits to her left, while the next most important sits to the right of the male host, and the next in importance after that sits to his left. If there is only one host, then the seat of honor is to the right of the host, and the second seat is to the host's left. [Then,] counting from the right are the third, fifth, seventh, and ninth seats [in order of importance], and from the left the fourth, sixth, eighth, and tenth, while the person seated opposite the host occupies the end seat."

77. Chen Bohai, *Shanghai wenhua tongshi*, Vol. 1, 157–58.

78. Xu Ke, *Qingbai leichao*, 6270.

79. Xiong Yuezhi, *Shanghai tongshi*, ed., Vol. 5, 511.

80. Cited in Hu, *Fuzhoulu wenhuajie*, 318.

81. For example, Zeng Pu's 1905 *Flowers in a Sea of Retribution* (Niehai hua), cited in Theodore Huters, *Bringing Home the World*, 44.

82. "Lun Shanghai xinzheng fancaiguan shengyi jian buru xi," *Youxi bao*, No. 617, 1.

83. "Lun Shanghai xinzheng fancaiguan shengyi jian buru xi," *Youxi bao*, No. 617, 1.

84. Huang Shiquan, *Songnan mengying lu*, 126.

85. Chi Zhicheng, *Huyou mengying*, 159.

86. Cited in Catherine Yeh, "Creating a Shanghai Identity," 118.

87. On the Ningbo riots, see Susan Mann Jones, "The Ningpo *Pang* and Financial Power in Shanghai"; and Bryna Goodman, "The Politics of Public Health," 816–20.

88. Xu Ke, *Qingbai leichao*, 6237.

89. "Lun fancaiguan yi jiangjiu pengtiao" [*Fancaiguan* should pay attention to cooking], *Youxi bao*, No. 778, 1.

90. *Doctrine of the Mean*, Chapter 4, Verse 2, following Legge, *Chinese Classics*, Vol. 1, 387, with slight modification; *Analects* 10.8, following E. Bruce Brooks and A. Taeko Brooks, *Original Analects*, 61, where the passage is numbered 10.6a. Legge's *Analects* passage reads, "He did not dislike to have his rice finely cleaned, nor to have his minced meat cut quite small" (*Chinese Classics*, Vol. 1, 232). The effect is the same, but the Brooks and Brooks rendition works better in the present context.

91. Legge, *Chinese Classics*, Vol. 1, 387.

92. Brooks and Brooks, *Original Analects*, 59.

93. "Lun fancaiguan," 1–2.

94. Chen Dingshang, *Chunshen jiuwen* [Old tales of Shanghai], 190.

95. *Huitu youli Shanghai zaji*, 7.10a–b.

96. Ge Yuanxu, *Huyou zaji*, 30.

97. On Zhuo Wenjun, see the biography of Sima Xiangru, in Sima Qian, *Shiji, juan* 117; or in English, in Burton Watson, *Records of the Grand Historian*, Vol. 2, 259–306.

98. Yeh, *Shanghai Love*, 270.

99. Yeh, *Shanghai Love*, 203.

100. Yeh, *Shanghai Love*, 266.

101. On learned women in the late empire, see Dorothy Ko, *Teachers of the Inner Chambers*; and Susan Mann, *Precious Records*.

102. Paul Bailey, "Active Citizen or Efficient Housewife," 319.

103. Bailey, "Active Citizen or Efficient Housewife," 318.

104. Gail Hershatter, *Dangerous Pleasures*; Christian Henriot, *Prostitution and Sexuality in Shanghai*.

105. Bailey, "Active Citizen or Efficient Housewife," 321–22. Although I have retained Bailey's translation of "*shenglizhe*" as "producer," I consider "consumer" a more balanced translation of "*fenlizhe*" than his "parasitic consumer."

106. On Wu and Shimoda, see Joan Judge, "Talent, Virtue, and the Nation," 765–803.

107. Wu Rulun, "Jiazhengxue xu," 1.

108. The *locus classicus* reads as follows: "The ancients who wished to illustrate illustrious virtue throughout the kingdom, first ordered well their States. Wishing

to order well their States, they first regulated their families. Wishing to regulate their families, they first cultivated their persons. Wishing to cultivate their persons, they first rectified their hearts. Wishing to rectify their hearts, they first sought to be sincere in their thoughts. Wishing to be sincere in their thoughts, they first extended to the utmost their knowledge. Such extension of knowledge lay in the investigation of things." Legge, *Chinese Classics*, Vol. 1, 357–58.

109. Shimoda, *Jiazhengxue*, 1–2.

110. Many of the earliest "food treatises" (*shijing*) have been lost, but recipe collections that circulated during the late imperial period can be divided into four main types: hybrid works on agriculture and food production; medical treatises or manuals for "prolonging life" (*yangsheng*); entries in household almanacs and encyclopedias; and eccentric works of individuals. See Wilkinson, *Chinese History*, 625–50.

111. Li Tiaoyuan, "*Xingyuan lu* xu," 3.

112. Li's posthumous publication of his father's collection was itself no less an act of filial piety.

113. As Edward H. Schafer notes, paraphrasing a mid-nineteenth century work: "In Lingnan you could make a good marriage if you could make good pickles; and if you were a perfectionist in the preservation of snakes and yellow eels, you were destined for wedded bliss." Schafer, "T'ang," 129–30.

114. Zeng's book was not written in Shanghai, but it was republished there in 1911, in *Funü shibao* 3: 71–75.

115. Zeng Yi, *Zhongkui lu*, 1.

116. The full poem, as translated by James Legge, reads as follows: "She gathers the large duckweed/By the banks of the stream in the southern valley./She gathers the pondweed/In those pools left by the floods./She deposits what she gathers/In her square baskets and round ones;/She boils it/In her tripods and pans./She sets forth her preparations/Under the window in the ancestral chamber./Who superintends the business?/It is [this] reverent young lady" (Legge, *Chinese Classics*, Vol. 4, Part 1, 25).

117. The custom dates to at least the Tang dynasty (618–907), when it was made the subject of Wang Jian's (fl. 775) poem, "Xinjianiang ci" (The new wife), which reads: "Entering the kitchen after three days/[The new wife] washes her hands and prepares soup./Not familiar with what her in-laws like to eat/[She] first asks her husband's younger sister to taste it." Cited by Chen Guangxin in Zeng Yi, *Zhongkui lu*, 1.

118. Li Gong'er, *Jiating shipu* [Family recipes]; Lu Shouqian, *Pengren yiban* [Fundamentals of cooking]. For a partial list of Republican-era cookbooks, see Ren Baizun ed., *Zhongguo shijing*, 939–40. It is difficult to gauge the size of the readership for these books, but many were reprinted several times, suggesting that the publishers considered the market a lucrative one. Li's *Family Recipes*, for example, was followed by three companion volumes of similar length (roughly four hundred pages each) in 1924, 1925, and 1926, respectively, while the first volume received its twelfth printing in 1946. Li's

was not the only cookbook to go through numerous printings: Lu's *Fundamentals of Cooking* was reissued in 1930; Pan Kan's *A Comprehensive Cookbook* (Shipin pengzhi quanshu), first published in 1924, was reprinted for the sixth time in 1934; the following year witnessed the fifth printing of Shi Xisheng's *Vegetarian Cooking* (Sushi pu), first published in 1925; Tao Xiaoyao's *Mother Tao's Cooking Techniques* (Taomu pengrenfa) received its second printing in May of 1936, a mere four months after its first printing in January of the same year; and Xiao Xiansou's 1934 *Techniques of Cooking* (Pengren fa) was reprinted in 1948. Nor were cookbooks the pet project of any one press; all of Shanghai's major publishing houses (including Zhonghua, Shanghai shijie, Shangwu, Shanghai guangwen, and Datong) counted cookbooks among their publications.

119. Li Gong'er, *Xican pengren mijue* [Secrets of Western cookery]. The China Modern Education Co. (Zhonghua xinjiaoyushe) published a work titled, *Xican pengzhi quanshu* (Comprehensive techniques of Western cookery). I have not been able to locate a copy of this work, but an advertisement can be found in the same publisher's 1934 reprint of the *Jiating wanbao xinshu*, opposite the copyright page.

120. Wang Yanlun, ed., *Jiashi shixi baojia*, 90.

121. Yi Han, "Xishi weisheng pengtiaofa," 25.

122. For a concise overview from the standpoint in Tianjin, see Rogaski, *Hygienic Modernity*, 22–47.

123. The reasons for this shift are complex and involve changing conceptions of the body, state power, and a new culture of nutrition. For a more detailed discussion of these issues, see Rogaski, *Hygienic Modernity*, 104–35, 165–92, and Mark Swislocki, "Feast and Famine in Republican China," 138–77.

124. Lu Shouqian, *Pengren yiban*, 2.

125. Yeh, *Shanghai Love*, see esp. 271–303.

126. Chen Duo, ed., *Riyong baike quanshu*, Chapter 37, 27 (non-continuous pagination).

127. On beef shopping tips, see the *Jiating leyuan, fu Shanghai zhinan*, 175, which notes, "The beef sold in common markets is mostly water buffalo or old ox; but the beef sold in [aristocratic] markets is all genuine cattle beef. Those who want food delicacies and who desire top quality beef, should seek it at top grade markets."

128. Hua Ting et al., *Jiating wanbao xinshu*, Chapter 1, 45 (non-continuous pagination).

129. On this development, see also Susan Glosser, *Chinese Images of Family and State*, 134–66.

130. *Jiating*, 6.6 (1940): 23.

131. An important exception is the movie star Hu Die, who opened her own chain of mid-priced Western food restaurants in the 1930s. See the discussion in Wang Dingjiu, "Chi de menjing," in *Shanghai menjing* [Keys to Shanghai], 5–6. Generally

speaking, however, even when women appear in the imagination of early-twentieth-century modernist writers as fixtures of Western restaurants and coffee shops, they appear there as waitresses, not as customers. On the image of the coffee shop waitress, see Leo Ou-fan Lee, *Shanghai Modern*, 17–23.

Chapter Four

1. Reprinted in Xiong Yuezhi, ed., *Shanghai tongshi*, Vol. 5, 521–22.

2. Ge Yuanxi, *Huyou zaji*, 41.

3. Late nineteenth-century Shanghai witnessed important initiatives in self-governance that helped fill the gap left by the gradual weakening of Qing power and authority. For example, a series of gentry-led public works projects undertaken at the beginning of the twentieth century yielded various local boards and offices that assumed responsibility for such matters as road building and upkeep, local policing, and schooling. In 1912, however, the government of the new Republic of China relocated members of these local boards to the office of the Governor of Jiangsu Province, in which Shanghai County was located, subsuming local initiative under a national political structure. The new central government then quickly faltered under President Yuan Shikai's monarchial ambitions, and when Yuan passed away in 1916, the country fragmented into spheres of interest controlled by military generals from Yuan's Beiyang Army, provincial armies, and local strongmen. Not until 1924 was a municipal office, the "Shi gongsuo," even proposed for Nanshi (the "southern city," the name by which the territory of the Shanghai county seat had become known), or for Zhabei, a new Chinese jurisdiction northwest of the foreign concessions. On these trends and developments, see Mark Elvin, "Administration of Shanghai," 239–62; and Christian Henriot, *Shanghai, 1927–1937*, 9–19.

4. This waning is evident, for example, in the growing control of the Shanghai Municipal Council over the Shanghai Mixed Court, which until 1911 had remained an arena in which Qing officials maintained considerable influence. Elvin, "Mixed Court."

5. The Bureau of Social Affairs would later draw on these figures for its study of Shangahi rice prices, "Shanghai zuijin wushiliunian lai mijia tongji," 1–25.

6. Wang Dingjiu, *Shanghai guwen* [Shanghai advisor] and *Shanghai menjing* [Keys to Shanghai]. Little is known about Wang himself, although in addition to his two Shanghai guidebooks, he was also the editor of a collection of sample letters and three anthologies of women's writings.

7. Liu Yanong, *Shanghai xianhua*, 69.

8. [Yan] Duhe, "Hushang jiushisi zhi bijiao," 389.

9. *Shanghai zhinan* [Guide to Shanghai] (1909), 8.5a.

10. *Shanghai zhinan* [Guide to Shanghai] (1912), 5.9a.

11. *Shanghai zhinan* (1909), 8.5b.

12. It focused, secondarily, on the prices of individual dishes.

13. *Shanghai zhinan* (1912), 5.10a–b.

14. *Shanghai zhinan* (1912), 5.11a.

15. *Shanghai zhinan* (1912), 5.11a.

16. *Shanghai baojian* [Shanghai precious mirror], 14.1a–2b.

17. *Changshi daquan*, Chapter Five, 3–10; *Shanghai zhinan* (1926), 5.3–5.

18. *Shanghai baojian*, 14.1b.

19. Xiong Yuezhi, Zheng Zu'an, Luo Suwen, and Xu Min, *Lao Shanghai daguan: mingren, mingshi, mingwu*, 48.

20. [Yan] Duhe, "Hushang jiushisi zhi bijiao," 389–90.

21. [Yan] Duhe, "Hushang jiushisi zhi bijiao," 392, 393.

22. [Yan] Duhe, "Hushang jiushisi zhi bijiao," 390.

23. [Yan] Duhe, "Hushang jiushisi zhi bijiao," 390.

24. [Yan] Duhe, "Hushang jiushisi zhi bijiao," 390–91.

25. [Yan] Duhe, "Hushang jiushisi zhi bijiao," 391–92.

26. [Yan] Duhe, "Hushang jiushisi zhi bijiao," 392.

27. [Yan] Duhe, "Hushang jiushisi zhi bijiao," 392.

28. Vera Schwarcz, *Chinese Enlightenment*, 70–71.

29. Xiong Yuezhi et al., *Lao Shanghai daguan*, 24; Liu Zengren and Feng Guanglian, *Ye Shengtao yanjiu ziliao*, 3–10.

30. Ye Shengtao, "Guojie," 98–99.

31. Ye Shengtao, "Ou yu chuncai," 111–12.

32. Ye Shengtao, "Ou yu chuncai," 112.

33. Ye Shengtao, "Ou yu chuncai," 112.

34. "Chuban shuoming," in Chen Boxi, *Shanghai yishi daguan*, np.

35. Chen Boxi, *Shanghai yishi daguan*, 67.

36. Chen Boxi, *Shanghai yishi daguan*, 67.

37. On the introduction of the automobile to Shanghai, see Cao Juren, *Shanghai chunqiu*, 166–68; on the racecourse, see Ye Xiaoqing, Dianshizhai *Pictorial*, 65–67; on the Great World, see Meng Yue, *Shanghai and the Edges of Empires*, 208–9.

38. Chen Boxi, *Shanghai yishi daguan*, 68.

39. Wang Dingjiu, "Chi de menjing," in *Shanghai menjing*, 26.

40. *Shanghai baojian*, 14.1b.

41. Shizhe, "Shanghai de chi, san," 33.

42. *Zhongguo mingcanguan*, 104, 106–7, 94–95.

43. Wang Dingjiu, *Shanghai guwen*, 216.

44. Wang Dingjiu, "Chi de menjing," 7.

45. Wang Dingjiu, "Chi de menjing," 8. On workers' wages, see Shanghai Bureau of Social Affairs, *Wages and Hours of Labor*, 148–53.

46. Wang Dingjiu, "Chi de menjing," 8.

47. Xiao Jianqing, *Shanghai changshi* [Shanghai common knowledge], 28.

48. *Shanghai fengtu zaji*, 47.

49. *Shanghai fengtu zaji*, 47.

50. Wang Dingjiu, "Chi de menjing," 9.

51. Wang Dingjiu, "Chi de menjing," 9.

52. Wang Dingjiu, "Chi de menjing," 2.

53. Wang Dingjiu, "Chi de menjing," 8.

54. Wang Dingjiu, "Chi de menjing," 16; Wang Dingjiu, *Shanghai guwen*, 221.

55. Wang Dingjiu, "Chi de menjing," 15.

56. Wang Dingjiu, *Shanghai guwen*, 221.

57. Lin Yin-feng, "Some Notes on Chinese Food," 299.

58. Wang Dingjiu, "Chi de menjing," 17.

59. Wang Dingjiu, "Chi de menjing," 14.

60. Shizhe, "Shanghai de chi, san," 33.

61. Wang Dingjiu, "Chi de menjing," 14; Wang Dingjiu, *Shanghai guwen*, 216.

62. Wang Dingjiu, "Chi de menjing," 27–28.

63. Wang Dingjiu, *Shanghai guwen*, 231.

64. Wang Dingjiu, "Chi de menjing," 28–29.

65. Wang Dingjiu, *Shanghai guwen*, 232.

66. Wang Dingjiu, "Zixu" [Author's preface], in *Shanghai menjing*, 2.

67. Wang Dingjiu, "Chi de menjing," 5.

68. Wang Dingjiu, "Chi de menjing," 30.

69. Wang Dingjiu, "Chi de menjing," 30.

70. Wang Dingjiu, "Chi de menjing," 14.

71. Wang Dingjiu, "Chi de menjing," 24.

72. Wang Dingjiu, "Chi de menjing," 10–11.

73. Wang Dingjiu, "Chi de menjing," 10.

74. *Shanghai zhinan* (1909), 8.6a. See also Tang Zhenchang, *Yizhishi*, 15–18.

75. Wang Dingjiu, "Chi de menjing," 25.

76. Wang Dingjiu, "Chi de menjing," 32.

77. Wang Dingjiu, "Chi de menjing," 33.

Chapter Five

1. Richard Gaulton, "Political Mobilization in Shanghai," 36.

2. Shen Hsi-meng [Shen Ximeng], Mo Yen [Mo Yan], and Lu Hsing-chen [Lu Xingzhen], *On Guard Beneath the Neon Lights*.

3. Shen Hsi-meng et al., *On Guard*, 33.

4. Shen Hsi-meng et al., *On Guard*, 48–49.

5. Shen Hsi-meng et al., *On Guard*, 46.

6. Shen Hsi-meng et al., *On Guard*, 116.

7. Noel Barber, *The Fall of Shanghai*, 147.

8. Barber, *The Fall of Shanghai*, 152.

9. For a more focused examination of this question, see Wen-hsin Yeh, *Shanghai Splendor*, which came out too late to consult for the present work.

10. Elizabeth Perry, *Shanghai on Strike*, 38.

11. Bureau of Social Affairs, *Standard of Living of Shanghai Laborers*, 110.

12. Hanchao Lu, *Beyond the Neon Lights*, 118.

13. Lu, *Beyond the Neon Lights*, 118–21.

14. For an itemized list of all the foodstuffs consumed by working families and the average quantity of each item consumed per family, see Bureau of Social Affairs, *Standard of Living of Shanghai Laborers*, 111–14.

15. "Street Procession in Shanghai's Big Famine Drive." I am grateful to Bryna Goodman for sharing this document with me.

16. Cai Wensen, *Shipin jingjixue*, 9–12.

17. Shanghai tongshe, *Shanghai yanjiu ziliao*, 305, 310.

18. Chen Wuwo, *Lao Shanghai sanshinian jianwenlu*, 1.

19. "Shanghai zuijin wushiliunian lai mijia tongji."

20. The *minshi* concept many be traced to the *Analects*, where it is said of the Duke of Zhou, "What he emphasized was the people, food, mourning and sacrifice." *Analects* 20.1; translation follows E. Bruce Brooks and A. Taeko Brooks, *Original Analects*, 192.

21. Pierre-Etienne Will, *Bureaucracy and Famine in Eighteenth-Century China*; Pierre-Etienne Will and R. Bin Wong, *Nourish the People*.

22. *Shanghai minshi wenti*, 238.

23. *Shanghai minshi wenti*, 238.

24. For a more detailed account of the events recounted here, see *Shanghai minshi wenti*, 199–210, and the analysis in Mark Swislocki, "Feast and Famine in Republican Shanghai," 124–33.

25. *Shanghai minshi wenti*, 207–208.

26. Tang Hai, *Zhongguo laodong wenti*, 178.

27. Whereas the BSA study indicated that price increases had not become significant until the surge in prices following Europe's recovery from the Great War in 1920, Tang argued that, from the standpoint of Shanghai's industrial workers, before 1920, the price of rice had already been hit by three waves of inflation, in 1898, 1913, and 1915 (Tang Hai, *Zhongguo laodong wenti*, 178–79).

28. Xia Yan, "Baoshengong," 17.

29. Emily Honig, *Sisters and Strangers*, 107.

30. Xia Yan, "Baoshengong," 18–19.

31. Henry Lester Institute of Medical Research, *Annual Report*, 20.

32. For a more detailed analysis of the debate, see Swislocki, "Feast and Famine in Republican Shanghai," 75–88.

33. Henry Lester Institute, *Annual Report*, 22.

34. *Shanghai minshi wenti*, 125–26.

35. Swislocki, "Feast and Famine in Republican Shanghai," 88–108.

36. Wen-hsin Yeh, *Wartime Shanghai*, 4–5.

37. Vanya Oakes, *White Man's Folly*, 357, cited in Frederic Wakeman, Jr., *Shanghai Badlands*, 54.

38. Yeh, *Wartime Shanghai*, 5.

39. Eleanor Hinder, *Life and Labour in Shanghai*, 45.

40. On the Shanghai rice supply between 1937 and 1945, see also Christian Henriot, "Rice, Power and People," 41–84.

41. On the importance of Shanghai's waterways for rice transport, see Rhoads Murphey, *Shanghai*, 133–46.

42. Oakes, *White Man's Folly*, 360.

43. Hinder, *Life and Labour in Shanghai*, 101.

44. Hinder, *Life and Labour in Shanghai*, 100.

45. Poshek Fu, *Passivity, Resistance, and Collaboration*, 122–24. See also Frederic Wakeman, Jr., "Urban Controls in Wartime Shanghai," 146.

46. Emmanuel Hsu, *Rise of Modern China*, 613.

47. Noel Barber, *Fall of Shanghai*, 37–39.

48. *Shanghai mishi diaocha*, 2–4.

49. Lynn T. White III, "Shanghai-Suburb Relations," 245.

50. Mao Zedong, "Report on the Peasant Movement," 434.

51. Mao Zedong, "Report on the Peasant Movement," 436–37.

52. White, "Shanghai-Suburb Relations," 244.

53. White, "Shanghai-Suburb Relations," 244–48.

54. Gaulton, "Political Mobilization in Shanghai," 60.

55. Gail Hershatter, "Regulating Sex in Shanghai," 169.

56. Robert Ash, "Quest for Food Self-Sufficiency," 238.

57. Personal Conversation with Zhu Gang, Director of the Shanghai Association of Cuisine and the Shanghai Hotel Association.

58. Xiong Yuezhi, ed., *Shanghai tongshi*, Vol. 15, 93, entry for April 27.

59. Shanghai Municipal Archives file (hereafter SMA), 325-4-1, 26–28.

60. Ding Ling, "Shanghai, 1930," 121.

61. Ding Ling, "Shanghai, 1930," 122.

62. Ding Ling, "Shanghai, 1930," 128.

63. Ding Ling, "Shanghai, 1930," 144.

64. Ding Ling, "Shanghai, 1930," 149.

65. Ding Ling, "Shanghai, 1930," 153.

66. "Yinshi fuwuye de jinxi," SMA B98-1-532, 1.

67. "Yinshi fuwuye de jinxi," 2.

68. The phrase became synonymous for Shanghai soon after the publication of *Shanghai: The Adventurer's Paradise*, by Mexican honorary consul, Mauricio Fresco, under the pseudonym G. E. Miller.

69. "Yinshi fuwuye de jinxi," 1.

70. "Shanghaishi yinshiye gongzuo huibao," SMA B98-1-134, 002.

71. "Shanghaishi yinshiye gongzuo huibao," SMA B98-1-134, 002–005.

72. Wan Pingyuan, *Shanghai Xiaoshaoxing yinshi zonggongsi jianzhi*, 72.

73. Wan Pingyuan, *Shanghai Xiaoshaoxing yinshi zonggongsi jianzhi*, 72

74. "Shanghai siying fuwuxing hangye de jiben qingkuang he jinhou gaizao yu anpai de yijian," SMA B6-2-139, 8.

75. "Shanghaishi yinshiye gongzuo huibao," SMA B98-1-134, 1–2.

76. "Shanghai siying fuwuxing hangye de jiben qingkuang," 21.

77. "Dui fuwuxing hangye youguan ganbu he congye renyuan xuanchuan jiaoyu cankao ziliao," SMA B6-2-138, 48b.

78. According to one account, 17 percent of all people registering to sell blood in 1954 at the Shanghai Blood Transfusion Company worked in service industries ("Baogao Shanghaishi siying yinshi fuwuye de qingkuang ji yijian," SMA B6-2-138, 21). For anecdotes about service industry workers living on congee and making ends meet by selling their own furniture, see "Jing'anqu fuwuxing hangye anpai qingkuan baogao," SMA B6-2-138, 77.

79. "Dui fuwuxing hangye youguan ganbu he congye renyuan xuanchuan jiaoyu cankao ziliao," 48–49a.

80. "Dui fuwuxing hangye youguan ganbu he congye renyuan xuanchuan jiaoyu cankao ziliao," 50.

81. "Shanghai siying fuwuxing hangye de jiben qingkuang," 20a.

82. "Guanyu siying fuwuxing hangye gaishan jingying guanli gongzuo de yijian," SMA B6-2-138, 12.

83. "Baogao Shanghaishi siying yinshi fuwuye de qingkuang ji yijian," SMA B6-2-138, 21.

84. Baogao youguan yinshi fuwuye de gongzuo qingkuang he jinhou yijian," SMA B6-2-138, 27.

85. Bruce L. Reynolds, "Changes in the Standard of Living," 236; Ash, "Quest for Food Self-Sufficiency," 199.

86. Ash, "The Quest for Food Self-Sufficiency," 188.

87. Wang Zheng, "Call Me 'Qingnian' but not 'Funü,'" 29.

88. Wang Zheng, "Call Me 'Qingnian' but not 'Funü,'" 29.

89. "Guanyu siying fuwuxing hangye gaishan jingying guanli gongzuo de yijian," 13–14.

90. Cited in Jonathan Spence, *Search for Modern China*, 547.

91. "Baogao Shanghaishi siying yinshi fuwuye de qingkuang ji yijian," 23.

92. *Shanghai xianzhi*, 517.

93. Cited in *Shanghai xianzhi*, 517.

94. *Shanghai xianzhi*, 517–18.

95. "Zuohao Chenghuangmiao yinshi gongying gongzuo de jingyan," SMA B98-1-730, 60.

96. "Zuohao Chenghuangmiao," 60–61.

97. "Shanghaishi yinshiye gongzuo huibao," 24.

98. "Guanyu peixun shangye yinshi fuwuye jishu renyuan de qingshi baogao," SMA A65-2-117, 15.

99. "Zuohao Chenghuangmiao," 61.

100. "Baochi he fayang teshu fengwei," SMA B98-1-730, 81.

101. "Zuohao Chenghuangmiao," 61–62.

102. "Baochi he fayang teshu fengwei," 80.

103. "Zuohao Chenghuangmiao," 62.

104. Chef participation in classroom work and text preparation is indicated on their personnel files. See SMA B98-1-164, 54–319.

105. Records of these exams are collected in SMA B50-2-208, 9–18.

106. For a list of the examines and their areas of expertise, see SMA B50-2-208, 8.

107. On Dong, see her memoir, Dong Zhujun, *Wode yige shiji*.

108. "Gaoji chushi shang kaochang," *Xinmin wanbao*, August 27, 1956, 4, in SMA B50-2-208, 35.

109. Xiao's piece summarized many of the points he had raised about the distinguishing features of Cantonese cuisine during his oral presentation at the competition. Xiao Langchu, "Tantan Guangdongcai de shaofa," 4, in SMA B50-2-208, 34.

110. "Guanyu tiaozheng chushi de jidian yijian," SMA B50-2-319, 1.

111. "Yinshi fuwuye," SMA B98-1-732, 2.

112. "Yinshi fuwuye," 1.

113. "Guanyu dai guowuyuan jiguan shiwu guanliju peixun chushi de chubu dasuan," SMA B50-2-398, 26.

114. Tan Tingdong personnel file, in SMA B98-1-164, 55.

115. Soon after the Liao fell, the Sixteen Territories became a part of the Jurchen Jin state (1115–1234), which in turn fell to the Mongols, who reintegrated the territories with China proper.

116. Feng Pei personnel file, SMA B98-1-164, 63.

117. He Qikun personnel file, SMA B98-1-164, 116.

118. Yu Hong personnel file, SMA B98-1-164, 75.

119. Ning Songtao personnel file, SMA B98-1-164, 103.

120. Burton Watson, *Chuang-tzu, Basic Writings*, 46–47.

121. *Zhongguo mingcanguan*, 108–109.

122. Personal conversation with Sha Peiwen, Head Chef, Meilongzhen jiujia, March, 1999, and Zhang Weimin, Public Relations Department Manager, Xinya Yuecaiguan, December, 1998.

Epilogue

1. On the various meanings of *bang*, see Bryna Goodman, *Native Place, City, and Nation*, 39–40.

2. In contrast to Shanghai, for example, the southern city of Guangzhou, strategically located near Hong Kong, was given a much freer hand in restructuring patterns of industrial and commercial employment. Moreover, most of the new forms of capital investment elaborated in the early post-Mao era for urban areas went into the cities of the new Special Economic Zones, such as Shenzhen. On Guangzhou, see Ezra F. Vogel, *One Step Ahead in China*; on Shenzhen's importance to the early reform period, see Kwan-yiu Wong and David K. Y. Chu, *Modernization in China*.

3. Jos Gamble, *Shanghai in Transition*, 10.

4. Gamble, *Shanghai in Transition*, 10.

5. Gamble, *Shanghai in Transition*, 11.

6. Personal conversation with Yangzhou Restaurant management.

7. "Red Chamber Banquet Overview," 1–7. Author's personal copy, provided courtesy of the Yangzhou Restaurant.

8. Xue Li, "Canyingye chuiqi huaijiufeng," 19.

9. Zhang Xudong, "Shanghai Nostalgia," 354.

10. Cited in Petra Saunders, "Shanghai Chic," 11.

11. Ban Wang, "Love at Last Sight," 91.

12. Chen Wuwo, *Lao Shanghai*; Yu Muxia, *Shanghai linzhao* [Shanghai tidbits]; Wu Liang, *Lao Shanghai* [Old Shanghai]; and, for example, Liu Yexiong, *Chunhua qiuye heshi liao*.

13. These included works by figures like Liu Na'ou, Mu Shiying, Shi Zhecun, and Ye Lingfeng. For studies of these bodies of literature, see Leo Ou-fan Lee, *Shanghai Modern*, and Shu-mei Shih, *Lure of the Modern*.

14. Hu Genxi, *Lao Shanghai*.

15. See, for example, Xue Yanwen and Wang Tongli, *Piaozheng jiushi*.

16. On Mao nostalgia, see Geremie R. Barmé, *Shades of Mao*; and Jennifer Hubbert, "(Re)collecting Mao," 145–61.

17. Zhang, "Shanghai Nostalgia," 354.

18. Wang, "Love at Last Sight," 672.

19. Wang, "Love at Last Sight," 681.

20. For a translation and discussion of this poem and its meaning, see Dore J. Levy, *Chinese Narrative Poetry*, 71–75, 129–33.

21. Xue Li, "Canyingye chuiqi huaijiufeng," 19.

22. For a recent collection of the key contributions to the early *Haipai* debate, see Ma Fengxiang, *Shanghai*.

23. Chen Xiande and Lang Hong, "Tiaohe dingnai baiweisheng," 16.

24. Chen and Lang, "Tiaohe dingnai baiweisheng," 17.

25. Chen and Lang, "Tiaohe dingnai baiweisheng," 17.

26. Chen and Lang, "Tiaohe dingnai baiweisheng," 18.

27. Cited in Chen and Lang, "Tiaohe dingnai baiweisheng," 18.

28. Lu Yaodong, *Duda nengrong*, 52.

29. Lu, *Duda nengrong*, 54.

30. Lu, *Duda nengrong*, 48.

31. Lu, *Duda nengrong*, 48.

32. Tejijiaodui, pseud. [Chen Mengyin], *Jinshan shijing*, 13.

33. Zhou Sanjin, "Mingsheng Zhongwai de Shanghai meishi zhongxin," 1–4.

34. Zhou Sanjin, "Mingsheng Zhongwai de Shanghai meishi zhongxin," 3.

35. See, for example, the listing of restaurants in the 1907 *Shanghai huashang hangming buce*, 112a–13b.

36. Liu Yanong, *Shanghai xianhua*, 69.

37. Liu Shoumin and Xu Wenlong, *Shanghai laodian, dadian, mingdian*, 54.

38. Zhou Sanjin, "Mingsheng Zhongwai de Shanghai meishi zhongxin," 8; and *Shanghai laodian, dadian, mingdian*, 54.

39. Wang, "Chi de menjing," in *Shanghai menjing*, 30.

40. Ruo Wei, "Fandian nongtang xiaoji," 17.

41. Yu Muxia, *Shanghai linzhao*, 92.

42. Ruo Wei, "Fandian nongtang xiaoji," 17.

43. Wang, "Chi de menjing," 31.

Bibliography

Adshead, S. A. M. 1992. *Salt and Civilization.* Houndsmills, UK: Palgrave Macmillan.

Alford, Jeffrey, and Naomi Duguid. 2000. *Hot Sour Salty Sweet: A Culinary Journey through Southeast Asia.* New York: Artisan.

Anagnost, Ann. 1993. "The Nationscape: Movement in the Field of Vision." *positions* 1.3: 585–606.

Anderson, E. N., Jr., and Marja L. Anderson. 1977. "Modern China: South." In *Food in Chinese Culture: Anthropological and Historical Perspectives,* edited by K. C. Chang, 317–82. New Haven, CT: Yale University Press.

Ash, Robert. 1981. "The Quest for Food Self-Sufficiency." In *Shanghai: Revolution and Development in an Asian Metropolis,* edited by Christopher Howe, 188–221. New York: Cambridge University Press.

Atwell, William S. 1998. "Ming China and the Emerging World Economy, ca. 1470–1650." In *The Cambridge History of China.* Vol. 8, *Ming Dynasty, 1368–1644,* Part 2, edited by D. Twitchett and F. W. Mote, 376–416. Cambridge: Cambridge University Press.

Bailey, Paul. 2001. "Active Citizen or Efficient Housewife: The Debate over Women's Education in Early Twentieth-Century China." In *Education, Culture, and Identity in Twentieth-Century China,* edited by Glen Peterson, Ruth Hayhoe, and Yongling Lu, 318–47. Ann Arbor: University of Michigan Press.

Ball, B. L. 1856. *Rambles in Eastern Asia, Including China and Manila.* Boston: James French.

Barber, Noel. 1979. *The Fall of Shanghai.* New York: Coward, McCann & Goeghegan.

Barmé, Geremie R. 1996. *Shades of Mao: The Posthumous Cult of the Great Leader.* New York: M. E. Sharpe.

Belsky, Richard. 2003. *Localities at the Center: Native Place, Space, and Power in Late Imperial Beijing.* Cambridge, MA: Harvard University Asia Center.

Bergère, Marie-Claire. 1981. "The Other China: Shanghai from 1919–1949." In *Shanghai: Revolution and Development in an Asian Metropolis*, edited by Christopher Howe, 1–34. New York: Cambridge University Press.

Bickers, Robert A. 1999. *Britain in China*. New York: Manchester University Press.

Bickers, Robert A., and Jeffrey N. Wasserstrom. 1995. "Shanghai's 'Dogs and Chinese Not Admitted' Sign: Legend, History and Contemporary Symbol." *China Quarterly* 142: 444–66.

Birch, Cyril. 1965. *Anthology of Chinese Literature*. New York: Grove Press.

Boym, Svetlana. 2001. *The Future of Nostalgia*. New York: Basic Books.

Brandt, Kim. 2007. *Kingdom of Beauty: Mingei and the Politics of Folk Art in Imperial Japan*. Durham, NC: Duke University Press.

Brockway, Lucile H. 1979. *Science and Colonial Expansion: The Role of the British Royal Botanical Gardens*. New York: Academic Press.

Brook, Timothy. 1997. "Native Identity under Alien Rule: Local Gazetteers of the Yuan Dynasty." In *Pragmatic Literacy, East and West: 1200–1330*, edited by Richard Britnell, 235–45. Woodbridge, UK: Boydell.

———. 1997. *The Confusions of Pleasure: Culture and Commerce in Ming China*. Berkeley: University of California Press.

———. 2001. "Xu Guangqi in His Context: The World of the Shanghai Gentry." In *Statecraft and Intellectual Renewal in Late Ming China: The Cross-Cultural Synthesis of Xu Guangqi (1562–1633)*, edited by Catherine Jami, Peter M. Engelfriet, and Gregory Blue, 72–98. Leiden: Brill.

———. 2002. *Geographical Sources of Ming-Qing History*, Second Edition. Ann Arbor: University of Michigan Center for Chinese Studies.

Brooks, E. Bruce, and A. Taeko Brooks. 1998. *The Original Analects: Sayings of Confucius and His Successors*. New York: Columbia University Press.

Buell, Paul D., and E. N. Anderson. 2000. *A Soup for the Qan: Chinese Dietary Medicine of the Mongol Era as Seen in Hu Szu-Hui's* Yin-shan cheng-yao: *Introduction, Translation, Commentary and Chinese Text*. New York: Kegan Paul International.

Bureau of Social Affairs. 1934. *Standard of Living of Shanghai Laborers*. Shanghai: Bureau of Social Affairs, City Government of Greater Shanghai.

Cai Wensen. 1924. *Shipin jingjixue* [Food economics]. Shanghai: Shangwu yinshuguan.

Cao Juren. 1996. *Shanghai chunqiu*. Shanghai: Shanghai renmin chubanshe.

Cassel, Pår. 2003. "Excavating Extraterritoriality: The 'Judicial Sub-Prefect' as a Prototype for the Mixed Court in Shanghai." *Late Imperial China* 24.2 (December): 156–82.

Chang, K. C. 1977. "Ancient China." In *Food in Chinese Culture: Anthropological and Historical Perspectives*, edited by K. C. Chang, 23–52. New Haven, CT: Yale University Press.

Chang, K. C., ed. 1977. *Food in Chinese Culture: Anthropological and Historical Perspectives*. New Haven, CT: Yale University Press.

Changshi daquan. 1928. Shanghai: Changshi baoguan.

Chen Bohai, ed. 2001. *Shanghai wenhua tongshi,* 2 vols. Shanghai: Shanghai wenyi chubanshe.

Chen Boxi. 1924. *Shanghai yishi daguan* [Compendium of Shanghai anecdotes]. Reprint, 2000. Shanghai: Shanghai shudian chubanshe.

Chen Dingshan. 1967. *Chunshen jiuwen* [Old tales of Shanghai]. Taibei: Shijie wenwu chubanshe.

Chen Duo, ed. 1925. *Riyong baike quanshu.* Shanghai: Shangwu yinshuguan.

Chen Wenshu. 1814. "Xu." In Chu Hua, *Shuimitao pu. Shanghai zhanggu congshu,* Vol. 2. Taibei: Xuehai chubanshe, 1968 reprint.

Chen Wuwo. 1928. *Lao Shanghai sanshinian jianwenlu* [Record of things seen and heard over thirty years in old Shanghai]. Reprint, 1996. Shanghai: Shanghai shudian chubanshe.

Chen Xiande and Lang Hong. 1995. "Tiaohe dingnai baiweisheng: 'Haipaicai' tanxun." In *Shanghai meishi daguan,* edited by Ji Bin and Xu Zhiming. Shanghai: Shanghai yuandong chubanshe.

Chen Yinke. 1973. "Taohua yuan ji pangzheng." Chen Yinke, *Chen Yinke xiansheng wen-shi lunji,* Vol. 1. Hong Kong: Wenwen chubanshe.

Chen Yuanlong. 1735. *Gezhi jingyuan. Wenyuange siku quanshu neilian wangban.* Xianggang: Dizhi wenhua chuban youxian gongsi, 2002.

Chi Zhicheng. 1893. *Huyou mengying* [Dream images of a visit to Shanghai]. Reprint, 1989. In *Shanghaitan yu Shanghairen.* Shanghai: Shangahi guji chubanshe.

Chow, Kai-wing. 2004. *Publishing, Culture, and Power in Early Modern China.* Stanford, CA: Stanford University Press.

Chu Hua. 1814. *Shuimitao pu* [Treatise on the honey nectar peach]. In *Shanghai zhanggu congshu,* Vol. 2. Taibei: Xuehai chubanshe, 1968 reprint.

Clunas, Craig. 1996. *Fruitful Sites: Garden Culture in Ming Dynasty China.* Durham, NC: Duke University Press.

———. 2004. *Superfluous Things: Material Culture and Social Status in Early Modern China.* Honolulu: University of Hawai'i Press.

Coble, Parks. 1986. *The Shanghai Capitalists and the Nationalist Government, 1927–1937.* Cambridge, MA: Harvard University Press.

Cohen, Paul. 1974. *Between Tradition and Modernity: Wang T'ao and Reform in Late Ch'ing China.* Cambridge, MA: Harvard University Press.

Cooke, George Wingrove. 1859. *China: Being "The Times" Special Correspondence from China in the Years 1857–58.* New York: Routledge.

Daruvala, Susan. 2000. *Zhou Zuoren and an Alternative Chinese Response to Modernity.* Cambridge, MA: Harvard University East Asia Center.

Dennys, N. B., William Frederick Mayers, and Charles King. 1867. *The Treaty Ports of China and Japan.* London: Trübner.

Dianshizhai huabao. 1884–98. Guangdong: Guangdong renmin chubanshe, 1983 reprint.

Ding Ling. 1989 (1930) "Shanghai, 1930." In *I, Myself, Am a Woman: Selected Writings of Ding Ling*, edited by Tani E. Barlow with Gary J. Borge, 112–71. Boston: Beacon Press.

Dong Zhujun. 1997. *Wode yige shiji*. Beijing: Sanlian shudian.

Downing, C. Toogood. 1838. *The Fan-Qui in China, 1836–7*, 3 vols. Shannon, Ireland: Irish University Press.

Drayton, Richard. 2000. *Nature's Government: Science, Imperial Britain, and the "Improvement" of the World*. New Haven, CT: Yale University Press.

Du Zhizhong. 1985. "Yetan Zhonguo de caixi." *Zhongguo pengren* 6.1: 9–10.

Duara, Prasenjit. 1997. *Rescuing History from the Nation: Questioning Narratives of Modern China*. Chicago: University of Chicago Press.

———. 2000. "Local Worlds: The Poetics and Politics of the Native Place in Modern China." *South Atlantic Quarterly* 99: 1: 13–45.

Duhe. 1923. "Hushang jiushisi zhi bijiao." Reprint, 1998. In *Jiu Shanghai fengqinglu*, Vol. 2, edited by Yu Zhi and Cheng Xinguo, 389–93. Shanghai: Wenhui chubanshe.

Dyce, Charles M. 1906. *Personal Reminiscences of Thirty Years' Residence in the Model Settlement, Shanghai, 1870–1900*. London: Chapman & Hall.

Eberhard, Wolfram. 1986. *A Dictionary of Chinese Symbols: Hidden Symbols in Chinese Life and Thought*. New York: Routledge.

Echikson, William. 2004. *Noble Rot: A Bordeaux Wine Revolution*. New York: Norton.

Elvin, Mark. 1963. "The Mixed Court of the International Settlement in Shanghai." *Papers on China* 17: 131–59.

———. 1974. "The Administration of Shanghai, 1905–1914." In *The Chinese City Between Two Worlds*, edited by Mark Elvin and G. William Skinner, 239–62. Stanford, CA: Stanford University Press.

———. 1977. "Market Towns and Waterways: The County of Shang-hai from 1480–1910." In *The City in Late Imperial China*, edited by G. William Skinner, 441–74. Stanford, CA: Stanford University Press.

Fairbank, John King, ed. 1968. *The Chinese World Order: Traditional China's Foreign Relations*. Cambridge, MA: Harvard University Press.

Farquhar, Judith. 2002. *Appetites: Food and Sex in Postsocialist China*. Durham, NC: Duke University Press.

Finnane, Antonia. 2004. *Speaking of Yangzhou: A Chinese City, 1550–1850*. Cambridge, MA: Harvard University Press.

Fortune, Robert. 1847. *Three Years' Wanderings in the Northern Provinces of China, Including a Visit to the Tea, Silk, and Cotton Countries; with an Account of the Agriculture and Horticulture of the Chinese, New Plants, etc.* London: J. Murray.

Frankel, Hans H. 1976. *The Flowering Plum and the Palace Lady: Interpretations of Chinese Poetry*. New Haven, CT: Yale University Press.

Freeman, Michael. 1977. "Sung." In *Food in Chinese Culture: Anthropological and Historical Perspectives*, edited by K. C. Chang, 141–92. New Haven, CT: Yale University Press.

Fu, Poshek. 1997. *Passivity, Resistance, and Collaboration: Intellectual Choices in Occupied Shanghai*. Stanford, CA: Stanford University Press.

Gamble, Jos. 2003. *Shanghai in Transition: Changing Perspectives and Social Contours of a Chinese Metropolis*. New York: Routledge.

Gaulton, Richard. 1981. "Political Mobilization in Shanghai, 1949–1951." In *Shanghai: Revolution and Development in an Asian Metropolis*, edited by Christopher Howe, 35–65. New York: Cambridge University Press.

Ge Yuanxu. 1876. *Huyou zaji* [Miscellaneous notes on travel in Shanghai]. Reprint, 1989. In *Shanghaitan yu Shanghairen*. Shanghai: Shanghai guji chubanshe.

Glosser, Susan. 2003. *Chinese Images of Family and State*. Berkeley: University of California Press.

Goodman, Bryna. 1989. "The Politics of Public Health: Sanitation in Shanghai in the Late Nineteenth Century." *Modern Asian Studies*, 23.4: 816–20.

———. 1995. *Native Place, City, and Nation: Regional Networks and Identities in Shanghai, 1853–1937*. Berkeley: University of California Press.

Goossaert, Vincent. 2005. *L'Interdit de Bœuf en Chine. Agriculture, Éthique et Sacrifice*. Paris: Collège de France, Institut des Hautes Études chinoises,

———. 2005. "The Beef Taboo and the Sacrificial Structure of Late Imperial Chinese Society." In *Of Tripod and Palate*, edited by Roel Sterckx, 237–48.

Gu Bingquan. 1993. *Shanghai fengsu guji kao*. Shanghai: Huadong shifan daxue chubanshe.

Guangzhou zhinan [Guide to Guangzhou]. 1934. Guangzhou: Peiying yinshuju.

Gujin tushu jicheng. 1936. Shanghai: Zhonghua shuju.

Guo Xian. 1st Century. *Dongming ji* [Record of caves of mystery]. *Wenyuange siku quanshu neilian wangban*. Xianggang: Dizhi wenhua chuban youxian gongsi, 2002.

Han Banqing. 1894. *Sing-song Girls of Shanghai*, translated by Eva Hong. New York: Columbia University Press, 2005.

Hansen, Valerie. 2000. *Open Empire: A History of China to 1600*. New York: W. W. Norton.

Hanson, Marta. 1998. "Robust Northerners and Delicate Southerners: The Nineteenth Century Invention of a *Wenbing* Tradition." *positions: east asia cultures critique* 6.3: 515–49.

———. 2006. "Northern Purgatives, Southern Restoratives: Ming Medical Regionalism." *Asian Medicine* 2.2: 115–70.

Hao, Yen-P'ing. 1970. *The Compradore in Nineteenth Century China: Bridge between East and West*. Cambridge, MA: Harvard University Press.

Harper, Donald. 1986. "Flowers in T'ang Poetry: Pomegranate, Sea Pomegranate, and Mountain Pomegranate." *Journal of the American Oriental Society* 106.1: 139–53.

Hay, Jonathan. 1999. "Ming Palace and Tomb in Early Qing Jiangning: Dynastic Memory and the Openness of History." *Late Imperial China* 20.1: 1–48.

Hayford, Charles. 1978. Review of *Food in Chinese Culture: Historical and Anthropological Perspectives*. *Journal of Asian Studies* 37.4: 738–40.

Henderson, John B. 1984. *The Development and Decline of Chinese Cosmology*. New York: Columbia University Press.

Henriot, Christian. 1993. *Shanghai, 1927–1937: Municipal Power, Locality, and Modernization*. Berkeley: University of California Press.

———. 2000. "Rice, Power and People: The Politics of Food Supply in Wartime Shanghai (1937–1945)." *Twentieth-Century China* 26.1: 41–84.

———. 2001. *Prostitution and Sexuality in Shanghai: A Social History*. New York: Cambridge University Press.

Henry Lester Institute of Medical Research. 1939. *Annual Report for 1937/1938*. Shanghai: North China Daily News.

Hershatter, Gail. 1992. "Regulating Sex in Shanghai: The Reform of Prostitution in 1920 and 1951." In *Shanghai Sojourners*, edited by Frederic Wakeman, Jr., and Wen-hsin Yeh, 145–85. Berkeley: University of California Institute of East Asian Studies.

———. 1997. *Dangerous Pleasures: Prostitution and Modernity in Twentieth-Century China*. Berkeley: University of California Press.

Hervouet, Yves. 1964. *Un poète de cour sous les Han: Sseu-ma Siang-jou*. Paris: Presses Universitaires de France.

———. 1972. *Le chapitre 117 du Che-ki (Biographie de Sseu-ma Siang-jou)*. Paris: Presses Universitaires de France.

Hightower, James Robert. 1970. *The Poetry of T'ao Ch'ien*. Oxford, UK: Clarendon Press.

Hinder, Eleanor. 1944. *Life and Labour in Shanghai: A Decade of Labour and Social Administration in the International Settlement*. New York: Institute of Pacific Relations.

Ho, Ping-ti. 1955. "The Introduction of American Food Plants to China." *American Anthroplogist* 57: 191–201.

———. 1998. "In Defense of Sinicization: A Rebuttal of Evelyn Rawski's 'Reenvisioning the Qing.'" *Journal of Asian Studies* 57.1: 123–55.

Hongzhi Shanghai zhi [Shanghai gazetteer, Hongzhi era]. 1504.

Honig, Emily. 1986. *Sisters and Strangers: Women in the Shanghai Cotton Mills, 1919–1949*. Stanford, CA: Stanford University Press.

Hsu, Emmanuel. 2000. *The Rise of Modern China*, Sixth Edition. New York: Oxford University Press.

Hu Genxi. 1998. *Lao Shanghai: bujinjin shi fenghua xueyue de gushi*. Chengdu, China: Sichuan renmin chubanshe.

Hu Yuanjie, ed. 2001. *Fuzhoulu wenhuajie*. Shanghai: Wenhui chubanshe.

Hua Ting et al. 1934. *Jiating wanbao xinshu*. Shanghai: Zhongguo xinjiaoyushe.

Huang, H. T. 2000. *Science and Civilisation in China.* Vol. 6, Part 5, *Fermentations and Food Science.* New York: Cambridge University Press.

Huang Shiquan. 1883. *Songnan mengying lu.* Reprint, 1989. In *Shanghaitan yu Shanghairen.* Shanghai: Shangahi guji chubanshe.

Hubbert, Jennifer. 2005. "Revolution IS a Dinner Party: Cultural Revolution Theme Restaurants in Contemporary China." *China Review* 5.2: 125–50.

———. 2006. "(Re)collecting Mao: Memory and Fetish in Contemporary China." *American Ethnologist* 33.2: 145–61.

Huitu youli Shanghai zaji. 1906. Wenbao shuju.

Hushang youxizhu. 1898. *Haishang youxi tushuo* [Illustrated guide to Shanghai entertainment]. Shanghai.

Huters, Theodore. 2005. *Bringing Home the World: Appropriating the West in Late Qing and Early Republican China.* Honolulu: University of Hawai'i Press.

Jiajing Shanghai xianzhi [Shanghai county gazetteer, Jiajing era]. 1524.

Jiangnan tongzhi [Comprehensive gazetteer of Jiangnan]. 1736. *Wenyuange siku quanshu neilian wangban.* Xianggang: Dizhi wenhua chuban youxian gongsi, 2002.

Jiaqing Daqing yitongzhi [Unified gazetteer of the Great Qing, Jiaqing era]. 1842.

Jiaqing Shanghai xianzhi. 1814.

Jiaqing Songjiang fuzhi. 1818. *Xuxiu siku quanshu.* Shanghai: Shanghai guji chubanshe, 1995.

Jiating leyuan, fu Shanghai zhinan. 1939. Shanghai: Shanghai chubanshe.

Jinshu [Jin history]. Beijing: Zhonghua shuju, 1974 reprint.

Johnson, Linda Cook. 1995. *Shanghai: From Market Town to Treaty Port, 1074–1858.* Stanford, CA: Stanford University Press.

Jones, Andrew. 2001. *Yellow Music: Media Culture and Colonial Modernity in the Chinese Jazz Age.* Durham, NC: Duke University Press.

Jones, Susan Mann. 1974. "The Ningpo *Pang* and Financial Power at Shanghai." In *The Chinese City Between Two Worlds,* edited by Mark Elvin and G. William Skinner, 73–96. Stanford, CA: Stanford University Press.

Judge, Joan. 2001. "Talent, Virtue, and the Nation: Chinese Nationalisms and Female Subjectivities in the Early Twentieth Century." *American Historical Review* 106.3: 765–803.

Kafalas, Philip A. 2007. *In Limpid Dream: Nostalgia and Zhang Dai's Reminiscences of the Ming.* Norwalk, CT: EastBridge.

Kao, George, ed. 1946. *Chinese Wit and Humor.* New York: Coward-McCann.

Karlgren, Bernhard. 1950. *The Book of Documents.* Stockholm: Stockholm Museum of Far Eastern Antiquities, 1950.

Keswick, Maggie. 2003. *The Chinese Garden: History, Art and Architecture.* Cambridge, MA: Harvard University Press.

Knechtges, David R., trans. 1982. *Wen xuan, or Selections of Refined Literature.* Vol. 1, *Rhapsodies on Metropolises and Capitals.* Princeton, NJ: Princeton University Press.

————. 1997. "Gradually Entering the Realm of Delight: Food and Drink in Early Medieval China." *Journal of the American Oriental Society* 117.2: 229–39.

Ko, Dorothy. 1994. *Teachers of the Inner Chambers: Women and Culture in Seventeenth Century China*. Stanford, CA: Stanford University Press.

Koehn, Alfred. 1944. *Fragrance from a Chinese Garden*. Peking, China: At the Lotus Court.

Kroll, Paul, 1986. "Chang Chiu-ling." In *Indiana Companion to Traditional Chinese Literature*, edited and compiled by William H. Nienhauser, Jr., 207–209. Bloomington: Indiana University Press.

Kuaiji zhi [Gazetteer of Kuaiji]. 1510. *Wenyuange siku quanshu neilian wangban*. Xianggang: Dizhi wenhua chuban youxian gongsi, 2002.

Lary, Diana. 1996. "The Tomb of the King of Nanyue—The Contemporary Agenda of History." *Modern China* 22.1: 3–27.

Laufer, Berthold. 1967. *Sino-Iranica: Chinese Contributions to the History of Civilization in Ancient Iran*. New York: Kraus Reprint. Original published 1919.

Lee, Leo Ou-fan. 1999. *Shanghai Modern: The Flowering of a New Urban Culture in China, 1930–1945*. Cambridge, MA: Harvard University Press.

Legge, James. 1967. *Li Chi: Book of Rites. An Encyclopedia of Ancient Ceremonial Usages, Religious Creeds, and Social Institutions*, edited by Ch'u Chai and Winberg Chai. Hyde Park, NY: University Books.

————. 2001. *The Chinese Classics*, 5 vols. Taibei: SMC Publishing.

Leung Yuen-sang. 1990. *The Shanghai Taotai: Linkage Man in a Changing Society, 1843–90*. Honolulu: University of Hawai'i Press.

Levy, Dore J. 1988. *Chinese Narrative Poetry: The Late Han through T'ang Dynasties*. Durham, NC: Duke University Press.

Li Gong'er. 1917. *Jiating shipu* [Family recipes]. Shanghai: Zhonghua shuju.

————. 1923. *Xican pengren mijue* [Secrets of Western cookery]. Shanghai: Shanghai shijie shuju.

Li Hua'nan. 1984. *Xingyuan lu* [Record of Xing garden]. Beijing: Zhongguo shangye chubanshe.

Li, Hui-Lin, trans. 1979. *Nan-fang ts'ao-mu chuang: A Fourth Century Flora of Southeast Asia: Introduction, Translation, Commentaries*. Hong Kong: Chinese University Press.

Li Tiaoyuan. 1984. "*Xingyuan lu xu*." In Li Hua'nan, *Xingyuan lu*, 1–4, noncontinuous pagination. Beijing: Zhongguo shangye chubanshe.

Li Weiqing. 1907. *Shanghai xiangtuzhi* [Shanghai local gazetteer]. Shanghai: Quanxuesuo.

Liangshu [Liang history]. Beijing: Zhonghua shuju, 1973 edition.

Lidai shehui fengsu shiwu kao. 1989. Shanghai: Shanghai wenyi shubanshe. Original published 1938.

Lin Yin-feng. 1937. "Some Notes on Chinese Food." *People's Tribune* 26: 295–301.

Liu, Lydia. 2004. *The Clash of Empires: The Invention of China in Modern World Making.* Cambridge, MA: Harvard University Press.

Liu Shoumin and Xu Wenlong. 1998. *Shanghai laodian, mingdian, dadian.* Shanghai: Shanghai sanlian chubanshe.

Liu Xin. 1st century. 2002. *Xijing zaji* [Miscellaneous notes on the western capital]. *Wenyuange siku quanshu neilian wangban.* Xianggang: Dizhi wenhua chuban youxian gongsi.

Liu Yanong. 1961. *Shanghai xianhua.* Taibei: Shijie shuju.

Liu Yexiong. 2005. *Chunhua qiuye heshi liao: pandian Shanghai shishang.* Shanghai: Shanghai renmin chubanshe.

Liu Yiqing. 1993. *Shishuo xinyu jianshu,* edited by Yu Jiaxi. Shanghai: Shanghai guji chubanshe.

Liu Zengren and Feng Guanglian, eds. 1988. *Ye Shengtao yanjiu ziliao.* Beijing: Shiyue wenyi chubanshe.

Loewe, Michael. 1979. *Ways to Paradise: The Chinese Quest for Immortality.* London: Allen and Unwin.

Loutang zhi [Gazetteer of Loutang]. 1772, drafted (1805, published). Reprinted in Shanghaishi difangzhi biangongshi, 2004, *Shanghai xiangzhen jiuzhi congshu,* Vol. 1. Shanghai: Shangahi shehuikexueyuan chubanshe.

Lu Shouqian. 1917. *Pengren yiban.* Shanghai: Zhonghua shuju.

Lu Yan. 1998. "Beyond Politics in Wartime: Zhou Zuoren, 1931–1945." *Sino-Japanese Studies* 11.1: 6–12.

Lu, Hanchao. 1992. "Arrested Development: Cotton and Markets in Shanghai, 1350–1843." *Modern China* 18.4: 468–99.

———. 1999. *Beyond the Neon Lights: Everyday Shanghai in the Early Twentieth Century.* Berkeley: University of California Press.

Lu Yaodong. 2001. *Duda nengrong: Zhongguo yinshi wenhua sanji.* Taibei: Dongda tushu.

Ma Fengxiang, ed. 1996. *Shanghai: Jiyi yu xiangxiang.* Shanghai: Wenhui chubanshe.

MacPherson, Kerrie. 1987. *A Wilderness of Marshes: The Origins of Public Health in Shanghai, 1843–1893.* New York: Oxford University Press.

Mann, Susan. 1997. *Precious Records: Women in China's Long Eighteenth Century.* Stanford, CA: Stanford University Press.

Mao Dun. 1976. *Midnight.* Hong Kong: C & W Publishing.

Mao Xianglin. 1870. Reprint, 1985. *Moyu lu* [Record of leftover ink]. Shanghai: Shanghai guji chubanshe.

Mao Zedong. 1992. "Report on the Peasant Movement in Hunan." In *Mao's Road to Power, Revolutionary Writings, 1912–1949,* Vol. 2, edited by Stuart Schram, 429–64. Armonk, NY: M. E. Sharpe.

Marmé, Michael. 2005. *Suzhou: Where the Goods of All the Provinces Converge.* Stanford, CA: Stanford University Press.

Mather, Richard B., trans. 2002. *A New Account of Tales of the World*, 2nd edition, revised. Ann Arbor, MI: Center for Chinese Studies.

McCracken, Donald P. 1997. *Gardens of Empire: Botanical Institutions of the Victorian British Empire.* London: Leicester University Press.

Medhurst, William H. 1873. *The Foreigner in Far Cathay.* New York: Scribner, Armstrong.

Meng Yue. 2006. *Shanghai and the Edges of Empires.* Minneapolis: University of Minnesota Press.

Meskill, John. 1994. *Gentlemanly Interests and Wealth in the Yangtze Delta.* Ann Arbor, MI: Association for Asian Studies.

Miller, G. E. (Mauricio Fresco). 1937. *Shanghai: The Adventurer's Paradise.* New York: Orsay Publishing House.

Milne, William Charles. 1857. *Life in China.* London: Routledge.

Min, Anchee, Duo Duo, and Stefan Landsberger, eds. 2003. *Chinese Propaganda Posters.* Köln: Taschen.

Morrison, Robert. 1815. *A Dictionary of the Chinese Language.* Macao: East India Company's Press.

———. 1828. *Vocabulary of the Canton Dialect.* Macao: East India Company's Press.

Mote, Frederick W. 1977. "Yüan and Ming." In *Food in Chinese Culture: Anthropological and Historical Perspectives*, edited by K. C. Chang, 193–258. New Haven, CT: Yale University Press.

Murphey, Rhoads. 1953. *Shanghai: Key to Modern China.* Cambridge, MA: Harvard University Press.

Naqvi, Nauman. 2007. "The Nostalgic Subject: A Genealogy of the 'Critique of Nostalgia.'" Centro Interuniversitario per le ricerche sulla Sociologia del Diritto e delle Instituzioni Giuridiche, Working paper n. 23, pp. 4–51. Retrieved from http://www.cirsdig.it/Pubblicazioni/naqvi.pdf

Needham, Joseph. 1986. *Science and Civilisation in China*, Vol. 6, Part 1, *Botany.* New York: Cambridge University Press.

Neskar, Ellen. Forthcoming. *Politics and Prayer: Shrines to Local Former Worthies in Song China.* Cambridge, MA: Harvard University Press.

Oakes, Vanya. 1943. *White Man's Folly.* Boston: Houghton Mifflin.

Oxford English Dictionary (online edition).

Pan Kan. 1934. *Shipin pengzhi quanshu* [A comprehensive cookbook]. Shanghai: Zhonghua xinjiaoyushe.

Perry, Elizabeth. 1995. *Shanghai on Strike: The Politics of Chinese Labor.* Stanford, CA: Stanford University Press.

Proust, Marcel. 1981. *Remembrance of Things Past.* Vol. 1, *Swann's Way: Within a Budding Grove*, translated by C.K. Scott Moncrieff and Terence Kilmartin. New York: Vintage.

Qianlong Shanghai xianzhi [Shanghai County gazetteer, Qianlong era]. 1750. Reprinted in *Xijian Zhongguo difangzhi huikan.* 1992, Vol. 1. Beijing: Zhongguo shudian.

Qian, Nanxiu. 2001. *Spirit and Self in Medieval China: The Shih-shuo hsin-yü and Its Legacy*. Honolulu: University of Hawai'i Press.

Qinding shoushi tongkao. 1747. *Wenyuange siku quanshu neilian wangban*. Xianggang: Dizhi wenhua chuban youxian gongsi, 2002.

Rankin, Mary Bakus. 1971. *Early Chinese Revolutionaries: Radical Intellectuals in Shanghai and Chekiang, 1902–1911*. Cambridge, MA: Harvard University Press.

Rawski, Evelyn. 1996. "Re-envisioning the Qing: The Significance of the Qing Period in Chinese History." *Journal of Asian Studies* 55.4: 829–50.

Ren Baizun. 1999. *Zhongguo shijing*. Shanghai: Shanghai wenhua chubanshe.

Reynolds, Bruce L. 1981. "Changes in the Standard of Living of Shanghai Industrial Workers, 1930–1973." In *Shanghai: Revolution and Development in an Asian Metropolis*, edited by Christopher Howe, 222–40. New York: Cambridge University Press.

Roberts, J. A. G. 2002. *China to Chinatown: Chinese Food and the West*. London: Reaktion Books.

Rogaski, Ruth. 2004. *Hygienic Modernity: Meanings of Health in Treaty-Port China*. Berkeley: University of California Press.

Rowe, William. 1993. "Introduction." In *Cities of Jiangnan in Late Imperial China*, edited by Linda Cooke Johnson, 1–16. Albany: State University of New York Press.

Ruo Wei. 1939. "Fandian nongtang xiaoji." *Modeng banyuekan* 1.1: 17.

Saunders, Petra. 1998. "Shanghai Chic." *iSH* 1.2: 11.

Scarth, John. 1860. *Twelve Years in China: The People, The Rebels, and The Mandarins*. Edinburgh: Thomas Constable.

Schafer, Edward H. 1963. *The Golden Peaches of Samarkand: A Study of T'ang Exotics*. Berkeley: University of California Press.

———. 1977. "T'ang." In *Food in Chinese Culture: Anthropological and Historical Perspectives*, edited by K. C. Chang, 85–140. New Haven, CT: Yale University Press.

Schwarcz, Vera. 1919. *The Chinese Enlightenment: Intellectuals and the Legacy of the May Fourth Movement of 1919*. Berkeley: University of California Press.

Shanghai baojian: lü Hu bibei [Shanghai precious mirror]. 1925. Shanghai: Shanghai shijie shuju.

Shanghai Bureau of Social Affairs. 1930. *Wages and Hours of Labor, Greater Shanghai, 1929*. Shanghai.

Shanghai fengtu zaji. 1932. Shanghai: Shanghai xintuo gufen youxian gongsi.

Shanghai Huashang hangming buce. 1907. Shanghai: Huashang gongyihui.

Shanghai minshi wenti. 1931. Shanghai: Shanghaishi liangshi weiyuan hui.

Shanghai mishi diaocha. 1935. Shanghai: Shehui jingji diaochasuo.

Shanghai Municipal Archives. File nos. 325-4-1, A65-2-117, B6-2-138, B6-2-139, B50-2-208, B50-2-319, B50-2-398, B98-1-134, B98-1-164, B98-1-532, B98-1-730, B98-1-732.

Shanghai tongshe. 1935. *Shanghai yanjiu ziliao*. Reprint, 1992. In *Minguo congshu* Series 4, Vol. 80. Shanghai: Shanghai shudian.

Shanghai xianzhi. 1993. Shanghai: Shanghai renmin chubanshe.

Shanghai zhinan [Guide to Shanghai]. 1909. Shanghai: Shangwu yinshuguan.

Shanghai zhinan [Guide to Shanghai]. 1912. Shanghai: Shangwu yinshuguan.

Shanghai zhinan [Guide to Shanghai]. 1926. Shanghai: Shangwu yinshuguan.

"Shanghai zuijin wushiliunian lai mijia tongji." 1929. *Shehui yuekan* 1.2 (February): 1–25.

Shaoxi Yunjian zhi [Gazeteer of Yunjian, Shaoxi era]. 1193. In Weiwan biecang reprint series, Vol. 43. Nanjing: Jiangsu guji chubanshe. Reprint, 1988.

Sheehan, Brett. 1999. "Urban Identity and Urban Networks in Cosmopolitan Cities: Banks and Bankers in Tianjin." In *Remaking the Chinese City: Modernity and National Identity, 1900–1950*, edited by Joseph Esherick, 47–64. Honolulu: University of Hawai'i Press.

Shanghai mishi diaocha. 1935. Shanghai: Shehui jingji diaochasuo.

Shen Fuxu. 2002. "Shanghai yuanlin goushen (2): liangge huangjia huayuan—yuyuan, wuyuan." *Yuanlin.* No. 8.

Shen Hsi-meng, Mo Yen, and Lu Hsing-chen. 1961. *On Guard Beneath the Neon Lights, A Play in Nine Scenes.* Peking: Foreign Languages Press.

Shepherd, John Robert. 1993. *Statecraft and Political Economy on the Taiwan Frontier, 1600–1800.* Stanford, CA: Stanford University Press.

Shi Xisheng. 1925. *Sushi pu.* Shanghai: Zhonghua shuju.

Shi Zhecun. 1996. "Chungeng." In *Shi Zhecun qishinian wenxuan*, edited by Chen Zishan and Xu Rulin, 758–61. Shanghai: Shanghai wenyi chubanshe.

Shih, James Chin. 1992. *Chinese Rural Society in Transition: A Case Study of the Lake Tai Area, 1368–1800.* Berkeley, CA: Center for Chinese Studies.

Shih, Shu-mei. 2001. *The Lure of the Modern: Writing Modernism in Semicolonial China, 1917–1937.* Berkeley: University of California Press.

Shimoda Utako. 1903. *Jiazhengxue* [Home governance], Wu Rulun trans. Shanghai: Zuoxinshe.

Shizhe. 1935. "Shanghai de chi, san." *Rensheng xunkan* [Livelihood weekly] 1.5: 33.

———. 1935. "Shanghai de chi, si." *Rensheng xunkan* 1.6: 36.

Sima Qian. *Shiji.* Beijing: Zhonghua shuju, 1982 edition.

Simoons, Frederick J. 1991. *Food in China: A Cultural and Historical Inquiry.* Boston: CRC Press.

Smith, Joanna F. Handlin. 1992. "Gardens in Ch'i Piao-chia's Social World: Wealth and Values in Late-Ming Kiangnan." *Journal of Asian Studies* 51.1: 55–81.

Smith, S. A., 2002. *Like Cattle and Horses, Nationalism and Labor in Shanghai, 1895–1927.* Durham, NC: Duke University Press.

Solinger, Dorothy. 1984. *Chinese Business Under Socialism: The Politics of Domestic Commerce, 1949–1980.* Berkeley: University of California Press.

Song Zuanyou. 2007. *Guangdongren zai Shanghai (1843–1940)* Shanghai: Shanghai renmin chubanshe.

Spence, Jonathan. 1977. "Ch'ing." In *Food in Chinese Culture: Anthropological and Historical Perspectives*, edited by K. C. Chang, 259–94. New Haven, CT: Yale University Press.

———. 1999. *The Search for Modern China*, Second Edition. New York: Norton.

Sterckx, Roel, ed. 2005. *Of Tripod and Palate: Food, Politics, and Religion in Traditional China*. New York: Palgrave Macmillan.

"Street Procession in Shanghai's Big Famine Drive." 1921. *Shanghai Gazette*, March 14.

Swislocki, Mark. 2002. "Feast and Famine in Republican China: Urban Food Culture, Nutrition, and the State." Ph.D. dissertation, Stanford University.

Sutton, David E. 2001. *Remembrance of Repasts: An Anthropology of Food and Memory*. New York: Berg.

Tang Hai. 1926. *Zhongguo laodong wenti*. Shanghai: Guanghua shuju.

Tang Zhenchang. 1997. *Yizhishi*. Hangzhou, China: Zhejiang shiying chubanshe.

Tao Xiayao. 1936. *Taomu pengrenfa*. Shanghai: Shangwu yinshuguan.

Tejijiaodui, pseud. [Chen Mengyin]. 1966. *Jinshan shijing*. Hong Kong: Xianggang xingyun maoyi gongsi.

The Jubilee of Shanghai, 1843–1893. 1893. Shanghai: North China Daily Press.

Thurin, Susan Schoenbauer. 1999. *Victorian Travelers and the Opening of China, 1842–1907*. Athens: Ohio University Press.

Tongzhi Shanghai xianzhi [Shanghai county gazetteer, Tongzhi era]. 1872.

Trubek, Amy B. 2008. *The Place of Taste: A Journey Into Terroir*. Berkeley: University of California Press.

Tuhua ribao. 1910. Reprint, Shanghai: Shanghai guji chubanshe, 1999.

Vogel, Ezra F. 1989. *One Step ahead in China: Guangdong under Reform*. Cambridge, MA: Harvard University Press.

Vogel, Hans Ulrich (trans., Yoshida Tora). 1993. *Salt Production Techniques in Ancient China*. Leiden: Brill.

von Glahn, Richard. 2003. "Towns and Temples: Urban Growth and Decline in the Yangzi Delta, 1100–1400." In *The Song-Yuan-Ming Transition in Chinese History*, edited by Paul Jakov Smith and Richard von Glahn, 176–211. Cambridge, MA: Harvard University Asia Center.

Wagner, Rudolf G. 1995. "The Role of the Foreign Community in the Chinese Public Sphere." *China Quarterly* 142: 423–43.

Wakeman, Frederic, Jr. 1996. *The Shanghai Badlands: Wartime Terrorism and Urban Crime, 1937–1941*. New York: Cambridge University Press.

———. 1998. "Urban Controls in Wartime Shanghai." In *Wartime Shanghai*, edited by Wen-hsin Yeh, 133–56. New York: Routledge.

Waley, Arthur. 1958. *The Opium War through Chinese Eyes*. Stanford, CA: Stanford University Press.

Waley-Cohen, Joanna. 2004. "The New Qing History." *Radical History Review* 88: 193–206.

Wan Pingyuan. nd. *Shanghai Xiaoshaoxing yinshi zonggongsi jianzhi*, Huangpuqu hangyezhi xilie, No. 10.

Wang, Ban. 2002. "Love at Last Sight: Nostalgia, Commodity, and Temporality in Wang Anyi's *Song of Unending Sorrow.*" *positions* 10.3: 669–94.

Wang, David Der-wei. 2000. "Three Hungry Women." *Modern Chinese Literary and Cultural Studies in the Age of Theory: Reimagining a Field*, edited by Rey Chow, 48–77. Durham, NC: Duke University Press.

Wang Dingjiu. 1934. *Shanghai guwen* [Shanghai advisor]. Shanghai: Shanghai zhongyang shudian.

———. 1937. *Shanghai menjing* [Keys to Shanghai]. Shanghai: Shanghai zhongyang shudian.

Wang Guoliang. 1989. *Hanwu dongming ji yanjiu*. Taibei: Wenshizhe chubanshi.

Wang Qiyu and Luo Yousong, eds. 1985. *Shanghai difangzhi gaishu*. Changchun: Jilin sheng difangzhi bianzuan weiyuanhui, Jilin sheng tushuguan xuehui.

Wang Tao. 1870. *Yingruan zaji* [Miscellaneous notes from the seaside]. Reprint, 1989. Shanghai: Shanghai guji chubanshe.

———. 1873. *Haizou yeyou fulu* [A Supplement to Record of Visits to Courtesan Houses in a Distant Corner By the Sea]. Reprint, 1992. Zhang Tinghua, *Xiangyan congshu*, Vol. 20a. Beijing: Remin wenxue chubanshe.

———. 1860. Preface, *Haizou yeyou lu*. Reprint, 1992. Zhang Tinghua, *Xiangyan congshu*. Series 20, 5:5633–84. Reprint, Beijing: Renmin wenxue chubanshe.

Wang Xiangjin. *Qunfang pu* [Treatise on many fragrances]. *Siku quanshu cunmu congshu bubian*, Vol. 80. Jinan: Qilu shushe, 1997 edition.

Wang Yanlun, ed. 1924. *Jiashi shixi baojia*. Shanghai: Shangwu yinshuguan.

Wang Yi. 1997. *Xinghualou*. Changchun, China: Jilin sheying chubanshe.

Wang Zheng. 2001. "Call Me 'Qingnian' but not 'Funü': A Maoist Youth in Retrospect." In *Some of Us: Chinese Women Growing Up in the Mao Era*, edited by Xueping Zhong, Wang Zheng, and Bai Di. New Brunswick, NJ: Rutgers University Press.

Wang Zhenzhong, "Qing-Minguo shiqi Jiang-Zhe yidai de Huiguan yanjiu." Paper presented at the 2003 Shanghai Academy of Sciences symposium, Ming-Qing yilai Jiangnan shehui yu wenhua guoji xueshu yantaohui.

Wanli Shanghai xianzhi [Shanghai county gazetteer, Wanli era]. 1588.

Wasserstrom, Jeffery. 2001. "New Approaches to Old Shanghai." *Journal of Interdisciplinary History* 32.2: 263–79.

Watson, Burton, trans. 1962. *Records of the Grand Historian*, Vol. 2. New York: Columbia University Press.

———. 1971. *Chinese Rhyme-prose: Poems in the Fu Form from the Han and Six Dynasties Periods*. New York: Columbia University Press.

———., trans. 1995. *Chuang-tzu, Basic Writings*. New York: Columbia University Press.

West, Stephen. 1987. "Cilia, Scale and Bristle: The Consumption of Fish and Shellfish in the Eastern Capital of the Northern Song." *Harvard Journal of Asiatic Studies* 47.2: 595–634.

———. 1996. "Playing with Food: Performance, Food, and the Aesthetics of Artificiality in the Sung and Yuan." *Harvard Journal of Asiatic Studies* 57.1: 67–106.

White, Lynn T., III, "Shanghai-Suburb Relations, 1949–1966." In *Shanghai: Revolution and Development in an Asian Metropolis*, edited by Christopher Howe, 241–68. New York: Cambridge University Press.

Widmer, Ellen. 2003. *The Beauty and the Book: Women and Fiction in Nineteenth-Century China*. Cambridge, MA: Harvard University Asia Center.

Wilkinson, Endymion. 2000. *Chinese History: A Manual*, revised and enlarged edition. Cambridge, MA: Harvard University Asia Center.

Will, Pierre-Etienne. 1990. *Bureaucracy and Famine in Eighteenth-Century China*. Stanford, CA: Stanford University Press.

Will, Pierre-Etienne, and R. Bin Wong. 1991. *Nourish the People: The State Civilian Granary System in China, 1650–1850*. Ann Arbor: Center for Chinese Studies, University of Michigan.

Wolff, E. 1971. *Chou Tso-Jen*. New York: Twayne.

Wong, Kwan-yiu, and David K. Y. Chu, eds. 1985. *Modernization in China: The Case of the Shenzhen Special Economic Zone*. New York: Oxford University Press.

Wu, David H. Y., and Sidney C. H. Cheung, eds. 2002. *The Globalization of Chinese Food*. Honolulu: University of Hawai'i Press.

Wu Liang. 1998. *Lao Shanghai: yishi de shiguang* [Old Shanghai: years gone by]. Nanjing, China: Jiangsu meishu chubanshe.

Wu Rulun. 1903. "Jiazhengxue xu." In Shimoda Utako, *Jiazhengxue*, 1–2, non-continuous pagination. Shanghai: Zuoxinshe.

Wu Zimu. *Mengliang lu* [Record of the splendors of the capital city]. *Wenyuange siku quanshu neilian wangban*. Xianggang: Dizhi wenhua chuban youxian gongsi, 2002.

Xia Yan. 1996. "Baoshengong." In *Xiayan gishinian wenxuan*. Shanghai: Shanghai wenyi chubanshe.

Xiang Xinyang and Liu Keren, eds. 1991. *Xijing zaji jiaozhu*. Shanghai: Shanghai guji chubanshe.

Xiangguotoutuo, *Shenjiang mingsheng tushuo* [Shanghai's famous sites, illustrated and explained]. Shanghai: Guankeshouzhai, 1884.

Xiao Jianqing. 1937. *Shanghai changshi* [Shanghai common knowledge]. Shanghai: Shanghai jingwei shuju.

Xiao Langchu, "Tantan Guangdongcai de shaofa." *Xinmin wanbao*, August 26, 1956.

Xiao Xiansou. 1934. *Pengrenfa*. Shanghai: Shangwu yinshuguan.

Xiong Yuezhi, ed. 1999. *Shanghai tongshi*, 15 vols. Shanghai: Shanghai renmin chubanshe.

Xiong Yuezhi, Zheng Zu'an, Luo Suwen, and Xu Min. 1997. *Lao Shanghai mingren, mingshi, mingwu daguan*. Shanghai: Shanghai renmin chubanshe.

Xu Guozhen. 1933. *Shanghai shenghuo* [Shanghai living]. Shanghai: Shijie shuju.

Xu Ke. 1986. *Qingbai leichao*, Vol. 13. Beijing: Zhonghua shuju.

Xue Li. 1999. "Canyingye chuiqi haijiufeng." *Xinmin wanbao*, June 23, p. 19.

Xue Yanwen and Wang Tongli, eds. 1999. *Piaozheng jiushi*. Tianjin: Baihua wenyi chubanshe.

Yao Zhiyin. 1721. *Yuan Ming shileichao. Wenyuange siku quanshu neilian wangban.* Xianggang: Dizhi wenhua chuban youxian gongsi, 2002.

Ye Mengzhu. *Yueshi bian*. In *Shanghai zhanggu congshu*, Vol. 1. Taibei: Xuehai chubanshe reprint, 1968.

Ye Shengtao. 1998. "Ou yu chuncai" [Lotus root and water shield], In *Jiu Shanghai fengqinglu*, edited by Yu Zhi and Cheng Xinguo, Vol. 1, 111–15. Shanghai: Wenhui chubanshe.

———. 1998. "Guojie." In *Jiu Shanghai fengqing lu*, edited by Yu Zhi and Cheng Xinguo, 98–99. Shanghai: Wenhui chubanshe.

Ye Xiaoqing. 1992. "Shanghai before Nationalism." *East Asian History* 3: 33–52.

———. 2003. *The* Dianshizhai *Pictorial: Shanghai Urban Life, 1884-1898*. Ann Arbor, MI: Center for Chinese Studies.

Yeh, Catherine. 1996. "Creating a Shanghai Identity—Late Qing Courtesan Handbooks and the Formation of the New Citizen." In *Unity and Diversity: Local Cultures and Identities in China*, edited by Tao Tao Liu and David Faure, 107–23. Hong Kong: Hong Kong University Press.

———. 2002. "Representing the City: Shanghai and Its Maps." In *Town and Country in China: Identity and Perception*, edited by David Faure and Tao Tao Liu, 166–202. New York: Palgrave.

———. 2006. *Shanghai Love: Courtesans, Intellectuals, & Entertainment Culture, 1850–1910*. Seattle: Washington University Press.

Yeh, Wen-hsin. 1998. *Wartime Shanghai*. New York: Routledge.

———. 2007. *Shanghai Splendor: Economic Sentiments and the Making of Modern China, 1843–1949*. Berkeley: University of California Press.

Yi Han. 1915. "Xishi weisheng pengtiaofa." *Funü shibao* 16: 22–27.

Youxi bao. 1897–1908.

Yü, Ying-shih. 1977. "Han." In *Food in Chinese Culture: Anthropological and Historical Perspectives*, edited by K. C. Chang, 53–84. New Haven, CT: Yale University Press.

Yu Jiaxi, ed. 1993. *Shishuo xinyu jianshu*. Shanghai: Shanghai guji chubanshe.

Yu Muxia. 1998. *Shanghai linzhao* [Shanghai tidbits]. Shanghai: Shanghai shudian chubanshe.

Yuding peiwenzhai Guang qunfangpu. Wenyuange siku quanshu neilian wangban. Xianggang: Dizhi wenhua chuban youxian gongsi, 2002.

Yue, Gang. 1999. *The Mouth That Begs: Hunger, Cannibalism, and the Politics of Eating in Modern China*. Durham, NC: Duke University Press.

Zhang Yushu. 1720. *Yuding yunfu shiyi. Wenyuange siku quanshu neilian wangban.* Xianggang: Dizhi wenhua chuban youxian gongsi, 2002.

Zao Yangfan shu. 1909. Shanghai: Meihua shuguan.

Zeng Yi. 1911. "Zhongkui lu." *Funü shibao* 3: 71-5.

Zeng Yi. 1984. *Zhongkui lu.* Beijing: Zhongguo shangye chubanshe.

Zhang Chunhua. 1968. *Hucheng suishi quge* [Folksongs of Shanghai seasons]. *Shanghai zhanggu congshu,* Vol. 2. Taibei: Xuehai chubanshe.

Zhang Suowang. *Yuegeng yulu* [Notes on reading and plowing]. *Siku quanshu cunmu congshu,* Vol. 101. Jinan: Qilu shushe, 1997 edition.

Zhang Xudong. 2000. "Shanghai Nostalgia: Postrevolutionary Allegories in Wang Anyi's Literary Production of the 1990s." *positions* 8.2: 349–87.

Zhang, Yingjin, ed. 1999. *Cinema and Urban Culture in Shanghai, 1922–1943.* Stanford, CA: Stanford University Press.

Zhang Zhou. 1984. "Shilun Zhongguo de 'caixi'." *Zhongguo pengren* 5.5: 17–18.

Zhongguo fangzhi dacidian. 1988. Hangzhou, China: Zhejiang renmin chubanshe.

Zhongguo jingjizhi, Anhuisheng Ningguo, Jingxian. 1936. 2 vols. Hangzhou, China: Jianshe weiyuanhui.

Zhongguo mingcanguan. 1982. Beijing: Zhongguo lüyou chubanshe.

Zhongguo Wannan Huicai yanjiusuo. nd. "Huicai fayuan jixi kao." Retrieved from http://www.newconcept.com/jixi/culture/HuiCulture36.html

Zhou Sanjin. 1995. "Mingsheng Zhongwai de Shanghai meishi zhongxin: Huangpu meishilin zonghengtan." In *Shanghai meishi daguan,* edited by Ji Bin and Xu Zhiming. Shanghai: Shanghai yuandong chubanshe.

Zhou Zuoren. 1938. "Mai tang" (Selling candy). In *Zhou Zuoren quanji,* 4: 319–21 (Taibei: Landeng wenhua chubanshe, reprinted 1993).

Zhu Xuchu. 1987. "The Songjiang School of Painting and the Period Style of the Late Ming." In *The Chinese Scholars' Studio: Artistic Life in the Late Ming Period,* edited by Chu-tsing Li and James C. Y. Watt, 52–55. New York: Thames and Hudson.

Zhujing zhi. 2005. In *Shanghai xiangzhen jiuzhi congshu,* Vol. 5. Shanghai: Shanghai shehuikexueyuan chubanshe.

Zou Yiren. 1980. *Jiu Shanghai renkou bianqian de yanjiu.* Shanghai: Shanghai renmin chubanshe.

Index